Paranormal Case File

(Volume F

Malcolm Robinson

Published by

FLYING DISK PRESS

4 St Michaels Avenue

Pontefract, West Yorkshire

England

WF8 4QX

CONTENTS

Other books by Malcolm Robinson

UFO Case Files of Scotland (Volume 1)

UFO Case Files of Scotland (Volume 2)

Paranormal Case Files of Great Britain (Volume 1)

Paranormal Case Files of Great Britain (Volume 2)

Paranormal Case Files of Great Britain (Volume 3)

The Monsters of Loch Ness (The History and the Mystery)

The Sauchie Poltergeist (And other Scottish ghostly tales)

Please Leave Us Alone (The true and terrifying story of an Irish family and their desperate fight against the 'Hat Man' and supernatural forces)

The A70 UFO Incident (Scotland's first officially reported UFO Abduction)

The Falkland Hill UFO Incident (Scotland's most controversial UFO case)

Available on Amazon and Lulu.

This book is dedicated to Brian McMullan (Snr)

A wonderful friend, musician, and family man.

(02/05/46 – 27/03/22)

GUEST FOREWORD
By Ron Halliday

I was delighted when Malcolm asked me to write an introduction to his latest book. Malcolm has spent a lifetime investigating, cataloguing, and publishing his investigations into a variety of supernatural phenomena from ghosts and poltergeists to UFOs and many more. I've known Malcolm for nearly forty years, and I can attest to his enthusiasm and energy in bringing the fruits of his research to the public. I've often heard Malcolm state that he is not trying to preach to or put over a specific point of view, but simply wants the public to be informed of all those strange and weird events that have been brought to his attention and appear to defy the natural world as we know it. Let the people decide for themselves has been Malcolm's view.

In keeping with that approach, Malcolm's latest book is a great contribution to our fund of knowledge on the supernatural. Covering a range of subjects, it demonstrates just how wide and even bizarre the range of inexplicable incidents people experience is.

Malcolm discusses some phenomena which will no doubt be familiar to those interested in the subject, including ghosts and poltergeists, but covers cases which will reveal just how frightening these events can be for those who go through the experience of poltergeist activity in their homes or are confronted by a phantom or spectre. Such events can be disturbing in demonstrating that the world we take for granted can turn into something which defies our understanding. But Malcolm's book also deals with incidents that will come as a surprise even to those who have investigated the paranormal. One example is the chapter dealing with underwater ghosts which I had not previously come across. However, given that ghosts seem to appear anywhere, an aquatic phantom appears as likely as one you might expect to come across in a more 'conventional' location such as a medieval castle. If ghosts are truly spirits of the dead then anywhere where a death has occurred, particularly if it has been in tragic circumstances, might well hold on to a phantom of the deceased. It's a fascinating possibility which I'm glad Malcolm has brought to our attention.

I'm personally intrigued by reports of nature spirits - more familiarly fairies, imps, elves, gnomes - and the relationship to modern UFO entity sightings. In 'UFO Scotland' I discussed one case I investigated where a UFO case combined with an encounter with small blue beings just like the traditional fairy folk of old. I was, therefore, fascinated by Malcolm's account of a UFO case which combined encounters with goblins. I think the link between alien entities and the tradition in countries across the world of fairies, elves, and goblins has been overlooked for too long perhaps because the idea that they may be connected goes against the concept that UFOs are spacecraft from distant advanced civilisations. It may well be controversial with those who believe in 'nuts-and-bolts' UFOs as a result, but that doesn't mean we should ignore it.

As usual Malcolm has produced a well-researched and documented volume. But in addition to examining specific supernatural phenomena, he has also examined more general areas including 'Cellular Memory' and 'Life after Death'. The latter is a topic which generates endless discussion, but it is always stimulating to read a fresh point of view and Malcolm Robinson has spent a lifetime investigating mediums and their messages from the 'beyond' so has a great deal of knowledge to impart on the topic. Cellular memory may be a less familiar subject, but is certainly a fascinating, and of course, controversial one! A typical case would involve a heart transplant patient behaving like the individual from whom the heart was received even including memories of events the deceased person had been through.

So, can heart cells absorb and then pass on memories? An astonishing possibility.

In conclusion, Malcolm has covered an amazing array of fascinating cases and I can thoroughly recommend it to the reader whether an experienced investigator or new to the topic. There is something in this volume for everyone.

Ron Halliday, Bridge of Allan, March 2023

***

AUTHOR'S FOREWORD

Welcome to book number four of my series of books providing you with weird and wonderful tales of ghosts and the supernatural from around the British Isles. Since volume three, I have been presented by numerous weird tales of unexplained phenomena from people who were right there at the very heart of them. Not only did it frighten them, but it changed the way that they looked at the world and made them realise that there are indeed more things in heaven and earth than ever dreamt of in anyone's philosophy. I've said it before, there is no point in people giving me their bizarre paranormal stories only for me to place them away in a filing cabinet, what would be the purpose of that? No, these stories simply must get out to Joe Public for them to make their own informed judgement about them. I am not expecting the reader to believe every tale in this book, what I do want you to do though, is to be 'open minded'. Accept that what you are about to read really happened to those that experienced them. We are living in strange times, not everything we see, and experience is so cut and dried. Mysteries are there to be solved. And whilst not every event is truly paranormal, there are enough cases which I have gathered as a researcher throughout my life, which have convinced me that strange things do happen.

I don't accept everything that comes my way. I make an informed judgment by ways of deduction. Talking to the witness, either over the phone or through e-mail and finding out what happened to them. I think of the questions that a sceptic would ask and ensure that I ask them. I look carefully at any submitted photograph, and, if need be, getting that photograph properly analysed. I've said many times before, that there is a lot of 'nonsense' out there, by that I refer to people making stories up.

People submitting what they claim to be real photographs of ghosts, when all along it's just something that they have cleverly made up on computer. I don't need to tell you how easy it is these days to make a ghost, or a UFO appear on a family photograph. If you have the right software or app, it can be plain sailing. Researchers like me, must be on our toes for this. But thankfully, as yet, I've not had to deal with things of this nature. We all know that there are a lot of strange paranormal stories 'out there' and I often say that these days, nothing really surprises me. Having said that, I was slightly taken aback when I received an e-mail from a gentleman who I will call Martin from the U.K. He said.

Hello Malcolm.
"A few days ago, I heard a male voice speaking to me at 06:00 am and he repeated your name to me a few times. And then I was shown a clear image of your book. I apologise but I've not looked at you or your books, so a friend told me to contact you. The book was, 'The Dechmont Woods UFO Incident'. I tried to get more information but lost the feed. Will try again".

I asked Martin if he had any ideas why my book was shown to him and of hearing my name. Could it have been a dream for instance? He replied by saying.

"I am an Alien Abductee from birth and MILAB experiencer. (*) I'm currently writing my first book. I never get information for no reason. I do get information at times that is not so clear such as you. My friend here said there must be a link. The voice repeated your name three times and then an image of this book was shown to me, and it was very clear. I will purchase your book as sometimes that helps.

The information is derived from different sources including non-humans and sprit guides, the higher mind, my future self, over soul and others. At the moment I'm learning to control this energy, as it has been in the past and now used by various military intelligence agencies. Sometimes information comes in and I can't find a link to why and forget about it. I write it down and then 'something' or 'someone'. helps create the link, a synchronised event takes place so to speak. I feel something, but I can't say for certain. Perhaps something you have missed or overlooked in your research papers. A piece of evidence that creates a new twist in the story. Have you been thinking about updating this book. Someone is trying to reach out to me I don't know who".

Michael

(*) For those that don't know. MILAB stands for Military Abduction. There are reports in the UFO literature, that some (not all) UFO witnesses, are abducted by small creatures known as 'the greys' and taken to underground establishments where they are surprised to see normal humans in military uniforms. Some may conclude this to be a collusion between the 'aliens' and Military personnel, but that's another story!

So, what am I supposed to take out of Michael's account? He implies that spirit has told him that I may have overlooked something when writing my Dechmont Woods book! This is a book which I wrote concerning a close proximity UFO sighting in woods near Livingston West Lothian Scotland back in 1979. I would like to think that I covered quite a lot of possibilities in that book. I gave 11 'possible' theories to account for what that witness saw that day. Did I leave out something? Well, apparently his spirit guides believe that I might have! As a researcher, I receive e-mails from people from across the globe, there are only a few in which I believe may come from a deluded individual.

That said, my favourite saying is 'never throw the baby out with the bathwater', meaning, some things are so bizarre, that they might well be true. Sadly, Michael shut down his Facebook account and, for the moment at least, is not contactable.

People who know me, know that I am a Spiritualist. The greatness of being a Spiritualist for me, is knowing for sure that when it is our time to pass to spirit, we know that we will see those family members who have gone before us (and our pets) Spiritualism which encompasses this knowledge, is a great comfort to me. Yes of course we all miss the physical presence of the deceased person that goes without saying, but to see them again in the afterlife is a wonderful thought. And what with being a paranormal researcher who has investigated claims of the afterlife, who has spoken and interviewed members of the medical profession who have related their dying patients last visions, all confirm to me, that we go to a better place when we die. There are a number of cases throughout this book which have puzzled me (and I hope they will you) Some of the following cases in this book, are word for word, written by the witness. I felt no need to elaborate on them. In a number of cases, some people have requested that I don't use their real name, and to give them a pseudonym. That is absolutely fine by me, and does not in any way shape or form, make their account any less real. Many people are just glad to get their own strange stories off their chest. However, at the same time they don't want to be labelled crazy, so it is understandable that they would request a pseudonym. People have asked me if we will ever get to the truth about UFOs, Ghosts, Poltergeist etc. Its one of those questions that you can have a ton of answers for. Each researcher has his or her own take on it. Needless to say, ghost sightings go well back into antiquity and are still being seen today. Can everyone be deluded?

I hope that you enjoy the collection of strange paranormal and UFO accounts that I have gathered in this book. It all goes to show, that these things are real, that they are still occurring, and that they deserve the attention of the public. So, sit back, make yourself comfortable and let's jump into the weird and wonderful world, that is the paranormal.

***

CHAPTER ONE

STRANGE GHOSTLY OCCURANCES

"I cast a gaze at it. It was shimmering, like sunshine on water, almost glowing. The figure was dressed in an old-fashioned suit with a Trilby hat. This apparition was visible for a few seconds, perhaps five at most, before fading away into the darkness".

Witness to a ghost. Patsy Sorenti.

In 2013, I gave a lecture to the Sauniere Society at the Newington Village Hall in Newington near Folkstone England. The Sauniere Society are a non-profit making organisation and were formed firstly to pursue the mystery of Rennes-le-Chateau and other mysteries. It was at this lecture there that I met a young lady with an interesting tale to tell. Here, in her own words, is what she had to say.

The Black Mass On The Hillock.
Location: Hawley, near Dartford Kent, England.
Date: 2010/2011

"It happened two or three years ago (2010-2011) and took place close to Hawley near Dartford in Kent in England. I was walking with a friend in the countryside. Part of the route went through fields. The fields had been ploughed following the harvest. It had rained the night before and it was extremely muddy, so we had to keep to the edge of the field. It was probably mid-afternoon and the light was very good. As we were walking, something caught our eye in the distance. I am not good with distance, but perhaps it was two hundred yards away.

It was the other side of the flat field, across a narrow country road, with a low boundary bush, and on top of a very small hillock by the side of the road. It was a black mass, slightly taller than 6 feet at a guess. It was standing sideways on, so we could see the profile. It was matt black from top to ground. No limbs were visible due to the total blackness. No facial features were visible due to the black covering over the whole of its head. On its back, was a pack of some kind, square rectangular in shape, again black. It was standing very upright, with no movement in its body. The only movement seen, was its head, as it slowly, and robotically, started turning its head to the right, which was the opposite direction to where we were standing. It was presumably scanning the horizon. We stood for a few minutes watching it, then, when it started to move its head towards us, we moved too. We had to leave the edge of the field for perhaps three or four seconds to walk around a small, high bush, as we did so, we lost sight of it during this time. When we got to the other side it had disappeared. We were unable to cross the field due to the muddy conditions to investigate further. The hillock was small so if it had walked to the bottom, it should still have been in view".

Kind regards. Linda Steadman

Our next ghostly encounter takes us to the village of Tivetshall in Norfolk, where, as you will read, strange things were afoot. This account comes from Patsy Sorenti.

THE GLOWING GHOST OF TIVETSHALL ST. MARY

Location: Tivetshall St Mary, Norfolk, England.

Date: June 2016

"The small village of Tivetshall St. Mary is situated in the county of Norfolk in England. It is a tiny place and shrinking. In 2001 it had a population of 302; by the time of the 2011 census, it had fallen to 298 souls. Today it isn't much more than a group of houses with a small village hall, and the church, which gives the village its name, is located about one-and-a-half miles away. This church is derelict and has fallen down, the roof eventually collapsing in 1947 after a low flying military aircraft sped overhead. The church was abandoned and worshippers from the village migrated to the church at Tivetshall St Margaret, around two miles hence. The place has been abandoned for many, many years. However, this did not, and does not, prevent residents and countryside ramblers from ambulating around the lanes and traversing the fields. The ruined church is imposing, especially at night. With its disused churchyard still bearing old gravestones, it casts an eerie quality over the landscape. For many years it has had the reputation of being haunted, but by what, and by whom? Just because this place has an air of creepiness, doesn't mean there is anything otherworldly to experience, or does it?"

"In mid-June of 2016, I visited the old church with a group of ghost enthusiasts. We arrived early evening, bringing our supper with us, for the place is so remote, not even a shop could survive in business there, and there certainly are no washing facilities. The church is surrounded by crop fields and the building itself nestles inside a spinney (small wood.) The road bends to the right very sharply and vehicle traffic have to slow down at this point for oncoming cars or people in the road. Parked cars have to be tucked well into the muddy layby outside the farmer's field. There were 10 of us, a mixture of sexes and ages and some believers and sceptics, a good mix. Towards midnight, and with only a few shadowy figures spotted by the brook at the rear, we decided to bring the night to a close.

I had to use the non-existent 'bathroom' and so before we left, I walked down the lane away from the church for privacy's sake. During the return walk, I heard footsteps behind me. Thinking it was one of my fellow enthusiasts, I turned around to greet them; nobody was there, yet the footsteps continued until I reached the church porch. The rest of the group members were standing very quiet and still, nobody was saying anything. I joined them, and as I did so, a figure, transparent and white, much whiter than any shade of the colour I had ever seen, stood between me and my neighbour. The figure stood still, unmoving. I cast a gaze at it. It was shimmering, like sunshine on water, almost glowing. The figure was dressed in an old-fashioned suit with a Trilby hat. This apparition was visible for a few seconds, perhaps five at most before fading away into the darkness. Nobody else had witnessed this phenomenon, but several members of the group felt 'icy cold' and 'driven with fear' for a few seconds during the apparition's appearance. I just felt privileged to have seen a full ghostly spectre, complete with footsteps and transparency. A few days after this, I contacted the Parish Council, asking for information about the ruined church and the ghost. A woman named Janet contacted me to say that she had twice before witnessed the ghost, just as I had seen it, and described it as it presented itself to me. These sightings were in daytime. Janet told me that in 1952 a man had been knocked down and killed by a speeding car on that blind bend and his ghost has haunted the place ever since. That would explain the old-fashioned clothes. Janet also commended me for going up there at night, for she confessed that 'no amount of persuasion would entice me up there in the dark". Sincerely. Patsy Sorenti.

Our next port of call takes us to Stirling Castle in Central Scotland. The town of Stirling is just over nine miles from where the author currently lives which is the small town of Sauchie in Clackmannanshire.

The following write up, comes from Paul Dale Roberts, a prolific writer on all things weird and wonderful. Paul lives in the United States of America and is a researcher for Halo Paranormal Investigations. Here he talks about his visit to Scotland not just to see our glens and lochs, but more interestingly, our supernatural places.

HAUNTED STIRLING CASTLE

Location: Stirling, Central Scotland.

Date: 1980's.

"When I was younger, I did a lot of international traveling. I clocked out with visiting 59 countries and territories. One of the places I truly loved was Scotland. When my ex-wife, my stepson Jason Porter and I, visited England, Wales, and Scotland, one of the places I definitely wanted to see in Scotland was Stirling Castle. I gravitated towards Stirling Castle because I knew it was haunted and I loved the history of this castle. This majestic castle sits atop a basalt crag, 250 feet above the Forth River. Talk about majestic. When I first saw this castle, my jaw dropped, I was in awe and felt like I stepped into a fantasy world. This castle was built in a strategic location in which you can observe the surrounding countryside. The poet Alexander Smith called the castle the 'huge brooch'. The castle was built in the 15th century and before that, there was a wooden fort 300 years on the spot where Stirling Castle sits today. From the castle, the king or queen residing could observe battles that were being fought for the independence of Scotland from England. Many kings resided at this castle. In fact, Mary Queen of Scots resided at the castle for a while, and she was crowned in the castle's chapel in 1543. Charles I also stayed at the castle briefly.

The Earl of Mar was the last reigning monarch that lived in this castle. The castle after that became a military centre and prison". *(Author's Comment. It's now a tourist attraction)*

The Green Lady

"One of the most famous ghosts in Stirling Castle is The Green Lady. Our tour guide told us that the castle is very haunted and most people in the darkness of night, encounter the Green Lady. Legend has it, that the Green Lady was Queen Mary's maid servant. This maid servant to Queen Mary, had a premonition that Queen Mary was in trouble. The maid servant rushed to the bedchamber of Queen Mary and discovered that the massive drapes were on fire and Queen Mary was asleep. The maid servant pulled Queen Mary to safety. It is said that if you encounter the Green Lady, she is somewhat a harbinger of doom, and that you should stay on high alert, because something bad could happen to you. I was told that there was a mess cook for some Scottish troops at the castle, and that the mess cook had encountered the Green Lady and passed out. I asked the tour guide if anything bad happened to the mess cook and the tour guide said 'no'

The Whipped

"Another ghost that haunts Stirling Castle is 'The Whipped'. Ewan Thomson of Plockton, was walking around Stirling Castle, when he heard an odd sound of moaning. Ewan went to investigate and came upon a man with his arms spread out in the air, tied to ropes. The man's bare back was bloody and full of red welts as if he had been whipped. He was moaning loudly. Ewan at first, thought that this was an actor playing out a historical scene, and to Ewan's shock, the whipped man disappeared, and when he vanished, the crackling sound of a whip was heard.

Ewan says that there were 3 crackling whipping sounds, and then a bloody scream, and the paranormal encounter that Ewan had, was now ended. I believe Ewan encountered a 'residual' haunting, something that has been imprinted into the atmosphere and plays out over and over again. This is strong negative energy".

The Stirling Archer

"Rowan Barland of Bellshill, Scotland was also on the tour with us. Rowan told us that she has visited Stirling Castle 7 times, the first time, was when she was 7 years old with her parents. Rowan said that she encountered a ghost at Stirling Castle, and that the ghost was an archer from long ago. The ghostly archer was pacing up and down the flanks of the castle, and she could see his bow that was shouldered. The ghostly archer wore a Scot's bonnet and a green lime (shirt). He had a long thick beard and moustache. He had long reddish hair. Rowan said she was petrified when seeing this archer, and then the archer started walking towards her and Rowan couldn't move. The archer walked right through her and disappeared into a wall. Rowan said that she is psychic, and that she is more sensitive to seeing ghosts, and that is probably why she had this encounter. Rowan said that she goes back to the castle hoping to come across the archer one more time. Rowan also stated that she is used to her psychic abilities and is no longer afraid when she sees ghosts".

Sincerely. Paul Dale Roberts.

Our next ghostly encounter comes from a good friend of mine, fellow researcher Darren W. Ritson. Darren is a prolific ghost hunter and author of several books on the subject. Here is what he had to say in regard to a haunting that he investigated at one of England's most haunted houses.

THE CHINGLE HALL HAUNTING

Location: Chingle Hall, Whittingham near Preston, England.
Date: 2006.

The following account has been taken from the pen of the renowned author and ghost hunter of many years Darren W. Ritson. It was first published in his book, Supernatural North (Amberley Publishers, 2009) and with Darren's permission; I have been able to reproduce the account herein almost word for word. It centres upon one of the United Kingdom's most haunted Manor Houses, Chingle Hall in Lancashire. Darren, over the space of a month or two back in 2006, spent almost a week at this historic location investigating its ghosts, hauntings, and its history. A few nights were spent there with his own group, the Northeast Ghost Research Team, which was founded by Darren in 2003, and a number of nights was also spent there with the Ghosts and Hauntings Overnight Surveillance Team that was co-founded in 2005 by Drew Bartley and Darren W. Ritson.

"The north of England in the United Kingdom has a wonderful accolade, an accolade to which the tiny hamlet of Borley on the Essex and Suffolk border once encompassed between 1863 and 1944, and that is, it is home to the most haunted house in Britain. Chingle Hall in Lancashire is described by ghost hunter James Wentworth Day as 'One of the best authenticated examples of a haunted house'. The Hall is a 700-year-old manor house that is reputed to house more than its fair share of active spirits and ghosts inside and outside the premises. The ghosts include a girl named Eleanor, who was allegedly held captive for twelve years in one of the small rooms inside the house, (now known as Eleanor's Room), a monk, a cavalier, and an abundance of children (inside and outside), a hanging man, a number of spirit animals including dogs, a demonic-like entity, and a poltergeist. For many years now Chingle Hall has been subjected to paranormal activity and ultimately this has led to the house being subjected to paranormal investigators, and plenty of them have visited over the years. Many radio stations have carried out live broadcasts there, and many TV programmes have been filmed here. The well-known psychic medium, Billy Roberts, filmed a TV documentary at Chingle Hall, as has Michael Aspel when he presented LWT's Strange but True series in the 1990s".

"Chingle Hall was built around 700 years ago, and originally it had a thatched roof and a wooden drawbridge. A moat, that can still be seen today, although minus its water, runs around the house and, from what I was told by house guide Pat, on one of my visits there, that it was a sign of stature rather than a defence mechanism or a safeguard during the sieges. When Adam de Singleton first built the house, it was named 'Singleton Hall' after the family that lived there. In 1620 John Wall was born there but when he grew up, he was sent away to be educated and in 1641, he became a Franciscan Priest and was known to be one of the last English Roman Catholic martyrs. During King Henry VIII reformation, it was illegal to practice Catholicism, so priest holes were constructed at Chingle Hall. If the Kings men raided the house, the practising monks had a place to hide. In 1678, John Wall was subsequently apprehended at Rushock Court near Bromsgrove as he was tendering 'the oath of supremacy,' and was taken to Worcester Jail where he was told his life would be spared if he turned his back on his religion. Needless to say, he declined, and was subsequently hung, drawn and quartered a year later in 1679. His body was distributed to his friends and his head is said to have been taken on a tour of the continent before being smuggled back to the hall and buried within the walls or in the gardens of Chingle Hall.

In his book 'This Haunted Isle', former correspondent of Darren, the late Peter Underwood recalls his many visits to Chingle Hall. He states that.

"Chingle Hall is a fascinatingly hidden house built in the form of a cross that lies at the end of a long drive. I have lost count the number of times I have been there, for the place has an intriguing and puzzling atmosphere and it does seem indisputable that ghostly forms have been seen and heard here many, many times".

He went on to say.

"I remember the late Mrs Margaret Howarth telling my wife and I unequivocally, *'this house is undoubtedly haunted'* And she went on,

"We hear ghostly footsteps constantly in some rooms and passages and sometimes heavy footsteps walk over the bridge across the moat, through the old front door and across the hall. Once, eight people heard these footsteps. Door latches move, sometimes night after night and then not for a while. Doors open by themselves. Dogs' hackles rise at something they can see, or sense. Objects are moved, water appears from nowhere, monk like figures have been seen inside the house and in the garden. Once my brother and I watched a cloaked form for fifteen minutes before it faded and finally disappeared. No, we were not afraid, now I can't think why we weren't, but we never slept in that room afterwards".

"Brilliant accounts of paranormal phenomena reported to Peter Underwood by a former owner of the house. It must be stressed now, that there are a couple of examples previously mentioned, that I could personally verify because I have had the opportunity to spend many a night investigating Chingle Hall. The aforementioned door latches being moved, and ghostly footsteps being heard in the rooms and corridors I have witnessed for myself at the house and have managed to catch them on tape. I was sitting in Eleanor's room late one night with colleagues that were fellow ghost aficionados from the North East Ghost Research Team, when we all heard the floorboards begin to creak and groan as though someone was walking on them. Footsteps although no one was there, made their way along the corridor and into the John Wall room where they ceased abruptly".

"My colleague Drew Bartley was downstairs in the Great Hall at the same time carrying out his 'sit in' and he too heard the ghostly footfalls. Drew actually bellowed up the stairs to us and asked us if we were moving around. We were not, and our video footage can prove this. Yes, we actually caught it on tape. It felt really strange to be looking through the doorway of the upper corridor, knowing and furthermore seeing, that no one was actually there, yet hearing the blatantly loud creaking and groaning of the floorboards with a chilling crystal clarity. There was definitely something otherworldly making its way down that corridor that night, maybe John Wall himself and if I have to be honest, it was quite unnerving yet strangely exhilarating"!

"During our many days and nights at Chingle Hall, I also managed to experience and capture an array of paranormal activity including many wonderful anomalous sound recordings. On one occasion, while carrying out a séance experiment in the Great Hall area, myself, and a number of investigators, including the aforementioned Drew Bartley, all heard what can only be described as the sound of coins hitting/landing/bouncing off the metal fireplace that stands in the room. No coins whatsoever could be found, and nothing could be identified as the source of the noise. It was a very perplexing occurrence which kept us all in heated and bewildered discussions for months to follow. On another occasion we recorded a number of anomalous voices that were definitely not any of the investigators present.

A male voice can be heard on one recording speaking the words, *"Dare come the dead",* followed by a female voice immediately after saying, *"Bring me the Bible".* Chills shot down the spines of those present when we played that recording back; it was very eerie. Another anomalous voice recording was made by one of my investigators called Claire Smith, and it said simply, *"Get out, get out my house".* It was said in a whispering tone and yet again, it was chilling".

"As well as hearing strange, disembodied breaths or sighs, one of which frightened myself and a colleague of mine somewhat in the John Wall Room, and many other kinds of strange paranormal phenomena, we can now wholeheartedly agree with the late Mrs Margaret Howarth when she said, *"This house is undoubtedly haunted".*

The attention this house has received for over fifty years now is most certainly justified and being able to visit it on numerous occasions, and investigate it from top to bottom, has to have been one of the many highlights of my long and successful ghost hunting career.

Regards Darren W. Ritson.

Witnessing a ghost is one thing, being touched by a ghost is another, as our next tale demonstrates.

I FELT A GHOSTLY HAND ON MY BACK!

Location: Dumbryden Gardens, Wester Hailles, Edinburgh.
Date: November 2019.

Hi Malcolm,

"I had a strange experience in November 2019 when I was working as an electrician on call in Edinburgh, Dumbryden Gardens, Wester Hailles. I was about to use my key to get into a low-rise block of flats. As I was about to pull the door open, I felt what I thought was someone putting their hand on my right side of my lower back, like they were pushing me aside to get past into the close before me. I reacted automatically and turned. To my surprise nobody was there. I could actually feel the pressure push on my jacket, then right onto the lower side of my back. It spooked me out as I was 100% sure that there was something pushing me aside. It gave me the chills, and I gave out a shout along the lines of *"What the f**k"!* I decided to look into the history of the area and found out that there had been a few local murders in the locality and a few there over recent years. One person was stabbed, and in a bad way, and was trying doors to get help, unfortunately the guy bled out and died. Maybe it was this poor fella pushing by me!"

"Another weird one, was whilst driving up from Dark Sky camping down in Dumfries and Galloway. It was August 2021 and we travelled up from Glentrool Campsite. It was an awful road, with room for only one vehicle with stop points to let cars past. We came up to a bend and I looked ahead and saw a blue car further up the road heading round. So, I pulled into the lay-by to allow the car to pass. The blue car which I had seen at a distance, had disappeared out of sight behind some trees in the middle of the bend as it approached. I sat talking to Sara and Lucas as we waited. Sara then asked why I was waiting, and I said that there was a car coming round. *"What car?"* Exclaimed Sara. I ended up having to drive on in case the car was also waiting for us to come round. As we drove round there was no car! There was no other turn off on the road, and we could see for miles in front. So, it had not turned around.

Where that car went to, I don't know. Albeit I was the only one that had seen the blue car. I was getting ribbed from my two passengers saying I was off my head, but there was a blue car for sure".

"Again, I looked into accidents in that area, and found an article about an old woman who lived in Glentrool. She had drove her car off the road and crashed on her way home to Glentrool and sadly died. You can guess what colour the car was, blue! Could it have a been a moment of time where the old woman was trying to complete her journey home, like a ghost ship lost, only to be seen momentarily before disappearing? Who knows. Some folks would think I have a vivid imagination with such tales, but like yourself Malcolm, we love to think about the unknown and what could be around us. I still believe we could be in a simulation where glitches or energies from the past appear".

Regards. Graeme Kelly.

A very dear friend of mine who goes by the well-known name of 'Alien Bill,' real name, Bill Rooke, who resides in York England with his wife Victoria and dog Foxy, has had many strange and paranormal events occur to him in his life. Many of which he has photographed. (See my previous book, Paranormal Case Files of Great Britain (Volume 3) where I devote a whole chapter to 'Alien Bill' and his incredible photographs). Anyway, I would now like to provide you with three more interesting paranormal tales from 'Alien Bill', one of which had a 'back up witness', more of that one in a moment. For now, let us take a wee walk in the rain, shall we?

THE GHOSTLY WOMAN IN THE RAIN!

Location: York, England.
Date: Thursday 3rd September 2020.

Author's Comment. The following is the testimony as told to me over the phone from my friend Alien Bill Rooke.

Abbreviations

(MR) Malcolm Robinson. **(ABR)** Alien Bill Rooke)

(ABR) "Here is what happened that night. This occurred on the 3rd of September 2020. I had departed early that night from the Lysander Arms pub at Rawcliffe. And what later happened, has blown my mind somewhat although I am used to many strange encounters over the years. As I left the pub and was unlocking my bike in the heavy pouring rain, which I was none too pleased about, I felt that I was being watched from behind and above. At the time, I turned around and looked into the rain-soaked sky and said, *"Are you watching me"?* I got no reply, but I wasn't expecting one. So, I got on my push bike to set off home. Five minutes later, I encountered three white lights dancing around the sky, then, I later found myself in a lane between two small woods which leads onto Shipton Road. I, for some reason, was heading in the wrong direction home, and I felt totally disorientated. Nothing to do with the pub I might add. Many other things happened before this, but at this juncture, I was midway down, this 15-feet wide lane. I turned my bike to the right, away from this lane to head in the right direction home. Suddenly, at the end of this lane, and still in the pouring rain, a black caped woman appeared out of nowhere. To me, I couldn't understand what on earth she was doing in the dark in the pouring rain, more so, as just around the corner, it was well lit up and I thought that she would have felt safer going the longer way round. I then gestured to her, that it was OK for her to go to the far side of the lane if she so wished. We did not speak to one another, and we were about some 80 metres or so away as she walked down the lane in the pouring rain, which, I might add, was very noisy. The figure, then stayed for a few minutes not moving at all. I then waved my hand again to the far side of this lane to say it's OK. This time, the woman who I thought was under this heavy-duty wool cape, ventured towards me. I stayed exactly where I was until I saw which direction, she was going to go in. To my surprise, she kept to 'my side of the lane'. I found this very strange as she got closer. My instincts, as to what had occurred earlier, seeing those strange lights in the sky, and finding myself at a different location from my normal route, told me that something was not quite right here. I then started to see if I could see any facial features inside the hood that draped onto her shoulders, but I couldn't see anything".

"Not afraid at all, I stayed put, and I started to notice that at the bottom of the cape, no feet appeared! There were puddles in this lane due to the heavy rain, and not a splash came from under the cape. Now I knew straight away that this was not normal. This black caped lady got closer on my side of the lane. Not scared or shy, this woman, (well I thought she was) Well I waited for her to pass me by onto my right. When within six feet or so from my bike, I picked up strange vibes and noticed the caped lady wasn't getting her cape wet and seemed to be 'gliding' along the lane. As I am a committed researcher, I would have taken pictures before this, but as I thought she was an innocent woman in a cape, I did not. However, when she got so close, and as she seemed to be floating to my right, and passing my bike, I tilted my bike headlight into the hood, and to my shock, the light hit the interior of the hood and went into 'total blackness'. I knew for sure, that there was no human of sorts in that cape, but I still felt a female presence. Research head kicked in again, so I laid my bike down onto the grass next to me whilst she passed by and I got my mobile camera out as it was best to use in the pouring rain, rather than my digital cameras. I thought that I would wait until she got to the end of this alleyway to turn left or right, and then I would dash to the end of the lane and photograph her from behind. The 'entity', as I called her then, stopped in the middle of the lane, and I waited to see which way she went. Lo and behold, it wasn't left or right, but 'she' changed into a light grey colour and dematerialised in front of me. I had taken too long to take the pictures and I was very annoyed with myself. I then phoned Vic after the event which left her shocked, as so many things had been happening that night. To this day, I have no idea, who or what! The caped lady was, or where on Earth she came from".

(MR) "Bill, can you confirm for me, how this caped lady disappeared and have you ever seen anything like this before".

(ABR) "She went totally grey from top to bottom and just faded away. Yes, this was the very first time that I have ever seen something like this, never before, and never since".

(MR) "Bill, you said that it was heavy rain and that there were puddles on the lane and when she was gliding towards you, she didn't appear to be getting wet, was this the case"?

(ABR) "It looked like a heavy wool cape and not a lightweight cape, it was like ancient old wool. I thought that it was soaked as she walked past me, but it looked dry! And I thought, that's odd, it doesn't even look wet. She had a jet-black cape, and it was down to the floor nearly to about an inch, to an inch and a half from the ground. It was a big full cape with a big, draped hood over her head".

(MR) "Now you said that you shone your torch into the hood of this caped lady and there was no face"!

(ABR) "Yes there was no face, it was just like a black hole in the cosmos you know when light goes in there and it just sucks it up and disappears. It reminded me of that, it was like a black hole. My light did not reflect off anything. The light went into the hood, and it was swallowed up".

(MR) "Was she taller or shorter than you"?

(ABR) "She was taller than me, I'd say about 5 foot ten inches".

(MR) "You mentioned that you got some vibes when you were near her".

(ABR) "Yes, when she got really close to me, I did feel something. Not scary vibes, I just felt strange vibes tingling through my body but nothing that spooked me".

(MR) "Did she appear solid looking then"?

(AB) "Solid yes. And I always felt that it was a woman, it felt feminine to me".

THE GHOST OF ROCKY THE DOG

Location: York, England.
Date: 2020.

(MR) "Now moving on Bill, you are a dog lover as is your wife Vic. You love your pets. Sadly, you lost little Rocky your dog a few years ago, but then again, maybe he is 'not gone', for I believe that both you and Vic have seen him in the family home".

(ABR) "Yes that's right. Rocky passed on about two years ago who we had for about 16 years. He was half chihuahua and half King Charles spaniel, so he was about the size of a terrier. A couple of days after Rocky had passed on, Vic was the first one to see him from the other side so to speak".

Author's Comment. At this point, Bill said that he would now read a statement about Vic's ghostly sightings of Rocky. This is what he said Vic had written.

(VR) Victoria Rooke. **(ABR)** Alien Bill Rooke.

(VR) "A couple of days after Rocky had died, I was looking out the French windows into the back garden, and there was Rocky, as clear as day running around the flowerpots on the patio wagging his tail. He wasn't the sixteen years old Rocky, he looked bright and brisky, and looked instead to be two to three years old. Rocky had always slept at the end of our bed near Bill's feet. A number of times in the first couple of weeks after he had died, I clearly felt him moving about on the bed and woke Bill up to tell him about this. Another time Bill was sat on the sofa with our new dog Foxy and suddenly I heard a scratching noise and I felt something jumping from the sofa and onto my armchair I turned around and asked Bill what Foxy was doing, and he told me that Foxy was fast asleep which he was at the time, on my lap on the couch".

(ABR) "I should point out here Malcolm, that at the time Vic was mentioning this to me, I felt and heard a bigger dog, because Foxy at the time was a tiny little pup a much smaller dog, spring off the bottom cushion of the couch onto the arm of the chair. I felt this and also heard it. And as he jumped from one arm of the chair to the other, you could hear his claws scrape across the arm of the chair from taking off and landing, this is what Vic has explained here".

Author's Comment. We continue with Vic's testimony of seeing the ghost of Rocky, her previous dog.

(VR) "The last time I saw Rocky was early one morning. Bill had taken Foxy or new dog downstairs to put him out as I was just getting up. I heard a noise in the hall, and I looked over the banister, and there was Rocky, 'with' Foxy running around following Bill from the lounge to the kitchen. Again, he looked like his younger self".

Author' Comment. We continue back with Bill, where he shares his own sightings of the ghost of Rocky. Here is what he had to say.

(ABR) "I have also seen Rocky appear in the bedroom and also on the couch and feeling him on the duvet on the bed on a few occasions. I have seen him on and off over a couple of months. Sometimes we get four weeks or six weeks or eight-week gaps before he pops up again. And one time I was coming down the stairs early in the morning with Foxy, I only got down the first three or four steps when Foxy suddenly stopped, dead in his tracks and just started up at me, then glanced downstairs and then looked back at me again and wouldn't go any further. So, I was wondering what was up with him, and I said, *"What's up with you Foxy"?* Then I looked down towards the bottom of the stairs, and lo and behold, sat there, right on the bottom step, is Rocky looking young. Every time we see him, he appears younger, no grey whiskers under his chin. So Rocky was sat there, looking up at me, tilting his head backwards and forwards. He slowly stood up, and he looked solid as well. He didn't look translucent like a ghost and walked through the lounge door which was shut. The next time I saw him, it was only the back of him which was quite a few weeks after that. Vic and I were watching a movie in the lounge and Vic wanted an ice lolly from the freezer in the kitchen. So I went through to the kitchen, and as I did so, I felt a 'pushing' on my right leg as I was lifting the lid up on the freezer. I then glanced down thinking that little Foxy had come through following me through to the kitchen.

But as I glanced down, I saw a bigger dog, a light brown colour, not the head of it, pushing against my leg. I got the ice lolly out then looked down again at my feet and there was nothing there. So, I came back into the lounge and asked Vic is she had just let Foxy follow me into the kitchen? She said, no, he has been with me all the time, and I said "Right, we've just had another appearance". And since then, he has made the odd appearance at times. I truly believe that dogs can come back in spirit as humans do".

Author's Comment. In the above statement by Bill, he mentions that it had been a weird night, more so before his ghostly encounter with the caped woman. I can't relate here what had previously transpired that same night, as Bill will be including this in his own book which he is currently writing. Bill was more than happy to discuss the latter part of that crazy night (you'll have to read Bill's book to find out what transpired before the caped woman encounter). Now, when Bill got home that night, he immediately telephoned his friend Nick Kyle, former President of the Scottish Society for Psychical Research. Nick has written up what transpired regarding that phone call. Nick states.

"Bill Rooke phoned me at 10.45pm approximately last night in a state of agitation to tell me of his experience minutes earlier. The gist of which, was that while cycling home from a pub, he saw a cloaked and hooded (possibly female) figure coming towards him, face hidden, and he thought it strange that she had chosen such a dark, quiet lane to walk, when there was a well-lit alternative route nearby. She was about six feet from him and about to collide with him, when she went around him, her black cloak swirling close to two feet from him. He watched her walk away and a few yards later, he saw her fade and disappear. That's when he realised that he had just seen a ghost. Reflecting upon this, he realised that she glided rather than walked along the road. He was aware during this encounter that he had lost his sense of hearing and touch (he could not hear or 'feel' the wind and rain) and then he realised that he was in a different location from where he had expected to be. He was a long way back down the road that he had just cycled".

"Disoriented, he began to cycle from his new position, when he passed two couples, spaced about 60 yards apart, who were out walking their dogs. Bill said that each dog went 'berserk' at him as he passed on his bike, with the owners showing their surprise at their dogs' aggression. Bill says that he also experienced 'missing time' of about 40-50 minutes, because a journey that routinely takes him up to 25 minutes took 1 hour 20 minutes on this occasion. When I asked him how he was feeling now that he was safe at home, he said that he was feeling better, though he still had an elevated heartbeat and was still shaken by what had happened. Bill phoned me this morning and went over his encounter(s) again, still trying to make sense of it all".

"I advised him to write, or video record his most detailed recollections of the above events as soon as possible and to monitor his health closely, contacting NHS 24 if he didn't feel well. I told him that he could have had a stroke or psychosis or 'turn' that led to auditory and visual hallucinations and a confused memory. I suggest that he researches the area involved, including speaking to local residents about that apparition".

Kind regards, Nick Kyle.

Bill didn't seek that medical advice, as he firmly believed that what happened that particular night was a supernatural event. He admits to having a few beers but was 'not' drunk as he made his way home. Our next ghostly tale from 'Alien Bill', is not only one of the most bizarre paranormal tales that I have ever heard about, but Bill's sighting also had the back up of a second witness, one Kathy Cogliano. Here is that incredible tale, firstly we hear from 'Alien Bill' himself, followed by Kathy Cogliano who also experienced this. Now, before we begin this mysterious tale, let me set the scene for you. It's the big, once a year Outer Limits Magazine Conference in Hull England, put on by the wonderful Chris Evers, where people come from around the world to be regaled by tales of UFOs, Poltergeists, and a whole lot more. Bill Rooke is sitting with his wife Victoria at one side, and American Kathy Cogliano on the other. Everything is fine, they are watching the guest speaker on stage, (which funnily enough was me. I was giving a lecture on the Sauchie Poltergeist) when all of a sudden, a strange ghostly 'floating arm' comes into view. So, sit back, buckle up, as your about to go into the 'Twilight Zone'.

THE STRANGE GHOSTLY ARM!

Location: Freedom Centre, Hull, Yorkshire, England. (Bill Rooke's Testimony)
Date: 2022.
Abbreviations. (MR) Malcolm Robinson. **(ABR)** Alien Bill Rooke.

(MR) "So Bill, you were sitting in a chair at the Outer Limits Conference at the Freedom Centre in Hull, and I believe you were watching my lecture on the Sauchie Poltergeist when this happened. Tell me exactly what happened, all you can remember, what did you see?"

(ABR) "Yes this happened at the Outer Limits Conference at Hull. I saw this 'thing' twice. Once on the Saturday afternoon, and then again on the Sunday afternoon. It was around three o clock, on the Saturday afternoon when I first saw it, and nobody else saw this with me at that time. I saw the forearm of an old man's arm. It was in a dark blue colour shirt. It was his right arm, as his thumb was facing towards me, and it flashed for a few seconds in front of me.

It looked 3D and was solid, and it was a foot or so above my kneecaps as I was sitting down. It startled me for a few seconds, but I sort of dismissed it and carried on watching the lecture. Now on the Sunday, the next day, the first sign of anything to do with this, is when I went down the corridor at the same centre to the gents' toilets, one fellow had just left before I went in, and nobody else was in there. I went over to the hand dryer, and it was a real powerful hand dryer which had blue lights on, and even although it was blowing out hot air, I felt a cold chill just round the back of my neck, and it was really icy cold, and I thought that's a bit odd. As I was going to go around and put my hand up and rub the back of my neck, suddenly in my left ear, and not telepathically, but like as if somebody was stood right next to me, I heard clear as day, a gravelly voice saying, *"You're all right mate"*. It was really loud. And I asked myself, what the hell was that. So, I looked behind me thinking that there would be somebody there having a bit of a lark, and I was only 2 or 3 metres away from two toilet doors which were pretty well close. And I thought, has somebody gone in there, hiding in the toilet and having a laugh? So, I went and checked, and there was no sign of anyone. Then I opened the door to the corridor which is a very long corridor, and there was nobody there, no sign of anybody in the corridor, and that was just a split second from when I heard the 'voice' on that Sunday afternoon. A few minutes after that, I met Chris Evers which is part of this story down at the cafeteria area, where I immediately told him about this voice, and he told me that there had been a few strange ghostly experiences in and around the cafeteria area. As I was also mentioning that Andy, who had been down that corridor with his daughter an hour or so earlier, told me that they had felt a cold chill go through their bodies which freaked them out. So, after all this had happened, I went back to the auditorium and sat beside my wife Victoria and Kathy Cogliano at the back of the auditorium.

Kathy had mentioned to me, that earlier she had heard loud banging on the ceiling of the female toilets. But separate to that, Vic is sat next to me, I'm sat on the right-hand side, and Kathy is on the left of Vic. Vic, my wife, had, unbeknown to me, spotted a white light energy light up to my right-hand side. At this point, you Malcolm, were on the stage talking about the Sauchie Poltergeist. Now seconds after this bright light that suddenly appeared next to me, (and I'm surprised that Vic never saw this), was a 'floating arm' which was moving this time, and it looked exactly the same as I had seen on the Saturday afternoon. Now this had got my attention, not just because it was an arm from the elbow onwards, it was 3D and solid looking, like an old man's right hand with the thumb facing us. This time it was in motion, moving, really slowly. And I just sat up, and it was so close, you could have grabbed hold of it to support yourself on. And I'm watching it slowly move off, and I never said anything. It went past Vic, and this is the odd part, Vic never spotted the actual arm, and I looked across at Kathy and I said to myself, *"I wonder if Kathy has seen this"?* So, I got up within seconds and asked Kathy if she had seen it, and Kathy described 'exactly', the same arm, looking like an old man's arm in 3D with a bluish sleeve of some kind on it with the thumb facing towards her. Where it disappeared to, I don't know".

(MR) "Wow, Bill, that's a fantastic account, and to have this vision backed up by Kathy is even more astounding. It's a shame that Vicky your wife never saw it".

(ABR) "But isn't it strange? I saw it going past, and I don't know if it switched itself off at that point. Vic never saw it, but she did see that bright white light next to me, and that was where this arm came from".

(MR) "So on the Saturday, you just saw the arm. Was it a vision, in the sense that it just flashed on and off for a few seconds, or was it there for longer on the Saturday?"

(ABR) "No it was just seconds, it just flashed in front of me. This was Saturday afternoon around 3:00pm, the middle of the afternoon. It 'wasn't' in motion this time, but it was definitely the same arm".

(MR) "Whereas on the Sunday, you saw it for longer, yes"?

(ABR) "Yes, it was moving in slow motion past me, and I almost went to grab it, that's when I wondered if anyone else had seen it. When Kathy had said that she had seen it, we put together the banging in the corridor, and the old man's voice only an hour or so before that that spoke to me in the toilet, and Andy and his daughters who felt a cold chill going through their bodies that freaked them out.

That was all around the same time that afternoon within an hour or so. There were no signs of any modern watch or any rings on this wrinkly hand. This floating arm' wasn't neatly chopped off at the elbow, it just sort of, faded off, it was a bit fuzzy".

(MR) "Bill, thank you ever so much for telling me about this. I'm pretty sure that you'll never forget this in a hurry".

(ABR) "You're right there Malc".

Now, is that weird, or is that weird! And to back Alien Bill's sighting up, here is what Kathy Cogliano saw.

THE STRANGE GHOSTLY ARM!

Location: Freedom Centre, Hull, Yorkshire, England. *(Kathy Cogliano's Testimony)*

Date: 2022.

"I travelled from the United States to attend the 2022 Outer Limits Magazine Conference held at the Freedom Centre in Hull, England. The Freedom Centre is reportedly haunted. Firstly, I had a personal encounter in the empty hallway with very loud knocks seemingly coming from the walls and the ceiling as I walked down the hall to the lady's room. There was no one else in the hallway at the time. I also had a ghostly encounter as I sat in the audience, I started to nod off, when the apparition of a male arm covered with a dark blue shirt sleeve, its hand extended out, appeared in front of me as though to catch me if I fell forward. I felt no fear with this encounter, it was as though this apparition was there to help, it felt as though it was an older gentleman's arm".

Regards. Kathy Cogliano, US correspondent for Outer Limits Magazine (OLM)

Needless to say, I just had to find out more, and I asked Kathy a number of further questions to ensure that I had dotted the I's and crossed the t's of this most unusual experience. I asked her if this shirt was checked, or had any patterns on it, she replied that it didn't. I then asked where the arm ended, was it at the shoulder or elbow? she stated that it ended at the elbow. She further stated that it was a right arm, with the thumb facing her and it was in view for a full 10 seconds. It was around chest high as she sat in her chair. There were no rings that were visible on this floating hand, and she didn't notice any thick veins protruding from the hand, but she had a strong sense that it was the hand of an elderly gentleman. Surprisingly, she felt no fear as this instantaneous floating arm moved in front of her from right to left. In the e-mail that Kathy had sent me, outlining the above events, she said that she would like to inform me about another bizarre event that happened to her. This is what she had to say.

"Malcolm, I will share with you one of my most frightful encounters as an experiencer, I have many as you well know! This experience still leaves me in chills! I am still trying to understand what happened. I was in bed just starting to settle into sleep, I was thinking that I'd like to have a sign from my teacher Xenos, who recently passed away. All of a sudden, I am grabbled from my bed by unseen hands from behind and taken up and through the doorway of my bedroom. I find that I'm suspended high up, almost touching the ceiling in my little den area in front of the fireplace. I can see into my bedroom and see my empty bed. I am in a total state of paralysis. I am desperately trying to scream out to God to please help me. I can't scream, I am so afraid I keep trying to scream and nothing comes out! I keep trying to cry out, when all of a sudden, I think of my teacher, Xenos and I am able to scream his name! I just kept screaming his name! All of a sudden, I am back in bed, I am lying down, and I'm not sure if I'm awake. I am stunned and shaking. What just happened? I must have drifted into sleep, only to wake up very early remembering every detail about what happened! I had a sense of calm surprisingly, and a 'knowing' that my teacher saved me, and he is guarding me from the other side! What I don't know Malcolm is, *"Did I wake up in the middle of an abduction"?*

Sincerely. Kathy Cogliano.

Author's Comment. Kathy has indeed experienced many strange events in her life. She went on to say.

"I'm a lifelong Experiencer of the paranormal and of extra-terrestrial encounters. I had my first Paranormal experience at six years old, having my grandfather appear to me in the television in my bedroom, only to learn that morning he passed away the night before. I had my first cigar shaped craft encounter at age nine while living on a nuclear submarine base, walking to school. I am clairvoyant, (communicate with spirit) clairaudient, (hearing) and clairsentient, (psychic ability) as well as an intuitive. I have studied the practices of mediumship, reading the Akashic Records, Tarot, and I am a channel to the multidimensional realms. As an energy healer I've trained in; Reiki, Avesa Quantum Healing, Egyptian Healing Rods; using the Wands of Horus and Integrated Energy Therapy; IET. I have been honoured to do several radio interviews with; Jeremy Vaeni for his show; 'The Experience' and also Whitley Strieber's 'Unknown Country'. I've also done Philip and Ronald Kinsella's show, 'Twin Souls' on UK Paranormal, and Bob Brown's show 'Over the Rainbow' on Beacon of Light Radio, and 'Tales from the Séance Cabinet' with Alex Lovelock and Vanessa Cole, and Wife of a Demon Hunter with Durinda Stewart. I am a U.S. correspondent for the Outer Limits Magazine, having numerous articles and experiences published. I've had my experiences published in two of Philip Kinsella's books; 'Guardians of the Dead' in which I shared my angelic experiences and 'You, The Public Deceived The Grand UFO Deception' where I shared my UFO experiences. I currently live in Plymouth, Massachusetts, USA with my Cavalier King Charles Spaniel, Kali. I am a proud grandmother to my dearest Elizabeth and Vivienne".

Having a ghost in your house is not something most people would want, but when you have to contend with a poltergeist in your house, well it isn't any wonder that some people just want to make a hasty exit as our next tale demonstrates.

THE BALORNOCK ENTITY

Location: Balornock, Glasgow, Central Scotland.
Date: 1979 till 1990.

Hi Malcolm,

"The following is a short account of the strange events that took place in my flat in Balornock, Glasgow. It all started off with typical poltergeist activity and progressed into something more sinister and ultimately evil. Whatever was taking place, in my opinion, was demonic".

"I was in the flat for about a year before the strange occurrences began. My eldest son who was around the age of 8, started to complain to me about heavy breathing in the hall when he was in bed, and then he said he heard something heavy being dragged down the hall. He was so scared he never opened his bedroom door to look. All this time, I heard nothing, so I thought that he was playing up. Then before I knew it, I heard, what I called, the 'bouncy ball'. The noise would come from the ceiling. It sounded like a billiard ball being dropped on a wooden surface then snatched up and dropped again. This would continue most of the day and would follow me around every room I went into. The loft of the flat was fully insulated, so if anything fell up in the loft, you would only hear a dull thud if you heard anything at all. I had workmen check the roof for loose slates etc, but the roof was intact. I even had my friend's husband go up into the loft when the noise was happening and he could not hear anything or see anything out of place, but still the noise continued in front of witnesses. Things started to disappear and reappear in the strangest of places. I had folded the washing one day and put the clothes in the cupboard in the hall until the kids were in bed and I would do my ironing. Strange as it may seem, two pairs of trousers and a jumper were missing. I hunted the whole place high and low, but to no avail. They were completely gone. One day, about 3 months later, I had been to the school to pick up my eldest son, I had my youngest son in his high pram, and when I got home, I put the high pram in the spare room as it was wet with the rain. When I went into the room to dry it off, there on the cover of the pram, were the two pair of missing trousers and the jumper".

"When my youngest son was about 4 months old, I got up about 3 in the morning to make him a bottle. When I opened the living room door, it hit off something, I didn't look right away as I was more interested in feeding my crying baby. I went into the kitchen and proceeded to boil the kettle to make the baby's bottle. While I was waiting for the kettle to boil, I thought about the door hitting off something and that's when I looked. I was horrified to see that one of my wall units had been moved a good two feet out from the wall. This unit was so heavy that it took two people to move it. I could not understand how this could have happened. It was as if it had been lifted up and placed two feet in front of where it should have been. One day my friend Sheila and her daughter Sheena had come to stay the weekend, we had our dinner then done the washing up and left the plates etc to drain. I never had a door on the kitchen as I had been flooded out and was waiting for a new door. I had heavy velvet curtains meantime. Well, the curtains were closed, and we were sitting chatting when we heard a terrible racket coming from the kitchen. It was as if all the plates, glasses, cutlery, pots, and pans were being thrown around and smashed. We were dumbstruck! Sheila jumped up and pulled the curtain back and the noise stopped. We went into the kitchen and could see that 'nothing was out of place'. The horrible thing that happened next was the mirror incident. I had a mirror with no frame sitting on the windowsill. As we were standing there at the sink wondering what the noise had been, the mirror rose up on its own, turned sideways and came straight for me. I don't know how Sheila managed to grab it, but if she hadn't, it would have sliced my neck open or decapitated me. I truly believe that. I took the mirror and immediately smashed it up".

"Another friend came up one day and asked to borrow some money. She was leaning on the living room door and looked down the hall then looked at me and said, *"Barbara, who is that wee woman standing there"?* I jumped up to see and she looked back down the hall and said *"Oh, she's not there now"*. This was all in the space of seconds. Another friend, Sandra, went to the toilet. The carpet in my toilet was so thick that you really had to push the door hard to shut it or open it. Well Sandra had just sat down when the door silently glided open. She came running through in quite a state of undress. She was physically shaking. Another friend, Margaret, saw a shadow person in the flat. I had asked her to watch my one-year-old till I went to phone the doctor as he was unwell. She was in the bedroom with the child and thought she heard something. When she looked out the room door, she saw the shadow figure through the open living room door. When I returned, she asked me why I had asked her to look after my son as there was already someone else in the house. I took her through every room to prove there was no-one else in the house. She never came back to my house after that. It really spooked her. Then there was the case of the bleach bottle incident. I had a pair of white cord trousers that I would occasionally bleach to keep white and bright. I put them into the sink in the bathroom and took a full bottle of bleach with me and poured some into the sink with water. I then screwed the lid back on and sat the bleach bottle down on a wee shelf beside the toilet bowl. Convinced that I had to put more bleach in, I reached for the bottle and before I could get it, it rose up in the air and flew through a gap at the sink. I asked my eldest son to retrieve it as I couldn't reach it, and when he pulled it out it was empty, the lid was still intact, but the bottle looked as though the very air had been sucked out of it. That was scary. When Sheila came back to visit, I took her into the bathroom to re-enact what had happened. She just laughed and said, *"Aye right"* Immediately the chain on the high up cistern was pulled by an invisible hand and flushed. We ran out of the toilet as fast as we could. My son and his friend were walking up the hall towards the living room when they noticed a big black shadow. It flew through the ceiling just outside the toilet door. My son said it was blacker than black, like a void. They got the fright of their lives and ran out of the house".

"I began to hear my name being called. It sounded normal at first then sounded menacing. I was in the kitchen with my back to the aperture where the door should have been, and I heard a loud B....A..... I ran out and felt as though I was running through a freezer till, I reached the end of the hall. It sounded horrible. A lot more happened in that flat, the hatchet marks on the main bedroom door, the chanting through my tape deck, the phone ringing at all hours of the night, and when lifted, just static noise, and my neighbour about to tell me something that had happened in the flat but was stopped by her sister. I think the climax came when I returned home from a weekend at my T.A. (Territorial Army) camp, and my son told me that he was cleaning the bath but could feel that he was being watched. When he turned round, he said he saw an old man and woman looking at him from the full-size mirror on the wall. Well, I hired a van next morning, packed up all I could, and fled with my kids to my friend's house in Tullibody".

"It was a horrible experience which lasted about 8 years, but I just couldn't deal with it any longer as I feared for our safety. The house was always dark and gloomy no matter how bright I tried to make it. It was just full of negativity and ended up with constant arguments with my then partner and we eventually split up. I've tried to find out if anything bad happened at that flat, but no joy so far. I know a lot of people believe that children can attract poltergeist effects when going through puberty, but my eldest son was only about 7 when the phenomenon started".

Best wishes. Barbara Anne McDonald.

Our next case comes from a woman who had to endure spirits in five different houses. I'm sure you will agree that It's bad enough having to suffer ghostly activity in one house, but in five! Here is what she had to tell me; it makes for horrifying reading.

SPIRITS JUST FOLLOW ME AROUND!

Location: Stirling X2, Sauchie, Glenochil, Tullibody, Central Scotland.
Date: 1989.

Author's Comment. Before we get into Christian's story proper, here is an overall general piece that she sent me via e-mail which helps to illustrate what she had to go through.

Hi Malcolm

"I am currently reading your book on the Sauchie poltergeist I have some knowledge of it as I stayed in Clackmannanshire for many years. I used to live in Sauchie main street in the flats above the library, I stayed there around a year before I had to flee with my kids due to poltergeist activity, I am originally from Stirling, and I lived in a house in Craighall Street in the Raploch. The house was so bad with activity, that my son and I had to huddle in a corner. Eventually I had to call a priest in the early hours of the morning. I was levitated in that house; my father and uncles saw this happen from the window and had to kick my front door in to get to me. I remember this thing sucking the breath out of me while it happened. My dad took me out the house and that's when the fire started soon after that. The house was set on fire, the fire chief said that it was a chip pan fire, but the cooker wasn't plugged into the mains!

I moved house but it followed me and caused more mayhem. I still have nightmares about that house to this day. I think the issue was that I was open to seeing things, because as a child, I met a man on the stairs of the close and no one else saw him, yet he spoke to me! I would also watch orbs fly around the light at bedtime. The house I lived in then, was actually attached to the house that had the haunting, it was part of the old railway that sat behind the house. The guy that haunted me was William Watt, he was killed between the buffers of a train, and lived in that house many years ago, he can be found In Stirling archives, he made my life hell, but I also feel there was something else there witnessed by others. It was a pretty terrifying time in that house".

MY EARLY EXPERIENCES AS A CHILD

"When I was 10, we moved into a house in Oak Street in the Raploch near Stirling, this is still where my family live to this day. The house is a 5 apartment with a bedroom downstairs. I remember viewing the house with my parents and I remember going into the downstairs bedroom and having a look around. There were stickers on the cupboard door of cats, and there was a ray of light coming in through the bedroom window and a haze of mist filled the room. My bedroom was upstairs at the end of the landing. I hated that room. I would lay in bed at night and feel something sit down on the end of my bed. One night I was looking out the window because it was snowing outside, my brother and I had never seen eye to eye because he always wound me up, so, as I had my head out the window, I felt my hair being pulled back with a short sharp yank! I immediately shouted stop! As I looked around my room door was closed, and no one was there, so I stormed out the room into my brother's room shouting at him about it, and he said it wasn't him! My wardrobe door would squeak and open on its own. I never felt alone in that room. One year, during the summer, we were playing with the neighbours' kids, and this day we were going for a walk, my sister was in her buggy, and I got to push her. We walked up towards the back walk, this was situated below Stirling Castle, it's a long path that led into Stirling at the Albert Hall, but instead of going that way, we walked straight ahead which took us to what is called the 'sandy bunks'. It was called that because there was orange sand on the rocks. So, further up past that, there was a path that took you to the top of the hill. At the top of that hill there was a very old swing park, and to the right of it was an old orphanage that was burnt down. There is a story that a young boy was killed in the fire, and while fire fighters went through the building they saw a young boy, but then he disappeared! This building sits on Upper Bridge Street in Stirling. It was a very calm day, and we were playing at this old park and running around when all of a sudden, one of the swings started swinging on its own? I remember my mum looking at her friend with a confused look. The swing got higher and higher, we could hear whispers which sounded like children, and I heard what sounded like a child crying. I looked to my right, and in the window, I saw what looked like a young boy! He waved at me, and I waved back, and that's when mum said we had to go".

"Years had passed, I was now 15, and decided that I was going to leave home. I stayed with friends until I couldn't. I ended up homeless and was taken to a building that helped people like me get back on their feet and get jobs. This building was on Upper Bridge Street, and I was given a small bedroom. As I was lying in bed that first night, I could hear a child crying, it sounded distant but close as well? It was strange. It kept me awake. I asked staff if they had ever heard anything, and their reply was *"This used to be the old orphanage"*. Well, the blood drained from me. I couldn't believe that I was now in this building in the room facing the park where the boy I had seen all those years ago had been.

HOW IT ALL STARTED. CRAIGHALL STREET, STIRLING

"I was 18, and I had just had my first child, and was living in homeless accommodation when I was offered my first house in Craighall Street, in an area known as the Raploch which is near Stirling. I was so pleased, because the house was on the block I grew up in, and when I was younger, my best friend also lived in that house. It was 1989 and winter when I moved in. I felt scared about having my own house but was excited to! All was well for the first 6 months, I would often hear noises through the night that sounded like it was in the kitchen, but I always ignored it, I was far too busy and exhausted just having a new born baby to look after. I lived with my partner at that point, so it was great to share responsibilities with my son so I could have a break, but in 1990 we broke up and I was alone with my son".

"Things were okay for a while, until one night, while lying in bed, a door in the house slammed shut! I jumped out of bed and checked all the doors, the only one that was closed, was the living room. I was really confused and tired. I ended up going back to bed. I could go through my daily life talking about how life was, but this is about how I was haunted and tortured in that house! The first time I physically saw something strange, was in 1990, it was through the day. My son was asleep, and I decided to wash my hair with the over the taps shower, as my head was lowered into the bath, I suddenly looked around and saw two brogue shoes and pin striped trousers! There was a man standing there beside me and, in a flash, he was gone! Some weeks were quiet, then boom, it would start all over again. The heavy footsteps on a wooden floor that would walk to my bedroom door then suddenly stop. There would be the movements of objects in the house, right in front of my face. As time went on, things just got worse. In 1991, as my son was getting older, he would be fixated to an area in the living room where he would chatter away.

I never thought too much about it at the time, I just thought that's what kids his age do, until one day I was in the kitchen, my son was in his chair in the living room while I made some tea. I suddenly heard a scream from him I quickly rushed through and grabbed him into my arms. He had a mark on his cheek which looked like a thumb print? I couldn't figure out what had happened, so I comforted him, and he fell asleep. Little did I know that things were about to get worse! My son would still babble at nothing, well nothing that I could see until he got older, and he called it guist. I never knew why he gave it this name, but I would catch him chatting away, and sometimes he would cry and say that the guist *(Ghost)* took his dummy".

"It had been 5 years in the house when my son started primary one, and I was able to get out more and visit my mum while he was still at school. Then one day my aunt stopped me in the street and asked me who the man was that stands and looks out the curtains in my house? I had no idea what she was talking about? She said she had seen him a few times on her passing the house. My neighbour upstairs would complain to me about the banging and constant noise coming from my house, but I wasn't in! I started to feel low, I could feel myself getting depressed with it all. I found myself napping instead of going out, and there were times when I would be attacked by something that would make me feel like I couldn't open my eyes! I know I was still awake, but I couldn't fight it. It would claw at my skin and strangle me as I lay there, then boom, I was awake! I tried to speak about my experiences but felt people thought I was crazy. So, for the longest time these things happened until one night my doors would open and close on their own. These were really old heavy doors, and there was no draft in the house to account for this. I held my son in my arms as the doors, one by one would open and close in front of me, then the lights would blow out, then the windows would rattle for no reason! I was terrified. I took my son and put him in his pram and went to the phone box to call for help".

"I ended up calling for a priest. I called a church that stands on upper bridge Street in Stirling, *(Author's Comment. This would be St Mary's Church)* The priest came to the house, and I remember him not wanting to actually come into the house. He brought me a wooden cross and asked me to hang it up on the wall and to pray when I'm scared. I had to stay in that house that night, I never slept at all through fear. Strange things still continued, I had nowhere to go, nowhere to stay, this was it! I was stuck here with this! In 1994 my son was in school I was having a nap on the sofa when I had some sort of attack! I woke up and saw a man standing over me pulling me up to his mouth, he was sucking the very life out of me.

I fought and fought but couldn't get him to stop! Then when I finally came to my senses it stopped. I was greeted with my dad and my cousin who had broken in through the door telling me that I had been levitating. My dad blessed himself and said come stay with me tonight. My dad had said that he and my cousin were just visiting me to see how I was. I found out, that there was a man by the name of William Watt that was killed by the buffers of a freight train on the railway. This house felt evil. The next day my aunt called my mum saying that my house was on fire! The kitchen was where it started? Apparently, the chip pan went on fire but wasn't switched on at the mains? I had to stay at the Portcullis that night with my son, after which it was back to my mum's. But I'd had had enough, the house terrified me! And I wasn't about to let something hurt me and my son. A girl approached me asking if I would like to swap houses with her, I agreed I needed out of there! But I soon found out that the move didn't help, it made things worse!

WEIR STREET RAPLOCH STIRLING

This was a house in Weir Street where I experienced the haunting of the 'burnt man'. I found out that a man was burnt to death while intoxicated on his sofa by a lit cigarette. This started from day one of the move. I felt unwell in that house, very sickly. My senses were heightened, and I felt immediately uncomfortable in that house. I didn't know about the guy that died in that house till after, when I asked about the place, I got the truth! The furniture would be moved; cutlery would come out of the drawers all bent. Loud running and tumbling sounds could be heard from upstairs when no one was in bed. I was levitating again and vomiting. I soon asked for my house back in Craighall Street and we agreed to swap back".

BACK TO CRAIGHALL STREET STIRLING

"It seemed that no matter where I went to, I was being haunted by 'something'. I stayed a little while back in Craighall before the council decided that they were going to renovate the houses. We were put into caravans by the time the houses were finished. I was offered another swap and I took it. I stayed for a short while, then moved away completely. I couldn't face that street any longer. It still haunts me to this day. I'm drawn back a lot and taken into the house in my dreams. I have battled demons most of my life".

"Many years ago in the 1980s, my sister, our brother, and his friend, were out at the park across from the house in Stirling, it's called Trotten park, we always played there, only one day was different. On the grass behind the fence was what we thought was a drunk man all curled up in a foetal position with his long dark hair covering his face. We called out to him a few times but nothing! Then my brother's friend poked him with a stick, and the man looked up and basically flew across the field next to the park at great speed!

This was witnessed by us all, my brother refused to talk about it, but my sister talks about it and how frightening it was. My brother's friend isn't with us anymore. The house we lived in then, is where I also had other experiences. An invisible 'someone' was sitting at the bottom of my bed. My hair would be pulled. I'd have scratches and bruises and my mum had scissors thrown at her, they stuck into the floor just missing her. That was a real bad house".

MY MOVE TO SAUCHIE

"As you will probably see I have moved house so many times because of the hauntings, when I moved to Sauchie near Alloa in Clackmannanshire, I was a stranger to the place. I got a flat above what used to be the library on the main street. I was there a couple of weeks when I began to notice some strange happenings. I was on a power card meter and had forgot to put the card in when I came home from the town. It wasn't until the power went off that I realised, so grabbing my purse and shuffling around in the dark, I made it to the hall cupboard where the meter was, and just as I was putting the card in, I instantly saw a little boy standing in the cupboard with me he was wearing a baby grow and couldn't have been any more than two years old. From then, I would find teddies in the hall that weren't my kids. I would hoover the hall then turn around and by the bedroom door I would see the little boy. He seemed harmless, but it did frighten me. Then one night around 9.30pm, the toilet would flush. Thinking it was one of the kids, I ignored it. Then it flushed again. So, I checked, and no one was in the bathroom? And for that whole night the toilet kept flushing! I contacted the council and they sent someone out and they had no idea what was wrong and in fact said jokingly, *"Maybe you have a ghost"!* I ended up moving again across the road into a private let before I moved to Glenochil, and that's where the really scary stuff happened".

MY MOVE TO GLENOCHIL VILLAGE

"So eventually I moved again to a private let in Glenochil Village near Alloa in Clackmannanshire. I had met my son's father at this point, and we lived together. We viewed the property, and everything seemed fine, so we paid our deposit and moved in. We were in the property two days when the first strange thing happened. I was upstairs and I had set the PC up in the bedroom and attached the speakers. As I sat on the computer chair, the speakers began to make a strange loud buzzing sound. Then I felt a cold breeze on the back of my neck. The floorboard squeaked as though someone had walked in, and as I looked around, the built in cupboard door swung open! I removed myself from the room and in a panic ran downstairs. There were days when things would happen and days that were quiet, but when things happened, they were always extreme in this property".

"My son was only 6 months old when we moved in, and when he was two, I fell pregnant. Connor my two-year-old was playing in the hall when I heard him screaming. I ran over to him, but he wouldn't breathe for me, he was terrified. I lifted him up and checked him over, and eventually when he calmed down, he said 'monster man'! I asked him where was 'monster man', and he pointed to the kitchen. So, I checked the kitchen, and to my shock all four of my dining chairs were tipped over. I decided I wanted to catch evidence of this stuff because I didn't want people thinking I was crazy, so I bought a new camera and thought I would take pictures. But when I tried with the flash on, something would flash back! A huge bright light would mimic the flash. One night my kids dad would go for a shower and we would be downstairs. I'd hear banging and I'd run upstairs thinking he had fallen in the shower, but when I got there, the bathroom door would be open, and he would be going mad saying that one of us kicked the door open?

This seemed to happen a lot, the door would be banged really hard when someone was in there. One day I was going into town, the house was empty at this point, but when I came home, I went to the toilet to find that the bathroom sink was smashed!

Everything had come off the windowsill and was scattered on the floor, apart from my bottle of ghost perfume which was sat on the toilet seat! This terrified us, it was getting worse! But we had nowhere to go, I didn't want to move again. A neighbour came to visit one night as I had invited her over, and as she stood in the hallway with me, she jumped in fear. When I asked if she was OK, she said she heard a voice in her ear telling her to get out! She was in tears with fear".

"I didn't know what to do. I had the kids to think about and I was pregnant. So, I stayed and put up with the banging stuff and things being moved. I would hear voices that sounded like they were coming from my pillow when I lay down. It was like women chatting, but I couldn't make out what they were saying. So, it was getting close to me going into hospital to have the baby. I needed to fetch some stuff that I had for my older son from the loft, so my partner went up for me and he would hand me the stuff down. He handed me a baby rocking chair; I sat it out the way as I was grabbing bags being handed down to me. Then all of a sudden, the rocking chair started rocking on its own! I couldn't believe my eyes. I stood and watched it for at least 30 seconds then it stopped! At which point the bathroom door burst open, and stuff was thrown about. I would often come home to weird things in places that there were not meant to be. For example, the chair in the living room would be up against the door. Pictures would be off the walls. Kitchen utensils were scattered over the kitchen floor which included bent cutlery and a chair broken from the dining area".

"Whatever this was, had power. I had a knife thrown at me in the dining area and it stuck into the floor. It caused me to have severe depression and nasty thoughts about killing myself and caused mayhem in the house. It seemed to attach itself to me I'm often taken back to that house in my dreams, and it still terrifies me".

MY MOVE TO TULLIBODY

"I had no choice, so at the end of my lease I moved again! I ended up in a house in Northwood Road Tullibody near Alloa in Clackmannanshire, where every night I was chased upstairs by something! There was no getting away from these hauntings.

BACK TO STIRLING

"So, I moved back here in Stirling. I blessed the house before I moved in, and I haven't had anything! For the first time in my life, I've become settled. These things have followed me since I was a child, I would say since I was seven years old. I feel protected here and safe, although my dreams still take me back to those haunted houses. I never used to speak about these things because I wasn't believed. It does sound crazy though. The demons though, they were something else. They sexually abused me. I've never spoke about that. The only time that they left me alone was when I was pregnant".

With regards. Christian.

Our next door that leads us into the paranormal, is a tale told by a lady who deals specifically with psychic phenomena, and, if called upon, will do her best to cleanse a property of its spooky conditions.

OUR PSYCHIC INVESTIGATIONS

(Gail Peacock and Jo Bradley).

Location: Hertfordshire.

Date:1980's.

"As a professional medium and psychic investigator with more than 40 years' experience, I am often contacted by people who have encountered extraordinary phenomena in one form or another asking for my assistance. Each case is unique with its own individual patterns and circumstance, and it is interesting to note that many people who experience poltergeist phenomena or hauntings simply do not know where to turn or whom to contact. One aspect of my work as a medium involves spirit release. I find it extremely fascinating and rewarding work and am still learning from each and every case I have been involved in".

"I hope that by highlighting just one of my cases, of which there are many, it will show what can happen to very ordinary people and how I work with my guides in helping them. What follows is just one such case. I received a telephone enquiry from a lady called Jade. She had got my name from a previous cleansing case I had worked on and asked if I could assist in investigating some ghostly happenings at her home in Hertfordshire. She said that for as long as they have lived there, her family have been constantly visited by spirits, and it started only a few weeks after moving in. Jade shares her home with her husband, a young daughter and son and two boisterous dogs, they are a very ordinary, loving, family living in a 70's style home located on a housing estate. Due to the unsettling activity, Jade was becoming increasingly agitated and distressed, and word soon got around about what seemed to be poltergeist activity in her home. Several mediums and paranormal groups became interested in visiting her in the hope of capturing and recording spirit activity. Their visits had done nothing to ease her fears and worries, and if anything, the activity had become more intense. She felt her only hope was to ask a local priest to come in and perform a blessing, but it was apparent shortly after his visit that her active spirit had returned, and an appointment was made for my visit. I prefer to work without having any prior knowledge of the haunted areas in the location I am visiting or the full facts regarding who the spirit has targeted. In effect this gives me a 'clear page' to work from and that way no previous stories are conflicting with my findings".

"In the first instance, I ask my spirit guides if I will be successful in investigating the case and I get a sign, a thumbs up or thumbs down, a very simple process. Then, sitting quietly with pen and paper, I tune into my guides and ask their assistance. I start to write this is best described as doodling. These doodles come direct from my guides and the information received is significant to the case, they are like pieces of a puzzle, and it is not always obvious knowing where they fit. Names, dates, and emotional sensations immediately start to flood my mind, prior to entering the location or meeting with the client. I ask my guides what rooms are being affected and if there are any portals (spiritual doorways) present, and if so where they are placed within the location. I also ask who is being targeted and why. In this case what was revealed in my doodling was that both the children were being affected. It was physical in the fact they were being harmed and were somehow physically weakening. The spirit was operating like a vampire and drawing energy in order to maintain its own existence. Jade confirmed this was indeed the case, and that both her children had an impaired immune system and that doctors could not find the cause. Numerous tests had been carried out on them both, but nothing concrete was discovered".

"Jade had told me, prior to my visit, that whilst she was watching her children playing in the garden out of her kitchen window, she had witnessed them both being swooped up in the air, levitating a few feet off the ground, then slapped back down, face forward. This was when she contacted a spiritual group and then the priest for help to bless the house.

She had never encountered anything of this nature prior to moving into the house. As with any investigation I prepare the night before, making sure all instruments are ready and charging, such as cameras, infrared video, and voice recorder. I asked that the father along with the children be removed from the house for the evening whilst I was there. Jade had her sister stay with her for moral support and was witness to what transpired. I was instructed by my guides to concentrate on both children's rooms, but especially the daughter's bedroom. The portal was identified as the attic. These portals are like worm holes of energy, which a spirit can travel through into our dimension. These artefacts are often associated with cold drafts and strong vibrations which are often felt once in, or near, them. The attic entrance is in front of their daughter's bedroom. The air when entering the bedroom was quite suffocating and very different to the rest of the house. Jade confirmed that this room was the height of spirit activity; and even the dogs would not enter".

"When we arrived, Jade explained that all hell had broken out the night before. She told me they were woken up at 03.12 am to a loud scratching and banging sound coming from the attic. Both now wide awake, they sat bolt upright in the bed awaiting whatever force was about to reveal itself to them, knowing in their logical mind that the noise was far too loud to be any bird, when suddenly the attic hatch door flipped open with astonishing force. They went on to say that this 'thing' had jumped down through the attic into the hallway, 'he', they were certain it was male, was almost solid. They felt extremely frightened for themselves and their children and were almost paralysed with fear when they heard the most horrible growling sound come from it. They instantly felt his anger. With great speed it took off into their daughter's room where it woke her. She screamed and was extremely traumatised by the experience. It is often the case that prior to my visit, the 'spirit earth walker' will increase in activity, almost as if aware and disapproving of my arrival".

"I had set up my equipment, but as on previous occasions the video recorder failed as the batteries were drained, even though they were charged the night before, as did the batteries in the camera. However, I am happy to say that the voice (or should I say the growl) of the 'spirit earth walker' was captured. He was very angry that I was able to identify him as a reverend who had lived in the home some years previously. It was later confirmed that a reverend had formerly resided there, but that Jade had never met him or knew anything about him as the house was empty for some time before they bought it. I asked my spirit guides to come in and work amongst us to assist in communicating with the troubled 'spirit earth walker'. To start up a form of communication to try to identify what it was it wanted from the property, land, or family. A connection was made with him and through direct spirit communication he told me he wanted his book and letters; he was very agitated. Jade confirmed that post addressed to this entity, does still on occasion come to the house, and that a letter had arrived only two days prior to my visit. She had it in her car, for re-posting. I asked her to get it for me. The post mark on the letter was from India, it was from other reverends and religious factions working at a children's sanctuary".

"Opening the letter had obviously sparked an anger in him so great that the whole room actually blackened. The room had become like a vortex of energy, almost like an echo chamber. Jade complained of feeling quite dizzy and sick. The aroma in the room was vile to say the least. Bad drains would not suffice to identify the smell. The freezing cold atmosphere was felt by all. I asked out loud for protection for us and started to pray for the soul of the 'spirit earth walker'.

I was experiencing a pain to my right arm, a feeling best described as a Chinese burn, I felt an intense pressure on my arm and held it outstretched for others to see. Fingertip bruising could be easily witnessed appearing like a hand grip around my arm. I continued praying even louder and had noticed that Jade had gone completely white; her face drained of all colour. I called her name to get her attention and her face had a glazed look on it. Dark circles surrounded both her eyes and she looked straight at me, but not focusing, I knew he was affecting her. I asked Philip to grab her as it was witnessed by all that she was levitating about two inches above the floor. At the same time, the back of her head was hitting the wall continuously. She could not speak and had a transfixed expression on her face. This was naturally frightening for her sister to witness. I demanded that the 'earth walker' release her, which he did, and that's when he recorded his anger, this can be heard on my website under 'audio' on the forum".

"He said, through me clairvoyantly, that he wanted his book. I relayed what I was hearing in my mind. Jade was recovering from her shock and was not aware what had happened. The 'earth walker', (the reverend), wanted his book then he would be gone. I felt what seemed like anger rising in me, and knew it was my guides working through me. I stormed out of the daughters' bedroom and into the sons' bedroom while Jade's sister followed in hot pursuit.

He pointed at the boys fitted wardrobe, to a top cupboard. Jade and her sister had said there were no books or anything in there, only her son's action men and Lego bricks. He was quite insistent, so a chair was brought in allowing the top cupboard to be reached he was talking so fast in my mind, he was getting very excited. Jade had told me that no items were left in the house prior to them moving in. A very large, white, ornate bible was found, it needed two hands to hold it exactly where he had told us to look.

A bookmark had been placed in the book, at a passage marked 'come unto thee little children'. The bookmark was a picture of their daughter's latest school photo, taken only a month previously. They had not seen that photo for some time and didn't even know of the existence of the bible in their sons' bedroom. Logic asks how can a book so large, materialise in their son's cupboard, which had not previously been there prior to their move and that a school photograph of their daughter was found being used as a bookmark, highlighting a children's passage Why? and how"?

"The investigation continued and whilst I had asked Philip to read the passage, I tore the letter up in shreds and asked for the reverend to reveal why he was angry and why he refused to enter the light. His answer was shocking as he revealed he was frightened of redemption. He was guilty of wrong doings to children and knew he would need to have to face the consequences. He had been hiding behind the security and camouflage of his dog collar for many years allowing him safe passage for his addiction. He knew this was wrong and that judgment day was beckoning. He preferred to stay in the grey matter the in-between realms, rather than face his sins. I asked the higher realms to collect him, for him to start his journey for forgiveness and to move on and leave this family in peace. Some moments passed, all was quiet, this was an important time of the clearance.

I had sensed reluctance from him at first, deemed as being caused by his own fears and then a release; I knew he had surrendered to what fate he must now face. It was done. I returned to the portal to close it down. A healing prayer was given to Jade and the home blessed. It was immediately noticed by all that the smell had gone, the room had warmed, and all had felt quiet and peaceful. I had destroyed the bible page by page once back at my home and said a prayer of forgiveness for him and asked for him to receive redemption and peace as I did so. I instructed Jade in the use of further protective measures and mind energy techniques; I do this in all my cases".

Information received from Jade after the investigation

"I received an update from Jade saying that they have not experienced any paranormal activity since my visit, which is a tremendous relief, especially as poltergeist activity was experienced on a daily basis. She told me that they are all sleeping through the night, and that both her son and daughter are getting well again and no longer require any further medical tests. What follows are excerpts taken from email correspondence received from Jade".

"The evening before Gail was due to visit, we had our newly decorated entrance hall destroyed, an extremely heavy mirror lifted off a cabinet it was resting on and flew through the air smashing everything in its way. It was at that moment all my fears were confirmed and I waited in anticipation for Gail's arrival. I decided to take photos of the incident before clearing away the debris, which I did not look at until Gail had visited. The mirror landed facing upwards, it clearly showed an elderly gentleman's (or man not very gentle) face and shoulders looking straight back at me. My son had been suffering with sleeplessness, and was often very scared at night, saying he was being woken by something/someone.

Gail advised me to tell my son to imagine himself wrapped in huge angel wings. Whilst he is wrapped in wings no one can wake him. So, my son did this and that night my husband and I were awoken by an almighty crash, we ran to my son's room to find Lego strewn across my son's bedroom floor. More surprisingly, my son was still fast asleep. The following morning my son said to me "Ha"! The wings work mummy, he tried to wake me, and I just laughed at him that really annoyed him didn't it'!

Gail reencountered the incident and conversations between my son, my husband and I, telling me the reverend got so angry at my son, he smashed his Lego house. This amazed me".

"The next thing I knew was I was feeling physically sick as I ran to the bathroom, I found myself in an almost dream state, everything was in slow motion, it took, what felt like minutes to realise my head was banging against the wall and I was frozen unable to move. I could see Gail mouthing something to me, but I could not hear her, it felt like I was under water. I eventually could hear Gail saying, "You are an oak tree, put your roots in the ground". As I looked down, I realised I was quite a few inches off the floor, and I was pinned against the wall. It took me some time to register what I had to do, but eventually I put all my energy into getting my feet back on the ground. Gail was amazing, she was very strong and took control of the moment, which I am very thankful for. Gail had recorded that moment on tape, the reverend was chanting at her and then as he pushed passed her to get to me, he shouted, "Move". Gail offered me the opportunity to listen to the tape, but I declined."

Gail Peacock (e-mail excerpt from Jade)

In a further communication that I had from Gail, she stated that both she and her friend Jo Bradley, (a fellow psychic) decided to combine both of their psychic abilities and to dedicate their time and effort into developing all forms of physical mediumship. Not only that, but she informed me that they felt a duty to pass their knowledge onto those who have an interest and an enquiring mind. Here is what Gail and Jo had to say about her work with spirit.

"For those who wish to explore physical phenomena, for themselves at first hand. We use a scientific approach to all our work with all the regalia of the Victorian era with the combination of modern equipment that can capture electronic voice phenomena (EVP) and more. There are no guarantees of results achieved, as each workshop or course is a unique experience and dependent on the collective energies. We have been focused in bringing forward an awareness and an understanding, that external spiritual forces can and do work amongst us. Our subjective energy is utilised by our guides with an objective view, to be able to capture and experience at first hand, and to deliver external evidence of another dimension at work and that life is continual, albeit in another dimension. It was thought that due to the mass speculation of the Mayan calendar, predicting the end of the world in 2012, highlighting many, to question the possible existence of another dimension. This in itself has increased popularity and opened people's minds with a renewed interest in physical mediumship. Will I see and be joined by my loved ones again? Or is it lights out for eternity! Working with various forms of lighting allows tangible physical evidence to be captured through photographs and on video to eliminate any form of trickery or fraud. We work on two levels, one of which is traditional ectoplasm as in Victorian times and secondly with a blue energy, which was an unexpected ingredient that spirit brought to our work, thought to be a new and highly evolved form of spirit energy. We are, still experimenting with this electric blue mass, showing intelligence as it responds on request, to changing colour and form. It has also been captured in daylight.

It is easily photographed, captured on many students' cameras. To date, we have discovered that the energy and the ectoplasm do not mix but do work side by side. Our experiments are continuing and are drawing attention from scientific communities".

"Daylight manifestation / etherialisation is very rare, as it is to capture ectoplasm which allows spirit manifestation, to occur. We encourage all attendees to experiment with their own equipment, should they wish to, and in doing so, eliminates any allegations of trickery or fraud. No enhancement is used on any of our images captured, they are all in their raw stage. We have a large portfolio of photographic and video evidence which we show at our workshops, courses, and lectures to further educate the understanding and principles of Physical Mediumship. We work to provide a controlled environment to carry out our experiments, to enhance the attendee's experiences and to ensure their protection and wellbeing. Although we have fun in learning and experimenting, our teaching is by no way random. We also host Ghost hunts, where our energy is utilised in a completely unique way from the norm. Our physical energy is used to draw out and connect with the spirits who reside and haunt the location, enabling them to increase and intensify paranormal activity, such as apports, external voices and sounds, touches and physically moving of objects. We do not only rely on gadgetry alone to record spirit energy or residual energy impregnated into the fabric of the walls. Our goal at all times, is to connect and provide absolute evidence that life continues".

Gail Peacock & Jo Bradley. www.spiritconnexions.com

As we know, there are many castles and hotels throughout Scotland which claim to have ghosts. Now whether this is just to garner publicity or not, is open to question.

Our next case comes from a man who worked in one such haunted hotel, and who witnessed something which to this day, he will never forget.

THE KYLE OF LOCHALSH HOTEL GHOST

Location: Kyle of Lochalsh Hotel.
Date: May 1990.

Dear Malcolm,

"Having given some thoughts to try and recall the strange experiences of which occurred to me whilst working at the Kyle of Lochalsh hotel in the Scottish Hebrides in 1990, I have decided to word these things as clearly as I can. Although this was now 33 years ago, occasionally these events still come back to me. Basically, I moved to the Scottish Highlands to take up a seasonal job in May 1990 as a day and night Porter. The hotel was known as the Kyle of Lochalsh hotel. During these busy months many people would come to work there. There would be lots of people especially from around Glasgow. I remember there were many people working also from France and our head chef was French. So, there was a real big variety of people. The hotel was exceptionally busy at times with tourists and coach tours. I had a very busy job and often worked flat out on over 7 nights a week. I didn't really have a lot to do past midnight apart from keeping the front of the hotel area tidy and being around for any calls at the reception desk. I had to do three key checks throughout the night at 1am, 3am, and 5am. This meant going and turning a key on all floors at all the fire doors".

"I cannot remember exactly the day or month this occurred, yet I know it was midsummer, as it was only a deep blue darkness for a couple of hours rather than really dark. I'm sure that this happened to me sometime between 03-05am. I remember covering my work college who was away on holiday to Blackpool, and I think I was on my 10th night shift in a row. I know I was pretty tired that night. I sat in the front of the hotel and decided to rest my eyes for a while, I knew I couldn't fall asleep as I'd the 05am key check to do. I closed my eyes briefly just for a few minutes to rest a bit. Then suddenly, from absolutely nowhere as I opened my eyes, I saw directly in front of me, these two people appear on the other side of the table sitting staring at me.

They were certainly not people from our time, they were definitely from a completely different part of time. They looked kind of transparent like cigarette smoke, in other words, you can see cigarette smoke yet see through it. That's the nearest explanation I could give to seeing them. Yet they were absolutely perfectly formed".

"There was a man and a woman. The man was on my left side and the woman was on my right side. They were both staring hard at me with these really deep small dark eyes. They had a huge grin or smile. They didn't seem to be unfriendly in anyway, yet absolutely scared me to a shivering wreck. The man was wearing a kind of stone necklace around his neck. They were extremely thin. Very thin faces and arms and wore some kind of fur clothing. Totally unlike any kind of people you'd ever see today. They looked like they didn't eat much. Perhaps that's just the normal for how people would have looked in those times. As I say, they just looked like they were from a completely different time in history. I'm not sure exactly when though. I'd say 100s if not 1000s of years ago. I immediately jumped up, shaking and extremely scared. I was on my own, there wasn't anyone around anywhere. All the residents were well away by now and the staff wouldn't be on until 07am where the breakfast staff and receptionist would be on to relieve me.

I remember panicking and running around the entire hotel checking all the doors over and over again going up and down for an hour in the lift. I even remembered sellotaping the front door up and stayed downstairs".

"I just didn't know what to say or think. I just got through the night. I didn't say a word about this to anyone. At 7am when the reception staff came on, I just slipped away out the back door. I think I was off for a couple of days after that night shift. It just wasn't the sort of thing that you'd really bring up or talk about. I never heard anyone ever talk about anything unusual that I can remember certainly, in the hotel itself. Most people were extremely busy working flat out. Also, I remember this feeling I had there which was extremely strong. I always thought it was some kind of chemical smell coming from the small coat room next to the front reception area. I just put it down to perhaps a cleaner leaving a bucket of cleaning equipment in where the coats were hung".

"At one point, I think on a night shift, the smell was so powerful that I decided to go and have a look in that coat room. I'd never actually gone in there before as I don't think I wore a coat. I was shocked to see that there wasn't any cleaning equipment in there whatsoever. I think I just remembered seeing a couple of old coats hanging up in there and nothing else, it was practically empty. I then realised that this wasn't an odour it must be a sensation or something else. It was more a kind of piercing energy which seemed to be going on right through the hotel. It just seemed a lot stronger in that area next to the reception. This was extremely bewildering. The next thing which occurred to me which I just couldn't fathom out, was several weeks later. I was doing kitchen porter work one evening about 7 or 8pm. It was extremely busy; I'd guess it would have been sometime in August 1980. The head chef was from France and most of the chefs were also French. I think his name was Jacuine. He would constantly be needing things handing back to him very quickly.

I remember him handing me a large pan and I placed it on the sink at the right-hand side of me which wasn't anything any different from any other night, yet what happened next was quite bizarre. The pan suddenly burst up into flames. I remember he quickly ran over to it, and I think he smothered it with a blanket. I paused for a minute thinking 'hmmm now that seemed really a bit odd'. Anyway, it was very busy so I'd to carry on with everything. Then, a short while later, the pan was handed back to me again. I don't think anything was said, and it seemed to be OK, not sizzling or smoke coming from it, so it must have been cooler than before.

I mean this head chef was an absolute perfectionist with the highest levels of vigilance I've ever seen in all areas, a brilliant man. Needless to say, I was still very cautious of it and placed the pan in the centre of the kitchen floor completely on its own away from everything else".

"I just couldn't believe what happened next and it wasn't instantly either, I'd guess it was a minute or two later, the pan simply burst up into flames again and he ran around and smothered it again. I was absolutely left speechless just thinking to myself, what was that? What is this energy around here? I did sense something from the chef as well. I don't know if he'd got more awareness about something going on, but I could definitely feel something, yet it remained mutual. I just don't know. Perhaps there's a kind of spiritual code or something you just don't go there. The light and atmosphere was very peculiar, that's the nearest I can explain in words about it all. It's by far the strongest sensation of any place I can ever remember being in. Yet I think there's absolutely very different energies right throughout Scotland. Very moving and extremely powerful. I have just drawn a brief picture of the two people who I saw directly in front of me for you Malcolm to try and bring some clarity to it". *(Author's comment. See photographic section)*

"As for the hotel today I've no idea, yet I'd be very surprised if it was the same as it was back then, yet having said that, I think that these energies or spirits must definitely still be very active in or around this hotel. I don't think they are bad or hostile either, I did feel extremely energised working in that job. I think the energies are actually good. Perhaps very overpowering though. It was a very energised place. Very spiritual".

With regards. Neil Attenbury.

In point of fact, I telephoned the hotel a few times but didn't get through, so I e-mailed the hotel but didn't get a reply. I had hoped to speak to someone there who could perhaps inform me if there were any recent ghostly sightings or strange happenings at the hotel. It may still be the case that uninvited guests, from the other side still haunt the rooms of that hotel. Now, moving on, let me take you the reader, to an aquarium where a strange photograph was taken.

AN UNDERWATER GHOST!

Location: 'The Deep' Aquarium attraction. Hull, England.

Date: The 2000's?

I posed a question on my Facebook page in May 2020 where I asked my readers if they were aware of any tales of ghosts being witnessed under the oceans of our planet. We have of course, thousands of ghosts being witnessed above ground, and I personally was only aware of a few ghosts that had been sighted underwater. And when one thinks about it, the loss of life at sea throughout the centuries is astronomical, and I'm not just talking about the first and second world wars. You could bring to bear the Napoleonic wars and more. So clearly with the immense loss of life at sea, one would expect to have numerous ghosts flitting about the depths of our oceans. Yes, it does sound weird, it does sound fanciful, but let's be honest, other than professional divers going into the depths, of the oceans, it's not a day-to-day thing for Joe Public to go diving into the oceans.

One response that I got from my post, came from author, lecturer, and tour guide, Mike Covell who told me that he worked on a case where a photograph was presented to hm which 'appeared' to be a ghost. This was photographed at a public aquarium called 'The Deep' which is situated at Sammy's Point, on the River Hull and the Humber Estuary in Hull, England. This beautifully stocked aquarium opened its doors in March 2002.

Wikipedia tells us that it's the world's only submarium of which the exhibits contain thousands of sea creatures. Holding back all the fish and sharks are 2,500,000 litres (550,000 imp gallons) of water. The Deep also has Europe's deepest viewing tunnel at 9 metres long (30 feet).

Mike himself was intrigued by this photograph which he told me he has featured in one of his books. He said that the girl who took the photograph Emma, was very genuine and a bit scared after taking the image. Apparently, Emma was walking along the tunnel feature inside the Deep, which leads you beneath the main tank which has thick reinforced glass. It was at this point that she took the photograph. On the bottom right-hand corner of the photograph, is, what appears to be, a head. What isn't clear is that we don't know, is if Emma actually saw this head at the time when she was taking the photograph, or she noticed it later. Mike went on to inform me that he had tried to recreate this photograph by using different cameras, lights, and positions, but never could. The photograph appeared in a local newspaper where they tried to tie it in with the Fever Hospital, but as Mike pointed out, this hospital stood some distance away. Then the newspaper tried to tie it in with the citadel, but as Mike rightly pointed out, the old castle was actually built some way back towards the main road. I think what the newspaper was trying to suggest, was that there might have been some tragic accident where the Deep now stands. However, Mike was quick to point out that The Deep was actually built on reclaimed land from the Humber. If we were to look at local tragedies which some might construe as to why we might have this ghostly face, then Mike tells us that the Humber itself was stricken with many tragedies, including the infamous R38 airship explosion of 1921 where 44 souls lost their lives.

Of course, it might not be a ghostly face at all (even although it clearly looks like one)

We have to consider that old but good explanation to account for many ghostly and UFO photographs that's known as, 'Pareidolia' also known as, 'simulacrum' Effectively, what Pareidolia is, is that the human eye is prone to make faces out of anything. It's all about perception. For instance, you may look up into the sky and see a cloud that is shaped like a horse. You may look at a tree and see what resembles a face from the leaves of the tree. This can be done by a combination of light and shade and the visual perception that this effect gives you. Pareidolia, has been the cause of many so-called ghostly photographs falling by the wayside. Was this the case here? Well, I guess we'll never truly known, unless perhaps, someone else comes up with a similar photograph.

I came across an article on the internet (link in reference section) where the lady who took the photograph, Emma, had this to say.

Emma stated. *"I took this eerie photo on my phone at Hull's £53million attraction The Deep"*. Boffins at the aquarium admit they are baffled by the appearance of the man's face, which appears to be gawping up at a shark. Emma continued. *"I only spotted the ghoulish face when I arrived home.*

My boyfriend said, 'what's that?' I replied, 'it's a shark'. He said, 'no, the face.' I was like, 'oh my Gosh'! It actually looks quite spooky. I'm easily freaked-out. Although my dad, aged 48, was standing next to me in the glass tunnel, he looks nothing like the man in the photo.

Bosses have spent hours searching CCTV footage, which confirmed the two of us were the only ones inside the tunnel. And they have even tried to recreate conditions in the tunnel where the reflection could appear, but with no success.

According to a report in the Sun newspaper, and also the ghosthoot web site, it states that it's not the first time that ghostly goings-on have been reported at this

attraction. There was a night watchman who claims to have spotted a shadowy figure in the TimeLine. This TimeLine charts the history of the world's oceans. Colin Brown, chief executive of The Deep, said: *"We are a scientific centre and we're sure there must be a logical explanation. It's just that we can't find it."*

OTHER UNDERWATER GHOSTS!

Doing research for this book regarding underwater ghosts, I found that there are a few good stories out there, but none that I could find concerning ghosts in the waters around the British Isles.

That said, and as this is quite an interesting subject (Ghosts seen underwater) I felt it remiss of me not to at least give you some of the better examples from overseas that I found. From the website 'Mysterious Universe' there is a page that deals with 'underwater ghosts'. It was written up by a chap called Brent Swancer who is an author and cryptozoology expert living in Japan. The following are but a few of those most interesting tales. See what you make of these.

THE RMS RHONE GHOSTS

We are told that there is a wreck of a 19th century mail ship called the RMS Rhone which was lost at sea due to a hurricane back in October 1867. This was near Salt Island which lies in the British Virgin Islands. The story goes that when divers are exploring this wreck, they often claim to see ghostly swimmers who are desperately swimming upwards as if to reach the surface only for them to vanish midway.

THE HUMANOID CREATURES OF THE BLACK SEA

Probably one of the more bizarre tales that I read from this web site, was the tale coming from a chap called B. Borovikov, who, whilst diving in the Black Sea hunting sharks in the Anapa area back in 1996, came across something that he least expected to see. Borovikov states that he was diving at a depth of around 8 meters when suddenly ascending from below him, were what he could only describe as some type of 'humanoid creatures'. They were milky white in colour and just over nine feet in length. They had human like faces, but tails like a fish. Needless to say, Borovikov was terrified. Suddenly one of these strange creatures stopped, to look and stare at Borovikov at which point Borovikov further describes this particular strange creature as having bulging frog like eyes. Another one of these creature's appeared to wave at him and as it did so he noticed that it had a webbed hand. A few seconds later they all swam away and were lost in the darkness.

Now admittedly, this has nothing at all to do with underwater ghosts, but as it was such a fascinating account, I felt that I just had to mention it here. For more information about underwater ghosts from this web site, please see the link in the chapter reference section at the end of this book.

Another web site which contained a number of unusual ghostly encounters, was entitled, 'Paranormal Authority'. Again, there is a link to this in the chapter reference section.

THE LAGOON OF GHOSTS

There is a lagoon in Southeast Asia which has the most beautiful of lagoons. It's called Truk Lagoon, and whilst on the surface the area looks peaceful and tranquil, it's a different story beneath the waves. For it was here, during the Second World War, that one of the most feracious Naval battles took place with the loss of around 3,000 people. Over five dozen ships which included several civilian merchant ships sank beneath the waves. The story goes, that in recent years a number of scuba divers have descended into the depths of the lagoon to view the remnants of these ships, and when they do, they encounter not just ships, but apparently shadowy figures walking along these sunken ships.

Even more disconcerting, is the fact that some divers claim to have heard voices shouting underwater.

THE ANDREA DORIA, A HAUNTED CRUISE SHIP

There are many beautiful ocean liners traversing the seas of our planet right now, but back in the early 1950s, there was an Italian cruise ship by the name of Andrea Doria. It wasn't the largest, nor was it the fastest, but at 697 feet, it contained three outdoor swimming pools, and an art gallery. For its time, the ship was 'state of the art' and had not one, but two radar screens, and its hull contained 11 watertight compartments. But tragedy would soon befall the Andrea Doria when it collided with another vessel, the Stockholm, off the coast of Nantucket in the Atlantic Ocean. This disaster resulted in the deaths of 51 people 46 from the Andrea Doria and 5 from the Stockholm.

Sadly, most of the passengers were killed on impact, but there were dozens who were fortunate to be alive, at least for a short while, as they clung for dear life on the ship's hull.

As with other shipwrecks, divers have descended into the depths of this wreck, and some divers claim of hearing shouts from long dead passengers as they echoed through the hallways. It's also claimed that some divers have witnessed figures at the ship re-enacting what could be their last moments. However, what makes this dive all the more spooky for those who dive down to the ship, is the fact that some of these 'ghosts' seem to try and engage with the divers! Some even report being grabbed or poked, or even slapped by the ghosts who lost their lives on this ship.

THE GHOST OF THE FEMALE DIVER

There are many beauty spots around our planet, one such beauty spot is the 'Blue Hole' at Santa Rosa New Mexico. This 'hole' was once known as the 'Blue Lake' due to its pristine blue hues, and it's one of the seven sister lakes which are connected underground by a vast system of water. We are told that it is a 'one-of-a-kind' waterhole, which incredibly naturally replenishes with a stunning 3,000 gallons of water every minute. The hole is actually bell shaped and has an 80-foot diameter at the top and a 130-foot diameter at the bottom. One would think that such a beautiful area would be the furthest away from any supernatural happenings. But you would be wrong. Again, we have tales coming from divers who have entered this hole, coming back with stories of witnessing one single female diver who has swum up to them wearing a pink oxygen tank and vanishing before their eyes! The story goes that these divers had been concerned about the welfare of this mysterious female diver and had reported their concerns to the local police, at which point they have been told that this wasn't the first time that divers have encountered the figure and were further told that reports of her went back several years.

THE GHOSTLY WATERS AROUND THE TITANIC SINKING

One of the biggest tragedies at sea, certainly concerning a passenger liner, was of course the sinking of the (so called unsinkable ship) RMS Titanic. This fateful tragedy occurred in the early morning of 15th April 1912 in the north Atlantic Ocean. The ship was only four days into its maiden voyage when it struck an iceberg. There were 2,224 people were on board, of which more than 1,500 tragically lost their lives. I was quite taken aback to learn from the Mysterious Universe web site, that apparently 'people' including sailors that have gone over the sinking site, have claimed to have seen strange mysterious lights hovering above the water. Not only that, but bright glowing orbs have been witnessed floating just under the water's surface. But it gets even crazier! It's also alleged that radio operators from ships passing the area where the Titanic went down, have received strange signals, the most prominent one being a message in morse code saying 'CQD' which is an old version of SOS.

The message translates into, 'Come Quick Danger'! This was one of the first distress signals which was used for radio by the Marconi International Communication Company, first used on the 7th of January 1904. I guess it's not any wonder that people like myself and you reading this book, have this fascination for all things weird and wonderful.

THE STRANGE GHOSTS OF THE USS MAINE

OK, we're not finished yet, I have one more bizarre tale to tell regarding ghosts of the deep. Let us now take ourselves across to the waters to Havana Harbour which is the main port of Cuba. Here we learn of the sinking of the ship the USS Maine.

The sinking of this ship on February 15th, 1898, is alleged to have contributed to the start of the Spanish-American War. The Maine was sent to Havana Harbour to ensure the protection of the United States interests during the Cuban war of Independence. During her stay in the harbour, she exploded and sank with the loss of 268 sailors which was three quarters of her crew. The USS Maine now lies on the seabed 3,600 feet (1,100 m) below the surface. Now, this is where things get a bit spooky, are you sitting comfortably? Then I'll begin. We are told that sometime after the explosion and sinking (We are not told how long after) the United States and Spain ordered an investigation of this explosion and also a clean-up of the area. We learn that a Captain John Magee Jnr was given this responsibility and despatched some Spanish divers down to the wreck site in hopes of gaining some evidence as to the cause of the explosion. Each diver only had around 15 minutes air in their tanks to get down and have a look. And here's the rub, each diver that went down to the wreck, came up after only five minutes or so. After taking their mask off, each diver was shaking, their faces were pale, and they were unable to speak of what they saw. However, the job of inspection still needed to be done, so eventually other divers were despatched into the water (the previous divers refused to go back

down) When the initial divers eventually regained their composure and were asked what they saw that so frightened them, they replied that they had seen the ghosts of the men who had died aboard the Maine who begged them for a proper and respectful burial. We are told that a proper funeral ceremony was held for the deceased sailors and that things went quiet for a while. But like all good hauntings, you can't keep a good ghost down! Other divers who dived down to the wreck, claimed to have seen the ghost of a fully dressed lieutenant whose face was wrapped up in a black shroud following them around. What is remarkable about this, is that Lieutenant Jenkins, one of the men who perished in the Maine, was allegedly not in uniform when the ship went down, indeed he was asleep in his bed when the explosion occurred.

Author's Comment. Strange indeed. Let's be honest, if those that have perished above ground can be seen in their spectral form, it stands to reason that those who have perished at sea should equally be seen! Death is death, no matter on land, sea, or air. That said, it would be interesting to hear of any pilots who have seen ghostly people in the sky who have died. I'm referring to deceased pilots of the First and Second World wars, indeed any aerial combat. There have been countless deaths of people from commercial airliners whose aircraft have exploded in air. One cannot forget the terrible disaster of Flight Pan Am 103 which exploded in the sky due to a bomb on board and fell onto the town of Lockerbie back on the 21st of December 1988 killing all of its 243 passengers onboard as well as 16 crew with 11 fatalities in Lockerbie as the remnants of the plane came crashing down on houses. All told, 270 people lost their lives that night. So, my question here is, if people see and 'hear' ghosts of the dead in water and on land, where are the spirits of those that have lost their lives in the air! Have there been any reports of ghostly passengers from the Lockerbie disaster?

One would think that out of the countless millions of people who have travelled across the skies of this planet in commercial airliners (and indeed in small Cessna and other aircraft) that surely some aerial ghosts have been seen. I am aware that actual ghostly aircraft have been seen flitting across the skies of this planet, way too many to go into here. So maybe it's not so much the people who have lost their lives on board these aircraft, maybe it's the aircraft itself that will be sighted, and has 'indeed been sighted'. One may ask, how is this possible?

What is the mechanism behind this aerial apparition to form and why? We can but wonder. Our next ghostly tale concerns the witnessing of an apparition which scared the bejesus out of a husband and his wife.

THE CASTLEBAR GHOST

Location: Not stated.
Date: Not stated.

OK, that's not a good start. Presenting a ghost case with no date and no location? How this one came about was that I received an e-mail from a lady named Rachel who wanted to tell me about the ghost that was in her house. She failed to mention in her e-mail to me, where her house was located, and when did these ghostly experiences start. Needless to say, I e-mailed her back asking for this information, but sadly never received a reply. Here is that e-mail in its entirety.

Hi Malcolm,

"We used to live at 4c Castlebar Road, and during that time we experienced strange things when we moved in. There was a panic button in the flat and all the doors were broken. When we were in the kitchen there was a sense of someone behind us or passing the kitchen door in the hallway.

When we stood in the kitchen to the right of the doorway just outside the kitchen, we could see a silhouette of an upper torso and head. One night my husband heard a dragging noise outside the kitchen window near the alleyway from the garden. There were three footsteps pulling something heavy, it felt like someone dragging a body, my husband was too scared to go out and have a look, he had not told me this until later. When he had told me this, I mentioned to him that a few days before, I had heard a digging noise in our back garden,

81

but I was too scared to look out the window myself to have a look. When we discussed this, we then realised that we could both feel some kind of presence whilst in our kitchen and could see a silhouette. Until then, neither of us had realised that both of us were experiencing the strange things in our flat. Do you have any information on anything? To this day it is still makes us have goose pimples just thinking about it! I should also point out that my husband did not believe in such things until he had these experiences".

Thank you. Rachel and Corry.

Author's Comment. As I mentioned above. I e-mailed Rachel back asking for more information but did not receive a reply. It would have been interesting for me to research that house and area, just to find out if indeed there might have been a murder or some nefarious goings on at that property, who knows, I may yet get that e-mail.

We now take our journey over to the Isle of Sheppy, where a gentleman by the name of Daniel Worthington presented me with a few ghost stories that he had looked into. Before we get to them however, he gave me his own thoughts as to what might be behind poltergeist effects.

GHOSTLY TALES

Location: Isle of Sheppy and Sheerness, England.
Date: 1990's.

Dear Malcolm,

"On the back of a recent review in Fortean Times, I picked up a Kindle edition of your book *'The Sauchie Poltergeist'*. Having a keen interest in all unexplained events for almost 35 years now (especially poltergeists, the reason for which I will explain below) I was surprised that I had never heard of this case before".

"I have now finished your book, and thought it was both informative and entertaining. Thank you for sharing your research on this fascinating topic. I found your commentary on 'what is a poltergeist' especially interesting, as well as the thoughts of your guest contributors. While it is frustrating to you not to have experienced any of this yourself as a key witness, (especially being so close but too young!) I think the research work you have done is both admirable and entertaining. Your book, as well as Darren W. Ritsons, *'South Shields Poltergeist',* and Guy Lyon Playfair's, *'This House Is Haunted'* takes pride of place on my bookshelf".

"Although from my experience as an 'armchair' researcher (I really do dislike that term) I think that it is true that just as you start to come up with answers, the Polt (poltergeist) changes the questions! The reason that Polts fascinate me, is that I have had an active interest in all things paranormal since I was about 8 years old, having been introduced to the topic by the *'World Of The Unknown'* book collection (as I imagine many people were of my age). This developed into a need to devour all material making me well read on most topics by my late teens. Now at the age of 44 my views have changed considerably. Maybe this is age, or wisdom, or just being more healthily critical. Who knows? Polt's, in my option, have stood the test of time and are unique among unexplained events".

"Most of the others (ghosts, UFOs, Nessie, UFO/aliens) do not stand up to much scrutiny once you get to the bare bones. Now, I am not suggesting that they are not real (of course they are, once you refocus what 'real' means) Nor is it to discredit any witnesses or researchers.

But Plots are in a league above, in that there has always been quality tangible first hand evidence to prove their existence, more recently supported by video and photos. Unlike other topics where I sit between 'does not exist' and 'I'm open to believe', but what actual evidence is there? I have absolutely no doubt that Polts are very real, and relatively common. My own personal view is that they are not disembodied manifestations of the dead, but are human in their origin, albeit with an independent intelligence, and one day will be understood by science. I could be wrong, of course. I do hope not, as otherwise I will have to subscribe to the very frightening concept of the dead making a nuisance of themselves at the expense of the living! But who knows, open minds open doors. I wrote to Darren Ritson once I had finished his book to congratulate him on his research and book, and I would like to extend this to you Malcolm for yours".

"Locally I collect strange stories from my own area The Isle of Sheppy (is there a better hobby?) I must stress that I don't claim to be a researcher or investigator, merely a collector. Although for the contributions I do like to interview the witness personally to get a feel for their authenticity and to probe a little deeper into their experience. I have collected a couple of Poltergeist stories which I have copied below for your attention hopefully they may be of interest to you".

Author's Comment. These cases are situated in the Isle of Sheppy, Kent, England.

"In 2005 my son purchased a small house which was in need of renovation. My son only had a limited budget, so he bought it as a working project, something I was only too happy to help with. Over a few months we gutted and renovated the house, but I was always annoyed as various tools would vanish, only to turn up after searching. As a professional tradesman, I am aware that this does happen occasionally (we blame it on gremlins) but the frequency at this address was alarming. Things came to a head when I was painting the kitchen ceiling. I put the brush into the paint tray to open a new can of paint. I turned back to see the brush missing. Cursing as I thought it had fell onto the floor, I found it wasn't there. Scratching my head, I searched the floor only for my son to return to the house holding the paint brush asking why I had left it on the front doorstep. A few days later I was fixing cupboard doors in the kitchen, (my son was present) and a couple of handfuls of what I can only describe as shingles rained down on us. There was obviously nowhere these could have come from, and on inspection they were slightly damp. I am as confused now as I was then about these weird things. My son lived at the address for a few years and never reported any else happening".

Author's Comment. We now move onto another story that Daniel has researched. Here is what he had to say about the family who occupied this house.

"I live in a small terrace house in Marine Town Sheerness in Kent with my partner. We have lived here for 5 years now. Every so often the clear sound of shoes walking across my hardwood floor in the front room can be heard. It is always in the same way, from the front door to the kitchen area at the back.

Even if we hear it from our different positions, it can always be clearly heard walking at the same pace in the same direction, just to suddenly stop as the footsteps get to the kitchen door. As silly as it sounds, the footsteps sound like clogs or tap dance shoes. My partner's parents stayed over a few years ago, and without ever mentioning it to them, they commented that they heard the footsteps in the same way that we had.

I must stress that this is a loud noise that would stop any conversation and not merely just a faint hush that you really have to listen for. We have become used to it, and I think I would miss it if it ever stopped".

Author's Comment. We continue with another ghostly tale from Daniel.

"I lived in a small bungalow in Minster village on the Isle of Sheppy for several years with my wife, and (at the time) newly born daughter. I never saw anything that I would consider a ghost, but there were certainly some very odd things that went on which coincided with the birth of our daughter. I say this, as nothing happened before her birth despite us living at the address for a number of years".

"One morning I took my daughter into the front room only to notice that her stock of nappies, wipes and other things previously stored away, had appeared to have been thrown all over the floor. On another occasion I filled her baby bathtub with water, anticipating her waking up from a nap. Once she had, I walked into the bathroom to notice that the baby bathtub was upside down and empty. Silly things like this continued until she was about 9 months old, nothing especially scary, more of a playful nuisance really. Until what turned out to be our final encounter. Baby was asleep and I popped out into the garden to put a black sack into a wheelie bin. Our back door was an old-fashioned wood and key lock, with no modern springs or mechanisms to allow it to lock automatically. As I waked into the garden, I pulled the door to (but did not close it) to keep the heat in. As I waked the short distance down the path, I heard the door slam closed. I dropped the black sack and rushed back to the door, initially thinking it was a rogue draft that caused it. To my distress I found the door shut fully and would not open. I could see through the glass panels into the kitchen with no-one present or anything out of place.

I immediately tried the handle which was stuck in position as if it was being held from the other side. Now frantic, I pushed all my weight onto the handle, which was not budging, and in doing so I cut the side of my hand as it slipped off. My mind was going into overdrive. As any parent in this position will understand my only thought was how to get the door open and not what had caused it. I turned to run to my shed to get a hammer to break a panel of glass just above the handle, and as I was rushing down the path back to the door, I saw the door gently swing open. I put the hammer down and went to check on my daughter who was sleeping soundly. That evening, as I was nursing a nasty cut to my hand, I had a chat with whatever it was. I think I said something like *"Enough is enough"*. After this day, nothing ever happened again. My wife and I moved from this house some time ago now, but I often drive past it and wonder if the new occupants have a mischievous tenant".

Regards. Daniel Worthington.

Author's Comment. For the reader's interest. Wikipedia tells us that the Isle of Sheppey is an island off the northern coast of Kent, England, neighbouring the Thames Estuary, centred 42 miles (68 km) from central London. It has an area of 36 square miles (93 km2). The island forms part of the local government district of Swale. Sheppey is derived from Old English Sceapig, meaning 'Sheep Island'.

Our next strange tale is not so much relating to a sighting of a ghost, more of what some might call, 'ghostly orbs'. That said, this equally could be along the lines of 'UFO Lights'. See what you make of this.

BALL LIGHTNING ON THE M74 - (Or was it!)

Location: M74 (Between Junction 132 and Junction 12 North).
Date: 2008/9.

Hi Malcolm.

"Around 2008 /9 I was driving home to Aberdeen from Dumfries up the M74 in a truck, I don't know the place name, but if you are going south of Glasgow you climb to the highest point on the M74 south, you go over the top, and start to go downhill. Then there is a level stretch before you go down to the services on the southbound side. One night at about midnight, I was heading north on the part where it levels out before the top, before you drop down on the Glasgow side. I saw five balls of light coming from my left side, maybe one mile ahead. They were heading towards Edinburgh way. They came right down the motorway about two /three feet off the road, till they were 100/150 feet from the truck. Then they went off the road following the low ground around the hills on the left of the road towards Edinburgh way. The balls were glowing white, and I could hear a fizzing sound from them. There was also a strange smell coming from them. I told my friend that the nearest thing I could think of that would be similar, would be if someone lit up 20 boxes of matches all at once. I looked in the newspapers over a period of weeks to see if someone had reported it but never saw anything. So, I thought 'OK' and forgot about it. That was until last week when someone gave me a book of yours, and it brought it all back to me.

More so when I read the part in which a man said that there was a smell like burning brake shoes. *(Author's Comment. This refers to the Robert Taylor Dechmont Woods UFO Incident)* That was what prompted me to message you. I know other car drivers saw it as well, as some stopped on the hard shoulder. I should point out that there was heavy rain at the time. At their closest, there size was close to one and a half meters round. I never saw them again".

Regards. Fergus Hayes.

I wrote back to Fergus where I stated.

"Wow. It looks to me as if you encountered ball lightning, a rare atmospheric phenomenon. But to see five balls together is even rarer. The size, the smell etc, is all consistent with this phenomenon. What a sight to see, I doubt very much you will forget this one in a hurry. Thanks for sharing",

To which Fergus replied.

"If it was ball lightning, how did they change direction and come right down the middle of road and verge off right in front of the truck? It was north of Abington services just before the highest part of the road north side. If you were standing at the services looking north, they went along the valley on the other side of the hills. They followed the contours of the valley towards Edinburgh south. They never struck the ground".

I could understand where Fergus was coming from, if you have never encountered something like this before, then you may well think that it must have a supernatural explanation. Of course, that's not to say that it might not have a supernatural explanation. That 'ball lightning' exists, is a fact. It has been with mankind for centuries, not just here in the U.K. but all over the world as well. Some cultures believed that it was demons, others thought spirits.

Science has confirmed that ball lightning is indeed a reality, albeit a rare reality. These balls of light are mostly luminous and have been reported from being a few centimetres in size, upwards to a basketball size. They usually appear during thunderstorms when the air is electrically charged and tend to hug the ground. Colour wise, there have been reports of blue, red, orange, yellow and white circular lights, and come with a hissing sound and a most unpleasant sulphur like odour. They normally only last for a few seconds either fading out, or, in some instances, exploding. There have been reports of ball lightning causing damage to houses by burning or melting, and of course ball lightning has been misconstrued as fanciful UFOs over the years. Experts are pretty much divided as to the root cause of ball lightning. Some believe that it could be air or gas behaving abnormally, or some kind of plasma phenomenon. It should be noted that ball lightning has in fact, been recreated in the laboratory, *(Letzter, Rafi (6 March 2018). "The 'Skyrmion' May Have Solved the Mystery of Ball Lightning". Live Science).*

During my research about the recreation of ball lightning in the laboratory, I came across a web site entitled 'Live Science' where I found an article entitled, 'Mysterious Ball Lightning Created in the Lab', written by Ker Than. The article was published February 23, 2006. I learned that researchers Eli Jerby and Vladimir Dikhtyar from the University of Tel Aviv in Israel, had created a laboratory version of ball lightning using a 'microwave drill'. (Whether this was intentional or not, the article doesn't say) Anyway, don't you just love scientists who think out the box! Here is how they went about it. They took a 600-watt magnetron from a normal household microwave. A magnetron is an electron tube whose purpose is for amplifying or generating microwaves where the flow of electrons is controlled by an external magnetic field.

They had this microwave beam to bore through solid objects and aimed the beam through a pointed rod straight into various solid objects made from glass, silicon, and other numerous other materials. As they did so, they noticed that the energy generated from the drill, had created a molten hot spot in the solid object. It wasn't until the drill was pulled away, that it dragged some of the superheated material along with it. What this did, was to create a fire column which then, to all their surprise, collapsed into a bright fireball that floated and bounced across the ceiling of the metal enclosure. The scientists noticed that this bright fireball looked like, what they described as, 'a hot jellyfish', quivering and buoyant in the air.

It wasn't the big, long fireball that they had 'created', it only measured just over an inch long, and lasted about 10 milliseconds. One of the scientists Eli Jerby said.

"Our experiment confirms to some extent the theory that ball lightning originates from hot spots in the ground created by normal lightning".

Eli Jerby further postulated that perhaps in the future, his laboratory lightning balls might one day find practical uses in industry. He went on.

"My imagination leads me to speculate on applications like 'bulb-less' light sources, coating and deposition or energy production".

And there's the rub. Work like this, may indeed one day lead to a multitude of possibilities, maybe even to harness its power. That said, we all know that when scientists go tinkering with other sources of power, bad things happen. Just take for instance, Hiroshima, Nagasaki, and the problems encountered by the islanders of Bikini Atoll. Best stay clear.

We now move on with our supernatural journey to the town of East Kilbride in Central Scotland where strange things are afoot.

THE GHOST DOG AND THE PHANTOM WOMAN

Location: East Kilbride, Scotland.

Date: Various. 1994, 1987/88, 2019, 2020

Hi Malcolm.

"I want to tell you something that happened to me last night. (5th April 2020) I was in bed at my home in East Kilbride and suddenly woke up. My T.V. was still on, but I had muted it before I fell asleep, and that was the only light in the room. All of a sudden, I heard the sound of breathing! and then I became aware of the sound that I was making while taking a breath in and out. This freaked me out because this noise wasn't matching my breathing. I froze in bed. So, I concentrated on my breathing, and when I took a breath in and out, I could still hear it, and then I realised it wasn't me! Then I heard some rustling at the side of my bed. The first thing I thought of, was that it might be mice or something, because that summer we had caught a few mice in humane traps in the kitchen. Before I had the chance to move, I felt something jump onto the bed and walk across the bottom of my legs and then stop. My dog Floyd passed away on October 18th last year (2019) and he was the love of my life. It really felt like my dog Floyd who did just that every night when he was alive. He would jump up onto my bed and sleep right beside me every night. Anyway, I looked to see if it was Floyd, and there was 'nothing', but I just knew It was a sign from my baby. I'm so thankful that I've been able to pick up stuff like that. It makes me realise that the afterlife is real and there really is something after. I know the difference between having a sleep paralysis and being really awake. The reason I got in touch with you Malcolm, is because you're into this kind of stuff. The only reason I found you in the first place was because of googling stuff that I'd experienced. I just wanted to tell someone.

I'm sane, and, as normal as everyone else, but I feel like an idiot. My mum always said I must be good at picking these things up because I've had lots of strange things happen in my life".

"Another strange thing that happened to me, was when I was 15. I was skipping school near a high-rise block of flats in Calderwood East Kilbride around 1994 and I was loitering about when an old woman opened her window and shouted out, *"Excuse me hen, can you go to the shops for me"?* And I shouted back *"Yes",* whereupon this old lady said she would come down.

So I went round to the main door that had a security entry and waited, and waited, and waited. I could see another woman cleaning inside and she was looking at me strange. This lady came to the door and asked me what I was doing, and I told her that a woman had shouted out her window and asked me to go to the shops for her. And the caretaker lady looked at me weird, then took me round to where the woman had shouted, and I pointed up. She shook her head and took me up to the floor above that, and below where people answered the door, and they said that they hadn't asked me to go to the shop for them. I said to the caretaker, *"But why didn't you take me to the flat I told you"*, and the caretaker looked me straight in the eye and said, *"No one lives in that flat, it's empty. The owner died and no one lives there"*. I was in shock and went on my way. All my family know this story".

"Probably my first experience with something weird, was in the late 1980s, 1987-1988, I think I was about 8 and I was in bed. I woke up with the day light starting to come through, when I noticed that there was a young boy standing at the bottom of my bed, standing side on. I remember the fear, and I pulled the duvet over my head terrified until I must have fallen asleep again. When I woke again later in the morning and went downstairs, I told my mum and dad about it, and they were spooked, but they said I must have been dreaming, but I wasn't.

I remember it vividly. The boy wasn't facing me, he was standing sideways facing the window, so I could just see his profile and curls sticking out at the back of his head. I don't remember what he was wearing, and he didn't move or speak. He didn't have a glow or anything and wasn't see through. He just looked like a solid person. I still have no idea who the young boy could have been, but I was terrified. He looked about the same age as me".

I asked Lisa what was he wearing, what did he look like, and did he try and speak to her? She replied.

"Well, he wasn't facing me, he was standing sideways facing the window, so I could just see his profile and curls sticking out at the back of his hair. I don't remember what he was wearing, and he didn't move or speak. As soon as I woke and opened my eyes, I saw him just standing there and I was so scared I pulled my duvet over my head and under the covers too scared to move. He didn't have a glow or anything and wasn't see through. He just looked like a solid person. I just thought I'd tell you Malcolm as I wouldn't know who else to tell, apart from close family and friends. I just wanted to tell you what happened".

Regards. Lisa-Ann Davie.

Our next case is a tale of premonition. That is, a feeling, a sensation, or even a 'knowing,' that something bad was about to take place. This was the feeling that Tom Scholes of Swindon England had back in June 1983. Here is what he had to tell me.

MY BAD FEELING CAME TRUE!

Location: Swindon and Penzance Airport, England.
Date: July 16th, 1983.

"We were due to fly to the Isles of Scilly on holiday, and for two weeks before this holiday, I had the feeling that something was going to go wrong. I even phoned British Airways to check the booking. Two days before the holiday, the feeling passed, and I felt that everything would be OK. We arrived at Penzance heliport to catch our flight, but we were a bit too early, and there were no early places available as the airport had been fogged in all morning.

We watched a helicopter take off, then a short time later, the tannoy announced that there would be a 4-to-5-hour delay in flight time. As we had a small child with us, we decided to catch the boat over. We arrived in Hugh Town *(Author's Comment. Hugh Town is the largest settlement on the Isles of Scilly)* When we got there, we watched as the accident services were unloading the wreckage of the helicopter that had crashed into the sea on the way over **(It was the flight we had watched take off!).** My father had died earlier that year and all along I had the feeling that it was him trying to warn me of the impending accident. I still can't explain the feeling that I had to this day".

Regards. Tom Scholes.

Doing research for this book, I found out that this tragic accident, occurred on the 16th of July 1983. It was a British Airways commercial Sikorsky S-61 Helicopter, Oscar November (G-BEON), which crashed into the southern Celtic Sea, in the Atlantic Ocean. It was en-route from Penzance Airport (Where Tom and his family saw it take off) to St Mary's, in the Isles of Scilly. According to an investigation that was carried out by the Accidents Investigation Branch (AIB) it was deemed that the crash was the result of pilot error, in that he failed to notice and correct an unintentional descent whilst flying at low altitude in poor visibility. Other factors involved with the crash, were the pilot's failure to monitor his flight instruments correctly and a lack of audio height warning equipment. Sadly, twenty-six people lost their life in that crash with six survivors. At the time, it was Britain's worst helicopter civil aviation accident.

SOME FURTHER PREMONITIONS

Why is it, that some people can see into the future and are aware of things yet to come? Surely the future can't be predicted, right! Does that mean that everyone's future is already mapped out for them. Is it 'Pre-Destiny'.

We Scot's people have a saying which is, *"What's for you, won't go by you"?* Well one thing's for sure, there is no denying that some people can foretell the future, and I'm not just talking about psychics with their card and palm readings. Probably two of the biggest names that some of my readers may well already be familiar with, are of course Nostradamus and Mother Shipton. What a lot of people found with the predictions of Nostradamus, (1503-1566) was that his predictions were a bit loose. By that I mean that they could apply to anything. Probably one of the best examples coming from Nostradamus, was his prediction that he saw two, 'Steel Birds. And a fire in a big city' Of course a number of people read into that, that this must be to do with the tragic events of 9-11, when two airliners, American Airlines Flight 11, and United Airlines Flight 175, crashed into the North and South Towers of the World Trade Centre in New York back on September 11th, 2001. We could of course speculate that Nostradamus was correct, and that he was only trying to put into words what he saw. How could he possibly know that steel birds would in the future be a flying aircraft! Nostradamus predicted other great tragedies, and I refer to the bombing of Hiroshima and Nagasaki. The Great fire of London, and the death of Henry 11. Another famous mystic was Mother Shipton who also had an array of prophecies. But it seems to me, the more disastrous the event, the more some people can foresee it. Some of course would say that certain disasters are only a matter of time, and they may well be correct, but then some disasters are so

'spot on' by those that predict them, that we must ask ourselves, is something else going on here! See what you make of the following examples.

THE ABERFAN DISASTER

There have been a number of tragic events here in Great Britain, one that comes to mind certainly as far as having been psychically predicted, was the tragic events at a small mining village in Aberfan in Wales back on October 21st, 1966. Admittedly, this may well have been a disaster 'waiting to happen'. It concerned a National Coal Board colliery spoil tip which reached over 100 feet high which sat on a hill behind the town. It was a mountain of coal built up from the spoils of underground mining. Sitting below this massive spoil tip, was Pantglas Junior School and Aberfan village. The powers that be, had not given great thought as to where they should have put this giant spoil tip, for they situated it over an underground spring. The sad thing was, that this tragedy could have been averted, as the villagers knew that this was a disaster waiting to happen. Indeed, back in 1963, three years before the disaster, a petition was sent to the NCB (National Coal Board) complaining about the potential dangers that this tip possessed. Tragically, no one listened, and on the morning of October 21st, 1966, this tremendous spoil tip slid down the mountain killing 144 people in the village, 116 of whom were children from the school.

This is where the premonition comes in. Two days before the disaster, 10-year-old Eryl Mai Jones had gone to bed where she had dreamt that she had gone to school and found it 'missing' and that there was some kind of 'black thing' covering it. She told this to her mother, and Eryl's mother stated that in the week leading up to the disaster, her daughter had repeatedly said to her that she wasn't afraid to die. I think you can guess the outcome here.

Yes, sadly young Eryl lost her life along with 143 others. A tragedy that could have been averted if only the National Coal Board had listened to the concerns of the villagers.

THE RMS TITANIC DISASTER

Some might say that the following story is more of a coincidence than a prediction of an event yet to come.

Nonetheless, it is interesting. It all stems from a chap called Morgan Robertson, who wrote a novella about a large passenger liner called, 'The Titan'. Nothing remarkable about that so far right! Wrong. Here is where it gets spooky. Morgan's book details this liner as 'unsinkable' and has it as the largest liner of its time. The ship is capable of travelling at 25 knots an hour and the 'Titan' sank after hitting an iceberg in the month of April. The 'Titan' only carried a minimum amount of lifeboats, way less than the amount of passengers that were on board. Is it looking familiar so far? It should do. For as we know, one of the biggest Maritime disasters of its day, was the sinking of the Titanic, which, as we know, sank after hitting an iceberg in the month of April 1912. Here we have a chap writing about the sinking of this seemingly 'unsinkable ship' 14 years 'before' the sinking of the Titanic. In his novella, he wrote about the sinking of the 'Titan', the real tragedy occurred to the 'Titanic.' Did Morgan Robertson have a 'vision of the future' which gave him the inspiration to write his novella, or was this just a pure coincidence, if it was a coincidence, then it sure is a belter. Come what may, 1,635 souls lost their lives that night, in a tragedy that could have been averted. But that's another story. Incidentally, I would recommend you read the book, *'Premonitions of the Titanic Disaster'* by Terry Keefe. He tells that some passengers of the Titanic cancelled their tickets due to a feeling of foreboding. He also states that there was a famous social reformer of that time who told those who would listen, (and remember, this was a year before the disaster), that he would be in danger from water in 1912. Terry also states that the inhabitants of the remote islands of Fiji, were aware of the Titanic's sinking well before the reports of the collision reached the Pacific. We are told that a dying girl, stated on the actual date of the sinking, April 1912, that she saw a big ship which was sinking in the water.

What's even more astonishing, is that she also knew the name of the violinist in the Titanic's orchestra!

THE WORLD TRADE CENTER PREMONITION

I mentioned above about the premonition that Nostradamus foresaw, which was 'two steel birds and a fire in a big city'. This of course could have been anywhere, but some have attributed it to the events at New York on September 11th, 2001. There have allegedly been many premonitions about the events of that day, probably the most unnerving would be that made by a gentleman by the name of Barrett Naylor. This is how it all come about. Picture the scene, we have Barrett Naylor, a Wall Street Executive walking to work at the World Trade Center on February 26th, 1993, suddenly, as he neared Grand Central Station, he had this horrible feeling that something bad was going to happen. It completely overwhelmed him, so much so, that he about turned and went home. It's as well as he did so, for later that day, he was shocked to learn that a bomb was detonated at the World Trade Center which resulted in the deaths of six people and injured over 1,000. Apparently, the terrorists had planned to bring down Tower 1 where it would crash and fall into tower 2, thankfully that didn't happen, and all told, five men were convicted of this terrorist attack. Had Barrett gone to work that morning, he may well have been one of the injured, or at worst, dead! His foreboding feeling had probably saved his life.

So, that was in 1993, this strange feeling may have saved his life. Fast forward to 2001. Barrett again is walking to work at the World Trade Centre when again, he got this sudden horrible foreboding feeling that something bad was going to happen. Like before, Barrett trusted his gut feeling, and quickly about turned and went home. We all know what happened next, two commercial airlines struck both towers which eventually collapsed causing the deaths of

2,996 people, a combination of office workers, firefighters, police, and emergency services. Once again, Barrett had probably saved his own life by trusting his gut feeling that something bad was going to happen. What he does trouble over, however, is the fact that he never told anyone else about his premonition that something bad was about to happen. Would people have listened to him? Probably not, but even if one person had have listened to him, that would have been one less fatality.

Allegedly former United States President Abraham Lincoln foresaw his own death in a dream. President Lincoln was assassinated by John Wilkes Booth on April 14th, 1865. Now here is a coincidence. The Titanic sank on April 14th, and President Lincoln was shot dead on April 14th. Probably one of the biggest controverses attributed to a premonition, was the one that Princess Diana gave in a letter to her butler Paul Burrell. Sadly, the princess of Wales died from her injuries which were sustained when her car crashed in the Pont de l'Alma tunnel in Paris in the early hours of 31st August 1997. A few months prior to the crash Princess Diana had given, what some would say, was a prophetic letter to her butler Paul Burrell, part of which is alleged to have said,

"This particular phase in my life is the most dangerous, my husband is planning 'an accident' in my car, brake failure and serious head injury in order to make the path clear for him to marry Tiggy. Camilla is nothing but a decoy, so we are all being used by the man in every sense of the word".

Of course, there is a lot of controversy about this letter. Some saying that it was a forgery, or that Paul Burrell himself had written it. Indeed, Paul Burrell was

acquitted at the Old Bailey in 2002 of keeping and hoarding a lot of Diana's possessions. In the Daily Express online article written by Sophie McCabe dated August 31st, 2022, she states that Duncan Larcombe, a Royal Journalist had told the Channel 4 Documentary which was looking into the death of Princess Diana, 'that the letter was a complete game changer, and was another piece of the jigsaw'. Duncan further stated, and I quote,

"Diana's fears that she'd be murdered, fits in with what Mohammed Al-Fayed had said".

Come what may, Britain and the world lost one of its loveliest souls that day, in a tragedy that was either orchestrated, or was the result of incompetent driving at speed. One truly wonders if we will ever know!

Did you know that there was actually a British Premonitions Bureau set up just so people could log their premonitions? One was set up in 1966 soon after the tragedy of Aberfan mentioned earlier. The chap that set it up, John Barker who was a psychiatrist and was involved in helping the parents of children who died in the Aberfan Disaster. During his time working with the parents, he was informed of two children who had dreamt of the tragedy before it happened, and who had also drawn pictures of the mudslide over the school. In 1967, Alan Hencher (who incidentally had predicted the Aberfan Disaster) telephoned Barker and informed him that he had a premonition that there would be a plane crash 'over mountains', and that either there would be 123 people who would die in the crash, or 124.

As it turned out, it was 124 people who sadly lost their lives when a Bristol Britannia passenger aircraft with 130 people on board, tried on its third attempt, to land in a violent thunderstorm at Nicosia airport in Cyprus. It crashed into a hill near the village of Lakatamia and burst into flames. Only four lucky souls survived the crash.

Doing research for this book, I learned that that the Premonitions Bureau received 469 predictions many of which did not come true.

Incidentally, many years ago a lady from Glasgow informed me that she had a very strong premonition that there would be a bank robbery in Glasgow. With trepidation I called the police to inform them about this robbery, wondering if the police would think that I was some kind of practical joker, or worse still, might be involved in the robbery. Anyway, I felt it best to do my civic duty, and, as it turned out, no robbery occurred? Could this have been due to an extended police presence in and around the bank? Or did the robbers decided not to go ahead and rob the bank, or was there never going to be a robbery in the first place, and that my caller from Glasgow just had a weird dream? Well, I guess we'll never know. Getting back to the Premonitions Bureau, it shut down in August 1968 when its founder John Barker died of a brain Haemorrhage. In a strange twist of fate, a memo was found in his estate which contained information from two phone calls, one from someone called Hencher, and the other from a Kathleen Lorna Middleton, both these individuals predicted John Barker's death. What I didn't learn unfortunately, was if they give his death in August of 1968? So, premonitions, are they just pure chance, or are they something else? One thing is for sure, as long as there are people on this planet, there will always be premonitions.

OK, moving on. Our travels now take us over to Central Scotland, where disturbing events befell a young woman who was troubled by the strange 'goings on' at her house, which, as we will see, were quite traumatic.

A HAUNTED LADY

Location: Somewhere in Central Scotland.
Date: 1993/94.

The following was originally an article sent into our society's web site. I asked the author of the following piece if I could include it for this book, to which she replied yes. What I'm not allowed to disclose however, is the exact location where the bizarre events unfolded. This is what she had to say.

"Where to begin really...?"

"I think the event that really triggered everything was the unexpected death of my mother. She was aged 49 at the time. It was very traumatic and led to a medical negligence investigation and possible court appearances over a period of two years after her death. Meanwhile, other things were happening, moving home, getting married, husband losing his job, then the birth of my son and subsequent post-natal depression all within a year of mum's death. This had happened within a couple of years of my grandfather and grandmother dying also. I mention all of this, as I feel these life changing events triggered something inside me".

"We moved into a brand-new built house, so no previous owners. However, the house was built over an old mine, as we were to find out later on. Everything was 'normal' for the first while. After my son was born in the June, we noticed one of the bedrooms just simply did not heat up, it was always freezing cold despite the radiator being turned up fully.

We duly got the gas board in to investigate in case the radiator was faulty. Outcome: nothing wrong with it! It was the correct size for a small bedroom. It should work. You could actually see your breath in that room it was so cold. Eventually after complaining to the builder, the radiator was replaced but to no avail. Still freezing cold. This was to have been my son's bedroom and had been decorated as a baby boy's room. By this point, we had also started to hear some strange, muffled bumps and bangs, and occasionally when upstairs you would think you could hear talking downstairs. We put all this noise, which was very frequent, down to the house settling".

"Toward the end of the first year in the house, my husband had started working and had to take his turn of night shifts, and it felt strange in the house on my own. Although my son was there with me, it often felt as though I was being watched. You know the feeling, hairs stand up on the back of your neck, draughts blowing in your face from nowhere. I had also started noticing strange golden mostly coloured balls of light, usually in two certain corners of the lounge up near the ceiling. One was the corner below the cold bedroom, and the other was below my son's bedroom. I could actually see them appear out of the ceiling and come down into the lounge. Then they would hover for a few seconds and disappear. These became very frequent. At first there was no other change in them, but, after a while, they seemed to get larger and a lot more obvious. Sometimes there were more than just one or two. At this point, our two cats would sit and stare into corners, then walk over to the corners, sit down, and stare up at 'nothing'. In the interim period, I had been diagnosed with post-natal depression and I actually put a lot of these happenings down to that. I was even investigated in case I had epilepsy or something else along those lines. Nothing was ever found. The orbs, as I now know them to be, continued, whilst the feeling of a presence got stronger and stronger.

When I married my husband, he was a total sceptic, but even he eventually began to feel and see things. Ornaments were moved about, and at first I blamed my husband for not liking where I had put things. He emphatically denied moving anything. One night we went out and my husband's brother was babysitting. When we came back in, he was sitting with his jacket on. We went in the back door. He immediately left, saying he was never coming back again! Obviously, we asked why, and he said, *"Because you live in a haunted house, that's why!"* We laughed at him and told him we knew the house made noises but that it was just settling. We were used to it.

He replied, *"OK, then. Go upstairs. It's up there."* I remember this because his face was a picture. It will always live with me. We went upstairs, and we couldn't see anything. My son was still fast asleep in his room. My brother-in-law shouted up, *"Look up."* The loft hatch was missing. He had heard a noise and gone upstairs, thinking it was my son. The loft hatch, which was above the top of the stairs, had started to rock and continued to rock all the way back till it had totally opened up. It was a very calm night. No wind outside. His face was actually very white, and he looked ill. He left very quickly, saying he would never be back to that house. He never did come back".

"Things progressed from there quite quickly. I could actually make out shady figures, although it was not clear if they were male or female. If you were in the kitchen and turned around quickly enough when you were aware there was movement, you most definitely saw shadows moving. Sometimes they would be right behind you. I was not the only one to see them, but I was the first. My husband saw them regularly too, in fact he became quite self-conscious, because it was as if there were a whole bunch of us living in that house. One night, when my husband had gone to work nightshift, I had put my son to bed and came back down. I had put out a drink of Ribena but left the bottle lying on the kitchen work top. I was sitting in the lounge, and I could see straight through into the kitchen. I heard a strange noise and looked up. The lid from the Ribena bottle was spinning in mid-air above the bottle, and then it simply shot off into the corner of the room. I was used to things like this by now and it really didn't scare me. I simply spoke to whoever it was, and asked that they stopped, as I didn't really like it when I was in on my own. Doing that did usually work. Sometimes we couldn't actually believe these things were happening, but I have always believed in spirits. I believe they visit us in times of need, and I had been very down for the first part of my son's life.

We decided to have a barbecue one afternoon. We invited a few of the neighbours round, and during this, one of the neighbours said, *"There's a large man just walked through your lounge."* He had appeared beside the fireplace and walked into an alcove at the back wall and disappeared. When investigated, there was no one there. It was becoming intolerable by this point. I was seeing greyish human shapes, hearing voices talking to me, saying my name. I could not get a minute's rest. Night was the worst time. Finally, we decided we were going to have to do something about it. We decided (pre internet days) to go to our local library and research the land the house was built on. We spent days trawling through old microfiche documents, newspapers etc. We found there had been:

(1) A Covenanter's battle fought on the ground our house had been built on.

(2) A Spitfire had crashed in WWII killing the pilot.

(3) A major mining disaster where numerous men were killed.

"We were by now convinced it could be any one or more of these spirits that were living with us on a daily basis. Meanwhile, the occurrences kept coming, and it was difficult to shut out. In fact, it was driving me mad.

I became so sentient at one point I could be sitting watching the television one minute, the next I would seem to zone out and time travel to another place where I had my back to a row of small pitch and straw roofed cottages in the Highlands, staring at what I thought were budgie cages lying in a garden. The sun was shining, and I could feel the heat. I spoke to a tall weather-beaten man who told me he was a fisherman. His name was Angus, but he was dead. He told me how he had died in a fishing accident in a storm but had lived in the cottage behind him when he was alive. He said I knew one of his relatives. This felt so real. I could hear him talking, I could smell the sea.

These episodes happened a few times and never lasted very long. My husband told me on umpteen occasions he tried to speak to me, but it was as if I was unconscious with my eyes open. This old man I had spoken to was my mother-in-law's great-grandfather. He had been a fisherman and died at sea. During these episodes I also spoke to children who had not made it into the living world. When we followed it up, most of the time the stories were confirmed; sometimes these stories were about children that people had not wanted others to know about. During all this time the other stuff still happened, toys rolling across the floor on their own, and shadows or figures beside us. My son was beginning to talk and toddle by now. I had a picture of my mum, whom he had never known. He pointed at the picture and said in his baby voice, *"Ganny"*. He then took me by the hand, went to his room, pointed at the corner of the room, and said it again. *"Ganny."* I'll never forget that feeling. We got up one morning, and every single ornament from a display cabinet was in the downstairs toilet. Nothing really surprised us anymore. There was almost no respite, and I was prone to bursting into tears or laughing depending on the mood of our extended family".

"One night something happened that would prompt us to get outside help. It stepped up a notch and got a bit sinister.

Things had been all quiet that night and we had gone to bed. I slept on the left as usual, and at one point through the night, I woke up and shouted at my husband that he was hurting me. I thought in my sleep he had put his arm over me and was pulling me towards him, but in fact I was being pulled downwards into the mattress. I had to struggle to get free from the grip that was pulling me. It was painful. Eventually my husband woke up. I was actually in tears it was so painful. We turned the light on and looked around. There was nothing to see, but on my left-hand side, (I was facing the middle of the bed) I had a very large red mark over my rib cage. I was still angry as I thought my other half had been having a dream and done this. Over the next few hours and into the next day it became very obvious it hadn't been done by him, as there was very evident bruising appearing, and it was a large handprint with the fingers facing the front of my body. The opposite way it would have been if it had had been done by my husband. This scared us".

"We then had to try and find someone who would come and help us. Looking through books and articles, remember, no internet then! we kept coming across the name of Professor Archie Roy, who investigated paranormal happenings and was lecturing in astronomy at Glasgow University. My husband eventually phoned the Uni to ask if he was still there. He was, and he did indeed phone us back. He was interested in our story and made arrangements to come out to our house with a colleague who worked with him and was also a Spiritualist medium. When he arrived at our door, we were amazed to see this quite tall elderly gentleman standing there, with an older lady. It wasn't what we had expected. They came in and sat down and we told them in detail what had been happening. They asked us if we had a history and if we believed in the spirit world, as well as asking us generally about ourselves. When we were telling them about our 'visitors', the lady simply looked at the corner of the wall and kept nodding. Every so often she would turn back round to us and affirm everything that we had said. They walked round the house and spent some time in each room, came back down, and told us that we were correct in assuming we had spirits living with us and explained the reasons why. The woman told me I was conduit for spirits, and I would probably find it very difficult to cope with because it was so strong. This was also the reason my husband and others could feel their presence and sometimes see things because it was so active around me. They told us there were some family members around, plus some others that maybe weren't so happy. However, they didn't mean us any harm. They were simply trying to get my attention. She also told me at that point that I hadn't been well, and it would get worse if I didn't 'shut myself down' at this point in time. However, it was up to me. This was actually a very difficult choice to make, because although it had sometimes been frightening and draining, I was quite happy with the spirits' company. Eventually, after discussion all round, I decided it would be for the best to learn how to shield myself and was duly told how to do this. The medium also performed a ceremony to send the spirits on their way. She said it was not the house that was in fact haunted, it was me! One day it would all return, but only when my son was old enough to cope on his own, and I was sufficiently able to cope with it all again. Things did quieten down slowly after this, but occasionally we still heard and saw things. They weren't as obvious as they had been in the past though. It got to the stage where I felt very alone at times, as I had become so used to hearing and seeing things. I hadn't felt on my own for a long time. I did regret it a bit. Time moved on and we moved house. I wondered if things might start up again. Occasionally I saw spirits. I smelled them and heard them, but not to the same extent. I didn't have my 'time travel' again, as I called it".

"The years have passed since it all started. My son is almost at the age to move on. I feel it coming. Things are building up. I have seen more clearly the other side again. I have had different experiences. They are taking shape again. I have been touched and scratched. I can't deny it any longer. I can't wait. I have missed them. My husband believed in spirits before but was sceptical of other things. His mind says, *"That's not the way it should be!"*

But I believe.

Sincerely. Gail Mackay

I received an e-mail from a friend called Colin Saunders, who has had his own very close encounter with a UFO, but that as they say, that is another story! Colin informed me about two bizarre tales regarding 'beings' that the thought I should know about. Colin is 100% sure, that what he was told, was real. See what you make of the following.

FAIRIES, ELEMENTALS, OR WHAT?

Location: Barwell in Leicestershire, England.

Date: 1993.

Hi Malcom

"I had a very interesting conversation this Saturday, in fact two conversations. The first one I had been told before by a Phil King in our village of Barwell in Leicestershire, and I believe him 100 %. It was 1993, and he was on a bus just leaving the outskirts of the village, when he spotted two very small human type beings, flesh coloured and about 1 or 2 feet high, walking up a lane next to the last house.

What unnerved him, was the fact that eye contact was made between one of the little creatures and himself, full eye to eye contact before the bus carried him out of sight. This guy like me has also seen a triangular UFO in the past".

Colin Saunders.

After Colin had told me about these two small 'beings' I had to find out more. So, I got in contact with the witness, Phil King and he had this to say about the event.

Hi Malcolm

"From what I remember it was a Friday night, and my cousin and I were having a pint in the king William in Earl Shilton and we decided to go up to the working men's club for a cheap pint, as we hadn't got a lot of money. We got there, said hi to John's mum who was working behind the bar, then we decided to risk £5 each on the bandit to see if we could win, and, as luck would have it, we won £110 which gave us plenty money. So, we drank up and walked to station road in Earl Shilton to catch our fox cab to Hinckley, which takes you through Barwell village. As we are just leaving the outskirts of the village, there is a small track and I witnessed two small flesh-coloured humanoids about 1 foot to maybe 18 inches, holding hands and walking. I couldn't look away. Then they stopped, and looked directly at me and we made eye contact and then I was out of range from them".

Regards. Phil King.

Colin Saunders now tells us about the other bizarre encounter that he was told.

FAIRY AT THE END OF MY BED!

Location: Burbage in Leicestershire England.
Date: 2015.

"The second story I heard, which I also believe 100%, was from a different local guy telling of his experiences with ghosts etc, and this is the big one. He was in bed at home in Burbage in Leicestershire back in the summer of 2015, and awoke to see a fairy at the end of his bed, approximately three feet high. The fairy was kneeling down on one knee looking at this Sam. Sam was frightened and covered his head with the blanket. Plucking up enough courage, he stuck his head out again and the fairy was still there.

111

He was brown in colour all over, displaying two wings at the rear and still kneeling. Again, Sam stuck his head under the blanket and the next time he looked it had gone! I have no doubt he's telling the truth as he has had a lifetime of experiences with ghosts. His mother was also a medium".

Kind regards. Colin Saunders.

Colin kindly sent me the details of Sam and I quickly e-mailed them asking for more details. Here is what Sam had to tell me about the fairy at the foot of his bed.

Hi Malcolm.

"Yes, that's right. My bedroom was in the loft, so in the summer the room was really hot, so hot that I had my blinds up and the window wide open. I don't normally wake up during the night, once I'm asleep it's hard to wake me up, but for some reason I woke up, and there 'it' was, on my small chest of drawers that's in between my bed and the window. It was all brown skin, brown hair and had a rag on it. As soon as I seen it, I brought my knees up to my chest and pulled the quilt over me while saying *"You can f**k right off"*. I then thought I was seeing things and put it down to being half asleep and that nothing was there. So, I looked over, and there it was in the same place, but kneeling over the bed.

So, I done the same thing again. About a minute later I looked again, this time I was going to touch it, but when I looked over it had gone. So safe to say I closed my window in the middle of the summer while my room was in the loft".

Regards. Sam Neal.

There are countless worldwide tales similar to the above, maybe one day I will get around to writing about them!

For now, let us continue with our mystical journey. The following case I presented in my first volume of Paranormal Case Files of Great Britain, the reason I present it again here is, because by a quirk of fate, a previous resident of the haunted property, came forward when he read my book and said, *"I used to live there"!* Needless to say, I asked him what had happened, and you will read about this after I inform you the reader, what happened at this property in Croydon in Surrey.

THE GHOST OF TAMWORTH ROAD CROYDON

Location: 83 Tamworth Road, Croydon, Surrey, England.
Date: 1970'S.

Back in 2007, I worked for a financial company in Croydon in England and during my time there, one of my supervisor's approached me and told me about a photograph of a ghost that her friend had in her possession. She asked if I would like to see it, needless to say it was a resounding 'yes'. I soon got in telephone contact with the photographer. The following is a bizarre tale (but they usually are, aren't they) So here ladies and gentlemen, is the strange case of the ghost of Norman Smithenbottom.

The story goes that a Mrs Bell who lived at 83 Tamworth Road in Croydon England, held a party in her home, it was either October 1979 or October 1980 (she can't quite recall the exact year) anyway, the party was in full swing, and everyone was having a rare old time. Mrs Bell wanted to capture the mood of the party, and for that reason got out her camera and started to photograph all the people in her home having a good time. The night went well, and all had a good time. It wasn't until a few weeks later when she got the photographs developed from the local chemist (this was pre-digital of course) that she came across one particular photograph showing a man to whom she didn't recognise. This man had clearly not been in her home on the night of the party. Puzzled, she decided to take the photograph out with her and ask some of her friends if they knew who this chap was. None of her friends recognised the man in the photograph and like her were bemused as to who it could be. Not to be outdone she decided on one last throw of the dice, she took the photograph next door to show her elderly neighbour, a chap who had lived in the street more or less all his life. Upon seeing the photograph, he looked up at Mrs Bell, and with a surprised look on his face exclaimed, *"Oh that's old Norman Smithenbottom, he's been dead for years"*. That remark only served to make things even more bizarre. Her neighbour went on to say that Norman had lived all his life in her house and that he was the local butcher to the community.

Now, the question remains, what is a dead man doing turning up in a photograph? There is no denying that the photograph was taken in Mrs Bell's home, as you can make out behind Norman part of a wall unit. Mrs Bell explained to the author in a telephone interview, that it was a new camera (a Kodak Instamatic) and a brand-new spool was used specifically for that party. Every single photograph on the spool was used up. She further stated that the camera was not left alone and used again at a later event. The whole spool was used on that particular night. A fellow researcher, Kathy Gearing from London's Ghost Club, was also interested in this case, and she too had a telephone interview with Mrs Bell where an even more bizarre claim was made.

And that was, on that that same night of the party, Mrs Bell took a photograph of her brother standing in the room and he 'failed to materialise' on the exposure at all! In his place, was this spirit of Norman Smithenbottom!

Of course, all this just served to confuse Mrs Bell and her family, and they were desperate to get to the bottom of it. Mrs Bell's niece took the photograph to several mediums and clairvoyants in an effort to find out who the man in the photograph was, all to no avail. Nobody could provide the family an answer. Mind you, what didn't help at the time, was when pictures in the family home 'jumped off the wall' for no apparent reason. Now when the photograph was given to me, I too was desperate to try and get to the bottom of it and find out who this Norman Smithenbottom was. I checked through the local records all to no avail. I telephoned some of the local butchers if the name Smithenbottom meant anything to them (or perhaps their fathers who were in the trade before them) Again, all to no avail. Maybe, as Kathy Gearing speculates, the elderly neighbour aged 93 at the time when Mrs Bell showed him the photograph, might have been mistaken about the surname. Maybe it was something that 'sounded' like Smithenbottom (although I did mention this fact to the Butchers and looked for that from the records) We also ascertained that Norman died fifteen years 'before' the photo was taken. My next step was to do an interview with the local newspaper the Croydon Guardian in an effort to see if any of their elderly readers remembered or knew Norman Smithenbottom. The article came out on Wednesday the 19th of September 2007 and I'm sad to say that I didn't get one phone call or letter from it. The address where the picture is alleged to have been taken, 83 Tamworth Road has since been demolished to make way for the Centrale development, which is a massive, big shopping complex. 83 Tamworth Road was formerly a six storey Victoria house which had old servant bells downstairs and horse stables at the back.

I decided to take this photograph along to a demonstration of mediumship in Cheam Surrey where I showed it to paranormal researcher and film maker Marq English. Upon first glance, Marq raised a smile and said, that's not a ghost, that's Jeremy Wilkin, a famous British actor and he's still very much 'alive'! *(He was when Marq gave that statement. Sadly, Jeremy Wilkin died later that year on the 19th of December 2017, he was aged 87).*

Jeremy was born in Surrey who later in life went onto work in television and films, he is well remembered for working with animator, Gerry Anderson and had appearances in the Sci Fi T.V. show, UFO, amongst many others. I checked the Norman Smithenbottom ghost photo with photographs of actor Jeremy Wilkin from the internet, and admittedly, there does appears to be a 'slight' similarity. It's hard to believe that a famous actor like Jeremy Wilkin would not go unnoticed at a party in Croydon. If it was him, which I very much doubt, then why did Mrs Bell not mention this fact? Did he know the family? I tend to go along with what Mrs Bell's 93-year-old neighbour had to say, that it was a former butcher by trade known as Norman Smithenbottom, but he had been dead for a number of years! But the story doesn't end there, as I mentioned above. I had a gentleman who had read my book where I mentioned this case and he wrote to me with some startling information. Which, as we will see, will go to show that there was always something spooky in that residence. Here is what that gentleman (Alex Maitland) had to say.

83 Tamworth Road, Croydon, Surrey

"We as a family moved to Croydon Surrey in 1970 after leaving Edinburgh. At first, we lived in a small, rented flat, and mum was determined to find something bigger to live. On her daily journey to work at Fords motor company in Croydon, she passed an empty house in Tamworth Road and subsequently made enquiries as to who owned the property.

After asking at the house next door, she discovered that the house was owned by Edward Leigh builders. We rented the house and moved into 83 Tamworth Road in the summer of 1970. It was an old four storey house in need of some attention, but mum made it a comfortable home. All was well until November, on Remembrance Sunday, that's when strange things started to happen.

Pictures flew off the walls, internal doors would open, ornaments would fall over and break. Also, the gasses on the top of the cooker would tun off. In the evening, lights would turn off for no apparent reason. At the time, we all laughed about this and thought no more about it. A few weeks later when my dad was going up to his bedroom at the top of the house, we heard him shout. He returned to the sitting room shaking and said that he had seen an old man at the top of the stairs and refused to return to his bedroom that night. A few nights later, when going up to my bedroom, I witnessed a figure at the top of the stairs, an old man was standing there looking down at me, distinctly dressed in a shirt and waistcoat with white hair surrounded by a mist. This really shook me up. At that time, there was no landing light at the top of the stairs, or a big light in my bedroom. For months afterwards, none of us used the top floor of the house and we moved our bedrooms to lower floors in the house, although we would go up there in day light hours only. My mum spoke to the next-door neighbours at number 84, Mr and Mrs Edith and Jack Warner about the events, and was told by them that our house had been an unlucky home for everyone that had ever lived there and to be careful. When the top of the house was rewired and lights fitted, I moved back into my old bedroom, this was when my worst experience of events in that house took place. I was woken up by my sheets and blankets being ripped off my bed, so I looked down to the bottom of the bed and saw the same figure as I had seen before. It was the same man who had a very angry look on his face tugging at my bedding and I heard a sort of growling noise.

I was trying to pull the cover back to protect myself. This terrified me so much that I actually wet myself. When it stopped, I went downstairs and sat in the living room all night.

During our years living in the house, things continued to happen. There were pictures flying off walls, doors opening, lights going out, and during the power cuts in the 1970's, our candles would blow out, despite there being no draughts. This vision of 'the man', was seen by myself as well as my mum and dad at the top of the house, and we all said things would seem to get worse when any improvements were made to the house. We lived with the events until leaving the house in 1977 after a compulsory purchase.

Best wishes. Alex Maitland.

Author's Comment. Clearly then the house at 83 Tamworth Road in Croydon was haunted. It makes me wonder if the residents who lived in the property before Alex and his family encountered anything strange. Clearly Mrs Bell, did, when she moved into the property in the late 1970's early 1980's. People say that you don't often get a good photograph of a ghost, well, I'd like to think that the photograph we have of this chap Norman Smithenbottom turning up at a party is a good example. (See photographic section) It gets stranger and stranger folks doesn't it!

OK admittedly the following strange stories do not come from the British Isles, but nonetheless I felt these stories to be intriguing enough to recount them here. They concern the strange experiences that befell my Facebook friend from America, Linda Napolitano.

MY DEAD FATHER WAS SITTING ON THE CHAIR!
Location: NYC (Downtown Manhattan Island), near the East River.
Date: October 1977 and 2005.

Hi Malcolm,

"Both of my sons went to parochial schools, so they had to wear uniforms. One night, at about midnight I'm not sure of the month but it might've been in October 1977, I was ironing their shirts in my living room, at New York City, (downtown Manhattan Island) near the East River. I had finished one shirt and put it on a clothing hanger then turned around to hang it on the wall unit behind me. I took another shirt and began to iron it, when noticed that one particular wrinkle wouldn't iron out. So, I concentrated on the wrinkle. I'd finished ironing the shirt, turned around to hang it on the wall unit behind me again, and grabbed another shirt to iron, when suddenly, I saw my dead father sitting on the sofa in front me. Startled, I quickly turned around, facing the wall unit, and said out loud, *"Dad, please don't scare me. You were a good father and I love you."* At that time, he had passed away two years ago. I turned around slowly to see if he was still there, but he was gone. If my children weren't at home sleeping in their beds, I would have run out of the house. I was terrified. After I had gotten over the initial fear and shock that night, I'd realized that my father looked smaller than he was in life. He didn't look at me or utter a word, but he stared at my computer that was across from him. His clothing was the same as it was when he was alive, a clean white long-sleeved shirt and a pair of dress pants. He just looked much smaller than he did when he was alive".

"It took me about 3 weeks before I'd realized that the sight of him was a gift. Like most people, I believed in a life after death, possibly in Heaven, but I still had a shadow of doubt.

This gift shot my tiny doubt away. I wasn't thinking of him at that particular time. In fact, he hadn't crossed my mind because I was concentrating on that wrinkle and ironing all 10 shirts for both my sons for a whole week of school each. I don't know why my father showed up two years after he died which was close to the 2nd anniversary of his death. All I know is he kept staring at the computer, and not once did he glance at me or say a word. I also noticed that he didn't have any particular expression on his face. His face was expressionless. My impression is, and I may be wrong, that he didn't know that I could see him.

So, he just sat in the same spot on the couch liked he always used to do when he was alive. He might have always been around after he passed away, but I couldn't see him. Although I consider it a gift, I'm hoping that I will never see that again".

"I do have another strange experience for you. In about 2005, my neighbour died. I took care of my dear friend because she had no family and was never married. She had developed dementia and I didn't want the State to put her in a nursing home, so I volunteered to be her caretaker.

I didn't want to get paid because that's not what good friends do. Those State nursing homes are awful. I remember that she used to knock on my door, at least, 10 times a day. Anyway, she passed away in February of 2005 or 2006. She had prearranged for her funeral. After the funeral, I took a white rose off her coffin then pressed it in a large book when I returned home.

On the 1st anniversary of her death, I heard someone knocking on my door a few times that day, but when I opened the door, no one was there. That day I checked the rose I had pressed in the book, and it was still alive but very flat. It stayed alive for the whole year then died the day after her 1st anniversary. Impossible? Yes! But it happened. There is a life after death.

No doubt about it. I'm completely convinced of it, especially, two years after my father passed and one year after my friend, Margaret, died".

Sincerely. Linda Napolitano.

And there's the rub. Many people the world over have encountered the spirits of their loved ones or people they once knew. When Linda happened to turn around and see her dead father sitting in the sofa in front of her, it took her by surprise.

She wasn't expecting to see him, and although it gave her comfort for a while to know that he was still around, 'albeit in a different form', she did say that she would prefer it if she didn't see him again. I can understand that. We all, to some degree, would like to see our loved ones who have gone before. Not all of them can come back for reasons we can only speculate. Is it the more psychic one is, the more chance you will have of seeing a spirit? Perhaps.

Again, I have decided to place one more paranormal encounter here from overseas, just to show you the reader that strange events happen the world over. However, this is quite a disturbing tale and clearly something that neither you nor I dear reader, would welcome into our bedroom.

THE BEAST ON THE BED!

Location: Fayetteville North Carolina, USA.
Date: 1972 till present day.

"The events started in 1972 (I was 22 years old). I lived with my parents in Fayetteville, North Carolina. The events happened over many years, mostly at night, roughly two times weekly. Some 'entity' that was big, heavy, and animalistic in nature (not alien), would pounce on my bed and proceed to run around me very fast. I could hear snarling, and it was heavy. The hot breath was the worst, only because I felt it so close to my face.

I could tell (I don't know how, but I knew) that it was crouched over me, and those eyes (I remember yellow pupils with red background) that I tried to avoid as much possible. This would happen whether the lights were off or on. Back then, I always slept with the covers over my entire body, including my head. My Siamese cat, Chino, would immediately jump off my bed and run out of the room before the cryptid (it was physical), would appear.

I could hear him, smell him, and have his hot breath all over me. I did see it a few times, and it was a canine. It looked like a wolf, not a dog, and those red eyes! It was intelligent as it deliberately showed its snarling teeth. I did not experience weight on my chest nor lack of air, as in the so-called old hag enigma. *(*)* This 'thing' walked and ran around on top of me, and I could feel each paw as it pressured me at the locations where they stepped. My feet, thighs, lower leg, my arms, my shoulder. I never felt any weight on chest, only on my upper arms, neck clavicle, even when its face was directly in front of mine! And it definitely growled, and sometimes there was that panting sound, so vivid now in my memory as then when it was happening. I should point out that I was always fully awake when this 'entity' appeared, and I would have bruises on my body the following day which neither I nor my doctor could explain. This entity followed me wherever I would move. Once while vacationing with my family, my sister-in-law heard the creature at night while we shared a room. She was terrified and told me the next day".

"Back then, I was seeing a Dr. Don R. Schulte, who was the Psychiatrist at Moore Memorial hospital in Pinehurst, N.C, for Manic Depression (Bi-Polar). I had informed him about this strange wolf like creature after my third visit since I was terrified. I knew that it was not a psychotic episode nor a nightmare. We tried various meds, therapeutic relaxation methods, nothing worked. Dr. Schulte was concerned, as this occurred with no explanation that he could see.

Unbeknownst to me, my mother had reached out to her friend in Columbia, S.C., for help. Then I was notified about a lady who was coming to visit us and do a spiritual cleansing! I immediately let my doctor know this. I said, *"Can you believe this, Dr. Schulte?"*. I was then taken aback, when Dr. Shulte, leaned forward, and told me to go ahead and have it done. He explained that nothing had helped, and that there were many things that were unknown in the scientific community. In short, the lady who was going to do the spiritual cleansing, was an elderly Puerto Rican woman (my family is from the island) She spread oil over my body from head to toe, said incantations to Saint Barbara, then I was told to wear on my body, a small red triangled scarf, and place the same under my bed (headboard side). There was also a glass filled with holy water with a rosary immersed within. Prayers to Saint Barbara were said twice daily. This stopped nothing! The same year we went on vacation to Texas, Colorado, and Fort. Sill, Oklahoma. In Oklahoma, while sharing the bedroom with my sister-in-law Betsy, myself on a bed (about 8 feet away from her), I was attacked by the 'thing'! The following morning, Betsy approached me quite concerned, and told me that she had heard the growl of a large animal and the shadow of a big dog, she was so terrified she stayed hidden under the covers and quietly prayed! Back in North Carolina, it continued sporadically. I married in 1977 (previously I, lived in Puerto Rico 1975-76), then lived in Kentucky 1978-81, Germany (1981-82), Fayetteville, N.C. (1983-1991), and Harnett County, North Carolina. (1991-2003). During these last places I lived at, I have no recollection of 'any' attacks on me. I have lived here in Sanford, North Carolina, since 2003 till present time. In my former apartment (directly across the street), I was attacked by the cryptid twice, within a 6-year span. It was there that I screamed for it to go away, that it was not for here, to go back to where it came from!

Not in those words, I was in absolute terror and saying what I could remember of the Lord's Prayer). Then earlier in the summer of 2022, this 'entity' attacked me again as I rested on my recliner. As always, the same terror, again more prayers. I kept uttering demands to leave and for it to go away and that it was not welcome here. After gathering my wits, I immediately, contacted my fiancé in Canada".

"In 1995, I found a letter addressed to my mother in her bedroom dresser drawer, and I was shocked to read that it was part of a long-distance exorcism by a Catholic priest from Ponce, Puerto Rico. I especially remember the part where the priest had directed my mom to steal a penny from someone's pocket. It was a very long letter and obviously there were others sent to her at various times in the past. So far, I have been freed of any visit by this entity, but yes, some nights in fear I think about its return".

Sincerely. Olga Perez.

(*) Author's Comment. The 'Old Hag' is a name that has been given to describe a dream like creature which some scientists would attribute to the phenomenon of sleep paralysis. The individual will awake and feel totally immobilized and feel a heavy pressure on their chest. Sometimes the individual may think that they see some kind of entity laying on their chest. However, in Olga's case, the following day she had bruises to show for her own particular account of what had come into her room, plus the fact that her sister-in-law Betsy also heard the growling noise in a shared room that they both were in.

I also had a Facebook friend from the United Kingdom who also had a strange experience whilst in bed. Michael from Liverpool stated to me that back in 2011, he was lying on his bed, wide awake in broad daylight. There was no one in the house he was totally alone.

As soon as Michael closed his eyes, he was pushed down into bed. He said that he felt the sensation of 'invisible fingers' pushing him down onto the bed for at least five minutes. This he stated, was quite painful. This, however, wasn't the first time that this had happened to him. He recalls the time when he was slapped around the head and again, nobody was there!

This was at a point in Michael's life when he was witnessing quite a lot of UFOs, from black triangles to balls of light.

Moving back to the British Isles, we again find ourselves in Scotland, the Isle of Skye to be precise, where there are tales of a haunted car and fairies.

THE GHOSTLY CAR ON SKYE AND THE FAIRY KNOLL

Location: Broadford and Portree. Isle of Skye.

Date: 1940's to present day!

I've mentioned many times in other books that I've written, and on the lecture circuit, that you don't just get ghosts of human beings, you also get ghosts of aircraft, ships and even cars, as our next strange tale relates.

It is said that there is a ghostly phantom car that haunts the road between Broadford and Portree on the Isle of Skye. Reports of this ghostly car start way back in the 1940's when drivers on this stretch of road, encountered the headlights of a fast-moving 1934 Austin Seven car, which upon getting close to them, completely vanishes. Since then, it has been seen throughout the years only to vanish once again. At that point in time, it was a single-track road but the road has since been upgraded. History has it, that a local policeman who was driving along this stretch of road, saw the car coming quickly towards him, but once again, the car completely vanished. Researching this ghostly car, I learned that one Dr Allan MacDonald was the first to report this ghostly car in 1941, there may well have been other sightings of this car before then, but witnesses might have been frightened to come forward with their tales due to either fear or ridicule, or not being believed. Clearly those drivers who encountered this speeding spectral car, were so concerned that there might be a crash, that they actually had to swerve up onto the grass verge to ensure that there was no collision. It is speculated that the driver of this ghostly Austin Seven, was a local church minister, who apparently lost control of his mind and was racked with guilt after having been involved in a fatal accident. It would be interesting to know, if indeed this was the case.

The Isle of Skye is steeped in beauty, no matter where you look, you will see some amazing sites, it isn't any wonder that thousands of tourists' flock to the Isle of Skye each year to soak up its beauty. I often wonder if these tourists are aware of the fairy lore that the Isle of Skye holds. Fairy pools, fairy knolls, where the 'wee folk' are said to inhabit. The fairy knoll on Skye, is one such spot. But beware, when visiting the fairy knoll because you might not come back! There is a legend (there always is, isn't there) of a fiddler who was sitting down comfortably at a fairy party one night. He must have enjoyed himself, but he sure got a fright in the morning. For in the morning, he was astonished to learn that 100 years had passed. Of course, this type of story can be found from many countries, in that people will come across either a fairy dance or some fairy gathering, where they will be enticed into joining the festivities only to find that on their return to what they believe is their own time, that hundreds of years have gone by. With the Isle of Skye story, legend has it that if you get close to the fairy knoll, you might just hear the sound of a fiddle being played. But don't get too close will you! OK, we move onto a combination of strange paranormal stories.

These come from a friend of mine who although is happy to get them off her chest, she prefers to have a pseudonym. See what you make of these.

THE STRANGE EXPERIENCES OF SARAH THOMPSON
Location: Central Scotland.
Date: From 1971 till 2003.

Hi Malcolm,

"When I was 7 or 8, I had to get a tooth out at the dentist. They gave me gas. As soon as the mask went on my face and I breathed in, I shot down a black tunnel, and at the end of the tunnel, the blackness ripped open in a pixelly-edged oval shape, exactly like a transition in a movie. I found myself on my bike cycling with two of my pals on theirs. I was 'really there', exactly like the world I left with 'no' memory of being at the dentist seconds before. It was a normal day. Real life and not a dream. I remember our conversation as we played on our bikes just along from my house.

After a short while, around 10 minutes or so, I'm suddenly back at the dentist being slapped, poked, and shouted at. There were tears, snot, blood, and saliva all over me, and I screamed the place down with the shock of being in there and remembering every second of where I had just been. I'd gone sideways into another dimension exactly like this one. I think that if I had died at the dentist I wouldn't have known, I'd have taken my bike home at teatime and continued my life as normal. Either that, or the experience was some sort of 'holding area' to pass the time till I was needed to come back into my body again. But who or what would create that"?

"I was 12 when I went to the swimming baths with my pal and her dad. I couldn't swim but decided I'd try a breadth across the pool with her dad alongside me. I kicked away from the side, got about 10 feet across, and went under. Instantly I was out of my body watching myself screaming and flailing about. Then I was back in, still screaming and kicking, then out again watching myself drowning. This 'in and out' happened about half a dozen times. When I was out, I was just observing and I was thinking it was 'very strange, and I'm not sure I like this.' It was creepy. Anyway, they pulled me out and I lived.

At no point did I go unconscious. That very same day, in the afternoon, I was playing in the park with some other friends, and we were running. I leaped up onto a bench and it was effortless and floaty and on top of the bench it felt like I could just keep floating upwards. I had zero weight just for a few seconds. Those two incidents on the same day were definitely connected. Around 1981, when I was 17. We moved house, and it was our first night there. I went to bed, and the next thing I know is that it's dusk, and I'm walking on a wide gravel path. I heard the crunching under my feet as I walked. The setting sun made the sky red, and I could see it through a row of small cottages on my left. There were holes where the doors and windows should be, and the red sky was shining through them. To my right there was a dry-stone wall with woods beyond it. I'm slowly waking up and starting to think *"Where on earth am I? I'm awake. What the...?"* It dawned on me I was really somewhere else. Then a fierce breeze started. The trees were bending and blowing really hard, and I heard dry leaves and I looked down and saw them rolling forward from behind me and between my feet. *"I'M AWAKE AND THIS IS REAL".*

"Immediately a noise from behind me on my right made me turn around. There was a field at the edge of the wood and the noise was a large wide cattle gate that had swung open and was swinging closed again.

A bar of blue light about a foot long, being held by someone I couldn't see, had come through that gate, and rushed towards me and touched me in the stomach. Blackout. I was lying down in blackness with what felt like a dozen hands gripping the skin on my belly and shaking it violently. (That could have been my adrenaline pumping) Next, I'm standing up at my bedroom door with the light on. I then put the hall light on followed by the bathroom light. Downstairs I put on every light. It was the middle of the night, but I even put the telly on.

My mum got up wondering what I was up to. *"I had a nightmare and I'm scared"* I said. She left me to it.

"1984. I'm now 20, and my boyfriend was staying over. He was in my single bed in the corner, and I was on a sofa bed along the wall underneath my window. Above me was my spider plant hanging from the ceiling. We were both sound asleep, but then I'm wide awake and running in absolute terror. It's dark but I'm in some metal thing, with curved walls. I think it's metal as my pounding feet were making 'do-ying, do-ying' noises. I'm gasping with fright as I run around curves in the darkness making sounds like you'd make if Freddie Kruger was after you. There was laughter somewhere behind me. Someone (maybe two or three people) thought this was funny. I fell through a dark opening in front of me and started screaming and stretched my arms out to catch my fall. Then I'm on the sofa bed screaming with my arms up in the air and looking up at my spider plant as a loud, electrical *'DZZZT'* sound moved quickly from my right ear and out through the window. I then realised nobody could hear my screams, and my arms were folded tidy under the covers. I jumped out of bed and into the single with my boyfriend. He woke up and I told him what had happened and then he became as terrified as me".

"1985, I'm sleeping over at my boyfriend's house when the phone rang early one morning.

I got out of bed and went to answer the phone which was at the bottom of the stairs. It was my mum telling me my grandpa had died last night. I went back to bed sobbing. He was my favourite person in the world. My boyfriend woke up and I told him, and he was upset too. After a few minutes it dawned on me that he didn't have a phone at the bottom of the stairs. None of what just happened was real! Fast forward about 6 years and I got the very same phone call from my mum. This time it was real, but our short conversation was exactly the same".

"1986 I went to a disco with a large bunch of girls. At happy hour everyone greedily ordered double vodkas. We probably had about 8 each or more. There was so much booze it was falling off the edge of our tables. I was very, very drunk when I got home. I went to bed and was fast asleep when suddenly a vicious dog barked right in front of my face. I leapt up and it was still there. Just the face, mouth open, saliva dripping, bared teeth, and angry eyes. Wherever I looked the face floated there. It was like when you get a photograph taken and the flash stays burned onto your retinas for minutes after. I put my lamp on and I could still see the dog's face. I was petrified. It was getting smaller, but I remember it still floating in front of my wardrobe when I looked there. I got up to put more lights on and found my living room door closed. When I opened it, there was a warm blast and a sucking of air. It was like an oven in there. I'd put my gas fire on full blast and closed the door on it. I would have been unconscious in bed, sleeping off the alcohol if this dog hadn't woken me and sobered me up in a flash. But was it warning me, or waiting for me? I remember mentioning to you that I've always had great first-time luck, usually followed by my own stupidity, well here is one example of many. On 18th or 19th of March 2003 I was in my garden. My partner came home early for work and came over to talk to me. Behind his head something caught my eye.

It was a jet-black UFO, growing into the air just behind the chimney of the house across the road. I shouted out *"UFO"*, whereupon he looked as well. It was like a manta-ray or stingray. The wing tips were curled up and ended in points, and there was a flashing light coming off it. We could have hit it if we'd thrown a stone. My boyfriend started walking down our drive towards it, while I decided to run into the house to get my camera.

In fact, all that morning I was saying to myself *"Get the camera out, there might be something to see"*, but I'd ignored that because I was busy planting stuff. Anyway, I got the camera and started switching it on while I'm heading out the front door. It was just a 2mp polaroid digital thing, but it took good pics. So, I started taking photo after photo, and this thing had by now already come from behind my neighbour's chimney and across the driveway and was moving higher into the sky and over the road. It's now morphed from a stingray shape into a ball with a narrow flange, and was bobbing and rocking higher over the road, moving like a mini submarine. Eventually it's high up over the road and it's a silver ball which got smaller and vanished. By the way, this was just after 3:00pm, maybe 3.20pm at the most. The school was not long out, and the street should have been busy, but it was silent, not a bird, no people, and no traffic while we watched this thing. The neighbour across the road was out by this time with his binoculars and his bathrobe on. He'd seen me appear from my door taking photos of the sky and came out for a look. He says, *"I think that was a child's balloon 'cos you could see the string"*. I didn't mention it was the size of a large car or a van and that it had come from behind his house, at lowest about 30 feet off the ground. It would have filled his driveway and his next-door neighbour's if it had landed. It was a beautiful cloudless sunny day, but you could see this light flashing every few seconds. I said to my partner later *"Did you see the red flashing light?"* and he said, *"It was pink"*, we argued about that, and so I said *"okay, it was a pinkish red"* then we agreed. However, when I put my card into my P.C. the photos were too huge to get a proper look at it. I had to scroll up and down the side of the screen and also across the bottom to see the UFO. I was quite new to computers in 2003, so I foolishly googled for a program to better view my pictures. There was one, and it cost me a fiver, I think.

Anyway, I shrunk them down in the program and clicked save on everyone, and they ended up absolutely tiny. How? I don't know. My bad luck again. I didn't know either that the pics would be recoverable on my memory card and also elsewhere on my PC. What a twit! My partner got a better look than me. We watched the old V series a few months back. *(Author's Comment. A science fiction series)* He said if you take a white scout ship from V, paint it black, make the body shorter, make the wings longer and curl them up into a point, then that's exactly what we saw. And it 'has' a red flashing light".

Regards. Sarah Thompson.

The strange world of the paranormal, holds a deep fascination for me. I often wonder, what is the mechanism to make strange things happen! I gave a lecture in Hull England back in 2021, in which part of my lecture comprised of a story that I was told by an elderly lady when I lived in England. This lady had come to one of my London lectures where she proceeded to tell me quite an incredible story. This is what she said.

It was during the Second World War, and this lady's son was in the Royal Navy patrolling the North Atlantic. The lady herself, was back at home in her North London house sitting in a chair in the living room knitting. Everything was fine, when all of a sudden, an instantaneous television screen appeared in her living room out of nowhere. The vision that befell her, was of a man thrashing about in water. And then she heard the words, *"Mother, Mother"*.

She looked closely at this television screen and saw that it was her son. He was slowly sinking beneath the waves. She dropped her knitting needles in shock as the vision slowly faded from view. A few weeks later, she received a telegram from the Admiralty, which stated that her son was lost at sea after his ship was torpedoed by a German submarine.

But here's the kicker, the date given on the telegram as to when his ship went down, was the very same day and time that she saw her son losing his life in this instantaneous television screen that had suddenly appeared in her living room. We could perhaps attribute this vision as the last throws of life from the son to his mother. That he desperately wanted to tell her what was happening to him. And due to some unknown paranormal mechanism, something happened to make this paranormal television screen appear in his mother's bedroom, hundreds of miles away in London. Now if that's not a strange story I don't know what is!

So, I've just come off the stage at the Outer Limits Conference in Hull, when all of a sudden, I see a conference delegate by the name of Deborah Singleton striding towards me, where she proceeded to tell me her own strange tale of an 'instantaneous' television screen. It would appear that my tale didn't stand alone! I asked her to put her account in writing to me, and the following is what she wrote.

THE INSTANTANEOUS TELEVISION SCREEN
Location: Tinshill and Bramley, Leeds, England.
Date: 1976.

Hi Malcolm,

"Firstly, it was lovely to meet you at Hull! Your Sauchie Poltergeist presentation was fantastic! It had me captivated!

And then, when you mentioned the lady who saw a television screen just suddenly appear in front of her, I knew I had to tell you what happened to me. So, where to begin. Let me set up a bit of the background".

"Going back to 1976, I lived in Tinshill in Leeds, and I sometimes used to go out with my mum when she walked the dog at teatime. This particular day, mum told me she was going into hospital for a few days, to be sterilised, so that she couldn't have any more children. I turned to her and said, *"You're having a baby, aren't you?"* She looked shocked, then said yes, but that she wasn't keeping it. and that was the end of the conversation. Over the years, I asked her occasionally why she didn't keep the baby, her response was always that her and my dad were going to split up, and that she wouldn't have been able to support me and another child as a single mother. Something about this didn't seem right, but she made it clear she didn't want to discuss it any further. Mum and dad did split up, in 1978".

"I lost my mum very suddenly in 2007, and being an only child, I came into possession of all mum's personal effects, including her diaries. The very first one was 1974, when I would have been 5 years old. It was a leather bound A5 size, and although there weren't entries on every page, I did notice, that starting on maybe the third month of that year, there was a date in the top right, and what I can only describe as coded notes. There were a series of tiny asterisk, either one, two or more than three on some occasions. Then there was tiny writing, *"Wife in"*, *"Wife out"* *"Not today"*. I began to realise that my mum had been having an affair! Now, among mums' personal effects, was a page torn out of a phone book, there was an address on there, quite a few houses up from us. But the name never rang a bell. From time to time over the years, this whole situation, bugged me, it just didn't make sense to me, it bugged me. I didn't feel I could approach my dad about this in case he didn't know that my mum had terminated a pregnancy, let alone had an affair. It was a bit of a tricky situation. But the puzzle was too much for me and I took a deep breath and went to see my dad.

I approached the subject carefully, and basically told him of my findings and suspicions. He said he once recalled seeing the coded notes in my mum's diary, but she passed them off as something else when he asked her about them. I broached the subject of the termination and said that this had occurred over two years before they actually split up. Then I asked the ultimate question *"Was the baby yours?"* He looked me dead in the eye and said, *"Put it this way, I worked long hours and went to bed early, your mother was a night owl and didn't come to bed much before 3am, what do you think?"* So, that was one penny that had dropped. The next was to work out who she had been having the affair with. Try as I might, I could not bring to mind any of the neighbours up the hill, who she could have become involved with".

"Over the next year or two, on and off, I puzzled over this, but still came up with no answers. Then one morning a couple of years ago, when I was living in Bramley in Leeds, I woke up and swung my legs out of bed, sat on the edge of the bed, readying myself to stand up, when all of a sudden, a television screen appeared on the wall in front of me. Not a big screen, about twice as big as a Kindle screen, but it was definitely a TV screen. It even had the 70's fuzzy, dull broadcast quality when it started. Then it cleared and I saw my mum, as if I'd been transported back in time to the 1970's. From the viewpoint I had, I was looking out of our bungalow window, and saw my mum walking past on the way out to walk our dog, who was on the lead she was holding. She was wearing her Burberry mac, that she wore around that time. She walked down the drive and when she got to the bottom, I was expecting her to turn right up the hill, she didn't, she turned left, and as she disappeared out of view, the TV screen shut down into the old white line and went"!

"As soon as I saw the direction she had gone, I knew exactly who the affair had been with, a local shop owner, hence the coded notes, *"wife in wife out"*. It was when his wife was working in the shop, 'or not'. Everything fell into place for me then and the puzzle was solved! I believe now that mum sent me the answer from spirit, to put my mind at ease and give me the solution to something that had puzzled me for a lot of years. It came totally out of the blue as I hadn't thought about it for a period of time when this occurred. So, Malcolm, there you have my T.V. screen story, to use as you wish".

Kindest Regards. Deb Singleton.

Just before we move onto another paranormal story, I'd just like to highlight the fact that I actually had my own 'instantaneous' television screen appear in front of me. Here is what I had to say in my previous book, *Paranormal Case Files of Great Britain (Volume 1)*

THE AUTHOR'S INSTANTANEOUS TELEVISION SCREEN!
Location: Tullibody, Central Scotland.
Date: 1967.

A strange incident occurred to me when I was around ten or eleven years of age. I was living in a village called Tullibody in Central Scotland and I have absolutely no idea as to what I exactly saw that day. It was a point in my life when I did a lot of hill walking. I used to enjoy walking up the Ochil Hills which were a few miles from my village of Tullibody, and I fondly recall those lazy days of summer strolling over the ferns and heather. This particular day I had just returned home after walking up those hills, and as I was feeling a little bit tired, I decided to go upstairs and lie down in my bed for a short while. After a period of time, I awoke and gazed lazily across the room.

It was a bright summer's day, and the sun was streaming in through the bedroom window. I thought that I had better get up as I had things to do. As I turned over onto my other side, my gaze was directed towards a small chest of drawers near the bed. Suddenly, and quite unexpectantly, I was shocked by seeing on this set of drawers, a small square, roughly two inches down, and two inches across, (like a small television screen) come into view. Contained within this small square, was what I can only describe as a small motion picture which featured the incredible scene of cowboys chasing Indians across a desert. This looked as real as can be. This vision suddenly became misty then completely 'vanished'. I would say that this whole vision lasted for roughly around twenty seconds. I remember I shot straight up out of bed and raced downstairs where I tried to convince my parents on what I saw. Now of course lots of people would put this down to an overactive childish imagination, and they would probably be right, as for me, I clearly remember that I was 'not' asleep at the point when I was looking at this vision. Indeed, I had been gazing across the room taking in the beams of sunlight that were coming in the window. I'm also sure that this was 'not' some form of 'waking dream' or some other form of sleep imagery. Was I interested in cowboys and Indians! Well, yes, I'm sure most youngsters of my age (10 or 11) were as well, and I'm sure I wasn't all that different from them. But I can't for the life of me understand why an image such as this should encroach into my reality on that day. The vision was so clear, so sharp. There was nothing mystical about this vision, and I'm well aware of similar stories the world over in which for an instance, images have been seen by people to suddenly appear on walls, ceilings, and other places. Sadly, this has never occurred to me in the life again, mores' the pity! If you the reader, have had an experience of this nature, please contact me by e-mail. The details are given at the end of this book.

There are many self-help videos out there in You Tube land, a lot of them are very beneficial. One such You Tube video concerns looking at your past lives. It's called, 'Past life regression, guided meditation, discover past lives.' It lasts for just over an hour and was placed on You Tube by the web site, www.newhorizonsholisticcentre.co.uk A friend of mine, Marina McGovern, decided to try it, and was amazed by the results. Of course, it might not work for everyone, and you have to give yourself over to it. But the calming words and soft relaxing music, certainly helps to bring forward a calmness and peaceful state. During the course of this one-hour session, Marina saw three past lives, and I'd just like to share them with you now.

PAST LIFE EXPERIENCES

Location: The Amazon, Camden London, and an Unknown City.

Date: Throughout time!

Marina wrote.

*"**First life.** Forest, large leaves, Amazon? I was called Maya, tee pee type houses but not red Indian, more like Aboriginal? Friend that I was destined to marry had black bob with a fridge but was a boy. I was late teens, early twenties".*

*"**Second Life.** I was called Poppy, 60's era. I was early thirties. Wore knee length boots, suede. A line mini skirt, light blue jumper, big light blue bag. I was walking along a road in Camden. I worked in a charity type shop, books, clothes, etc".*

*"**Third Life.** I was called Adrianna with a baby called George in a papoose. I was in a big city with large buildings, but I was more like a hippy with long dress and chunky boots.*

I died of breast cancer with my son beside me as a grown man. My husband was killed in a road accident, so I was a single mum for many years".

Of course, some people might say that Marina's visions above were just some wishful daydreaming on her part, or that her mind dragged up something that she had seen on the television or a movie. That's as maybe, but for me, there is no denying that when the mind is in an altered state, in can bring forth recall like this, some of which can be terrifying. They are not always nice events.

Some people claim to see themselves at the point of death. Either in their death bed through illness or being drowned or shot. Regressive hypnosis can also bring forward certain memories, all of which, go to show, that the human mind is a wonderful thing, which for this author, is still a marvel.

We now move onto a case where a famous British UFO researcher who sadly passed away, 'might' have come back to place a lost diary in order for it to be found for a friend. That friend was Colin Rees. Here is what Colin had to say.

THE MISSING DIARY TURNS UP!

Location: Stourbridge, Worcestershire, England.
Date: July 2022

Hi Malcolm.

"As you know my best friend, Kevin Goodman, recently passed away and it has been my task to sort out his house in Stourbridge in Worcestershire England. dispensing of his belongings and making sure his research materials were taken care of. For a number of years, Kevin and I were a little perplexed, as we had lost a very important diary which detailed our first two visits to Warminster in 1976.

I was in fact a little annoyed, as I had entrusted this diary to Kevin's care, and it had gone missing. Try as we could, we had looked everywhere, but had to admit, it was gone! As you know, I had collected all Kevin's materials together and had stacked it together in what was his front room. It ran to several boxes, and they were stacked neatly ready to be transported to a fellow researcher in Warminster itself. It was a couple of weeks before I returned to the house to pick up the material to take it to Warminster. Imagine my surprise! On top of the boxes of research, was the very diary that had gone missing. I can swear that the diary was not there when I left the house, and no one had access to the house in the intervening time period! I would like to think that after his passing, Kevin had finally managed to track the diary down and placed it on top of the boxes. I have always been sceptical about such things, but this has me scratching my head!"

Regards. Colin Rees.

If no one had access to the house, and Colin swears that this diary was 'not' there when he left the house on a previous visit, then one could surmise, that the recently departed and well-loved Kevin Goodman, had indeed placed that diary there to be found. I've lost count of the many stories that I have heard of similar instances like this.

We now journey over to a mystical part of Scotland, where, it's said, numerous strange events have occurred. One man, Gavin Dow, a Shamanic practitioner confirmed that strange things 'do happen' at Cairnpapple Hill near the town of Livingston Central Scotland. Here is what he had to say.

WEIRD EXPERIENCES AT CAIRNPAPPLE HILL

Location: Cairnpapple Hill, Central Scotland.
Date: 2012 to 2015.

"There were three hills I frequented over these years, they are named Ravencraig hill, the knock hill, and Cairnpapple hill. Cairnpapple hill has an ancient 5.500-year-old burial henge on top of it. Let me share some of many of these beautifully profound spiritual experiences that happened during the years from 2012 to 2015. I am in no doubt that my 'Higher Power' was guiding and protecting me over this time. I will take you on a journey through the first of these experiences as it happened to me. I hope to bring out the childlike innocence and naivety I felt during this time. With this experience, I had for two

weeks, been going up the hills searching for a piece of oak wood long enough to make a staff (walking stick). I had spent hours looking for one up the hills all to no avail. What I did get this night, will stay with me all my life. It was between the 21st and the 23rd of December 2012. I would like to think it was the 21st, this being the end date of the Mayan long count calendar. It was for me the beginning of a new way of seeing the world of spirit and the multiple dimensions that exist all around us. I feel blessed to have been chosen by the spirit world to receive these experiences up the hills and trusted enough to pass them on in this book as they happened to me. On one of the above days, I heard my 'Higher Power' repeatedly telling me to go up the hills, all day this went on. I had spent every day during the previous two weeks up the hills looking for a staff and I just wasn't doing it anymore, no matter how persistent the voice was in my head. It was raining, and it had been overcast all day. By 9.30pm I was starting to ask my 'Higher Power' why it was repeating this to me. By 11.30 pm, I'm putting my clothes on arguing with the universe about the stupidity of going out on this damp wet night to look for a staff a few days before Christmas. At all times of the day and night for a number of months prior to this night, I had been beating my shamanic drum up the hills. Why may you ask? To tell you the truth, at that time I had no idea.

I was led to do it through some readings I've spoken about already. I know now that shamanic drumming clears negative space and opens portals to other realms. I was being taught an ancient drum beat that I now use for raising my vibration and the vibration of the landscape environment around me".

"I drove for five or ten minutes up the hills and stopped at Cairnpapple hill. This is where I spent a lot of time during 2012 to 2015. As I arrived, I looked at the time, it was 11.45 pm. I then looked outside and said 'OK 'Big Man' I'm going out for five minutes and that's it; then I'm going home. I stepped out of the car into this miserable weather. The rain had calmed down somewhat as I walked a short distance along the bottom of the hill. I'd searched this area before over the last couple of weeks and didn't expect to find anything. I walked up the hill and turned to walk back along the top ridge where halfway along I stopped. Two small oak trees stood 10 feet below me on the slope of the hill. I looked at them both and said pleadingly, *'Please even just a small one',* none of these trees had dead branches or fallen ones I could get. Both trees were small and dense having grown on the windswept hillside for 60 to 70 years or so. I went down to the trees and leaned into them, holding on for stability. As I did, I felt a lump under my foot. I kicked it slightly and it made a kind of hollow thud. Bending down I pulled up a five-foot piece of old wooden stump that had been covered over by years of grass and mud. This miracle of a find was still slightly attached at the base. This tree had grown in the middle of the other two trees and had fallen many years previous. It had rotted most of the way through, but it was still slightly attached at the base of the tree. I separated it and cleaned off as much of the grass and mud as I could. I thanked my 'Higher Power' and the spirits of Cairnpapple then carried it down to the car".

"After putting it in the boot I got in and shut the door; within seconds, I saw the brightest flash I've ever seen. It came from over the other side of the hill.

I looked at my clock in the car. It was midnight, the digital numbers read 0.00. This time, and the numbers associated with them, become relevant further on. I remember thinking that it may be a fault with a windmill that sits on a farm on the other side of the hill. About 20 seconds later it happened again. At this point, I jumped out of the car and ran up the steps to the top of the hill. I was looking in the direction of the windmill when suddenly the brightest bolt of lightning struck the top of Cairnpapple burial site. It was an amazing thing to see, and it happened only 100 meters away from me. The lightning came straight down and across the sky simultaneously. *"Wow"*, I thought, as it happened again at the same spot-on top of the cairn. Then it struck about 30 meters to the right and then over to Witchcraig hill no more than a third of a mile away. Then again to the next hill. In all, the lightning struck seven small hills or raised areas on the landscape around me in a clockwise direction. It was an awesome sight to see. I don't think I had noticed at the time, but as I recall now, the weather changed completely from damp cold drizzle to a warm muggy atmosphere. I could see the landscape for miles in all directions. Whereas five minutes before I couldn't see more than a hundred meters in front of me because of the dampness in the air. As the lightning stopped, I scanned the sky waiting for it to happen again. It never did, but what I did see was a large cloud above me between three to four miles in circumference. The edges glowed orange all the way round which at the time I thought were the lights from Grangemouth oil refinery that sits to the north and the town of Livingston to the south shining up onto it. This cloud was perfectly circular. I'd never seen a cloud billowing at the edges as it did. It was like something you would see in America or over the plains of Australia. Months later I viewed videos and read more on this subject of cloud formations. I found out that it looked very much like a lenticular cloud. I was directly underneath and in the centre of it.

Whether it was a lenticular cloud or not I can't be sure. With the highly charged atmosphere that night I am inclined to look at this as some sort of energy transfer between something in the sky and the natural earth energies. Whatever the case, it was an amazing sight to have witnessed. When I look back now the lightning seemed to have waited on me to get up the steps before it moved to the other hills around me. I went home that night highly charged knowing that the two weeks spent looking up the hills for a staff had paid off, although it was not a long piece of oakwood, it was oakwood just the same, and I am in no doubt it was gifted by the elemental spirits of Cairnpapple hill"

"This was the first night of many that I gave little thought to other than it was a strange but spectacular experience that my 'Higher Power' gifted to me. I was blind to what was shown to me over these years. Everything happened so quickly over this period that I didn't find time to think about any of my experiences seriously until I came back down off of the hills in the latter part of 2014 early 2015 at which time, I spent another couple of years trying to make sense of it all. I see from the geological map of the area that there are several fault line's near if not in the exact places the lightning struck that wet December night in 2012. I am in no doubt these faults in some way we're responsible for the lightning and strange cloud formation. Might there be some sort of telluric earth currents interacting with Luna or solar energies? For instance, Paul Devereux found that all of Britain's ancient stone circles occur within a mile of faulting. Paul is a British author, researcher, lecturer, broadcaster, artist, and photographer based in the U.K. I spent the next few months working on the piece of oakwood that I'd been given by the tree spirits. I began to go up the hills a little more regularly over this time. I sat up Cairnpapple hill for hours in all weathers. Most times I would take my animal skin drum that I kept warm with a hot water bottle.

Animal skin tends to soften in cold weather making it just about impossible to get any sound from them. Taking the water bottle would give me around five or ten minutes of good drumming. As I look back over this period, I feel slightly embarrassed by some of the things I was doing, but grateful that I was chosen to receive these experiences. I feel blessed to have been trusted to bring my experiences to you with childlike innocence. I knew nothing about all the stuff I was shown back then, and I know even less now after many long hours of study. I remember another night standing drumming and connecting to the energies of Cairnpapple. The sound of the drum was muffled by the hissing of the electrically charged atmosphere caused by heavy snow falling around me. Madness you might say. Looking back and re-entering the energies of that cold winter night fills me with comfort. Only the light and warmth that comes from the 'Creator' could have removed the negativity I might have felt this night, leaving me with the nice memories I have today. Some people said that over this period I was enchanted by the elemental kingdom. I like the idea of being enchanted by faeries and guided by our ancestors and spirits from beyond the veil. It feels magical to me now that I've had time to look back. I was lost and lonely during these years but strangely I was loving it. I was like a child opening my eyes for the first time to the multi-dimensional world of spirit and what I now fully understand as the age of Aquarius and the entrance to the new eon. This experience is by no means the strangest of the mystical world that I was taken into over these years. To follow the rest of my journey through the realms of fairies, orbs, entities, and UFOs, look out for my upcoming new book to be published during 2024, entitled, *'To our Children, children's, children'*.

Regards. Gavin Dow.

(*) Wikipedia tells us that Cairnpapple Hill is a hill in Central Lowland Scotland. It was used and re-used as a major ritual site for around 4000 years.

In its day would have been comparable to better known sites like the Standing Stones of Stenness. The summit lies 312 metres above sea level and is about two miles (3 kilometres) north of the town of Bathgate. In the 19th century the site was completely concealed by trees, then in 1947–1948 excavations by Stuart Piggott, found a series of ritual monuments from successive prehistoric periods. In 1998, Gordon Barclay re-interpreted the site for Historic Scotland. It is designated a scheduled ancient monument.

Back in July 2020, I brought out a book about Scotland's most famous and biggest poltergeist event, 'The Sauchie Poltergeist'. After the publication of the book, a man wrote to me and explained that it was he who broke the story to the world. Here is what he had to tell me.

THE MAN WHO BROKE THE SAUCHIE POLTERGEIST STORY
Location: Sauchie, Clackmannanshire, Scotland.
Date: 1960.

Hi there.

"My name is Jack Taylor, and I am a retired journalist now living in Australia where I have lived and worked since emigrating from Scotland after my newspaper, the Scottish Daily Express, closed in 1974. I don't know if you know this, or even if you want to know this, but I am the reporter who broke the story of the Sauchie poltergeist in 1960 when I worked for the Alloa Journal. I then sold the story on to the Express for 12 quid (a lot of money for a cub reporter in those days) and although I got no by-line nor much recognition at the time, I was better rewarded by the Express which gave me a job, and I worked there from 1961 until it closed in 1974. It would be true to say that the poltergeist got me this great job, so it was a happy ghost for me as it played a

146

very important role in my life from that day forward. My sister Evelyn who has also had an interest in the poltergeist since 1960, emailed me today to tell me about your work and upcoming lecture on the subject. It was actually my other sister Alicia, a classmate of Virginia Campbell at Sauchie Primary, who told me about the poltergeist. I have written about the poltergeist at various times since then, although not very often after I moved to The Sydney Morning Herald in 1974. There has never been much interest in the Sauchie poltergeist in Australia. You asked how did I first get to know about the poltergeist? One night in 1960 I was having dinner with my parents and two young sisters, Alicia, who was then 11, and Evelyn, a bit younger, when Alicia told the family *"Virginia got sent home today."* We all asked: *"Who's Virginia?"* It turned out Virginia was Alicia's new best friend and she had been sent home because the other kids were becoming alarmed at happenings in her class, like objects being thrown, doors being opened then slammed shut in her face, jotters thrown from her desk, etc. So, the head mistress called her parents in then sent her home".

"As I've said, I was then 17 and a cub reporter with the Alloa Journal, so I told the editor, Henry Murray, who at first laughed it off as a joke. Then, since I was not doing anything better the next day, he told me to go to the school, talk to the teachers and kids then try the parents. I was known in the school because I used to take Alicia to school on the pillion of my AJS, and so the kids and teachers knew me, and they all talked their heads off about what had been happening. The headmistress confirmed the story but was otherwise a bit more reticent and said that she needed the parents' permission before she could speak about it. She told me Reverend Lund had been asked to help, and I should see him which I did. Mr Lund was helpful but none of the other ministers were, and the parents refused to talk to me at that time. Anyhow, I did a story about all this, and the story was published with only minor editing changes.

We didn't get by-lines on the Journal. But Nobody thought then that it was much of a story, so I didn't keep it or any record of it. It would be hard to get it now because the paper doesn't exist anymore".

"But the next day I tipped off the Daily Express who sent a reporter (Tom Grant) and photographer who used me more or less as a guide and gopher for which they paid me 12 quid, an awful lot of money for a 17-year-old in these days. (Actually, I spent it on new brake pads for my bike.) I also helped out an STV team by taking them to the house and introducing them to some of the kids. It was the first time I had met their cameraman, Morris Allan, who also gave me a few quid (a fiver, I remember). This is now 63 years ago, and although my recollection of some of it is still crystal clear, other memories may have been clouded or wrong. I was in the house as I went in with an STV crew, I found the family to be frightened, media shy, reluctant to talk, although the mum did, because she was paid to do so, but I do not remember Virginia ever saying anything. The most puzzling of all is this, I have a memory of a wicker basket being raised over her head as she lay on a bed, and this is supposed to have occurred in front of a TV crew. I have said this quite honestly to many people over many years, but a few years ago somebody said that didn't happen. I was not deliberately lying, but I can't swear to it that I definitely saw that. I never took any photographs. We reporters were not allowed even to hold a camera. That was a photographer's job then and still is. There was no diary that I ever saw. I went to the Dollar residence but can't remember where it was".

"I had an Interview with Reverend Lund and took shorthand notes of it which were not kept, as every word was published either in the Journal or in the Daily Express. I do not recall interviewing any of the other ministers, although I could well have done. The only thing I would add is that I returned to the house in Sauchie when I was home a couple of years ago.

I knocked on the door and whenever I introduced myself the lady who answered said: *"You've come about the ghost. It's always about the ghost. Well, I haven't seen hide nor hair of him all the years we've been here. So, he must have moved on."*

She explained that when they moved to the house, they knew nothing about the ghost and it was sometime later that she learned about it from a neighbour *"But it's not here now,"* she said.

Regards. Jack Taylor, formerly of Alloa Scotland and now living in Sydney Australia.

O.K. dear reader, we stay in Clackmannanshire Central Scotland, and our next case is less than 3 minutes car drive away from the Sauchie poltergeist house mentioned above. A lady wrote to me sharing her own weird story. Was this just a mist? And if so, how did it enter the car?

THE STRANGE MIST

Location: Sauchie, Central Scotland.
Date: 2007.

Hi Malcolm,

"I am in New Zealand. I am a Sauchie lass born and bred and remember my mum telling me the stories of the Sauchie Poltergeist. As for ghost stories, I can tell you hand on heart, that in 2007 my partner and I were traveling (in a car) over Sauchie brae, just outside Sunnyside cemetery, when a snake like cloud moved from the passenger side floor up around the gear stick towards me and vanished.

I turned to my partner and said, *"Did you see that, that did you see it"?* After discussing it, we both had seen the same thing. It was the strangest thing I have ever seen, not scary just weird".

Sincerely. Kathleen Jones.

We now head down south to England for our next weird case. This one was given to me when I lived in Hastings East Sussex and was working with the paranormal group, 'Ghost Office' along with colleagues Darren Garcia and his colleague Damien Brooks. Sadly, after the individual contacted me looking for help, he just went off the radar, and after repeated e-mails, he never got back in touch with me again. I give the case here, so that you the reader can understand the types of cases that were coming to my door. Now whether this individual got help from other parties I don't know; he may even have left the house and area. I just hope that he received the help he was so desperately looking for. Here is what he said.

HAUNTED FLAT

Location: Southwest London.
Date: 2018.

Hi Malcolm.

"Can you put me in touch with organisations in Southwest London who can investigate a case of haunting in our one-bedroom flat? We are on the ground floor in a communal building made up of three floors which is managed by, and rented from, a housing association. We have been in this flat coming up to three years now. There has been an increase of noticeable activity since last year. This however is not the only residence where activity is occurring. Our previous residence also had noticeable activity, but not as strong as we are experiencing it right now. We had CCTV installed in our previous residence but did not record any obvious signs of spirit activity/shadow etc on film. We are wanting an investigation of our flat. This spirit seems to have attached itself more to my wife than me. My wife is experiencing consistently being touched in different parts of her person. I too have experienced being touched as well, amongst other activity. We have both experienced sightings, touching, temperature drops, which are sometimes raised to an unacceptable level, despite the outdoor temperature being the opposite to the inside room temperature. We have had clothes torn and also go missing. There have been knocking sounds and crashing sounds and things falling We have seen something like cats eyes shining, and the physical manifestation of a cat shaped black shadow with sparklingly bright eyes walking past in front of us. There are other things that we've both experienced, such as low-level sound, whispering, (unfathomable) similar to a prayer recital. Each time my wife has a meal she notices the food disturbed with the shape of cat's feet. and on one occasion in the previous residence, when I was lying down in bed fully awake, I actually saw a doppelganger of my wife walk towards the bedroom door, smile at me, and then disappear in an instant down the stairs which ran adjacent to the bedroom. I stayed in bed totally confused with what I had just witnessed, more so as I could hear my wife across the landing asleep in the living room snoring. I tried to remain calm and mentioned what happened to my wife the next morning. Where we live now, I experienced a similar doppelganger incident whilst I was at home. It was my wife again, but my wife was at work when I saw her! Depending on whether my wife agrees, we are ready for an investigation anytime with your team. We'll reply to you tomorrow with an answer".

Kind regards and thank you in advance. Colin Gray.

Sadly, as I mentioned above, the couple never got back in touch with me. All e-mails went unanswered. I just hope that the couple have now found peace from these disturbing intrusions into their lives. We now hear from a gentleman who has had his fair share of unusual occurrences in his life, as you are about to see.

ESP, THE GHOSTLY DOG, AND THE STRANGE BOX

Location: Winchester, Hampshire, England.

Date: May 2015.

Hi Malcolm,

"In response to your message regarding ghostly activity. I would start off by saying that I have heard my own name being said out loud or into my ear on more than one occasion, it was so clear, that I literally jumped out of my chair, that's happened randomly over the years. Now having meditated many times before, my state of mind is to focus purely onto UFO related contact. We call this meditation CE5. Anyway, one night during May 2015, I did the meditation before taking my dog Lucky out for her evening walk, no special reason why I did this, but at the time I was having daily sightings of UFO's, some of which were captured on film, but that's another story. I am now assuming that the same state of mind during a meditation, puts yourself into this state where you attract or open yourself up to everything! Ghosts, supernatural/UFO craft etc. Now, having done a half hour meditation, I've taken my dog Lucky for a walk over the road to the park where we always go which is near the Winchester Science Centre and Planetarium. There is a circular pathway that goes around the outer edge of the green field. So, whilst walking around on this circular pathway while Lucky is on the grass, I'm all eyes on the sky as I always do every chance I get! The second time around the pathway, about three quarters of the way round, I felt a heavy touch on the shoulder, heavier than a tap, more like a grab, my heart nearly stopped. Now there is nothing there, and I saw nothing.

With my adrenaline pumping now, I'm calling my dog to me, *"Lucky come here! Lucky come on"*. She won't come, instead she is looking straight at me, I'm freaked out by this even more, and I kept calling her several times to get back on the lead thinking to myself this is certainly not UFO related. Lucky wouldn't come near me. It took way too long to get her to come back to me which wasn't normal, she was great normally. But the thing here was, that I had just been grabbed on the shoulder by something that I cannot see, wow. I've also had tones projected into or around my head at the planetarium in Winchester".

"I have a recording of a spirit telling me to f**k off during a session I did with my son Jake and his friend. Now the thing is with spirits and ghosts, I have only personal experiences, and I'm learning and finding out along the way. On this particular occasion we had three objects inside my shed which were thrown at us, and the spirit was laughing at me in a deep crazy sounding voice, that was so creepy. While this is happening, I have a K2 meter electromagnetic field device which I use every time, and this was going nuts. At certain times we would ask the spirit to grab the K2 meter in response to a question if it can't use the app or make something move, then it would flash on the correct colours that we had asked for. This is mind blowing to see right there in front of you! I asked for the spirit to hold the K2, and they did exactly that, with the lights staying solid for some time. Fascinating stuff but how on earth is it connected to UFO related consciousness thought projection"?

"Some years ago, I found out that I could do certain things like ESP (extra sensory perception) where someone would have a pack of the cards with various shapes on them, square, circle, triangle, wavy lines, cross etc *(Author's Comment. These are called Zener cards)* the other person would then choose one, then hold it up so only they can see it.

Then they would have to think hard on what shape has been chosen, whereby you answer when you see the shape in your head, well, I'd got every single one right and freaked everyone out in the room, including myself. I did this around 12 times and got 'none wrong'! I thought this was insane but would soon learn that it wasn't a one off, because I've done it many times since then. However, the other person must be 'tuned in' if you know what I mean. Now having said that, I arrived home one evening, my Dad Gary Cooper, along with his girlfriend at the time and my uncle Peter Cooper, were playing cards while enjoying a bottle of wine.

I walked into the room to say hello, and my dad who was holding up one playing card which was facing him said, *"What's this card"!* I paused for a few seconds and replied with *"The Queen of spades".* I turned around to take my coat off and went back into the room where I found them all looking at each other confused, because out of 52 cards, I've just blown them away by getting it right. I'm not sure if this is something we learn or simply born with. Now, if that's not weird enough, I'm out in the field doing a CE5 contact session when all of a sudden, I see what looks like a 3D box settling itself onto the ground with its shadow being cast onto the ground. I took a photograph of this, but more shockingly, was the second photograph that I took, its truly mind blowing to me, because it's looks like a Yorkshire terrier dog.

I was literally speechless, because this is my dog that I lost years before when I was younger. I have the ghost of my dog right in front of me and I have truly no idea how this is happening, more so because I was meant to be making contact with ET, and similarly related things. Speechless is an understatement. Do we have a connection between ghosts and Ufology out in the field? It would seem that way to me, and that's something I did not expect.

Is it me who has gained the ability to consciously contact both spirits and UFO related beings while in a peaceful meditative state of consciousness?

Regards. Darren Cooper.

They say that everybody has latent psychic ability within them. Some have it more or less perfected from an early age, whilst others can bring this to fruition by various means, it would appear that Darren held this ability which, when used, convinced others! Our next tale comes from a lady who soon found out, that she too had psychic ability.

MY FAMILY LEGACY

Location: Gosforth West Middle School, Newcastle Upon Tyne, England.
Date: 1970's.

"Growing up in a family that took paranormal encounters in their stride, doesn't appear abnormal, especially some of the experiences that my mother had been part of. My Grandfather on my dad's side was a Spiritualist medium and read from the rostrum. My mother's grandmother would often be called to contact loved ones because of her mediumship abilities. So, I didn't think it was strange when kids started to take an interest in my family's history. My story begins in Gosforth West Middle School, Newcastle Upon Tyne England in the 1970s. My friends wanted to see if I could contact the dead, so we wrote our letters on paper and arranged them into a circle. I asked for us to all join hands and call on whoever was present to come forward. Windows started to bang; the letters were blown across the classroom. We all ran out of the class as if being pursued. I felt a really strong heat on my back, which later revealed a red mark. I was reported to the deputy head teacher for scaring the class. I was threatened with thrashings from the belt if I did it again.

I talked to my grandfather after it happened. He said, *"You have the gift, but you are not wise enough to use it yet."* I have always been able to sense the presence of spirit, sometimes I have been scared and other times reassured. My grandfather said it can be a blessing or a curse. I have known both sides. I have been involved with vigils and I have heard and seen things that I can't explain. My mother would often dream of things that would come true. One night, when she was young, she dreamed of her brother Cud having an accident down the pit. She awoke screaming, my nana went in to see what was happening, my mother still distraught, was in a state of being half asleep and not fully conscious. She shouted that the pit sirens were going, and that her brother was being carried on a stretcher covered in blood. My nana tried to reassure her that all was OK and that it was just a nightmare, that was until she heard the sirens go off, she raced to the pit and waited to see if her son was safe. As my mum had predicted my Uncle Cud was covered in blood and carried on the stretcher".

Sincerely. Debbie brown.

Our research group, Strange Phenomena Investigations (SPI) have always worked with psychics, as they can assist on any ghostly investigation that we take part in. In early 2023, our psychic Steven Bird came to visit me at home, and in all his many stories about spirit (and believe me there are many) one stuck out. And it is this story that I would like to share with you now. I interviewed Steven on my digital recorder, and this is what he had to say.

THE DAY I SAW A DEMON!

Location: Cornton, Stirling, Central Scotland.
Date: October 2020.

Abbreviations. (MR) Malcolm Robinson. **(SB)** Steven Bird.

(MR) "Steven you've had many strange paranormal experiences throughout your life, one of which concerns a Demonic Entity. So, what happened Steven?"

(SB) "Well it was at the back end of the first Covid lockdown and I wasn't working because of Covid, and I was taking a walk down by the river forth just behind my house where I lived at that time. And as normal, I was conversing with a few of my spirit guides and family as I was taking this walk around the river which I did quite a lot. My guardian angel, who I also work with, said, *"Just be careful Steven, I think something is opening"*. The next thing I saw was my guardian angel standing next to me, my guide, who was also standing next to me and two of my family members, my grandad and my great uncle George, and I thought, 'something is opening'. I looked towards a gap in the hedge on the Cornton Road, and I saw, what I can only describe as a vortex, a whirlpool of energy opening up in the actual gap in the hedge. And my guardian said to me that there was a Demonic entity just about to enter our dimension. I started to get a little bit nervous at that point. There is nothing in this kind of business that scares me, but I was actually a little bit nervous about this. And then I saw, what can only be described as, well, do you remember the Tasmanian Devil in the cartoon"?

(MR) "I do yes".

(SB) "Well it was like that, but it was transparent. And it was running like you wouldn't believe towards me, gnashing its teeth together, basically trying to get to me. Well, it got to about 20/30 feet away from me and it was stopped in its tracks by my spirit team who were around me. The next thing I knew, was that I saw three angels, walk out of the vortex, and then they grabbed a hold of him, and pushed him back through, which was quite amazing, because you don't often see angels. I've seen one or two but these three put him back through this portal. It's a hard thing to tell people because it's a bit weird. And when I was going through the experience, I put a protection bubble around myself and covered myself in rainbows and other things that I know that Demons really don't like. In other words, I wrapped myself in positivity. I then came back onto the road and walked through the trees at the back of my house and my guardian angel was standing next to me and talking away to me. And I said, *"What is it about me and Stirling"* because there is a long story about me getting to Stirling. I've always been fascinated by the Wallace Monument. The reason that I am fascinated by Stirling, is because I was actually here in a previous life. In 1297, I was at the battle of Stirling Bridge with Wallace. After that battle, Wallace then went to Newcastle and sacked part of Newcastle and then he was going to head to Durham, but then changed his mind. The villagers on the other side of Newcastle, came down to the River Tyne and goaded the clansman who were on the other side of the river. The actual village was called Ryton and that's where I was born. So, it begs the question, did I sack my own village. Now this is historical fact that Wallace sacked the village that I was born in. Maybe that is why I have this fascination with Wallace, and Stirling. In 1974 we came to Stirling on holiday, I was just a wee fella and we had a tent at the camp site in Cornton. And I remember that weekend, we went up to the Wallace Monument and I looked over towards the Carse and towards the West Highlands, and I said to myself, *"This looks familiar".* I was just a six-year-old boy thinking, *"I've been here before"!*

(**MR**) "Can I take you back to your early years, when did you first realise that you had these psychic abilities and at this time, did you think it was natural, that everybody had these abilities"?

158

(SB) "It started when I was six. I used to have a spirit boy that used to visit me in my bedroom. And my best friend was with me one time on a sleepover, and he saw the spirit boy. One of my neighbours who lived directly next door, also saw the spirit boy from her house. And this spirit boy still visits that house. Subsequent nephews have seen him. One nephew is in his early forties, and one is in his late twenties, they have both seen him".

(MR) "Can you describe what the little boy was wearing? Was it traditional clothing or……."?

(SB) "I would describe him as a Victorian looking little boy. Scraggy pants, scraggy shirt and he had a cat with him on his shoulder".

(MR) "Did he try to speak to you? Was he aware of your presence"?

(SB) "He just smiled at me and waved at me"?

(MR) "And did he appear solid or look transparent"?

(SB) "Transparent. You saw his outline and you saw some detail, but you didn't see a solid object".

(MR) "Now as you have progressed through life, your psychic ability that you have, has remained with you. You now attend churches and give clairvoyance to the members of the audience. What does your mediumship mean to you, what does it bring to you"?

(SB) "My mediumship brings to me confirmation that there is far more to life in the universe as we know it. It brings me fascination every time I think about the subject or see something strange. I think about what's just happened. It brings me comfort in the fact that I know if I am feeling really bad, something will happen to make me realise that I am not on my own. It brings me a lot of comfort knowing that at any given time I can request to speak to one of my late

159

relatives and they will just appear. Also, I can speak to any angel if I wish to, that gives me great comfort. And just as much as anything else, it gives me great comfort to know that I can heal people, it's a nice feeling knowing that you can make a difference in some people's lives".

(MR) "Well thanks very much Steven for providing that information you sure have been on some journey".

(SB) "I sure have. Thank you".

The following strange tales were told to me by Ann Deans. Ann had been working on developing her psychic healing abilities with Sheila Wishart in Livingston West Lothian. Needless to say, Ann herself had psychic abilities and due to her psychic abilities, this ensured that she could 'see and hear' into spiritual dimensions as you will soon find out.

THE STRANGE EXPERIENCES OF ANN DEANS

Location: Shotts, near Glasgow Central Scotland.
Date: 2010. 2007.

Hi Malcolm,

"It was 2010 and I was staying in a one-bedroom flat in Nevis Place Shotts along with my dog, a border collie named Sam. I had been asleep when something woke me up, it was around 02:00am or 3:00am. I can remember seeing what looked like a very long wispy feather retracting from my bedside and recoiling into a tall swirling column at the bottom right-hand side of my bed. It was just above door height and hollow inside, and it was whirling on the spot clockwise. I remember that my first thought was *"That is pure spirit"* it seemed as if it was a dirty white and light grey going onto deeper shades of

160

grey. It was identical to whirling smoke, and I could make out that it was long feathers, and they were swirling quite fast. Then it started moving, continually swirling at the same time, and moved up along to the top of my bed, stopped, then went straight 'through me' to the other side of my bed. It stopped again at the other side, then proceeded down to the foot of the bed, again stopping, and again proceeding to where it first started. I waited for a few seconds, and then it repeated exactly the same again, this time I actually tried to duck when it came across my bed for the second time. All the time this was happening, my dog was lying beside my feet on top of the bed and the dog never moved an inch or reacted in any way. I was completely calm and went back to sleep. In the morning, I phoned my friend Sheila, and she said it was my door keeper, and it was to assure me that all was safe. So, I asked Sheila why did it go around me twice? *"Ah ha"* she said knowingly, And I said, *"Is it because I'm a bit slow on the uptake and needed it explained twice?"* Sheila replied, *"You've got it girl"*.

Ann had a further strange account to relate to me. She stated.

"It was December 10th, 2007, and it was a really sharp frosty night, when about 5.30pm before leaving to travel to Livingston to attend a Spiritualist development circle, I had called in to see my mum who was fast approaching the end of her natural life. She was lying in her bed in her bedroom where she had been for a few weeks, and on entering her bedroom she wanted to touch my hands, but I didn't want her to, because my hands were frozen. Anyway, she managed to, and it was so special, the feeling I received from that touch. I then went up to the Bon Accord area to pick up a girl going to the circle for the first time. On returning home after dropping the girl off, and as I was going along the road near the Bon Accord, there, lying in the middle of the road, was a long-stemmed red rose, I had drove past it before thinking 'I need to get that for my mum'. So, I got out the car and walked back to where it lay and picked It up, it was perfect. Where had it come from? This was Shotts at 10pm on a really sharp frosty night and a perfect long-stemmed rose is lying in the middle of a busy road? Anyway, I headed back to my mum's house to gift her this rose that I'd just found, and as I opened the front door, I was met by my older brother Robert walking out my mum's bedroom door, *"Look what I've got for my mammie"* says I so excitedly. Robert very solemnly relied *"I think she's gone"*. Was this a gift from Spirit? It would have appeared just as my mam had been drawing her last breath".

Ann followed this story up with another strange encounter that she had. She went on.

"When I was about 6 years old, my mum had given me a shilling (old money) 12 pennies, to go to the shop to get a 3 pence bar of Cadbury's chocolate for my younger sister. We lived in Currieside Avenue in Shotts which was just yards away from Dykehead Cross. Between Currieside Avenue and the cross, there were the remains of a farm that my dad's family had, and my dad's brother Tam was keeping hens and pigs there, an old farm bailing tractor stood on the piece of ground facing down towards Currieside. I had bought the chocolate and had sixpence and a thruppenny bit change in my hand. When taking the short cut through the wire palings at the side of the farm, I dropped the money, and on bending down to pick it up, something made me turn my head, and I was looking at this old farm machine. It now had a young girl with long hair and dress standing on it between two men, one was at the back, and one was at the front of her. The man at the front was pretending to pull the large lever beside the seat, and the man at the back was watching as the big circular forks would soon be moving and tearing into whatever lay on the ground beneath it. The girl was screaming in terror, and all the two men did was laugh mockingly. They were both dressed in 3-piece suits.

I remembered that I dropped the money, and as I looked away to pick it up, everything went back to normal. No girl, no men. I told my mam about it saying that I'd seen my dad and uncle Tam up at the farm, (to my child mind it was all it could be) my mam replied, *"Don't be silly, your daddy is doon the pit at Polkemmet"*.

Ann had one more story to tell, this one, concerns the time when she believes that her life was saved by a guardian angel. Ann now takes up the story.

"It was 1965 and I had been to the pictures that night at the Regal with my friend Agnes Weir, we were both 14. Agnes was meeting a lad she had been seeing, so that left me on my own going home. There was a lane between Torrance's the draper and Stevenson's Ironmongery buildings that led to where I lived at Currieside Avenue in Shotts. This lane was unlit, so you always did a double take looking back to see you weren't being followed. When I got to the entrance between Torrance's and Stevenson's, I first checked the lane was clear and that no one was behind me. Just more than halfway down the lane, I turned to see that I'd not been followed, and there, just at the start of the opening, was this man, a stranger starting to come down the lane. He was very handsome and was sort of looking back at me and I felt comfortable that there was sufficient distance between us. I didn't hear running footsteps behind me, and I proceeded on my way home. Just as I got to the almost safety of Currieside, I'd reached the fence railings of the swing park and heard the quickening heavy footsteps behind me. Then an arm came round my neck, and instinctively I reached out and grabbed at the fence to stop him pulling me down on the ground. The lights were on in the houses nearby, and Mrs Strirrat's curtains were wide open, and I was mentally saying, *"Mrs Stirrat please look out of your window"*. My attacker was saying *"Scream and I'll kill you"*. Scream, I couldn't breathe!

Next thing I know, his arm is off my neck, and I let out a hard terrified scream at the top of my voice. At the same time, I could hear hard running footsteps coming down from where I stayed. The attacker on hearing these footsteps, made a fast escape across the swing park towards Rosehall Road. I was now sitting on the ground where I'd fallen after being mercifully released from the stranglehold that I'd had been placed in. A split second later, I could see my older brother running up towards me who was in complete shock and shouting *"What the f***s happened. Where did he go"?* I said someone jumped me, and at the same time I pointed across the swing park in the direction of where my attacker had fled. My brother was like a hare running after him, I was sitting stunned when an elderly neighbour, returning home had come across me, and without breaking her stride asked, *"Oh dear what's happened?"* On telling her I'd just been attacked, she walked on saying *"Oh, that's terrible" and left me sitting"!* When I look back on it, I know that my attacker was not the man I'd seen earlier at the start of the lane. My feelings are that what I saw was a Guardian Angel that intervened and saved my life that night".

Best wishes. Ann Deans.

Our next few tales, come from Karen Wilson who wanted to recount her own strange sightings of paranormal phenomena.

THE BLACK DOG AND THE BLACK SHAPE
Location: Livingston West Lothian and Carnwath South Lanarkshire Scotland
Date: 1977 and 1993/4, 1995.

"My first strange experience was when I was about six, (1977) I was in bed at home in Livingston West Lothian reading a book and a shadow appeared, more like a grey fog. As it came in my room it formed into the shape of a black dog.

164

This thing had red eyes and looked like a Doberman. It came around the side of my bed, opened its jaws, and bit my arm. It scared me so much that I slept with the light on, right up till the age of fourteen. I also dreamt about dogs chasing me for years. In 1993/1994, I was having a very hard time as I was in and out of hospital with pains in my stomach. I woke during the night at my home in Carnwath and saw something black at side of my husband. I just thought that if I looked at it, it would kill me. Then in 1995, same house different bedroom, I saw a full body apparition of a woman looking at my baby in the cot. She was there for a good ten minutes".

Regards. Karen Wilson.

Our next few strange tales, come from Don Walker, who shares with us, his sightings of what could be termed, angelic 'beings'.

THE ANGEL, THE GHOSTLY BOY, AND THE CINEMA GHOST
Location: Paisley and Lenzie. Central Scotland.
Date: 1977, 2001, and 2005.

Hello Malcolm.

"I had several instances of angelic beings in my life during the time that my father was dying of cancer and hospitalised. I was training as a mental health nurse, working on wards, and attending the West of Scotland University in Ayrshire and also Paisley. I was keen on fitness at that time, and when I was not able to get to the gym I used a rowing machine, stepper, and cycle in my bedroom. I was in my bedroom; it would be around June or July 2001 before my father passed away. I was cycling on the stationary, when the room brightened, and time seamed to slow down. I was aware that my body was stopped, then I felt the weight of hands on my shoulders and feet behind me on the saddle. An Angelic being made of light appeared behind me, and its golden wing like trails rose up towards the ceiling, whereupon I felt a huge feeling of love and compassion. I was told that my dad loved me, and he was happy to go. The light went out in an instant and I was back cycling pretty much dripping with sweat. A few days later I was visiting my dad in hospital, although he was weak, he had eaten a salad and tomatoes, he seemed to go sleepy, and limp and his head sunk lower into the pillow. He stopped breathing and went pale. I went to find a ward nurse thinking he was dead. But on return with the nurse, he was sitting up and smiling. He said he was in a beautiful garden but was told to go back. He told this to my mother also. Next day he was unconscious and sedated by the medics due to not having effective pain control due to his tumours affecting an area of the brain. By this time, staff had said that he would pass away pretty soon, and we were also concerned about my mother's health. However, I felt a presence at times, and felt the angel was there with us".

"Much later, probably months later, I was having a bath in my rather enclosed bathroom of my flat. On this occasion, the ceiling opened up with light, and the vision of golden feathers floating down was spectacular, they even floated down into the bath water. This beautiful 'being' was more physical though and was now straddling me, and in the rather cramped bath, I had to move my legs to make room. This 'being' was more alien than angel and blinked slowly with piecing blue eyes. He seemed to morph from a smooth small body of a teen to a more adult golden face like a Roman statue. Strange but there was no message. Just a feeling I was being observed. Then things suddenly went back to normal. It only seemed to be minutes, but the bath water was pretty cold. I got out the bath and thought that this was very strange indeed".

"The third incident took place in Lenzie near Glasgow in the summer of 2005. A friend had a beautiful old mill house by a river. I was there to attend the wedding of my friend who was a prison governor and a police inspector. There was a large marquee erected in the large garden and lots of friends and family were attending with children running around it was lively. I was alone, as my relationship of twenty years had ended. It felt strange. I hadn't made up my mind if I was staying over at my friends or driving home, so right up till about eleven o clock, I had not drunk any alcohol. My friend said she would let me sleep in the mill room where the river ran under the house, and she set up a mattress and quilt there. I went through to the kitchen and was still drinking tea, but I had bottle of champagne ready. During this time, I noticed a boy standing on the stairway leading to the mill room, he was maybe eleven years of age and had a tremendous shock of black curly hair and a dark complexion. He walked confidently and sat next to me at the kitchen table. *"Your sober",* he said, *"My mom is drunk",* I said yes most of the party goers were like that. He then said, *"It's quiet here, can I stay with you"?* I said *"Yes, we can talk".* But honestly, I didn't know what an eleven-year-old would talk about. However, he told me he was from grand Brazil, and it was a very nice place with flying birds and colourful gardens, he said nobody there grows old. I was completely confused by this, but he was pretty intense with his story. I was happy to talk to him and thought this boy had maybe read a book or two. I said I'm going to sleep, and he said, *"OK I'll stay in the kitchen".* So, I went down into the mill room with my bottle of champagne and a glass. Changed out of my clothes and was soon under the duvet. I was pretty warm and having drunk my drink, felt quite relaxed. The noise of the party soon drifted into the distance. I was then disturbed from my sleep by a shaking, and was aware of the 'boy' sleeping, curled up next to me on the top of the duvet.

That aside, the shaking seemed to be coming in waves from the air around me. A figure then appeared in front of me very clearly, but not like an angel, he had dark shiny skin with blue veins clearly visible. I was feeling uneasy to tell the truth and sort of paralysed. The figure seamed to read my thoughts, and I could hear a voice saying, *"We will not harm you"*. Then the hand of this 'being' pushed through my body, and I felt my heart stop. Then, after a second, it started racing. The voice then said how easy it is to die or live, and further said *"You will have a mission, but I can't tell you what to do. Don, you will have hard times, but you will come through it"*. The 'being' stayed dark with purple shades moving over its skin and did not rise but sunk down into the floor as it disappeared".

"After this vison, the boy woke up, and I said, *"Did you see that Angel"?* he said he was not an angel, he was a messenger, I know these people, from the city under the earth. I said to him, *"Look you need to go back to your mum's room. She will look for you"*. The boy then smiled and got up and left. I fell back to sleep. In the morning my host and others were later to rise, but eventually the smell, of breakfast came through to where I was. I got dressed and went to join them. During the conversation I described the boy with the big curly hair, and asked if his mother was up yet. Nobody at all had seen the boy and there was no woman from Brazil on the guest list. My life has had ups and downs since then, but I've not had any similar experiences since".

"One of my earliest strange experiences was back in 1977. It was at the afternoon showing of Star Wars which had just come out. My sister and I were upstairs in the old cinema in Titchfield Street in Kilmarnock and were going up the stairs to leave, when all of a sudden, we were pushed aside by a man wearing an Arran jumper. It all happened very fast. When we turned around, he was gone, the cinema was empty!

168

We spoke to the staff at the admission and sweet shop downstairs, and they told us that this happens a lot, and it's a ghost from a fire that happened there years before. What was alarming, was the force of the push I felt".

Regards Don Walker.

Our next tale comes from a hotel which, as far as I know, is not haunted. However, guest Alan Brown would beg to differ. Here is what he had to say.

WHO OR 'WHAT', MOVED MY BAG!

Location: Western Isles Hotel, Tobermory, Isle of Mull, Scotland.

Date: 2011.

"It would be 12 years ago now (2011) I was working in Northern Scotland and stayed at the Western Isles Hotel in Tobermory on the Isle of Mull which had an unusual revolving door. I checked into room number 1 on first floor, and I placed my Tesco's hessian bag 'on the floor beside the bed', which contained a bridge camera and other bits and bobs. I then placed my baseball cap on top of the bag, thinking to myself, *"OK, if that cap moves, someone's been in my room"*. I then locked the door and went downstairs for a meal and a drink. 40 minutes later I came back up, I unlocked the door, and my eyes went straight to the hessian bag and my baseball cap which was now sitting 'on my bed'. The bag wasn't moved, the cap had moved from the top centre of the bag, onto the bed, there would no reason for anyone to come into a locked room and lift the cap like it was, and place it on the bed, this creeped me out. Annoyed, I went down and asked the manager if anyone had been in my room, I told him that my bag had been disturbed, he was genuinely surprised and said, *"absolutely not, was anything taken"?*

They were a new husband and wife couple who had just moved up from down south. English accent and seemed quite nice. I checked my bag, nothing else was touched or missing, I spent all night up with the lights on and never slept a wink. I left next morning without having breakfast, very pissed off. Never went back. I now prefer to stay in B&B's".

With regards. Alan brown.

Some might say that a member of staff had been in the room and lifted his bag with the cap and moved it so that it was not in its original position where Alan had placed it, but then again! We now hear about a tale from the First World War, but one which did not have a happy ending.

BACK FROM THE GRAVE!

Location: Chislehurst, Southeast London.

Date: During the First World War.

"Not sure if this is of any interest, but my now deceased nana, as a young girl, was at home with her mother in their home in Chislehurst. Her two older brothers were in France fighting in the war. They heard the front door open and close, and the sound of a heavy duffle bag drop onto the hallway floor. They both rushed out to welcome home one or the other boys to find the hallway empty. A day later, the telegram arrived to say he had been killed in action, in fact neither boy came home".

Sincerely. Kimberley Jones.

Over the years, I have read about a number of such cases, and the above case highlights this fascinating phenomenon. Our next tale comes from someone who was sceptical of ghosts but admits that what happened to him on a ghost Investigation, still has him puzzled today. Here is his tale.

TOUCHED ON THE ARM, BUT NOBODY WAS THERE!

Location: Tretower Court and Castle/ Llys a Chastell Tre-twr. Wales. UK.

Date: 2005.

"My potential physical encounter with a ghost was at Tretower Court and Castle/ Llys a Chastell Tre-twr in Wales. I was part of a camera crew on a paranormal ghost investigation show. My job was to film the action and just basically blend into the background. After a day filming pieces to camera and generic shots of the location, the crew would break into small groups and go off around the location looking for a paranormal activity. Each week they would try different techniques to bring in 'spirits'. This week's gimmick was chanting, so after a few minutes of *"OMMMMMMM-ing"* something weird happened. I felt something hit me on my left arm. Not a massive force, just as if a mate had given you a friendly tap on the arm in the pub. In our small group was a psychic medium, so I took it upon myself to ask had I just had a muscle spasm on my arm or had something indeed actually hit me. The psychic then went on to tell me that there was a presence behind me, and it was someone that knew me. Now, because of the nature of the show, I'd always kept information of people that I know who had passed away from the cast and crew. The medium, then went on to tell me personal information about this person, a nick name that they used to have, there real name and how that person died. I was in shock, I had indeed known a person in my youth who had sadly been killed in tragic circumstances, and all the information the medium had given me was spot on. I am a very sceptical person when it comes to ghost investigations and psychic mediums, but this experience did make me start questioning a lot of things. I have to say I am always aware of things around me while filming so that I don't break anything or trip over anything, and due to the nature of the way I used to film this show. I would always hang back to catch some of the action, so I know that no one was around me when I was tapped on the arm".

Sincerely. Iain Cash.

One thing that always intrigues me, is the fact that on some occasions, some ghosts will mimic one's voice, pretend to be that person to other members of a household. It would seem to take great pleasure in doing so. I had this effect in one of my SPI cases from the 1980's in a house at Gartmorn Road in the town of Sauchie. The ghost would mimic the daughter and the mother's voice to other family members, yet both mother and daughter were not in the house at the time. Well, our next case features the same effect, as you will see.

THE MIMICKING GHOST!

Location: Asply, Nottingham, England.
Date: 1988/1989.

Hi Malcolm

"In 1979 my family and I moved into a house on Seaton Crescent in Aspley Nottingham. I was 8 years old at the time when strange things seemed to happen. Things would vanish then reappear days or weeks later, but we never really paid attention to it, nothing scary in fact. It was not until I was living alone in the house from 1988 (my parents bought another house in Grimsby and moved there leaving myself with the house in Nottingham). That's when strange things started to happen. I would hear my name being called, but I was alone in house! again it was scary. I just thought it was my imagination playing tricks on me. Then what I call the 'mimic' started to show itself. I would be in bed asleep, I would then hear the outer front door open, then the inner front door open, and the alarm key turn in the house alarm.

172

I would then hear my parents shout upstairs to me *"It's OK Paul its only us"*, I would then hear them go into the living room then I would hear my mum say, *"I will just wash these few pots you have left",* then I would think to myself, I have not left any pots. Then I would get extremely cold and frightened and would not be able to open my eyes. My whole body would go stiff. This feeling would last for what seemed like several minutes but was probably only seconds. I would then go downstairs and shout *"Mum, dad are you here"?* but get no answer.

I would notice however, that the house alarm had been turned off, but the front doors were still locked, this happened two or three times a month. I spoke to my parents, but my father dismissed it, saying that there were no such things as ghosts. My mum on the other hand, told me out of ear shot of my dad, that she also had that, but in the day when she was awake. She said that she would hear me come home from school early and have a conversation with me though my bedroom door! In 1989 I had my girlfriend Karen over for dinner, the old romantic that I was. She had been to the house several times but never in the house on her own. On this particular day, I told her that I just had to pop to the shops, she said 'yep fine', and that she was just going to the bathroom. As I was backing the car out of the drive, I saw her put the bathroom light off. By the time that I had got the car off the drive, she had finished, then turned the light off, then came downstairs, and turned the stair light off.

But then the bathroom light came back on again! So I went to the shops, got what we needed, and when I got home the bathroom light was still on. I got in and said, *"Just popping up stairs to turn the light off".* When I got into the living room she was standing there with her coat on and said *"Can you take me home please, you know I like you, but I think from today we should just be friends"* I was confused, and I could see she was pale.

As I drove her home, I asked her what had brought this on, as only an hour before we were laughing and joking and making plans. But she wouldn't tell me what had happened whilst I was at the shop. And to this day, I still don't know. We did lose contact in the late 1990's".

"In 1990 I came home from work after a night shift, my father had come over to see me for a few days. When I got in at 7am, my dad shouted, *"Is that you Paul"?* I replied, *"Yes just got in from work."* To my surprise he said, *"No you got home at 2am, I was talking to you through the bedroom door for about 20 minutes, you said that you had come home early as the machinery had broken down and was going to take several hours to fix".*

I told him it was not me he was talking to but the ghost, and he was convinced I had come home, and then gone back to work. Other things happened in the house, it felt sometimes that someone or 'something', would get into the bed at side of you. You would feel the bed clothes move and the mattress sink as though someone had just got in, then the sense of fear would kick in, and I would not be able to speak for a few seconds then it would be gone. One thing I would say, is if this thing didn't like you or felt threatened in any way, it would make its self-known.

Like I said, Karen would never tell me what happened. I sold the house in 1999 but if I go back up to that area, I am still drawn to look at the house. In fact, I would now love to investigate the place knowing what I know and have seen over those 15 years".

Regards. Paul Croft.

1934 Austin 7

Alien Bill Rooke and Rocky

Chingle Hall, Lancashire UK (c) Darren W. Ritson

Close-up of Croydon Ghost

Main Croydon Ghost Photo

Drawing of ghosts seen at Lochalsh Hotel Neil Attenbury

Ghostly arm at OLM Con (c) The Author

The lane where the caped woman appeared.

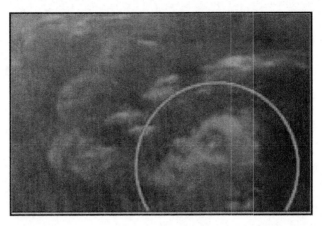

Underwater ghost. The Deep. Hull, East Yorkshire England

Where hooded lady appeared (c) Bill Rooke

CHAPTER TWO
THE HAUNTING AT GLADSTONE VILLA

"We experienced activity that simply defied rational explanation. My grandfather Bill claimed to have had a glass bottle thrown towards him as he entered the main bedroom, missing him by inches".

Andrew Dexter. Former resident of Gladstone Villa.

One of the more interesting tales of paranormal activity, was presented to me back in 2018, when a gentleman by the name of Andrew Dexter wrote to me informing me about the property that he had previously lived in (Gladstone Villa) The Villa stands in the Caerphilly County borough of the South Wales valleys in the United Kingdom, and it was a property that caused his family a lot of sleepless nights. In his e-mail to me he stated.

"My family and I had numerous paranormal experiences in the former mining town of Bargoed (Pronounced Bar - goyd) from 1969 to the summer of 1978. Bargoed was once part of the Rhymney Valley, and is 17 miles from Cardiff, 8 miles north of Caerphilly. We experienced things that defied rational and scientific explanation and left me and my family, in no doubt that the paranormal is most certainly real. These strange events lasted for a whole nine years and were entirely genuine".

We will come back to those strange events shortly. For now, let us take a look at the property and what Andrew himself had to say about it. He recalls that Gladstone Villa, was a three storied pale grey Victorian high building with a twin gabled front and a veranda. The building he states, loomed ominously over the other houses in Cardiff Road.

Andrew recalls the building as having a damp gloomy interior as there were no central heating, but there was a coal fire in every room. He also remembers whenever there was a windy draughty day, that the linoleum would lift up in the small, cramped kitchen. The furniture, he stated, was old fashioned even by 1960's standards. A tasteless two-seater brown leather settee was set against a wall with two chairs to match, each side of the open fireplace facing the dining table and television. There was also a boxed wireless and record player straight out of the 1950's. An interesting fact to note, was a building called the 'Rafa Club,' which was situated directly across the street from Gladstone Villa, this also, was reputedly haunted.

THE STRANGE EVENTS AT GLADSTONE VILLA

The story begins when Andrew and his parents, William, and Caroline, moved into the property in 1969 to live with his grandparents, William (Bill) Higgs and his grandmother Rita Higgs. Initially things were quiet, but then the family started to experience mild poltergeist activity such as house lights being switched on and off by unseen forces. Furthermore, electrical cables were witnessed being pulled by invisible hands. More disconcerting was the figure of a Monk that was witnessed by Andrew's mother Caroline, although he admits that during the nine years that he lived at the villa, he never saw the monk himself. Andrew further stated.

"It was so bad we slept downstairs with the lights on. It left us all in no doubt that this phenomenon was real, and there is indeed a spiritual plain of existence, though what it is I really don't know. But from a biblical point of view, it would be demonic, but we came to no serious harm, not physically anyway, but mentally it disturbed us to the point it made my mother a nervous timid person, and me obsessed with this kind of phenomena".

Thankfully, even with all the paranormal events occurring to the family, they still tried to live their lives as normal, and try not to let these strange occurrences bother them. And whilst the strange events were not a daily occurrence, it still kept them on their toes. More often than not, it was the 'footsteps' heard in the main master bedroom that freaked them out. On inspection of the bedroom, nothing was to be seen. These footsteps were heard on a daily basis and could be heard by all the family as they all sat downstairs watching television. Indeed, Andrew states that they would turn the volume down on the television to hear the footsteps more clearly, and that his grandfather Bill would point up to the ceiling and say, *"He's by here"* and *"He's by there now"* trying to make out where the footsteps were coming from and going to. Sometimes the sound of the footsteps would change, like that of a woman in high heels. Most of the paranormal activity occurred in the master bedroom where Andrew's grandparents slept. Another source of annoyance was that the family television would often switch itself on and off when no one was near it. I should point out here, that Andrew's grandfather Bill Higgs, had a strange experience when he was younger. I've learned that after leaving school, Bill took a job working down the mines, which many Welshmen did back in those days as it was the main source of employment. Anyway, the story goes that Bill, and some friends, were out cycling around the village of Six Bells Abertillery. The rain was incessant and was coming down with a vengeance, so they all decided to seek shelter in an old, deserted house. After a short while, they managed entry into the boarded-up house where they sought refuge for a while, and that's when strange things started to happen. Suddenly they all heard noises coming from one of the rooms upstairs, and being curious, they all decided to go upstairs in search of those noises. According to Bill, as they entered the bedroom quarters, the noises would cease, and suddenly be heard from an adjacent room.

Each time they went into the room with the noise, the noise stopped, and was heard in a different room! I should point out here that near this area, back on the 28th of June 1960, there was a disaster at the Six Bells Colliery. Wikipedia tells us that (and I quote) "At approximately 10:45, an explosion took place in the West District of the Old Coal Seam, caused by an ignition of firedamp. Coaldust in the air ignited, and the explosion spread almost throughout the district. Killing 45 out of the 48 men who worked in that district of the mine, the tragedy would have been even worse had it not been for maintenance work was being carried out on the 0.10 face where otherwise 125 men would have been working.

Lethal concentrations of carbon monoxide gas were found to be present. This suggested that the men lost consciousness rapidly, and that death occurred within minutes. A public enquiry into the disaster took place, at No 2 Court of Newport Civic Centre, between the 19th and 28th of September 1960. The Inspector of Mines reported that the probable cause of the explosion was firedamp, ignited by a spark from a stone falling onto a steel girder. Could the ghostly noises that Bill and his friends heard in that boarded up house, have been a place where those miners had stayed prior to the explosion that took their lives? Incidentally, another interesting point I should make here, is the fact that Bill Higgs's own father George Higgs, is reported to have said the following words just before he died in June 1969, *"I will haunt you all"!*

Now, what I would like to know, is 'why' he wanted to say those words? Was he just being jovial! That said, I should also point out here that both Andrew's mother and Grandfather Bill (George's son) clearly smelt the smell of pipe smoke in one of the rooms at Gladstone Villa. George, it should be pointed out, loved smoking a pipe. Could we speculate that this was indeed George who had passed away coming back to visit his family? We can but wonder.

ANDREW AND THE STRANGE EVENTS

Andrew Dexter was born on the 24th of August 1969 and came to live in Gladstone Villa on the 9th of September 1969. But as a baby, strange things were still afoot in Gladstone Villa, and as he grew older, he was in a position to notice things more clearly. Andrew's mother Caroline stated that things were fine for a while, but then strange noises could be heard coming from the attic. These noises comprised initially of gentle tapping's and rapping's which grew in intensity. With my previous books regarding ghosts and hauntings throughout the U.K., I always like to give my reader the tale as told by those who witnessed these events, so here, in part, in his own words, is the strange case of the ghosts of Gladstone Villa, as told by one of its former occupants, Andrew Dexter.

"We experienced activity that simply defied rational explanation. My grandfather Bill claimed to have had a glass bottle thrown towards him as he entered the main bedroom, missing him by inches. I didn't personally see this myself, but I still recall the time he came from the room with the broken bottle in his hands and he told us what happened. There were five members of the family that were living at Gladstone Villa. My maternal grandfather William Higgs, known as Bill to family and friends. Bill was a retired minor who worked at the local colliery. He was a short bald man who liked nothing more than to listen to his country and Western L.P.'s, Johnny Cash and Glenn Campbell and so on. He also liked Westerns on T.V. that starred John Wayne or Clint Eastwood. Also staying at the Villa, was my maternal grandmother Rita Higgs. She was a short woman who was a housewife, she was completely tee total but liked a smoke. She also liked collecting garden gnomes and liked watching soap operas on T.V. My mother, Caroline Dexter, met my father at the local bake house in Baldwin Street, where she was on day shift regularly whilst my father

worked the night shift. He would stay behind to make her a cup of tea and chat. They dated for three years before they got married on Monday the 1st of April 1968. They did not get a place of their own, but they decided to live with my grandparents at Gladstone Villa which was in Cardiff Road. I was born on the 24th of August 1969. I was just a baby when she said it all started off rather quietly, like a small tapping here and there, but nothing too noticeable. But in time, the activity gradually increased. My mother told me that when I was a baby sleeping in my cot, my pillow was suddenly and unexplainably torn in half by an unseen force. One time my mother said the family heard a noise like someone jumping down from the attic and onto the landing. Naturally, thinking that someone was trying to break in, they went to see what was going on. When they got there, they found nobody there, but the hatch to the attic was open! Whatever it was, eventually occupied itself in the main bedroom, which incidentally was my grandparents' room (Rita and Bill). It soon made its presence felt by walking around the bedroom and the sounds of dragging could be heard.

One evening, my mother went upstairs to that bedroom to get my father up for work so he could get ready for his night shift. When she got there, she was confronted by the sight of the ironing board placed on my father's torso as he slept! His slippers were also thrown out on the landing where they shouldn't be. When my father awoke, he was astonished to find the situation he was in. He suspected my grandfather Bill was playing pranks, but in time, he knew my grandfather was not responsible for it and he told his work friends what was going on. It soon got around town that Gladstone Villa was haunted. My parents separated in 1972, and my father left Gladstone Villa, but it wasn't because of what was going on at Gladstone Villa, it was just a breakdown of the marriage,

They finally divorced on the 25 of April 1975, I have no major memories of my father living at Gladstone Villa, but he would come to see me every Saturday to take me to see my paternal grandparents and to the local cinema. Great times, even though the paranormal activity still continued."

"As I got older, I too witnessed the poltergeist activity for myself. It was an Easter Weekend in April 1977. (Sunday, 24th April 1977) I saw the long brown coaxial electrical cables being pulled from the back of the T.V. through the hole in the ceiling by unseen forces. As it was an Easter Weekend, I clearly remember my family and I watching the final episode of Jesus of Nazareth, who was played by actor Robert Powell. At the crucifixion scene, my grandfather Bill sternly shouted out, "This is a mockery." On Saturday the 30th of April, my grandfather Bill moved the TV back into the corner of the room and the settee was put in its place. My dad came up Saturday 30th April and I wanted to draw the crucifixion scene for him as I recalled it from the television, but my grandfather Bill saw this and was very angry with me because of the blasphemy and smacked me! Sadly, my father didn't do anything to stop him, a dysfunctional family wouldn't you say! I recall a lot from 1977, the Jubilee in June, Elvis Presley's death the following August and it being on News at Ten. We also heard the sound of unaccountable footsteps that day as well. I saw the house lights switching on and off. Every time my grandmother would watch the T.V. show 'Songs of Praise' on Sunday, 'Johnny' (That's what we called our ghost) would start. It was as if he was taking exception to religious music being played. And when my grandfather Bill would play records on Sunday as the family sat down for dinner, the music would suddenly switch off. 'It' took exception to the 70's British band Slade. On one occasion, my granddad Bill played their album 'Old new borrowed and blue' from 1974 in the bedroom, 'Johnny the ghost' would turn the electric off.

This would annoy my grandad Bill."

"Another family friend Derek would also come to experience the phenomena. One night Derek came up to paint the living room door green for us, my mother was cooking sausages in the kitchen when the noises would start, this would quite naturally frighten Derek into stopping for a while until the noises stopped, but Derek was determined to finish the job he had started, and he did so. One day all the family went out and when we got back, we found, much to our astonishment, that the furniture in the living room had been turned upside down. There were no signs of a break-in, and nothing was missing, and there was no forced entry that we could see. My father William was quite suspicious of my grandfather Bill, thinking that it was my grandfather doing it, but as time passed, he realized it wasn't him doing it at all, and my father became convinced that this was a genuine haunting.

What I also found most interesting about the ghost of Gladstone Villa was when Andrew informed me that the local police had got involved! Even at his young age, Andrew recalls them coming to the property and popping their heads into the attic where some of the strange sounds had been reported. However, Andrew didn't say whether they were scared or not, and whether they went all the way into the attic for a proper look, stating instead that the noises coming from the attic may have been caused by Andrew's father playing a prank on the family!

Andrew continues.

"A family friend, Mrs. Ivy France, was more of a friend to my grandmother Rita, she would be in her 50's at this time and she enjoyed a game of bingo at the old people's hall next to Gladstone Villa, she used to read the tea leaves from the cup but was rather skeptical when my grandmother told her Gladstone

Villa was haunted. I can still remember Ivy going into the main bedroom, looking around and saying that it was the vibration from the traffic outside which was causing the noises, but she was soon to change her mind when she experienced it for herself. It was then she suggested that a medium should become involved, and a short while later, a medium by the name of John Matthews, a short man with glasses and black hair in his 40's, came to Gladstone Villa. He started by asking the family questions, after which he began by challenging the spirit to perform by knocking on the ceiling, and sure enough, it responded by knocking back at him! At some point John went into a trance to try and make contact with it, but he failed to get a name. He later confirmed the obvious that there was indeed a presence there and it was an earthbound spirit and that it had unfinished business."

"A priest by the name of Graham Jones was also called to Gladstone Villa. He blessed the property, and after a few prayers, he duly left, but before he left, he told the family to 'watch' baby Andrew, his tone sounded as if it was a warning! Thankfully, after the blessing it was quiet for a few short months, with no incidents to speak about. But sadly, it did return, and with a vengeance, and this time it decided to show itself! One evening, my grandfather Bill, my mother Caroline and I, were watching television, my grandmother Rita was reading a book, when all of a sudden, my mother just so happened to look to her left and she saw the full solid figure of a monk standing behind the sofa that Rita was sitting on. She described it in detail as a monk in typical brown habit complete with hood over the head, so she didn't see the face. It sounded very much like a 16th century Benedictine monk. My grandfather and I didn't see it as we were watching television. She said it was there for a few moments and it was gone. There was another sighting, but this took place in the daytime! My mother and I were in the front room, when my mother went over to the sofa to get something,

she looked to her left and I saw the confused expression on her face. I didn't see this as I was behind the door that was wide open, obscuring the hallway, but she later told me that she saw the face of an elderly man with a shock of white wavy hair looking into the room from the hallway that lead up to the bedroom."

"Fred Davies was a friend of my grandfather Bill, they worked together at the local colliery, and he would visit most evenings. Fred was a slim man who would wear a flat cap and glasses and smoked homemade cigarettes that hung from his lips when he spoke. He would sit in his favorite chair by the open fire and talk to the family and watch T.V. with us. One day, Fred was with us, in his usual place by the open fire, I was quietly playing with my toys by the sideboard. It was quiet when suddenly there was a very loud bang! It was so loud that Fred ducked his head, and I ran to my mother for comfort. When it was quiet, we all went upstairs. My grandfather, Bill, would always be first and I would be last. When we got to that bedroom, we found nothing that could account for that noise. Fred later told us that he ducked his head as he thought something was going to come through the ceiling! Fred also told us of another experience that he had had at Gladstone Villa. My grandfather Bill liked to look out of the landing window that overlooked Cardiff Road and across into Bargoed town center. This time Fred joined him, he said that he felt something brush pass him, but when he looked, there was nothing there! The most frightening experience that I personally had, was when I was alone in that particular bedroom. I made sure the light was on as I was scared of the dark. It was very quiet, and I was lying on the bed facing the window that overlooked Cardiff Road, when I suddenly felt something heavy pounce on the bottom of the bed. I heard the bed springs go just once, and I felt the bed bounce. I was too scared to look straight away as I was only a child at the time, but when I did eventually look, there was nothing there.

I went downstairs to tell my family and we all went back up. When we got to my bedroom and looked down towards the bed, we all saw three distinctive 'paw marks 'on the bed, like that of an animal. I later found out that my grandfather Bill had a black Labrador dog called 'Tovy' who had died before I was born. My grandfather Bill and my mother Caroline claimed to have heard a baby crying in that room, but as I didn't hear that at the time, I took very little notice of what they said. The activity got so bad that my mother, grandmother, and I, all slept downstairs with the lights on. It was only my grandfather Bill who was supposedly brave enough to sleep there. My grandmother Rita has had her own experiences. One day she went upstairs into that room to get my grandfather up, when suddenly, she saw the boiler door start to open wide by itself. She didn't stay there long to see what it was, as she quickly rushed out of that room. On another occasion, she said that she had the sensation of something being pulled from under her foot, like she had stepped on the ghostly monk's gown! As I mentioned before, we had the ghost for so long that my grandmother Rita gave it a pet name, she called him 'Johnny' and my grandfather Bill would shout out that name to provoke a reaction, but nothing would happen. A friend of the family by the name of Charles, who was Ivy Frances's son, got to hear about what was going on at Gladstone Villa and he came along with some friends, and, with my family's permission, they went into the bedroom. Something clearly happened. It frightened one of his friends so much that even to this day, his friend still says that the Villa was a spooky place. My grandfather Bill claimed to have had an unpleasant experience in the haunted bedroom. One night he was alone there, when all of a sudden, he said he felt a presence, and heard what sounded like floorboards creaking by the door. He then told me that he was completely paralyzed on the bed, he just couldn't move, not even to shout out to call us to help him.

But he managed to look, and saw a dark shadow appear at the foot of the bed and as quickly as it appeared, it disappeared."

It's fair to say that nearly everyone who visited Gladstone Villa came away with their own strange experience. Take for instance this account. Andrew's mother Caroline had to go into hospital for an operation on one of her toes, and, as a result, ended up on crutches to support her. One day the local nurse attended the Villa to ensure that the healing process on her toe was coming along. So, picture the scene, Andrew's mother is sitting on a chair with the nurse kneeling down beside her when the nurse says to Andrew's mother that there was no need to hold her. Andrew's mother looked at her mother Rita, who was also in the room, in amazement, as she was 'not' holding the nurse at all! Needless to say, Andrew's mother believed that it was their ghost that was doing the holding. In his narrative to me, Andrew goes on to say.

"The only time I heard the ghost being vocal, was the time we were all in the room. One of us wanted to use the bathroom and we couldn't get in there. My grandfather Bill said, "He's behind there!." (Meaning that our ghost was stopping the door from opening) I then heard quite distinctively, the sound of a Gregorian chant and that was it, nothing more. Another story about the bathroom, was when on Wednesday 22nd October 1975 my family and I heard a loud crash in the bathroom. We went to see what happened and we saw the tin bath on the floor. I think the nail fell off, but my mother Caroline still attributes it the 'Johnny' the ghost. (Author's Comment., the tin bath was held by a nail on the wall) A film was on T.V. that night, 'The fiend without a face.' I researched a T.V. archive and that's how I got the exact date of that incident. I saw the electrical cable from the back of the television being pulled at the back from the ceiling because that's where the aerial was.

My grandfather Bill took the T.V. from there and put it back in the corner by the window, this was Easter week. As I got older, I experienced the phenomena for myself, I too heard all the footsteps in the main bedroom. As I stated earlier, only my grandfather Bill slept in that room, he was the only one who was supposedly brave enough, but my grandmother Rita knew that he was just as scared to be in there, because every time he would go upstairs, he would whistle a tune."

On another occasion Andrew's Grandfather Bill was out in the garden one day, when he happened to look up at the house and was astonished to see two people looking out at him from one of the windows. It was a young man and a young woman. Andrew wonders if this could have been Michael and Evelyn Kimmiett who had lived in the house during the 1920's.

LEAVING GLADSTONE VILLA

"We left Gladstone Villa in June of 1978 when two local Italian businessmen by the name of John and Aldo Ricci bought the property, and the name was changed to 'Parc Villas.' It was curious that when the owner's son John moved in, there were no claims that the property was haunted. In the 1980's it was converted into a hotel and the name was changed again to 'The Parc Hotel' The then proprietor was a Londoner by the name of Roland Butler, but he also made no claim that the place was haunted. It wasn't until new management took over (The McBurney family) that rumours surfaced that it was actually haunted. The name was changed again to 'Redz Parc Hotel' (which itself closed back in 2014) The building was boarded up for a while until Gethin Mills took over who still presently owns the site. It's now a care home called 'Ty Parc.'

But before Andrew and his family left Gladstone Villa, it held one more surprise for them. Andrew now takes up the story.

"The night before we left Gladstone Villa, there was one final bizarre incident, it was as if 'it' knew we were leaving, and that was its way of saying goodbye. Our belongings were packed in black plastic bin bags in the hallway, we were getting ready to settle down for the night, ready for the big move the next day. My mother, grandmother and I got ready to go to sleep. The light was still on, and then we heard the doorknob turning, as if someone was trying to get in. At first, I naturally suspected my grandfather Bill, as he was the only one who slept upstairs in that room, and we thought it may have been him playing a prank. I called out to him, but there was no answer, no laugh that would give him away. We then heard our belongings that were packed in the hallway being thrown around. The next day we asked my grandfather Bill if it was him playing a joke on us. He insisted it wasn't him and to this very day I believe him."

So, the family moved out in the summer of 1978 and moved to a council estate in Gilfach Bargoed, and, as we have learned above, the property was converted into a hotel then finally a care home. But before it was turned into a care home, Andrew, who by now was living elsewhere, often wondered if, now that it was a hotel, (This was before it was turned into a care home) strange things were still happening! Well, he soon had the opportunity to find out. In August of 2009, he decided to hold his 40th birthday party at the hotel and, after speaking to some of the female staff there, he quickly found out that strange ghostly happenings were occurring there. The staff were experiencing lights being switched on and off whilst no one was there. Strange shadows would be seen flitting about in the bar area. There was also the occasional sighting of a monk in room five, and strange footsteps could be heard from various part of the building when no one should be there. There was always an 'eerie feeling' about the place. One place that the staff clearly didn't like was the cellar. This was because numerous unexplained noises could be heard coming from there, when they all knew that nobody should be down there. Not only that, the sound of a baby crying was also heard by the staff in the hotel. Let us recall that the Dexter family had also heard the sound of a baby crying 30 years before, when they stayed there when it was a Villa. Andrew found out from the staff that no baby was ever in the hotel when its cries were heard. Once the member of staff had finished telling Andrew all about the strange ghostly goings on in the hotel, Andrew then told the staff member about what had happened to him in the very same building 30 years before when it was Gladstone Villa, this drew a shocked expression across the face of the staff member.

ANDREW SEEKS ANSWERS

Not one to rest on his laurels, Andrew decided to do some digging of his own. He felt a need to find out more about the property and the Cardiff Road area in general and spent some considerable time looking through records from his local Bargoed Library and newspaper archives. What he found was most intriguing. He learned that Gladstone Villa dated back to 1900, and it was named after the former British Prime Minister William Gladstone. Andrew further discovered that the previous people that lived there, a family called the Kimmiett's, took up residence at Gladstone Villa in 1924. They were newly married Michael and Evelyn Kimmiett who had a son named Elvin Rowlands Kimmiett, who sadly died on Thursday the 29th of May 1924 at the property when he was just four months old. He was buried on Monday 2nd of June 1924. Of course, one may speculate that this may well explain the sound of a baby crying which was heard by Andrew's mother and grandfather at the property when they were in residence many years later. Incidentally, baby Elvin Kimmiett is buried in the cemetery of the village of 'Bedwellty'. Andrew further learned through the archives of the Cardiff newspaper 'The Western Mail,' that

Mrs. Evelyn Kimmiett died in Newport Wales in 1970 aged 68. This was a year after Andrew was born. Andrew speculated that maybe, the death of this child might have started all this strange paranormal activity! During his research on the Villa, Andrew uncovered that during the Second World War, a family by the name of Jones lived there. Andrew came across a letter that was written by Henry Jones from Gladstone Villa, stating that his son had been taken prisoner. Andrew also learned that the Mills family were also there at some point, and that Edgar Mills had claimed that Gladstone Villa was haunted, this was the first official record of the property being haunted.

As Andrew read through the history of the area, he learned that there was also a Monastery between Baldwin Street and Henry Street, where his parents had met and worked in a bakery that was situated there at that time. This might explain the monk that Andrew's mother saw. There was also a priest hide in this old, listed building that dates back the 17th century. The building allegedly has tunnels leading up to the local villages of Gelligear. Nearby there is an old manor house called Llancaich Fawr manor, this manor was featured on the T.V. programme, 'Most Haunted.' Andrew went on to inform me that some television stars had connections with the town of Bargoed. Actress Doris Hare who played the mother in the comedy 'On the Buses' was born there in 1905, her brother was born there in 1907, Doris left Bargoed when she was seven years old to become an actress. Rod Hull (Of Emu fame) spent his childhood in Bargoed as he was evacuated to Bargoed during the war. Andrew also met the actor Jon Pertwee, who played Doctor Who during the time that they filmed an episode of the popular series. That episode was entitled, 'The Green Death', and it was part filmed at the local pit where Andrew's grandfather Bill worked. As the years rolled on, Andrew's father Douglas Dexter died in 1991, aged just 44.

His grandfather Bill died in March 2014, aged 88, and his grandmother Rita died in July 1982. Ivy France who as we have read was a good and dear friend of Rita, died in 2002 aged 82. Fred Davies died in March 1982, and Charles France died in about 2017. Andrew's mother Caroline is still with us.

OTHER PEOPLE BACK ANDREW UP

In August of 2022, I received an interesting e-mail from Edward Williams, who did not know Andrew Dexter, but was aware of the hauntings at Gladstone Villa. This is what he had to say to me.

"Hi Malcolm.

"I read your book about the Sauchie Poltergeist, and it got me quite interested, if not obsessed, with wondering if Virginia Campbell is aware of your book about her? I'm fascinated by this subject and the Enfield case and Borley Rectory. I used to live in Merthyr Tydfil, South Wales. I moved to a nearby town called Bargoed (pronounced Bar-goyd) in the 1980's, but it wasn't until the mid-1990's that I heard a rumour of a haunting in the Cardiff Road area of the town. The Rafa Club is one of the oldest properties in Bargoed, going back to the 15th century and since I heard about it, there have been persistent rumours about this, and a property directly opposite, formally known as Gladstone Villa. I've been to both of these properties but saw no ghosts there, but I did experience something at Gladstone Villa when it became 'Redz Parc Hotel' in the 1990's. I tried to rationalise it by saying it might have been the wind causing the occurrence, but the staff say they've experienced things there, and at the Rafa Club opposite. Gladstone Villa apparently convinced a sceptic as did the Rafa Club. This is not a well-known or famous haunting, but I know the local press were interested. I also know that investigators tried to get access and were unsuccessful.

Having said this, 'The Capel Hotel' which is in very close proximity of Gladstone Villa and the Rafa club, have been investigated and researchers picked up some interesting EVP's, (Electronic Voice Phenomena) so that's evidence. There has also been a number of alleged UFO sightings in Bargoed by a couple of witnesses, Radio host Nicky Campbell interviewed one of them".

Sincerely, Edward Williams.

Another person who wrote to me to inform me about his strange experiences at Gladstone Villa, was Colin C. Evans from Andrew's former hometown of Bargoed. He had this to say.

"I knew Andrew when I was a lot younger. I can remember going to Gladstone Villa with my friend Charlie Flello, his mother (who was a medium) and another friend of ours, who's name I can't remember. While Charlie's mother was contacting the spirits that live there, Charlie and I went upstairs into the attic. While we were up there, unbelievably there appeared to be a big hole that seemed to be bottomless. We dropped a coin into the hole and never heard it land. Then there was a sudden whooshing sound, like something coming up the hole at speed. We panicked and got out of there as fast as we could. It scared the life out of us. We never went back there again. But. The weird thing is, whenever we walked past there. There was always someone (looked like a monk) that would be looking back at us. There are two windows upstairs at the front of the building with a solid wall between the windows (they were two separate rooms) yet as we walked past, the monk would instantly appear in the other room. The only explanation for this would be the monk had gone through the wall. I hope this helps".

Regards. Colin C. Evans

I also interviewed Andrew's mother over the phone, and she completely backed up all of what Andrew had said. And like Andrew, was equally puzzled as to the strange goings on in that house. Andrew suggested that I should go onto the Bargoed 'Past and Present' Facebook site where there have been a few posts about the haunting at Gladstone Villa. This I duly did. I sent e-mails to most of the people who said that they had experiences at the Villa but got little success with a reply. So, as these comments are already out there in the public domain, I will use some of them here. What I won't do however, is to use their real names. I'll give them pseudonyms, (p) but what they have said, is what they related on that site. I've had to tidy up some of their text, but in the main, what they have stated can be found on that site.

Henry Harkins (p)

"I remember the Higgs family, daughter Caroline living in Francis Street. Bargoed. Must have been in the 70s. I can recall going to Gladstone Villas to repair T.Vs. on a couple of occasions! Not so reliable then, (talking black and white) with valves! It was always so dark and dank! Curtains hanging in Hallway, I presume to stop draughts, but also excluded light! I remember pulling back said curtain and climbing stairs, always taking away T.Vs for repair, as there was not enough light to see properly! If they had ghosts, it wouldn't come as a surprise to me".

Alison Burns (p) This account concerns the RAFA Club.

"I'm in my daughter's account. I worked there. And when I was there, I used to hear the side door open to come into the bar like someone was coming in. I worked quiet a lot of day shifts so it was quiet.

I always used to go and check if someone was there, and there never was. I also worked upstairs cleaning the rooms, it was a very weird feeling up there.

I also saw a few shadows, like someone walking past, I checked but found nothing. I thought it was my mam, because she was up there to, but she was in a different room doing her jobs".

Alison Earnshaw (p)

"I've been to the Rafa Club a few times and heard or saw nothing. I stayed at the Redz many times, and yes, I did experience a few things like a door slamming and I tried to find a rational explanation for it. I did experience something in one of the rooms upstairs that frightened me so much that I couldn't move. I will not say what happened, but I never forgot it. I would advise anyone not to stay there alone! Someone I knew also stayed in one of the rooms and experienced something there, they had a breakdown soon after".

I received an e-mail from Nick Jones, who backed up the claims of others about the haunting at Gladstone Villa. Here (in part) is what he had to say.

Hi Malcolm.

"I live in the Bargoed area, and I heard you are writing a book about Gladstone Villa, or at least dedicating a chapter to it. May I confirm that what has been said about this property is actually true and 100 percent genuine. I went there once as I child and I heard disturbances footsteps on floorboards. I went to school with the boy that lived there in the 1970s. I won't say exactly what went on there, but the people who lived there were very honest and sincere in what they were saying. The boy I went to school with is a decent, honest person, and others who know him will vouch for that".

Nick Jones.

Now it's fair to say that my post on the Bargoed Past and Present Facebook page caused quite a stir. There were a number of people who stated that it was all rubbish, and that there were no such things as ghosts. One chap stated that he had lived at Gladstone Villas and never heard or saw a thing, but Andrew Dexter himself put that gentleman straight when he said that it wasn't until Andrew moved in, that strange things started to happen, and that just because he didn't experience anything, that's not to say that what was happening when Andrew was there didn't happen. A friend of Andrew's, Nick Jones, who we heard from above, came to Andrew's defence and stated to me.

Hi Malcolm,

"I'm here in Andrew Dexter's defence. It was mentioned on Bargoed Past and Present Facebook site that the Thomas family say the story is rubbish. May I state here that the Thomas family lived there 'before' Andrew was born, and the paranormal experiences started a few months 'after' Andrew Dexter was born. Andrew's family lived there without any incident before his birth. It's possible that his birth may have been the centre of the phenomena. There have been rumours about the Rafa Club as well for many years, and a bloke by the name of Daniel Collins (p) experienced something there and he mentioned a monk, his relatives are Dee Collins (p) and Karen Halliday, (p) I think they are cousins or sister and brother. Karen Halliday claims to know something about both properties. I've known Andrew since 1977 and I know he's an absolutely honest, sincere person. I visited him once at the Gladstone Villa property and footsteps were heard on bare floorboards; I never went there again".

Regards. Nick Jones.

Karen Halliday (p)

"My experience is from 1969, but my great grandparents came to Bargoed when my great grandfather came down from London to assist in the sinking of Bargoed pit. He stayed at Bargoed Farm for a month. He didn't like the place, said it was cold and austere, and that something very bad was present. He was a staid sensible man who didn't scare easily but he never set foot in the place again. I can remember as a young child in around 1967/68, walking down Park Drive and seeing a figure in the top left window of Gladstone Villas, the one in the left as you come down past the old RAFA Club.

I pointed it out to my friend who could see it as well. As we passed the RAFA Club, I had a horrible sensation and was sure I saw someone hanging from a tree in the club front garden. From then on, I had vivid dreams about the place. I have told Andrew Dexter what I saw a long time ago. Then in 2014 I went to see a medium show in there. It was the first time that I had set foot in the place, but I had vivid visions of men dressed as monks and a young person dying in the basement. This has happened several times, and each time someone I know has passed away I do feel something very bad has happened in the club, or in the farm prior to that building.

I was told as a child it is linked to Capel Gladys on the mountain, and that there is a tunnel that goes under the Park Villas down to the river. My great grandfather told us that and he was an engineer at Bargoed pit. He came down from London to help sink the shaft and spent time at the farm as a guest. He, referred to it as Tir Fargoed fferm."

Regards. Karen Halliday.

Susan Harmer Thomas

Hi Malcolm.

"Andrew asked me to contact you with reference to the Rafa Club in Bargoed. I remember being shown the priest hole in the cellar and was told of several strange things happening to the old men that were playing cards there. One card went missing and has never been found".

Regards Sue Hamer-Thomas Cllr Bargoed ward.

We now turn to a friend of Andrew Dexter, a young woman who shared a strange experience with Andrew whilst they were both young. This experience also shows that strange activity was indeed occurring at Gladstone Villas. There now follows an arranged interview that I conducted over the phone with Leanne Pritchard from Bargoed.

INTERVIEW WITH LEANNE PRITCHARD

Abbreviations. (MR) Malcolm Robinson. **(LP)** Leanne Pritchard.

(MR) "Hi Leanne. I'm calling in regard to Gladstone Villa and the Rafa Club. I'm devoting a chapter in my book to the strange goings on there and I have been speaking to a number of people to get their re-call on the incidents that they experienced. Now I believe you have a story to tell me, something about a rocking horse. Tell me more about that"?

(LP) "Yes I think I was about six, and there was a room in the attic".

(MR) "Is this Gladstone Villa"?

(LP) "Yes. I've grown up with Andrew, we have known each other since, oh, God's knows, certainly since we were tiny".

(MR) "So what did you see in this attic then Leanne"?

202

(LP) "I remember going up to the attic, and this place was enormous and sometimes we would hear banging on the walls as we were walking up there. I was just a small kid, and I didn't take much notice of it. So we went into the attic, and there was a little rocking horse, I can't remember if he was white, I think it was. And we started playing with his toys and out of the corner of my eye I could see something move. So, I turned around to have a proper look, and saw the rocking horse rocking on its own. I told Andrew and he looked at it, but we started playing again. I was young, and I didn't understand. So, we were playing for around a minute, and I looked around again and the rocking horse was still going, then all of a sudden it just stopped dead. It didn't slow down, it just stopped. I thought it a bit strange, but I didn't take any real notice of it. I didn't think anything of it because when you are that young, you don't tend to think about things like that, and we just carried on playing. It was so strange, and I can still vaguely see it in my mind".

(MR) "I know you said you were young. But what age do you think you were. Do you have a rough idea"?

(LP) "I know that we both had just started junior school, so I must have been about six".

(MR) "Do you recall what year that would have been"?

(LP) "Well I was born in 1968, so that would have been 1974".

(MR) "Other than the rocking horse experience that you had, do you recall anything else about Gladstone Villa or was that your only experience"?

(LP) "It was always cold in the place, even although they had the fire going. It always felt cold, especially in the attic. Walking up to the attic was always cold and like I said, you could hear banging coming from the walls.

I didn't understand what that was. Every time I went there, there was always banging or someone tapping on the walls. After that, when I went home, I didn't feel right in myself, I always felt that there was something there with me. Even in my own property when I was living at home, I felt one or two things happen to me, and this was after leaving Andrew's place".

(MR) "Yes this is quite common. Sometimes the phenomena follow people to their own homes".

(LP) "I can remember for about three or four years, I used to walk up the stairs in my own property when I was living with my parents, and it was like someone was tapping my shoulder. And that went on for months that did. Then one day, it really tapped hard as if I got punched, and I tuned around but couldn't see anything. So, for about three or four years I used to walk up the stairs with my back to the wall and I never knew what that was. But something had kept tapping me".

(MR) "I take it that this has all stopped now"?

(LP) "Yes. My aunt and father started seeing things, bless him he is gone now. But my father has seen ghosts in the past. It wasn't to do with our house, but it wasn't far from our house it was the park just up the road from our house. But like I said. I always used to feel uneasy when I went to Gladstone Villa, I always felt cold there, there was something not right about that place, but you don't tend to think about that when you are a kid".

(MR) "Do you still see Andrew"?

(LP) "Yes, but I haven't seen him for a while, but I keep in touch. I've been to Bargoed a few times and the Villa was turned into a hotel, and then it went into a home or something, and every time I walk past the building, I always get nervous, I don't know why, I just feel anxious. You know when you get palpitations"?

(MR) "Yes. Are you aware of anybody else apart from Andrew who had experiences at Gladstone Villa"?

(LP) "My grandma, she is no longer with me now. My grandma Ivy used to read tea leaves, she was psychic in a way, and she always knew that there was something that wasn't right about the place. And I know that there was a lot of strange activity once in there, and I'm not sure if it was an aunty of mine that took Andrew out of there".

(MR) "Have you heard tales about the Rafa Club"?

(LP) "Oh yeah, that's the little club opposite. There was something about monks and tunnels or something, and the monks used to go back and forth. I've known about this since I was a young child. Obviously, this was told to us when I was a young child about the monks going back and forth from the Rafa Club to the Villa. I also heard when I was in my late teens, that a Priest had supposedly gone into the building, and they reckon that he found a lost soul in there. I don't know how true that is".

(MR) "Yes there are so many stories about these buildings that sometimes you don't know what is true and what's not true. There is no denying however that there are some substance to the stories from Gladstone Villa, I mean you've had your own experience with the rocking horse".

(LP) "Oh Yeah"

(MR) "I mean, you know it's true".

(LP) "Oh yes, I love the paranormal stuff now, I'm into a lot of this stuff now, because it has always fascinated me. But that rocking horse was something that I did experience, and it is something that you can never forget".

(MR) "Leanne I'd just like to thank you for your time today and confirming the strange experience that you had at Gladstone Villa".

(LP) "No problem. I think the living are more scarier than the dead"?

(MR) "Yes, I'd have to agree with you on that one, that's for sure".

As stated above. Andrew Dexter had supplied me with many names who could back up the ghostly stories that occurred at Gladstone Villa and the Rafa Club, but sadly after giving it a few months and a few gentle reminders, only a few would come back to me. However, it was clear to see, that those that did come back to me, clearly had experiences there themselves.

FINAL WORDS

I shall leave the final words to Andrew Dexter.

"What I have told you Malcolm is true; I wouldn't discuss this if I couldn't possibly back this up. I have used real names as I have nothing to hide, and all I have said can be verified by the family of those people I mentioned. Sadly, some of the people I have mentioned are no longer with us. It's true, it all happened."

Andrew Dexter aged 6. Back garden of Gladstone Villa 1976

Andrew Dexter

Caroline Dexter Andrew's mother

Gladstone Villa, Bargoed

Gladstone Villa boarded up

The Parc Hotel, Bargoed

William Douglas Dexter. Andrew's father.

***

CHAPTER THREE

THE NOTTINGHAM HAUNTING

"They would be about no more than three and a half to four feet tall. I couldn't really see their faces, as when they were moving, they were like, 'blurred'. They moved at speed with such ease. It was amazing".

Andy discussing with the author, witnessing imps in the loft of the Lewis home.

HOW IT ALL STARTED

You know there are paranormal cases that come up from time to time that are head and shoulders above any other paranormal case. This is because of the sheer volume of bizarre paranormal events which includes the testimony from those that were there to view them. Some cases are so huge and comprise of so many different elements, that sometimes as a researcher, you wonder where to start. Well, such a case was presented to me back in 2015. At the time I lived in the lovely East Sussex town of Hastings on the south coast of England. The lady who notified me of this case, Sandra Collins (pseudonym) stated that she knew the couple who were at the epicentre of these horrible disturbances and said that it was making their life sheer hell. The elderly couple were Colin Lewis (pseudonym) who was in his mid-70's, and his wife Gail Lewis (pseudonym) who was in her late 60's.

They both lived alone in their Nottingham bungalow. Sandra knew that I was a paranormal researcher and asked for my immediate help. As I was 163 miles away in Hastings, East Sussex, I decided that I needed to act swiftly, and get someone on the ground who could attend the family home and find out what was going on. This is what I did. With this particular case, I feel it best to give you the reader the timeline of events.

It all begun on the 5th of August 2015, when I received the following e-mail from Sandra Collins, (pseudonym) who, I should point out, is a medium herself. She stated.

Hi Malcolm,

"Is it possible to speak to you privately please? I am working with a couple who have been, and still are experiencing what could be alien phenomena. The Spiritual side has been explored and dealt with, but this is something totally different".

Sincerely, Sandra Collins.

Needless to say, I e-mailed Sandra back, where she kindly gave me her phone number to call her direct which I did. That phone call, clearly showed to me, that this was indeed a major case and that I had to act quickly. I also found out that prior to Sandra contacting me, the Lewis couple had had a number of other 'so called' paranormal researchers who had visited their home and left it in a worse state than when they found it. Some even had the audacity to charge the couple money just for the privilege of their services! I informed her that as I was so far away, there were a team of researchers from the Nottingham area, who would be best served to get boots on the ground and see what they could do. What Sandra told me on the phone that day would have troubled anybody.

THE STRANGE EVENTS

Not only were there apparitions being spotted throughout the couple's bungalow in Nottingham, but there were also phantom voices, whispers, items being moved to different locations. Items going missing, only for them to turn up in completely different places. There were banging and thumping noises coming from the loft, there were intense cold spots at certain areas throughout the house (even in summer) There were UFO sightings in the sky around their property. It didn't stop there. There were also pieces of furniture moving around of their own accord. Probably the most worrying if not terrifying thing, was that both Gail and Colin were attacked in their bed by unseen hands! And as if that lot above is not enough, they had to deal with the ghosts of Roman soldiers walking down their hallway and also horses galloping through their house! Most surprisingly, was the observation of imps in the loft, and also a tall African looking gentleman who vanished in the back garden, but more amazingly, two researchers saw a small man turn into a frog, then disappear completely in front of their very eyes. I did say it was a bizarre case.

So, as the Lewis family wanted someone there immediately, and as I was too far away and also had work commitments, I called in the services of Sean Cadman and his wife Sarah from a group called, 'Past Hauntings' they were later joined by Vivien Powell, and Nery Kirby from a group called RAPS. More researchers would join the investigation later, and I will be discussing them in due course. Vivien and Nery would stay on this case for a full two and a half years. For the record, 'Past Hauntings' formed by Sean & Sarah (husband and wife) and long-time friend Simon in 1990, are a close-knit team, still with their founding members which now include their children who began investigating in their late teens. They have investigated numerous private cases over the years and were the first team to host team share events. They published an online paranormal magazine, hosted radio shows, teamed up with another team and organised two paranormal conventions. They also managed and organised paranormal events for the Codnor Castle Heritage Trust and have their own YouTube channel.

And so it was, that 'Past Hauntings' and 'Raps' took on this case, but due to work commitments with members of 'Past Hauntings', it wasn't until the following month, September 2015, that Sean Cadman and his team could attend. I had asked Sean to inform me of what his team found on their first visit, and he replied with.

Hi Malcolm,

"We had a very interesting night at the clients last night, they come across as very genuine people, sadly from what they have said, they have been ripped off by many people demanding money from them and not helping them. We have taken readings all over the house and got a few strange peaks. We also discovered that the house has an old mine shaft underneath, with a stream running through it, and is also on ley lines. The housing estate was built across the road on land that we believe was the site of an old abbey and churchyard. We are going back on Saturday to do a full overnight investigation and have told the couple that we will do everything we can, regardless of how long it takes, to get to the bottom of it. We will do everything to help them. It is looking like there are many layers of activity that we are going to have to peel back to get to the root cause".

I quickly replied to Sean stating,

"Hi Sean. Fantastic report on your visit. My heartfelt thanks to you and your team for helping this couple out. Really appreciate it my friend. Keep me informed with any more updates".

A week or so later I received another e-mail from Sean Cadman where he had this to say.

Hi Malcolm,

"Not sure if you have seen the footage, photos EVP's (Electronic Voice Phenomena) etc on our private investigation page? We went to see Colin and Gail on Saturday night with John Lee, a demonologist and we all felt a threatening unpleasant feeling in the properties back garden. John did his walk around and picked up on a very strong entity inside the house, it's not demonic or malevolent, but strong. He did his binding on it to hopefully calm things down until he can get back down in January to do a proper cleansing on the house. However, when we went into the rear garden, he became very nervous of whatever is there, he said it's definitely not spirit in any way shape or form, and he is sure that it's some form of alien presence of which he hasn't encountered or had to deal with before. He felt very threatened by whatever it is. He also picked up, like the rest of us, that the ground there is massively energised, and it feels like a beacon attracting everything and anything to it. After our investigation and chat with the couple, we concluded that there are definitely two separate, or linked happenings. Which are, the house haunting, and extra-terrestrial goings on! John said he will be in touch with you shortly so he can discuss it with you".

But Sean wasn't finished in a further e-mail he brought forward quite an astonishing revelation. Sean said that a close family friend of Gail and Colin had been coming round to their house for three years and it was Sean's belief that they were exacerbating the phenomena in the home. He stated.

"It's a fascinating case. I should have mentioned in my last e-mail that there is a third element too, a human one. A family friend and her husband initially went to the property to try and help, as the friend is a medium and they seem to have been going round to the Lewis's house for three years and have become 'close friends'.

215

We have been listening carefully to little things that have been said, and it seems that they are trying to keep Colin and Gail in a constant state of worry and fear. We spent a few weeks calming Gail down and explaining to her how to deal with it all until we can get a proper clearing done. It was working very well, Gail started to seem more settled and happier. Next thing the family friend announces that whatever is haunting them has followed her home which has sent Gail tumbling back down again. She now feels guilty that it's her fault. We are just guessing here but Colin and Gail are clearly not short of money and have no children, that part I will leave to your imagination! John after meeting them for the first time, and without me telling him about our opinions on them, told me what he thought of them, and it was exactly the same as us. We do feel that the hardest part of the whole case will actually be dealing with this family friend and her husband and getting them to stop dragging things up".

Sean went on to inform me about other aspects of his first visit to the Lewis household that he felt were important to highlight. He stated.

Dear Malcolm,

"On our first visit on 5th September 2015, we concentrated on taking some photographs and readings around the property and interviewing the owners. A couple of the photos did show some anomalies that we thought required further analysis and we did get some unexplained readings at various places around the garden and house. Colin and Gail come across as very genuine and trustworthy people and it is evident the toll the activity is having on them both. Whilst sitting talking with them, we heard what can only be described as 'footsteps' walking across the loft area. The loft is completely boarded on the floor, and accessible from a hatch in the utility room, nobody was up there at

the time. We were told that there is an old underground stream running underneath the property from old mines and also that ley lines cross underneath too. Across the road from the property is a new housing estate that was built around 4 years ago just before the activity started. It is believed that the site used to be a monastery and cemetery at one time. The couple were a major part of a local campaign to prevent the estate being built which they did win, but then it got overturned and the land built on. We had to consider that maybe the building work disturbed something from the past, but then that leaves the question that if it did, why has whatever's been disturbed, been attracted to their property"?

"We returned to the property again on another night in September with two mediums, Vivien Powell and Sandra Dunne and also more team members who supplied CCTV and extra equipment to do an overnight investigation. We arrived at 6:00pm, and before entering the property, we went for a walk around the new estate to get a feel for the area and see what our mediums could pick up. The mediums worked independently of each other, so we could compare notes and see if there were any matches. A couple of names came through that were matched, and also the sense of there being underground vaults/caves. Whilst walking, we also all had the very strong sense of being followed. Around 7:00pm, we began to set up the equipment around the property. We placed CCTV cameras at one at the end of the garden, one looking down the driveway, and one covering the front garden. There was also one in the client's bedroom, and one in the loft with the monitor set up in the kitchen. We also set up a camcorder in the hallway. We kept our cars off the property and parked on the street. Vivien had a good chat with Gail and found that she has a gift of mediumship which may have a bearing on some of the activity that is happening, she spent some time with her explaining about closing down, and *this will be an ongoing thing until Gail is comfortable with what she is able to do. All team members experienced something throughout the night from hearing things to being touched, we did voice recording sessions all around the house and gardens and did sessions with meters, one of which was very interesting. One of the main entities there, seems to be a man who uses a stick whilst walking, he seems to like to keep near to, but not close to, Gail. She calls him, 'the walking man'. During one session with a meter, it appeared we made contact with him through a question-and-answer session. It seems he is there to protect the couple from extra-terrestrials that are present at the property"?*

"Not long after this session, I had an experience that I can honestly say shook me up more than anything else has in 20 plus years. We were monitoring the CCTV and seeing what appeared to be something moving around in the greenhouse at the end of the garden, I decided to go and investigate. As I walked up the garden, I was using my torch on the ground so I could see the CCTV cable and not trip over it, as I was about to step over the cable, I lifted my torch. Now in the middle of the garden there is a pagoda type building with brick pillars, and I saw an arm come around the centre pillar followed by a head. The figure appeared to be around 4 feet tall and dark grey in colour, with very long fingers. I presume it saw me, as it ducked back behind the pillar. I was completely shocked. I've seen ghosts, but never anything like that. As I went back to the house in a bit of a panic, Luke, one of our team, came out. I explained what I had witnessed, and we then went all over the garden but couldn't find any trace or see anything, although we did hear some unexplained noises. Around 5:00am, a few of us were having a cigarette break and we noticed a bright light in the sky, we watched it for a while but couldn't see any other lights that would indicate it was a plane or helicopter.

What made it stranger, was that Vivien had on her person, an extremely bright cree torch, and each time she shined it towards the light it seemed to dim. When she turned the torch off, it would get bright again. There was no sound at all, it seemed quiet far away, but then looked like it kept getting closer then backing off again. We finished the investigation around 7:00am. I have lots of footage to now review and watch, so I will let you know as we come across anything".

Best Wishes Sean.

Sean Cadman mentioned in his report that he had invited a Demonologist along to help in this case, a chap by the name of John Lee (pseudonym) I kept in constant communication with John and asked him to give me a write up of what he encountered at the property. Before we read that write up. Here is some information about John which I found on his web site.

My name is John Lee I'm a practicing Demonologist and Occult investigator and reside in the City of Glasgow, Scotland. I was born in Southern Rhodesia (Zimbabwe) and moved to Scotland in 1977. Raised by my mother and Grandmother, both of whom were powerful Mediums and Sensitives, I developed mediumship skills at a young age. As the years progressed, my psychic attributes allowed me to specialize in Psychometry and Past Life Regression, along with tuning my third eye for Spirit recognition and detection. I began training in Demonology and Dark Arts at the age of 23, and by the turn of the millennium, I was actively conducting investigations into malevolent entities, negative forces poltergeist attacks and demonic possession. I regularly travel globally conducting investigations and offer professional lectures in Demonology. I am available to lead investigations, offer guidance on demonic cases and do guest speaker roles at conventions.

This is what John had to say about his first visit to the Lewis household.

Dear Malcolm,

"*Situated deep within Sherwood Forest, Nottingham, lies a small village of around a dozen cottages and self-built bungalows. Just off the main road, sits a row of six, small homes, mainly occupying elderly and retired couples. One of these homes is owned by a friendly, outgoing retired couple, by the name of Colin and Gail Lewis. Both former self employees, Colin and Gail bought the land over fifteen years ago and built their stunning little home from scratch. Around four years ago, (2011) building contractors moved into the small village and put out plans to redevelop the vacant grounds opposite the homes. The community rejected the proposals but were unsuccessful. The grasslands were part of the grounds of Newstead Abbey, the infamous Abbey used by Lord Byron and his secret coven of Satanic worshippers. In accordance with Colin and Gail's claims, within days of the building works commencing, supernatural occurrences began to occur within their home. Was this in conjunction with the uprooting of un-sacred grounds at the abbey? Did the contractors dig too deep and severe some kind of protection binding?*

The legend claims that Lord Byron had put a curse on the grounds of Newstead Abbey, stating that if any person were to build upon the land, an evil would spread across the fields and curse those who lived upon it. Myth, legend, a load of rubbish? Many locals believe it's total nonsense, but some do think it's a curse that's been unleashed as part of the building works. I was contacted by a good friend and owner of a paranormal research team called Past Hauntings. Sean Cadman telephoned me at home in Scotland to say that he received an urgent phone call from Colin and Gail.

They claimed they had been a subject of malevolent forces within their home. Dark figures, shadow people, extreme bangs and scratching, furniture moving on its own, and unseen hands attacking the couple in their bed at night. This had been going on for four years, ever since the disruption made by the contractors. Although only in the past few months, has the activities become very negative and malevolent. Prior to this, they had been experiencing a lot of residual hauntings, ie, Roman soldiers marching through their house, monks appearing in different rooms, and the sounds of horses galloping through their hallway. Colin and Gail stated they had got used to the residual happenings, although initially scared at first, the ghosts did not cause them any harm. This new activity was far worst, far more intelligent and with an intent of harming them".

"As one of only a few genuine professionals, and Scotland's only officially recognised Demonologist and expert in cases of violent house haunting, I was contacted to step in and investigate this case. I travelled down for my first interview in November 2015. I spent a considerable time interviewing Colin and Gail, taking detailed notes of everything they have experienced over the past four years, and more in particular, the events over the last few months. I did my initial walk round their home, and picked up on two very dark energies, one being situated in the couples' bedroom, and another in the hallway. I laid down a protection prayer in every room in the home and guided the couple to recite St Michaels prayer daily. I couldn't tell at this stage what kind of forces I was dealing with. They felt intelligent, and they did feel far more darker than the residual energy that flowed through the house. The home was a vortex of high-level energy. It sat directly upon a powerful ley line, and the ley line ran directly towards Newstead Abbey. In the back garden, there were copper pipes covering the entire garden, sitting only a few feet beneath the soil. (Water

irrigation and drainage) Copper, as we know, is a powerful conduit for energizing spirit. In conclusion, the home was a 'superhighway' for spiritual activity. Over the Christmas and New Year period, the elderly couple stated the darker forces were at play once again, but this time far more sinister and aggressive. Sean, from the Past Haunting team, phoned me again and gave me an update. I immediately telephoned the couple to offer them reassurance. I asked them to recite several prayers of protection around their home, and to place a small crucifix or religious icon in the hallway. I promised them I would be back down as soon as I could manage".

Clearly then, John had picked up on some quite disturbing energies and 'entities' at the property. On the 17th of November 2015, I received an e-mail from Vivian Powell, here is what she had to say to me.

Hi Malcolm,

"Can you let me know your thoughts on Alien hauntings? Can this happen? I think this is what the problem is at Gail and Colin's house. Everyone is shying away from this, but I firmly believe in this. As a medium, I am prepared to try communication with them to see how we can help. What are your thoughts on this and what kind of questions to ask other than the usual. I am not sure if it will work, but worth a try what do you think? Thanks for your help, Sean's friend and medium on the case".

Vivien Powell.

Like I say, this extraordinary case would seem to have lots of elements to it, from ghostly apparitions to UFOs. I think I have only ever dealt with one case similar to this one, where not only did the witnesses see ghosts in their home, but they too had UFO activity around their home as well. This included small grey 'beings' appearing in their bedroom at the same time as a ghost! I kid you not! I replied to Vivien with the following,

Hi Vivien,

"Many thanks for your e-mail. Yes, this would appear on the surface a very extraordinary case with some bizarre elements and a cross over between UFOs and spirits. It's rare, but it does happen from time to time, and we 'may' have that here. As for your help on the case, just be yourself, allow yourself to get into that zone so to speak and see what transpires. Don't forget, it may be a spirit pretending to come from outer space etc (but then again!) Have a go, see what happens and keep me informed. Good luck and happy hunting".

Malcolm Robinson.

Some may find my e-mail to Vivien off the wall, that I was asking her to consider that the spirits in the Lewis home were out to deceive and play games with the researchers. Those who are involved in psychic research, know all too well that it is a fact that some spirits will impart information which is blatantly false. They may try and convince you that you are speaking to your uncle Harry when all along they just want to play a game, get into your head. What is factual, and without a doubt, is that there were a number of UFO sightings around their property, verified by independent witnesses. It was only right that Vivien looked into the UFO aspect whether it had any bearing on the haunting at the family home or not.

In January 2016, John Lee the Demonologist paid another visit to the Lewis household and stated the following.

"Following a lecture, I had given in Derbyshire, I was driven to Nottingham by the Past Haunting team to meet up with Colin and Gail. This time I was prepared. I knew whatever was at play in this house was potentially evil in nature, maybe even demonic. This was my ball game! We arrived mid-afternoon, and from the first instance I stepped through the front door, I felt a heavy and oppressive atmosphere. Before getting a chance to sit down, I heard the voice of a disembodied spirit whisper in my right ear "Go home, not welcome". I took the warning on board but stood my stance. Sitting down for a coffee, and listening to the latest happenings from the couple, I looked around my surroundings, making eye contact with each of the team members. Sean and his wife were sitting opposite me, and our two spiritual medium friends sat in the other corner. I tried focusing on Colin's talking but kept being interrupted by this clear audible voice in my ear. This time it was being blunt. It said, "Get out!" I ignored it, but it kept talking.

I was surprised no one else could hear it. "Leave, or they will suffer" it stated clearly. Sean could see I was disturbed by something and gave me a nod. We stood up together and exited the sitting room, giving our apologies. In the hallway, I said to Sean what I had experienced. Sean looked a little apprehensive, but he stood firm and confident. "I'm going to carry out a minor rite of exorcism" I told Sean. I gave him a quick briefing of what the rite entailed and what I needed from him. I said to him, "You know this is not a real exorcism. I don't have the authority to perform one. Plus, I'm not clergy. However, I have been trained to carry out a minor rite. This is very similar to the real thing, and in most cases, is quite sufficient at banishing anything dark and malevolent. I'll talk through with you what you need to do for me. You OK with this?" Sean agreed.

We spent fifteen minutes going through the procedures of the task. Sean was to act as my assistant. He would give responses to prayers and film the event on camcorder evidence".

"I briefly re-entered the living room where Colin and Gail sat along with the three other ladies. I told them that I felt it necessary to carry out a minor exorcism on their property, as the intensity of the entities would require a more religious provocation approach. They all looked at me with eyes wide and jaws dropped. I explained the importance of staying together as a group and keeping totally silent, no matter what they hear or see. They agreed and huddled together. Sean and I collected the tools I required and entered the spare bedroom. I laid out my crucifixes, blessing each one and kissing Our Lord. I spread out my green stole that I used to keep my sacred books wrapped in. A bottle of blessed holy water, St Benedict medals and White Sage incense resin. I began reciting Our Lord's prayer followed by our Hail Mary. Burning the Sage, I began the ritual starting from the bedroom we were in. I cannot reveal exactly the procedure I use when carrying out this rite, but in general, what I do is enter each room, bless the burning sage as it fills the room with white smoke, begin reciting the first of three exorcism prayers, with Sean giving the responses, and ending with placing a blessed St Benedict medal at the doorway. This prevents evil forces from entering the room, and the sage and prayers banishes the entities. It's like an invisible protective field around each room. The whole exorcism ritual lasted just over two hours. At the end, Sean and I took a well-earned rest. After a quick break and a strong coffee, I asked Colin and Gail plus the whole team to take a walk around the house and tell me what they felt. The couple immediately felt an uplifting presence, a sensation of peace and tranquillity, something they have not felt for over four years. Even the team members claimed a sense of brighter, calming atmosphere.

This was a key sign to me, that the blessing may have worked, that whatever was inside the home had left. Only time will tell at this stage. However, the activities within the home were strong, and extremely negative. Hopefully they have been banished now, and the couple may have their home back again. There is also another flipside to this story. There have been unexplained phenomena occurring outside the confines of the house. Strange events which included hovering objects above their house, bright lights shining into their bedroom window, lighting up the room with an intensive white glow. There have been small grey skinned beings seen in their bedroom and back garden not only by the couple, but by several team members. A terrible sensation of impending doom and watching eyes every time you step foot in the back garden. Scurrying feet in the attic. Peering eyes through the kitchen window, and a host of other, unexplained incidences.

A lot of what's happening inside the house is of very malicious poltergeist type behaviour very heavy and oppressive. A hell of a lot of residual apparitions and intelligent entities. It's a vortex of high energy Hovering objects above their house. I felt extremely uneasy being out in the garden. Felt I was being watched. As a Demonologist, I tend to only stick to cases relating to spirit and demonic forces. Theses occurrences lean more towards alien phenomena. My thoughts on this have been validated by numerous others who also strongly agree to the synopsis of what is going on. Currently, this home is still under investigation, not for the darker forces at play, which I am confident have been resolved, but the alien activity which seems to be continuous and is now terrifying the elderly couple. I don't scare easily, but this house really makes my skin crawl".

Regards. John Lee.

In a further e-mail that I received from John on the 21st of January 2016. he reiterated some of his earlier points that he made in a previous e-mail. He stated.

Hi Malcolm.

"A lot of what's happening inside the house is of very malicious poltergeist type behaviour. Not saying it's demonic but very heavy and oppressive a hell of a lot of residual apparitions and intelligent entities. It's a vortex of high energy being directly above a powerful lay line and the house has underground connections to the ancient abbey across the road which I was told had satanic rituals and buried bodies carried out by monks. I can deal with the dark forces and malevolent entities, but the couple are also describing what I believe is alien/UFO phenomenon. Bright coloured lights shining in their bedroom, small grey skinned beings seen in their bedroom and back garden. Hovering objects above their house. I felt extremely uneasy being out in the garden. Felt I was being watched. I don't scare easily but this house really makes my skin crawl".

After John Lee's visit to the Lewis bungalow, I sent an e-mail to Gail. Prior to the e-mail, we had the odd telephone call where she kept me up to speed with what had been going on. Here is what I wrote to her on the 6th of February 2016.

Dear Gail,

"Thought I would drop you a letter explaining a few things. Firstly, I am in the fortunate position to put certain people your way, who, fingers crossed, may be able to help your situation. You've had Sean Cadman and John Lee pay you a visit to help the situation, and I believe John will be paying you a further visit in

due course. Now if things don't improve after their visits, I shall endeavour to find some other people who might be able to help. It seems that the vast majority of happenings are of the paranormal kind, and although you state that there have been UFO sightings above your property, I'm afraid that is an aspect, which sadly at this point in time, there is nothing anyone can do about. This is an aspect of your case which unless it has some spiritual aspects I couldn't help with. No one truly has the answer to explain the UFO enigma, what we do have are many speculations. There is not a magic wand to stop these worldwide UFO sightings, so unfortunately, I personally couldn't help with what's occurring near your property. As I say, it is with great hope and expectation that John Lee has worked his magic with the paranormal side of things, which we hope will once more bring peace to your house. I believe he will be back with you soon again. let me know how it goes".

"Wishing you and your husband good luck with Jason's process and I really and truly hope that things sort themselves out for you both".

Sincerely, Malcolm Robinson.

SO MANY RESEARCHERS!

During the course of Sean and his team, and Vivien and her team visiting the property, both Gail and Colin had been having visits from other paranormal researchers as well, but after the completion of their work, things were just as bad. One such psychic medium to attend the family home, who was not welcomed back, was Jim Bell, (pseudonym) Gail and Colin were none too pleased with this chap. They stated that they paid his travel and hotel.

However, it wasn't until they took Jim out for a meal which they paid for, that Jim turned around and dropped his 'bombshell', he stated,

"My spirit guide is telling me that it would be bad for me to visit your home so I'd best not to".

And with that he walked off into the sunset never to be seen again. It must have been heart breaking for both Gail and Colin. Here was someone who they hoped would cure their problem only for the rug to be pulled from under them in the cruellest of circumstances. So, back to square one, where both Gail and Colin still had to endure, hours of relentless banging's and rapping's and strange lights coming through the bedroom curtains into their home.

Needless to say, I just had to give this chap a phone call. Over the phone he sounded very efficient and knowledgeable about Spiritualism and the paranormal. He was the author of several books, and I found out that he does church services where he provides clairvoyance and the philosophy of Spiritualism. He readily confirmed that, yes, he had been invited to attend the family home to do a clearing back in February 2014, and that yes, he did get paid his travel and hotel (which is fine by me) but denied ever asking Gail and Colin for money. He also confirmed that they did take him out for a meal (paid by Gail and Colin) and he also stated that his spirit guides had advised him not to go to the family home, that there was something Demonic there with bad vibrations. This he said, was not strictly his line of work, and he was quite happy to leave it to others. Now dear reader, because we have one bad egg, does not mean to say that all eggs are bad, in other words, some mediums are more proficient than others. Some mediums charge for their services, and some don't. My society, Strange Phenomena Investigations (SPI) have 'never' charged for our services.

Of course, a debate like this, 'should you take money for your services or not', is always a big one. I accept that if one is travelling far, then they may have to stay the night, which of course would require a hotel or a bed and breakfast. Why did he not just say over the phone to Gail and Colin, that he couldn't do this, that this case was bigger than him, that they should get someone else on it? But he didn't, he took travel expenses, hotel accommodation, slap up meal and was out the door quicker than you can say 'Goodnight Vienna'. But wait, there's more to this story. I also learned in an e-mail that I received from Sandra where she confirmed that Jim Bell had attended the house and what happened when he did so. She stated.

Hi Malcolm,

"I think there's one more thing you can confront him with if you manage to contact him. He asked for travel expenses before he could visit them, and told them he would be travelling from Wales, so they sent him money before he came. Unfortunately for him, he had posted where he was that day on Facebook and he actually came down from Bradford or Leeds, can't quite remember which now, but certainly not Wales. He also rang them from Ireland and said he had crashed his car, and it was because of what was happening at their home! Unbelievable! It did upset Gail and Colin at the time and worried them even more".

So, Jim Bell and others had attended the Lewis family home to try and rid the property of its evil influences, all to no avail. On the 14th of February 2016, I received an e-mail from Sandra Collins who had initially asked me to go along and investigate this house. she stated.

Hello Malcolm,

"I'm so pleased that we have now found people who can help in some way, although there is still a long way to go. The person who you are referring to is Jim Bell he well and truly did everything that you 'wouldn't' expect a Spiritual person to do. That experience, along with several other people who let them down, really devastated them. Thank you for your post, and for your interest and guidance in this case".

Kind regards. Sandra.

Knowing that this was a big case, I knew that witness testimony and a few photographs might not convince certain members of the public. What we needed to do, was to get a professional cameraman in to film the testimony of Gail and Colin. I had someone in mind and duly told him next to nothing on the case, other than strange events had been occurring in this family home. On the 16th of February 2016, I sent off an e-mail to Sean Cadman informing him that I would like a cameraman to record a 30-minute interview with both Gail and Colin. I was therefore quite surprised to hear a week or so later, that this would not now go ahead. In my e-mail to both Sean and John Lee I said.

Hi Sean and John,

"I'm a bit disappointed to hear that I have been stopped from bringing in a chap to film the testimony of Colin and Gail for historic posterity. I explained to Colin and Gail that this footage was for SPI purposes only, and would not be broadcast anywhere, which is standard procedure for our society. I now have to go back to the chap and tell him that his visit to the couple has to be cancelled and he took a shift off work to go there as well. I fully respect the fact that you want to leave things the way they are in order to see if the house will remain quiet, but like I say, this chap was not there to chase ghosts, he was only there

to film testimony. I was asked to go on this case to help, to get people involved and to hopefully resolve the case but will accept the wishes of you both".

Sincerely Malcolm Robinson.

Almost immediately I received an e-mail from Sean which read.

Hi Malcolm,

"We didn't mean to annoy you, Gail had asked me what I thought about someone doing some remote work, a couple of mediums being involved and someone going to film them, my advice was to wait until after next week because Steve Mera is coming with us next Wednesday for an overnight investigation to get his take on the phenomena. The other reason is when John Lee did the house cleansing, Vivien spent time with Colin and Gail teaching them how to close down, and we advised them not to have anyone in the house until we are sure that the cleansing has fully worked. I'm sure you appreciate that they have some trust issues with new people coming in, and that's why we will be there with Steve".

This all made sense, and I could fully understand the need to see if, after the cleansing, the house remained quiet. I e-mailed Sean back saying that he and Vivien were doing a great job and that I would look forward to hearing if the 'cleansing' was a success. Sean again replied.

Hi Malcolm,

"I appreciate you asking us to be involved mate, hopefully find out answers to whatever it is lurking in the garden. Almost every one of the team doesn't like it out there, there is a constant feeling of being watched/stalked. At first, we thought that it might be down to some underground cabling causing a high EMF field, but after many sweeps of the garden there was nothing showing

above 0.2 so that's been ruled out. The lights we saw, and the humanoid figure just blew us away".

Regards. Sean Cadman.

In late February 2016, fellow researcher and author Steve Mera and Don Philips became involved, more on this shortly. On the 29th of February 2016, I received a further e-mail from Sean Cadman where he said.

Hi Malcolm.

"Just to let you know we are hoping that we have finally cleared Colin and Gail's house. After everything, it looks like it was all caused by old school black magic. There was a well on the property that was filled in, and these entities (Demons) call them what you will, were using it as a portal. The UFO phenomenon we now believe, was being caused by these entities to try and confuse the situation. On Friday night we went through some pretty extreme clearance steps that seemed to have been successful".

Regards. Sean Cadman.

Well, sadly those steps were not successful. Sean sent another e-mail which said.

Hi Malcolm,

"Just another update on the Nottingham case. After things quietening down, its 'back again'. We are now taking it to another level, as whatever it is, seems to hide whenever we go there, so we are now planning to attempt to draw it out. I believe a family friend has been speaking with you about the case. Please be wary of her, as we are very suspicious that she has something to do with what is happening there. We will have to have a phone conversation so I can give you more details very soon".

Cheers Sean.

Again, in late February 2016, I received an e-mail from Steve Mera which said.

Hi Malcolm,

"Quick update about Nottingham. We could not find any evidence in support of UFO phenomena; however, it would seem that they do have a paranormal footprint, low severity and frequency. Lovely folk, they have been confused by the many varied people visiting and giving their theories. All visuals on this case, lie with Phenomena Project and not me. I have also informed Anthony Beckett today that such information will be passed over to him and yourself. Was pleased to assist them, and they have our contact info via Sean. Any specifics required, let me know".

Sincerely. Stephen Mera.

NO MORE INVESTIGATORS PLEASE!

So, the years rolled by investigators came and went, and still the bizarre frightening events transpired at the Lewis household. It would seem that whatever was there at that house, had firmly cemented itself, onto Gail more than the house itself. For the moment, I was just happy to stay in touch with Sean and Vivien who were still there at the house trying all sorts to entice whatever was there, to go. On the 9th of June 2018 I sent a further e-mail to Vivien Powell asking her how things were at the house. She stated that they were continually peeling back layers and that there was clearly a 'residual' side to these strange events which sadly they could do nothing about. Moreover, the activity she said had increased over the past few weeks and had become a bit more violent. Both Colin and Gail had reached the stage where they did not want any more investigators coming to the house other than Sean, Vivien, and their team. Vivien went on to say that they were doing everything that they possibly could to help, but it was a slow process. In a further e-mail she stated.

Hi Malcolm,

"Andy and Nery are working on the case very hard as well. We have managed to remove a number of things, and that larger entity. But OMG Malc! The Negro man who we saw, was an absolute shocker, but he wasn't an issue. The UFO side seems to have calmed down and we have seen some really strange 'beings' that have kept their distance as if they are watching us. I have brought two things home with me. It's been with me for months, but it's now gone. It's taken its toll on me but I'm getting better with each day. So, I go back in a couple of weeks and start the process again, sleeping with lights on while I am there".

On the 10th of June 2018 I received another e-mail from Sandra Collins in which she confirmed that both Colin and Gail did not want anymore investigators going to their house. Here is what Sandra said.

Hi Malcolm,

"Mr and Mrs Lewis have still got the same problem! I saw them today and told them that you have been in touch and what you said in your message. They have had so many different people around there in the past four years, all claiming to be able to help them and get rid of the problems, but no one has been able to do so! They are now feeling, and quite understandably so, that they don't want anyone else there unless they can remove the problem fully, or at least give some solid help! I have only dealt with Spirit rescue and have never experienced anything like I've seen and heard there! They have been let down by so many people over the last four years, and don't want to put themselves in that position again, which I'm sure you understand".

Best regards. Sheila.

What did come as a surprise to me, was when Colin and Gail decided that they only wanted Vivien and Andy to stay on the case and told Sean Cadman and his team to step down. This was a great shame as Sean had been a big part of this investigation since its inception. He had taken time off work and was there when the Lewis's needed him. But at the end of the day, one has to accept the Lewis family's wishes. They wanted no more than three investigators in the house from now on. They saw it as there were far too many people traipsing through their house, which, even though those other people were there to help, they just wanted to cut the numbers down. Sean surprisingly took this well, I would have been miffed if it had had been me, but it's not about us, it's about the troubled family and their wishes, of which again we have to respect. That then left Vivien, Nery, and Andy on the case.

I knew that I just had to get this incredible case out there. I knew that it would feature in this book, so in that regard I went back to some of the players who were involved in the case and asked their opinions. So, in January 2023, I interviewed Vivien Powell for her thoughts on the case.

INTERVIEW WITH VIVIEN POWELL

Abbreviations. (MR) Malcolm Robinson. **(VP)** Vivian Powell

(MR) "How did you first become aware of the case in Nottingham, who drew your attention to it"?

(VP) "I was asked by Sean's team (Sean Cadman at 'Past Hauntings') That there was a case which was quite serious, and he said, as I am a medium, will I come in with his team. He said, I don't want you to do anything, just sit, listen, and observe, which I did. I had heard all the stories.

Gail and Colin and told me everything, and I said to Colin, can we have a walk around and you can show me the places where things have been happening. So, he said yes, and we had a walk around and I felt absolutely 'nothing'! I did the medium thing, I opened up quietly, I didn't tell anyone, but I felt nothing. He even took me up to the loft space, it felt different up there but not uncomfortable. I say I felt nothing, but I felt 'something', but it was nothing to worry about. Then he took me into the garden, it was night-time, it was pitch black, so I couldn't really see the garden. We walked up to the front garden and along the driveway, 'nothing'. We then went to the back garden and around to the garage. I did get a funny feeling around the garage, but I couldn't attribute it to anything. And then when we walked to the bottom of the garden and I stood on this particular spot, and I was jumping up and down on the grass and I said to Colin, *"Oh, it's really spongy here"*. And he said, *"I beg your pardon"*. I said, *"It's very spongy, was there a well over here"?* and he replied, *"Yes"*. And I said, *"Oh was it a deep well, or did you have a pond here"?* and he replied that it was a proper well. And he informed me that it was one of the six wells on the pilgrimage to Newstead Abbey. I said that this was interesting, and where I was standing felt really weird.

He asked if I was picking up on anything, and I just said no, it felt a bit spongy, a bit weird. I felt uneasy about that place, more so the actual grass bit where he had this well. I walked right to the back edge of the property and felt nothing. So, I came back into the house. Then I got called back to the property the following month by Sean who told me that they had a lot of activity. I asked them to show me what they had caught, and it was absolutely nothing. They said that there was a strange mist next to the house, and I said that I could explain that, that it was an air duct from the central heating, and that's causing the mist. Gail explained to me that she could hear things, she called 'him' the 'creature'. She described it like, a 'step and a thump', a 'step and a thump'. Anyway, I went outside, and I heard a 'step and a thump' a 'step and a thump'. And I said to myself, *"Oh, I can hear what she is hearing"*. So, I tried to debunk it straight away. I went into mediumship mode. I ran down the street to see if there was somebody coming along with a walking stick, there was nobody. So, I went back inside, and I stayed very late, until around 2 or 3 0 clock in the morning, just so I could debunk what she is hearing. And then she said that she saw an orange glow. So, I looked out the windows, but I couldn't find anything. I couldn't see anything, but I did hear this 'step and a thump.'

"Anyway, it ended up with just me and my fellow investigator Nery, and Andy who was into the darker stuff. We stayed over about 3 or 4 nights, and while we were there, we managed to get a photograph. What we ascertained, was that these balls of orange lights and this 'step and a thump' that she had seen and heard, were coming from the back garden at the very far end and then coming down by the side of the house. We photographed, a handful of figures appearing at the far end of the garden.

And in the next picture, tons of them. What we believe it was, was a reply of a procession of people coming through the garden property and walking to the old Abbey that was across the road which was knocked down. We've actually got a photograph of it, it is really weird. I said to Nery, *"Take pictures now, take pictures now"*, but she had put the flash on the infra-red camera, so you have got the flash from the bush, we know what that is, because the light from the flash is hitting it, but then you have all these 'people'. I don't know how many Investigators have ever photographed what I call a residual haunting where they are just passing through like that. We never ever showed that picture to Gail because we knew that it would frighten her, we actually told her that we didn't get anything. We had to lie.

At one point, Gail rang me up at midnight in tears telling me that it had all been kicking off in her house. She had noises which were running up and down on the ceiling, she had strange voices whispering, she heard banging and the thumping and the walking, and she was in a right state. I said that I would take time off from work and come down to see her. I said what do you want to do? I'm not going anywhere, I will be with you right till the end, what do you want to do. She said, *"I want an exorcist here"*. It got to the point where she wanted an exorcist. I said, *"OK, leave it with me"*, and then she further stated that she wanted a Catholic exorcist, priest. She said that she wasn't a Catholic, but she wanted a proper Catholic exorcist priest. She also said that she was fed up with all the charlatans that had come to her house. So, we found one, his name was Father Eastwood, he was based in Leicester.

There are only two registered priests that can conduct an exorcism in Great Britain, him, and one other. And the first thing he said to us was, that whatever he did, had to be sanctioned by the Vatican. So, it had to go through his diocese to the bishop, then it goes down the chain. He said that it won't happen overnight and that he needed me to collate evidence. He said, give it a couple of months, collate this evidence, bring it to me, and I'll give it to my Bishop, and we'll start the ball rolling, which we did. I think it took about seven or eight months. So, he rang me, and he said that he had been granted permission, and he asked me how he should approach it.

So, I gave him the number of Gail. I asked him to ring her directly, that he had to speak to both Gail and Colin in person. So, he made an appointment and visited them. I learned that he had walked around the house, and whilst he was sitting in a chair drinking tea in their living room, he heard the footsteps running up and down the ceiling, and at that point he said that he would agree to do a house blessing exorcism.

At this point Gail got her diary out and said when do you want to do this Father, and he said, *"We'll do it now"!* and with that, he went and got his case. It went very quiet when he did it. He did warn her, that when he left it would go one or two ways, it would either clear it, or it would make it worse. He said that this would not be a one-off job and that's it, that he would need to keep coming back. Apparently, it kicked off to the point where she couldn't handle it, and Gail said that she didn't want him back. She said that she wanted all this to calm down and that she didn't want to anger 'it'. So, I said 'OK, we won't have him back'. At that point, she refused to have him back, or anybody else".

(MR) "So was he definitely a Catholic Priest"?

(VP) "Yes, he was a Catholic Priest. This went right up to Rome. He said it went to the Pope's office and they had to give permission. And they granted permission to do it. On another occasion, I went up to see Gail and Colin with my husband to try and calm her down, and I asked her if I could bring one of my friends with me because I can't always bring my husband".

(MR) "How many miles was it for you to travel up to Gail and Colin"?

(VP) "For me, door to door, it would be an hour and a half. I said to my colleague Nery, who is part of my paranormal team, that I didn't expect her to do anything. I didn't expect her to get involved, I just need somebody there with me to back me up. But you know what? She fell in love with both of them as they did her, and she got involved in the case, more than I think she bargained for. It then got to the point where Gail wanted this thing gone so badly. I did research, and I found out that the Hell Fire club are involved in this".

Author's Comment. The Hellfire Club was founded in Britain and in Ireland in the 18th century and was partly set up for people who wished to take part in what could be termed, 'immoral acts.

A lot of high standing academic people were alleged to have joined this club, who tried to keep their presence secret from other members of society.

(VP) "There was a very old and ancient Abbey across the road that got levelled to build houses. That was connected to Newstead Abbey where the Hellfire club used to do their thing. Something was done there. I can only surmise what Lord Byron and that lot were doing. Anyway, long story short, Gail and Colin were saying that they saw what they described as imps. Colin had seen one. And I thought they must be off their head, that was until 'I' saw one! Colin described what he saw as scaly. I didn't see scales. They looked like loveable things, very cute".

(MR) "How tall were they"?

(VP) "I'd say that this thing was no higher than my knee. A bit gargoyle looking".

(MR) "Were they wearing any clothes"?

(VP) "No. It seemed to have grey skin, very dark nails. Beautiful eyes and a most beautiful smile, quite humanoid looking in the face. So, I saw one, and I couldn't believe what I saw. I told Colin, but I didn't tell Gail, I kept that away from her because she was so nervous as it was. At that point I said to Colin, *"Look, that is not good, we have an option here. I know someone who deals in some really dark stuff"*. My belief is you really need to know about the dark stuff to get rid of the dark stuff. So, I said to Colin that I could get this chap on the phone, see what you think, and if he was happy, then I would bring him with me to meet him, and we could use this to see what we could do. I didn't tell this other chap what I saw, I didn't tell him anything. All I told him was that there is a really bad case, and that he really needed to come".

(MR) "Was it John Lee (P)

Author's Comment. *I was referring to another Demonologist that also came to the house.*

(VP) "Oh, the John Lee thing. I went absolutely ballistic. I was made to sit in the front room, Sean Cadman took him around the house, he anointed the doors and placed medallions around the house. I didn't think anything of it, nothing happened, it was a load of rubbish. Months later, I went back to the house with Nery, as Colin had said that there were more noises coming from the loft which woke him up, and I said, *"Right, I'm going up there"*. I opened the trap door of the loft. And as I pulled it down, where it had been dusty, stuck to the inside of the loft door, was an upside-down cross staring at me. Nery was with me as I opened the trap door, and as soon as I saw that, I just burst into tears. That Demonologist, the other one, not Andy, wasn't what he said he was, and made it ten times worse.

It's one thing putting a cross on the door, but when you are putting it upside down, that's just not on. Nery said, *"That's it"* and went into the kitchen and got a bowl with soapy water and a dry cloth and we washed every single door in that house, front and back, just in case his anointment oil was still on there. I said to Gail, where are all these medallions that John had placed, she told me, so we collected them all and I said to Gail, *"When is your bin man coming, we are going to put all these medallions in the bin, get rid of them. what that man has done, is not right"*. I'm not kidding you Malcolm, we saw blood appear on the walls, well I say blood, it was like an orangey sticky substance. I'm describing it as blood. We even touched it, we felt it. It wasn't in just one room; it was in all four rooms".

(MR) "Was it wallpapered walls or painted walls"?

(VP) "Both. And we took photographs, we touched it we smelt it. Nery was even brave enough to taste it, she licked it, and she said that it didn't actually taste of anything. Afterwards we went out into the garden for a cigarette, and we were sitting down with Gail who had made us a cup of tea. We had been away from the house for a couple of hours, and when we came back into those rooms where this had been on the walls, and it was all gone, not a trace of it".

(MR) "Did that only happen just the one time"?

(VP) "Just the one time".

(MR) "How big was this? How long was it, an inch or longer? Was it a trickle?

(VP) "It wasn't just a trickle it was a splodge. There were loads of it. Some of it was long, some of it was just like a splodge on the wall. But it was just weird how it appeared then suddenly disappeared. It never ever came back. And this was at the time when we were staying there. All three of us witnessed that. I got pulled out of bed by my elbow by unseen hands".

(MR) "Wow".

(VP) "Yes, it was scary".

(MR) "This was at their house I take it"?

(VP) "Yes, at their house. We stayed over, and I would always stay in the end bedroom. But on this particular night, I slept in the bedroom closest to Gail. And I like the curtains to be closed and the room to be really dark so I can sleep. I got into bed, turned everything off. I was just dropping off when I heard footsteps. I thought that I was imaging that. By now I am lying wide awake, just listening. The next thing was that I felt a 'presence'. It's hard to describe it. You know when there is somebody next to you, but you can't see them. It was like that.

243

This 'presence' then leaned over the bed, my arm was above the covers, holding the covers, and I felt a hand and the fingers go right up to my elbow and pull me out of the bed. It pulled me out of the bed seriously. I jumped out of bed and turned all the lights on starting with the bedside light then the main light. Then I opened the door and went into the hallway just to make sure that there was no one messing around. I knocked on Andy and Nery's doors. I woke them up, and they said, *"What's going on"*, I asked them if they had been sleeping and they said 'yeah', and I told them that I had just been pulled out of bed. They went, *"No Way"*. I wouldn't go back to sleep that night. Another thing that happened, and this was in broad daylight. I was with Colin in the garden, we were talking about plants and gardening, and we got to the very far end of the garden where the greenhouse was. Colin looked at the fence, and he said, *"Look at that, they are there just trying to get on my nerves"*. There were three cats sitting on the end of the fence in a row, looking at us. And I said to Colin, *"Ah, it looks like you have got some friends"*, and he said, *"They better not come in my garden"*. Then, all of a sudden out of nowhere, and I can't believe I am telling you this, all three cats started 'barking' like dogs".

(MR) "Could it not have been dogs in an adjacent garden making barking sounds"?

(VP) "No. All three cats were barking like dogs. So, I looked at Colin, and I said, *"Are you hearing and seeing what I'm hearing and seeing"?* and he said, *"Yes, they are barking like dogs"*. You could see their mouth going as well. I even tried to research it, can normal household cats bark like dogs, or make sounds like a bark, they can't".

(MR) "That's crazy, absolutely crazy".

244

(VP) "It sounded like a small dog, like a chihuahua or a terrier or something like that, that type of bark. Colin looked at me and said, *'If you hadn't been standing right next to me to witness that and I had told people that I had seen something like this, they would think that I'm off my rocker".* I said, *"You're not, I'm witnessing this with you".* So, he ran towards them and chased them off. At that point I said to myself, this is more than your average day haunting".

"Right, the things in the sky. When the hauntings had been at their highest there have been strange lights hovering over the house in the sky. At one point, I was outside having a cigarette and there was a strange light in the sky. I have one of those telescopic torches, it's a really powerful one. I put it on the beam, and I shone it to a 'thing' that was shining in the sky. When I did that, it sort of retracted and went away. I turned the torch off, and it came back. So, I shone the torch at it again, and it went away. I did that a few times. Sean Cadman witnessed one incident when I did that. And I don't know anything that could do that in the night sky. I don't know what it is. It couldn't be a star; it couldn't be a helicopter as you would hear it".

(MR) "Did it appear far away this light"?

(VP) "No, I think that it was quite close to the house to be honest. And I thought that this was very, very, strange. And I have noticed this quite a lot through the years that I have been investigating there".

(MR) "So there have been quite a lot going on there"?

(VP) "Well I wasn't the only one to have been dragged out of bed. I called Luke who lived in Mansfield and asked him to come to Gail and Colin's house to help. We stayed the night, and Luke got dragged out of the 'very same bed' that I had been dragged out of. However, Luke got dragged out by his foot. It scared him so much, that he wouldn't go back".

(MR) "When you got grabbed on part of your arm by this invisible 'thing'. How would you define the touch? Was it a coldness, a clamminess touch?"

(VP) "It happened very quickly. I felt the hand, I wasn't aware of anything else. But the next thing that I was aware of, was that I was on the floor. And at that point on the floor, I felt cold. I felt that whatever it was that was there, was quite big. There was a photograph that was taken in the loft of a picture showing a knight on his horse. Superimposed in front of that, is a man with his head tilted and is wearing a long tweed coat. I believe that it was the man in the tweed coat that pulled me out of bed. Luke, who also got pulled out of bed, said that he was aware of a man standing in the room with glasses and a tweed coat, and he didn't know anything about that picture in the loft. So, the horse and the knight thing. There was another night we were there, we were upstairs in the loft, and me being me, said, *"Who's farted, that's disgusting, it smells like manure"?* Nery was taking pictures and said I didn't fart it must have been you, and she took a picture of the horse and the knight".

Author's Comment. *It was at this point that the significance of this knight that was in the picture in the loft came to prominence. At this point in my conversation with Vivien, she stated that a Shaman became involved in the case. Things got a big ugly in the back garden as we shall see.*

Vivien Continues.

(VP) "There was a friend there that day, he was a Shaman, and he was doing his thing. Anyway, long story short. The Shaman got it. We believe that this knight that was in the picture, jumped into Andy, and for a good two and a half hours the Shaman was being thrown around the garden while this, 'whatever it was', was in Andy. It was so frightening. 'It' just threw the Shaman four feet across the garden like he was a rag doll.

And Andy turned round to me and said, *"Is he dead"?* and I said *"No".* And he threw him again, and he asked me again, *"Is he dead"?* And I said "No".

(MR) "The person that was saying 'Is he dead'? Is that coming through Andy"?

(VP) "Yes. We got as much information as we could out of it because what this Shaman was trying to do, because there was a presence there. He wanted 'it' to jump into me. I didn't know anything about this".

Author's Comment. We will learn more about the astonishing events of that day later on in this chapter, where you will read from what Andy himself said to the author, on what transpired that afternoon.

(VP) "Later on, Andy called me and said that I needed to take a break, go out to the garden with Nery, have a cigarette, have a drink, chillax. So, me and Nery were in the garden, and the garden is quite long, we were sitting in a Pagoda when Nery said that she was just going to go out and take pictures of the garden. And Nery is tough, there is not a lot that bothers her. Well, she came running back to me, and threw herself over this little garden wall, saying, *"Oh my God, oh my God, footsteps, footsteps".* I said to her, *"What are you talking about"?* So, she said that she went up to the back part of the garden and she heard, 'thud, thud, thud,' on the mud, it was like somebody was running after her. So, she ran and jumped over the wall back to me. But she said that as she jumped over the wall, 'they' ran past me towards the house. The patio doors were open. This 'thing' had run, straight down the garden, through the patio doors, and straight into Andy. The next thing that we heard, was that I was being called to come down. I'm not kidding you; one side of Andy's face had dropped, and I thought that he had had a stroke, and he had a cut that was from his nose right across his eye, it was like a big slit and all that side of his face was covered in blood".

(MR) "Wow".

(VP) "And he said *"Viv, I can't see, I can't see"*. And I looked at him thinking, 'what do I say'. So, I said to him, *"Andy, are you OK"*, and he said *"I can't see, I can't see. Take my glasses, take my camera. Look after these"*, and then he just dropped to the floor. I managed to stand him up and I said *"Come on Andy, walk with me, keep talking to me. And he looked at me, and it wasn't Andy staring back at me"*.

(MR) "Wow".

(VP) "It wasn't Andy staring at me. He kept calling me the Devil. There was a lot of conversation, this went on for around two and a half hours, basically, he wanted to kill all of us. Long story short. I believe he was the knight with the horse that we saw on that painting in the attic, and he was trying to find his way back to the Abbey but couldn't. He was seeing 'us' as the Devil because we were wearing different clothes from a different era. He did tell us his name, he told us where he was from. When he was talking, it sounded like French, but it wasn't French. And I said to him that he needed to talk in a language that I could understand, and could he talk to me as I was speaking to him, but he kept jumping back into what I can only describe, as being 'old French".

(MR) "Right. Okay".

(VP) "So Andy had been throwing this 74-year-old Shaman around the garden like a rag doll. Just before the Shaman left to go home, we checked to see if he was alright".

(MR) "Oh yes, you would need to"!

(VP) "Colin was about to call for an ambulance, but we stopped him. Nery was threatening to call the police *(laughs)* It all came to a head, it all calmed down. As I said, we checked on the Shaman guy, and he was OK and Andy got into the car, and they were talking for a bit before he left. And I said to Andy, *"What did he say"?* And the Shaman said that the next time that anyone needs any assistance at this house, please don't call me. And Gail told us a couple of weeks later that the Shaman had admitted to her, that when he got out of the car and he got to his front doorstep and put his key into the door, he soiled himself, as Gail's house had bothered him that much".

(MR) "That's incredible".

(VP) "You know, that's nothing. I've sat in that house having a cup of tea in the afternoon with Gail and I've heard the house crack. It sounds like the house is splitting in two. Then something fell from the ceiling to the kitchen floor and then I heard it scurry away. Gail said to me, *"Did you hear that"?* I said *"Yes, it's just the house cracking".* I thought to myself, that I can't tell Gail what I've just heard, this thing scurrying away, as it would send her into a frenzy. I also heard a woman and a man talking, but you can't quite hear what they are saying. She heard that all the time, I used to hear this all the time when I was there. I heard a woman singing. Gail would play the organ; she'd play hymns and things like that, and I could hear a woman singing along with her and it wasn't Gail singing. There was nobody else in the house. I believe that Ley Lines played a big part in this, and I believe that a Ley Line was created, and it was cracked when they demolished the Abbey. So, whatever was there, in that Abbey, looked for somewhere to run to. I asked Gail's neighbours if they had had any hauntings or problems in their house and the neighbours said, *"Oh no, don't be silly".* That was both sides of Gail's house. Now, about six or eight months before Gail got really ill, the neighbours admitted that they do have problems. So, it wasn't just Gail's, it was happening at both sides of Gail's house as well".

(MR) "It would be strange if the neighbours didn't have strange things happening in their property with what was going on at Gail and Colin's".

(VP) "I have to tell you. I was in the car when this happened. We were all going to go out for lunch. I got in the car in the garage, normally Colin doesn't allow you to, he pulls the car out first. But I jumped in the car, and as he was driving the car out of the garage, it sounded like a plastic pipe was being thrashed onto the car roof, 'bang, bang, bang, bang'. I'm sitting there thinking *"Oh God, what has he reversed into"*. So, he took it out of the garage, we jumped out of the car and looked at the roof, not a scratch, nothing. Got back in the car again, then once more, 'bang, bang, bang'. And it wasn't the car that was faulty, there was something on the roof hitting the top of the car. Anyway, Gail gets in the car, and once more, 'bang, bang, bang'. I said to Colin, *"Oh come on, let's get out of here, let's go"*. When we got down the bottom of the drive. The noise had stopped, it had gone. Colin told me that this has happened before when they were going out to do shopping. And while he was in the supermarket car park it happened again".

(MR) "Wow. But was it really loud, or was it just little taps"?

(VP) "No. It was like it was being hammered *(laughs)*. It was really hammering it down. One time they went to the supermarket, and Gail wasn't feeling very well so she stayed in the car and Colin did the shopping, and when he came back to the car, Gail was outside of the car shaking and there were people around her. It had happened again, but this time it had happened 'inside of the car' trying to get at Gail. They go on holiday, and this 'thing' follows them.

250

They moved out for three months and this 'thing' followed them. So, they just couldn't get away from it".

Author's Comment. *At this point I broached the subject of Gail's passing which I had just learned.*

(MR) "Do you know how Gail died, was it an illness?"

(VP) "You know she had Parkinson's"?

(MR) "Yes".

(VP) "Well, she had been given this wonder drug and she was doing fantastically, she was running around like a young woman. The hospital decided that they were going to change her drug to a cheaper one. Gail and Colin fought and fought and fought, to keep the same drug as it was working for her. But the hospital said 'no' and that they had to put her on this cheaper drug. The minute they did that, the Parkinson's became a lot worse, more aggressive to the point where she became hospitalised. She stopped eating, she was like a walking skeleton. Colin had had enough of the way that they were treating her, and Gail had said to Colin that she didn't want to die in hospital and to take her home. The hospital were refusing to discharge her, so Colin just scooped her up in her nightie and said that he was taking her home. He said that as he picked her up, she didn't weigh anything. Colin said that the activity was still going on when they were home. Not as much around the house, it was more in the bedroom and around Gail. There were knocks on the window and lights flashing inside the room and outside. He said that she passed away at home and that she knew that she was going. There were Valentines cards and Christmas cards and presents all ready for him".

(MR) "That's really sad".

(VP) "She did get attacked in bed. Well, I say she, they actually attacked Colin. There were scratches all up his legs. He said to me that he was sleeping next to his wife, and yes she could have done it, her toenails finger nails whatever. He is quite a tall man. And these cuts on him were quite deep and they drew a lot of blood. He said that he had to change the sheets as there were blood all over the place. I kept my mouth shut at this point".

(MR) "Did that happen when she came back from hospital, or was that before"?

(VP) "That was before. He said that he did feel something in the bed with them".

(MR) "When did she die"?

(VP) "She would be dead three years ago next month (February 2023), so 2020".

(MR) "Now Colin is still living there just now. To your knowledge have things quieted down now"?

(VP) "Colin did say to me that there is activity that is still occurring. Colin, bless him, walks around with a huge cross on him. He said that he trusts in his God, and that he believes in his God and that his God will keep him safe. He said that he is not bothered about 'them' and that 'they' won't harm him. He said that he firmly believed that 'they' were there for Gail anyway. The thing is, it never went away, it's still there. He said that he could ignore it and not feed it, but Gail couldn't. So, what with the Sauchie Poltergeist, the Enfield Poltergeist, and the one that Darren Ritson wrote about, the South Shields Poltergeist, well I think this one tops the lot. Oh, and here's another thing. Colin got locked in the toilet. He went to the bathroom, he took the key, and locked the door, he done his business.

But we all said, *"Colin has been gone a long time, oh well, he must be busy, we'll leave him to it"*. Two hours had passed, no Colin, two and a half hours later, he turns up on the patio saying, *"Do you want a cup of tea"?* We all said, *"Where have you been"?* He said, *"I've been in the bathroom, thanks for checking".* What happened was, he locked the door, done his business, unlocked the door, went to open it, and he couldn't open it. Now the door was unlocked, and the handle was turning. So, it looked like 'they' were trying to keep him locked in the toilet. He said that he was pulling and pulling and pulling, and he is a strong man. He locked the door again, then unlocked it but still the door wouldn't open".

(MR) "Did he not shout or bang the door to get attention so that someone would come and get him out"?

(VP) "Well we couldn't hear him because we were out in the garden on the patio. He said that he just sat on the toilet and talked out loud and he said, *"Look, come on you guys this is not fair, I have company and I'm supposed to be entertaining, the least you could do would be to unlock the door."* He said that the door was already unlocked and then he could see the door handle move ever so slightly and the door just slowly opened itself".

(MR) "Wow, jeez oh. I take it that you have a lot of stuff on this case"?

(VP) "I did have. I've saved a lot of stuff. A lot of the E.V.P's camera work. I've got photographs of us all sitting there in the garden".

Author's Comment. *Unfortunately, although I asked for this to be sent to me to be included in the book, it wasn't!*

(MR) "I think the back story on this case is interesting. The Abbey, the Hell Fire Club.

It's possible that something has happened from that Hell Fire Club that something must have been done there, and it's somehow impregnated on the area where the Lewis household is".

(VP) "Do you know, that knight we got, his name sounded to me like Llewyn. He did say where he was from, he wanted to go to Aziah, (*) wherever or whoever that is! We had to take him in Andy's body across to where the Abbey used to be. When there, Andy threw up, he was retching, and the next thing that happened was that Andy was lying on the floor in a state. And I said, *"Are you Andy or are you Llewyn"*. He said, *"I'm Andy, where the f**k am I"* and he said, *"Why am I lying next to somebody's grave"?* He wasn't, it was a patch of grass. But I believe it was Llewyn's grave".

(MR) "Well Viv, I'd like to thank you ever so much for informing me what went on at the Lewis household. It certainly was a trying time for both of them".

(VP) "You're welcome, Malcolm".

(*) When Andy was taken over and said that he wanted to go and see Aziah. I decided to check the internet and see what I could find. From the web site *'Got questions? Your questions, Biblical answers.* I learned the following.

Ahaziah of Israel was king from 853-852 BC. He was the son of Ahab and Jezebel, who were among the most wicked rulers Israel ever had. Ahaziah's parents brought Baal worship into the land and turned God's people away from Him; although Ahaziah reigned for only two years, he was just as evil as his parents. He "aroused the anger of the LORD" (1 Kings 22:53) due to his own worship of Baal, which continued to lead the people into sin and idolatry. At one point King Ahaziah of Israel tried to ally with King Jehoshaphat of Judah, but, after a warning from one of God's prophets, Jehoshaphat severed ties with the wicked king (verse 49; cf. 2 Chronicles 20:37).

Now whether the above has anything to do with what Andy in his 'out of mind state' said, is open to question. But it is now part of record.

On Thursday the 9th of February 2023, I contacted Sean Cadman who was one of the Investigators on this case. I wanted to know from him what he had experienced at the Lewis household. In a telephone recorded interview, Sean had this to say.

INTERVIEW WITH SEAN CADMAN

Abbreviations. (MR) Malcolm Robinson. **(SC)** Sean Cadman

(MR) "Sean, nice to speak to you. As you know, I was asked to go on this case by a lady called Sandra Collins, but as I lived in Hastings at the foot of the U.K. I was too far away, and we needed to get someone on this case immediately as it was quite clear that this was a real nasty case. So, I passed it onto yourself and Vivien. Who else went with you on the day"?

(SC) "Initially it was myself and three members of my team. My wife, my daughter and her boyfriend and Simon".

(MR) "Now Colin and Gail, how did you find those two people. Describe them to me".

(SC) "They were a really nice couple, very friendly, really nice. They were very open at what they had experienced but also nervous about talking about it. Because nobody had believed them in the past".

(MR) "Now prior to you going, were there any other paranormal teams that went there"?

(SC) "Yes. Before we went, they had at least another two teams go. There was a Shaman who used to go quite often. But Gail got the impression that these people weren't particularly interested in finding answers, they just wanted the experiences".

(MR) "So they were there just really to take in any experiences then"?

(SC) "Yeah".

(MR) "Now over the course of the time that you and the team were there, what did you experience, what did you see"?

(SC) "Everything imaginable. From full apparitions to lights in the sky. Sounds that we couldn't explain. Meter readings which were off the scale. A whole spectrum of everything that you could class as the paranormal or supernatural".

(MR) "The apparition that you saw, was it solid looking or could you see through it? Was it male or female"?

(SC) "I saw a solid one in the garden that I can only describe as a 'creature'. It was definitely not of human form, but it was solid. In the house, we saw several un-transparent figures".

(MR) "The creature you saw in the garden. Talk to me a little more about what it looked like, how tall it was, how long did you see it for"?

(SC) "We've got a CCTV system set up in the garden which had been turned on all night. I went out into the garden to collect all the cameras in and to turn it all off, and I was looking down, and I have a torch in my hand which I was pointing at the floor to check where all the wires were, so I didn't trip up over all the cables. I heard three clicks, so I looked up with my torch over at a brick pagoda, and I saw something that had an arm around one of the pillars showing long fingers.

It was grey in colour and looked old. I can't say that it had almond shaped eyes, but the eyes were black, and it was peeking at me from around this brick pillar straight into my torch light. I got a shock at this, and sort of yelped, at which point it disappeared behind the pillar and I've disappeared straight through the back door of the house. I would describe it as more alien than human".

(MR) "And how tall was it"?

(SC) "I'd say at least seven feet tall, judging by the pagoda".

(MR) "Wow, seven feet tall"!

(SC) "Yeah".

(MR) "And you say that it didn't have those almond wrap around eyes"?

(SC) "No, they were round eyes, pure black. Quite big, but not like the wrap around almond shaped eyes. It had very, very, long spindly fingers".

(MR) "Do you think that it was surprised to see you"?

(SC) "Yes, I think it was surprised that I suddenly caught it in the torch light, as I was to see it".

(MR) "The lights in the sky that both Gail and Colin claim to have seen. Do you know much about these, did you see them yourself"?

(SC) "One night we had gone out for a cigarette break, and we were stood out the front. We happened to look up, and there was a solitary white light in the sky. At first, I thought it was probably a helicopter. Viv was stood with me. So, I turned my torch on it, it was one of those bright long-range torches with a big, long beam. I shone it up towards the light, and it moved backwards and got smaller as it was moving away. I turned the torch off, and it came forward again. There was no sound, and it was about 3 or 4 o clock in the morning.

All of a sudden, another light appeared next to it in the sky. I did the same thing, I shone the torch up to them, then it would back off. And then, without a sound, they both shot straight up into the sky and disappeared".

(MR) "So, was it more of a light, or was it a structured object"?

(SC) "It was just a very bright white light".

(MR) "Were you aware of a gentleman by the name of Jim Bell (pseudonym) who was a psychic medium who came to the house"?

(SC) "I do recall the name, but I can't say I can recall anything that he said".

(MR) "Now we also had a chap called John Lee attend the house who was a Demonologist. First of all, tell me what you thought about him. What was your take on John Lee and what he did".

(SC) "At the time, I thought he was an alright guy, since then, things have happened that have changed my view. He came to the house, he sensed things, and he picked things up at the house at the spots where we had. He went around the house, did the exorcism rites, and placed some Benedict Medals in various places around the house where he felt that he had to place them. He put crosses in various places using a blessed olive oil that he brought. After that, for about two weeks it went very quiet. Nothing happened and Gail said that things were lovely and then all of a sudden, it started up again".

Author's Comment. *Wikipedia tells us that the Saint Benedict Medal is a Christian sacramental medal containing symbols and text related to the life of Saint Benedict of Nursia, used by Roman Catholics, Lutherans, Western Orthodox, Anglicans and Methodists, in the Benedictine Christian tradition, especially votarists and oblates.*

This religious object is also a Christian symbol of opening doors and opening difficult paths. Tradition holds that it protects from curses, evil and vice, protects against diseases and protects good health.

(MR) "So did you actually spend the night at the property or were you just doing daylight vigils"?

(SC) "Yes, I was there all night investigating until 5, and 6 o clock in the morning. Some nights it would be quiet, there suddenly there would be bits and bobs going on, and then other nights it was just non-stop, from the moment you got there, till the moment you left".

(MR) "When you were there, did you hear any banging's or rapping's"?

(SC) "Oh yeah. The first big thing that we experienced while we were there, was when we were sitting in the front room, and Gail and Colin were telling us about the things that had gone on, when suddenly there was a very large 'thud' right above us in the loft. Now this was a long bungalow with a big central corridor with rooms coming off it. The loft was all boarded so that you could walk around the loft. So, we heard this loud 'thud' and I said, *"What was that"?* so I got up and walked into the hallway, and as I got into the hallway, I heard footsteps in the loft. I followed their progress and I thought that's a bit odd. I walked down the hallway, and the footsteps above followed me all the way down. They followed me into a bedroom, but when I went up into the loft, 'nothing'. There was a lot of that. There were a lot of banging's there were a lot of tapping's on the windows. There were knocking on doors, all sort of things like that they would just randomly happen throughout the night".

(MR) "I believe there was a fellow researcher by the name of Steve Mera involved".

(SC) "Yes that's right. Steve Mera and Don Philips came. I contacted Steve and asked if I could get his take on it. He came, and they got a lot of voice recordings. One of them actually said, *"It's the aliens"!* So, I had a chat with Steve to see what he thought, and he said that there was definitely activity in the house, also in the garden. But the main cause of 'it' being there, was Gail".

(MR) "I've learned that when Gail sometimes played the piano in the house that certain things happened as well, is that your recollection"?

(SC) "Yes, she has a piano in one of the spare bedrooms and she would sit and play it, and you could literally hear 'someone' walk up the side of the house and start tapping on the bedroom window. We sat there with her once and she was playing the piano and there were taps at the window, so we opened the curtains and there was nobody there. I would say that the side of the house wasn't wide enough between the house and the fence for somebody to walk up there. But we could hear clear as day, footsteps walking up and down outside. And when she would stop playing the piano, the sounds and banging's would stop".

(MR) "Now there is a back story of sorts about the area and the land where this house was built which possibly, could bring something paranormal into her house. And a long time ago, there was an Abbey that sat across the road which is no longer there. What do you know about this Sean"?

(SC) "I think it was in the 11th or 12th century. There was an Abbey virtually across the road where now sits a new housing estate. And it was one of only two Abbey's in the whole country where the monks were permitted to wear white. There is also the story from Newstead Abbey that the grounds in which Gail's bungalow is built on. The grounds originally belonged to Lord Byron at Newstead Abbey. He sold it all off as he needed the money. He put a covenant on the land saying that it wasn't to be built on until a thousand years, and obviously it has been, and it hasn't been a thousand years. So, whether that has stirred things up or not, I'm not sure".

(MR) "Now there were also tales about the Hell Fire Club in that area. Have you heard anything about this"?

(SC) "Yes, Byron used to have Hell Fire Club meetings at Newstead Abbey which is literally a mile away from where Gail's bungalow is. And they have two statues in the grounds of Newstead Abbey of the God Pan. Rumour has it (and it is one of the myths of the area) that these statues come to life and wander around the area. Now what we found weird about that, is that Colin told us that one morning they woke up, and all over the bedroom floor carpet, they have a white carpet in the bedroom, were dirty hoof footprints. They came from one window at the side which couldn't open so nobody could get in. And these footprints went round the bedroom, across the foot of the bed and towards the other window at the front. And the window at the front, that went into a sunroom. And these footprints were hoof shaped, they were dirty, tarry like muck that were left on the floor".

(MR) "And this is in Gail's bedroom in the house"?

(SC) "Yes this was in Gail's bedroom".

(MR) "And who saw this"?

(SC) "We didn't see it. It was when Gail and Colin woke up, they saw it. It was later when we went back, that they told us what they had seen, these dirty footprints. Gail and Colin took the photographs, gave them to another group, and never got them back".

(MR) "Do you know who these other researchers are, are you in touch with them"?

(SC) "No. All I know is at the time, they were called something like Nottingham Paranormal, and I've never heard of them. And I remember Gail saying that they started to charge money for them to go. So that's when she stopped them going".

(MR) "Yes, that's naughty isn't it"?

(SC) "Yes".

Author's Comment. I tried very hard to find this Nottingham paranormal group. I got in touch with a couple of groups from the Nottingham area, but they all said that they had never heard of this case. So, if you reading this book, were given these hoof print photographs, please get in touch with the author on the e-mail address at the end of this book.

(MR) "So, you have been on a number of investigations, you are a paranormal researcher yourself with many years of investigation under your belt. How would you rate this Nottingham case"?

(SC) "I'd rate it as the biggest case that I have ever been involved in. It was one of those cases where I would have liked to have seen a conclusion, but to have reached a conclusion there, would have taken many, many, years. There were so many layers of things that were happening that we'd experience there. But I think that it was mainly to do with the grounds. The history of the grounds, and Gail. Sandra Collins originally contacted you saying that Gail was psychic, and I think that once Gail experienced what she could be being a psychic, she couldn't close down. She was almost like a beacon for things in the area".

(MR) "Yes some people are like that, some people just seem to draw in spirits as they have that energy".

(SC) "I'll tell you the weirdest thing that I ever experienced. I was with a friend of Viv's, Andy. And we went out into the garden, just me and Andy. In the garden they have a big greenhouse and we saw a black cat walking across the lawn. As the black cat reached the greenhouse, it morphed into the figure of a man in black shadow".

(MR) "What"!

(SC) "And carried on walking to the back of the greenhouse. So, we both went running up the garden thinking 'what the hell was that'! Andy went one way, and I went the other around the greenhouse and there was 'nothing'. When we both met at the back, we both looked down to the floor, and there we saw the brightest, yellowy enormous, large toad. I've never seen anything like it. And I went right up to it with my torch, shining the light on it, and then, all of a sudden, there was this audible 'pop', and it disappeared right in front of our eyes".

(MR) "Wow. And how big was this toad would you say"?

(SC) "Very large. It was sat on its hind legs as they do and was probably eight inches high off the floor. It was bright yellow, almost luminous yellow. In the past, Andy has been involved in a lot of black magic rituals and things, and he said to me, that is a Witchcraft thing, it's got some link to Witchcraft".

(MR) "To your knowledge, did the next-door neighbours have any problems with paranormal things happening in there house"?

(SC) "Not as far as I know. I did ask one of the neighbours briefly asking if they had experienced anything and they just said no."

(MR) "Do you think that they were being honest with you, that maybe they were just trying to get rid of you at the door"?

(SC) "I think probably they 'had' experienced something, but they might be the type of people who deny it, who didn't want to know".

(MR) "To you as an investigator, what is your bottom line, what I mean by that is, do you think that it was (a) Demonic. (b) Ghostly. (c) Paranormal. Or could it have something to do with UFOlogy considering that both Gail, Colin, Vivien and yourself saw strange lights around their property. Or could it have been a bit of everything? What is your take on it all"?

(SC) "I think that it was a bit of everything. I think that they were all feeding off each other. Whenever we experienced anything to do with UFOs, the paranormal side would seem to bump up. And when Gail had stopped playing the piano or tried to ignore things it would ramp right up to almost full Demonic nasty".

(MR) "So by the sounds of it, this was your biggest case then"?

(SC) "Oh definitely yeah. Really, it's one of the most intense places that I have ever experienced in my life".

Author's Comment. I don't know about you dear reader, but what is mentioned above about that 'grey creature' with the long fingers seen in the Lewis's back garden near the pagoda, and also the cat turning into a black shadow figure which then turned into a toad which suddenly vanished, freaked me out. It's clear to see that there was a multitude of strange things happening in that property. I mean, can you imagine waking up one morning to see muddy cloven hoof prints on your white bedroom carpet! Not a pleasant sight I would imagine. As for the ancient Newstead Abbey which lies just over a mile away from Gail and Colin's bungalow, well it's interesting to note that poet Lord Byron allegedly held Hell Fire Club meetings there. Whether those comprised of black masses which allegedly were staged at other Hell Fire clubs, I don't know. I've learned that Lord Byron sold the Abbey to a Thomas Wildmam in 1818. Sean Cadman stated above that this was because Lord Byron needed the money, but what he needed the money for, I don't know.

It was important that I spoke to Andy who was also on this investigation. Andy only wanted his Christian name mentioned in this book, which is fine. Andy works on the darker side of things, but the Lewis family were at the stage where they would try anything to get rid of the menace that was invading their bungalow. Here is part, is what Andy had to say about his part in the investigation.

INTERVIEW WITH ANDY

Abbreviations. (MR) Malcolm Robinson. **(A)** Andy.

(MR) "Hi Andy. First question, when did you first go to the Lewis household, who invited you, can you remember what year it was"?

(A) "I can't remember the year; my memory is not that great to be honest."

(MR) "It may have been 2015 that's when basically people started to go there".

(A) "Yeah, 2015/2016 sounds about right".

(MR) "Was it Sean or Vivien who invited you, or how did you hear about it?

(A) "A bit of both really. They both invited me, and they said, 'you do all this black magic stuff and I said yeah'. Well, they said we need your help. So, I went along and discovered some things that weren't too nice".

(MR) "Yes, we'll come to that. How many times in total were you there for"?

(A) "Well over 10 times. At one point I spent about a week there".

(MR) "Wow. So obviously you got to know the couple fairly well then"?

(A) "Yes, they were like a mum and dad to me they were they used to look after me".

(MR) "Ah, bless them. OK, let's now talk about when you first arrived at their house. What was expected of you, what did you do, what did you hear? Just go through with me a number of these strange experiences".

(A) "I don't know if Viv told you, but when I first got there, 'a person' showed themselves up alongside the bungalow on the left-hand side of the driveway. So, I put up a chase and he actually got through a locked gate. I couldn't get through it so I couldn't catch up. So, I went around the back straight away, trying to find out where he went, and the figure was still at the bottom of the garden on the left-hand side next to the bushes. I wasn't the only one to see him, Viv saw him as did someone else to, I think it was Sean Cadman".

(MR) "What did he look like Andy"?

(A) "Bloody tall and quite big built. He was easy 6 feet 2, 6 feet 3, a very big built character. He was quite intimidating to be fair".

(MR) "Did he look human looking, is that what you are saying"?

(A) "Yeah, definitely human looking. Big and burly, and as I say, very intimidating".

(MR) "Can you recall what clothes he was wearing"?

(A) "No, it was quite dark. His clothes were fairly dark by the look of it".

(MR) "How did this playout. I mean, were you staring at each other"?

(A) "I approached him, asking who he was and what not, and all I got was a sort of grunt from him as he disappeared. He just walked 'through' the fence at the bottom. I got a shock at that.".

(MR) "A lot of people talk about the garden, not just the house, but the garden, that it felt very weird. Is that your recollection"?

(A) "Yes, I found out what was going on in the garden which was the strangest thing. I think it was me and someone else who were out in the back garden one night, and I saw this woman standing in the garden, she was just going about her daily chores, it was like history acting itself out again. I believe that this 'lady', was a Witch. And it turned out that the house was built on top of the foundations of another old building, which turned out to be a Witch's house. So, there were a few weird things going on with that. They've got a ley line that goes through there as well, so I knocked the ley line out of it which calmed things down a little using my old black magic stuff. But there are still things in that garden that are staying there, like crystals and stuff, and they are staying there permanently, I left them there".

(MR) "The work you do Andy, well its different from a psychic medium, I guess. When you go to a property or any location, how do you go about doing what you do"?

(A) "There are no rules. I just go along as me. It's just what I do, I don't know how to explain it really. It's just something that I have always been able to do. My nan was a Witch, so I was able to gather up her bits and pieces. I spent a lot of time with my nan as a child, so I guess it kind of rubbed off on me. I get feelings and stuff like psychic mediums do. Viv says I am a medium, but I don't class myself as a medium. I can actually see spirit and talk to spirit; I don't know how to explain it".

(MR) "No that's absolutely fine. Now when we talk about inside the property, what were your experiences inside the property"?

(A) "It was weird. I was lying in bed there one night on the week I stayed there. I woke up, it was like a pressure on the bed, and there was a man on the bed. He was sat on the bed staring at me. I thought 'wow'. I sat up and said, *"Who are you, what do you want"?* He said something, but I couldn't make out what he said, and at that point he disappeared. And as he disappeared, Gail came running out of her room shouting, *"Who's in the hall, Who's in the hall"?* And there was no one there. And I just walked down the hall and said to Gail that there was no one in the hall. And she said, *"Well I just heard someone walk up to my door".* And I said that there was no one there. So that was a bit of a weird one, and we both ended up having a drink of coffee and chatting in the kitchen. And then she said, *"Can you here that"?* and I said, *"What",* and she said, *"The footsteps, they are outside, he wants me".* And I said, *"No, he's not going to get you, don't worry, I'll go out and chase him off".* And I went out, and there was that big figure again, that big burly man. He was carrying something this time, how can I put it? It was like an African staff. The chances of him being coloured, were very strong. That would explain the height and his build. I haven't got a clue what he was doing there and what it was all about. He was there, but he didn't want to play ball if you know what I mean"?

(MR) "Yes". "So, I continued to put little spells around the garden, to try and drive him out, keep him away, because Gail was getting very agitated that week. Gail said that she was frightened, and I said don't be frightened, I'm here, nothing can hurt you. Viv was consoling her to make sure she was OK, and I carried on outside doing my bits and pieces. Colin came out and brought me a cup of coffee asking me if I was OK, and I said that I was fine. He said that he had seen 'him' earlier as I was walking back down the garden, he walked up behind you past the greenhouse.

So, I said, *"Did he now"!* and I went up and sat beside the greenhouse for a few hours, but he didn't show. The following night, whoa, that was something else. That was a weird night. I don't know how to explain it. It was like a dense atmosphere in the whole house and garden. In some parts of the house, it felt like static. You knew there was something there. And we could hear things up in the loft, a lot of footsteps running around in the loft. So, I asked Colin if I could go up in the loft, he said, *"Oh bloody hell, if you want to you are welcome to Andy",* and I said *"OK, I'll go up and have a look".* I got up there, Colin came up there with me. Now this is the thing that got me, now whether you believe me or not, well its just crazy. The only way to describe this, is by saying 'little imp characters. Two or three of them".

(MR) "Right".

(A) "When I go to places, I use my black magic staff and other things. It's all magic emblems and crystals. And Colin said, *"Did you hear what it said"?* and I said, *"What"?* and Colin said, *"Get the one with the stick."* (laughs) I was quite worried about that and said he's not having it. That was a funny old night. The following day, Viv had to go home, but she came back the following day. And Gail then invited a Shaman guy round".

(MR) "Yes".

(A) "Did Viv fill you in on him, the French guy, the Knights Templar guy"?

(MR) "Yes. Is that the occasion where something took you over in the garden and you were throwing this Shaman guy around"?

"Yes, this happened. I was bleeding from the ear, nose, and eyes. It was a strange experience. I mean, I was out of it. I was speaking fluent French and I cannot speak fluent French for the life of me.

And when I went unconscious, Viv said I looked almost dead, she thought I was dead. The thing is, I could hear Viv saying, *"You can get off my uncle Andy, let my uncle Andy go, let him come back".* Then apparently this Shaman bloke started pouring lots of water over my head as I am lying on the floor, at which point I got up and grabbed him by the scruff of his neck and threw him, and he went flying about eight feet up the garden. I'm not capable of that sort of s**t. I've got a bad shoulder, and this guy went flying. It was crazy. I don't know what happened. Viv was recording it, but it never came out! Everything else came out, but that didn't come out. That threw me, that's pretty strange for that video camera just to go down".

(MR) "Have you ever been possessed before, is that the first time that this has happened to you"?

(A) "No, it's part of my trade, that's what I do. If spirit wants to talk, it can come through me, I don't mind".

(MR) "So this person who inhabited your body for that short period of time where you were speaking French, did you get the impression of who this might be that was coming through you, what time period etc"?

(A) "He told Viv his name. And apparently, he was a Knights Templar, which is quite a weird one. After all this happened, Colin told me the story that the leisure centre across the road and up the hill in the old days, there used to be a Knights Templar. I don't know what you would call it, a keep or something on that site. But that wasn't good enough apparently, he came back into me later on".

(MR) "Was that the same day, or a later day"?

(A) "The same day. He wanted something, I don't know what it was. This happened. Apparently, I ran off and shut myself in a bedroom, and there were four people trying to get into the bedroom by pushing the door open, but they couldn't, and there was no lock on the door. And I don't remember all this. The next thing I know, there was a lady who I had been seeing for a little while, she was apparently punching, and kicking me. Apparently, I just got in her face and laughed at her. She was trying to get 'him' out of me, but it didn't work. Now afterwards they all went out and sat out the front and I somehow got past them out the front without them seeing me. Now there is no way I could have got past them without them seeing me, that is impossible. You've got a driveway, that's your only port of access, in and out. And apparently, I got past them, and they found me outside by what used to be an old temple, where this leisure centre was. I crawled up there on my hands and knees apparently. Some old boy saw me. It was a weird night".

(MR) "Going back to the loft episode inside the house. You said you entered the loft with Colin and saw a few imp-like figures. Talk to me more about that. What height were they, what were they wearing, what were their faces like"?

(A) "They would be about no more than three and a half to four feet tall. I couldn't really see their faces, as when they were moving, they were like, 'blurred'. They moved at speed with such ease. It was amazing".

(MR) "Did Colin see this as well as you, these imps"?

(A) "Yeah. But he only saw them out of the corner of his eye, and he said that he could hear them talking".

(MR) "Wow. Now, there was also a chap called John Lee who attended the house as well, and he anointed the house with holy oils and placed medallions around the house. Did you get a chance to meet John, and if so, what was your interpretation on what he was doing"?

(A) "My interpretation of John, is that I've never met him, never want to. What he done at that house was an awful lot of damage. He opened up a few doorways, trust me. Those medallions you spoke about, I disposed of every single one of them".

(MR) "So effectively, he made things worse then?

"100 times worse to be honest with you. He was absolutely rubbish. I'm not being horrible, but he is one of the biggest fakes that I have ever known. He just causes trouble. Those medals, medallions, as soon as I picked them up, I noticed that there was a cast of St Christopher and something else on the back of them. They were something that you can pick up in any old shop you know. Apparently, he had done a cleansing spell on them, and when I picked them up, I said that these were bad news. Because what I was getting up my arm was numbness, and that's not a good thing to have. So, I said to Viv, they've got to go. So, I offered to get every single one of them out of the house and destroy them".

THE MAN TO FROG INCIDENT!

(A) "There was another thing which Sean Cadman will verify as well. Me and Sean Cadman went out to the garden and Sean said, *"Who's that man up there"*. So, I said come with me, Sean looked scared. I said look, just come with me, you'll be fine you'll be safe, and Sean said, *"Well I've never dealt with this sort of thing before"*. So again, I said, just come with me, you'll be safe. He then said, *"Who is that man"?* and I said, *"Exactly"*. So, he said to this man, *"Who are you"*, and this man just stood there, he looked at us, and vanished. And we've walked around the greenhouse where he was stood, and I'm not lying to

272

you, on my honour, I looked down at the floor, and I could see this effigy of this little man, and this little man turned into a frog. Now this is going to sound really weird, Sean Cadman went, *"Fuck off, no way is that happening"*. And I said, *"It's happening"*. And the frog had its back towards us, and I said *"Oi, I know who you are, and what you are. You turn round and look at me"*. Well, that 'thing' turned around and looked up at me and Sean, and Sean said, *"Fucking hell"* and turned white as a ghost. Then, in front of our eyes, this frog did 'not' jump away, it just vanished"!

(MR) "Now I have spoken to Sean about this, and he definitely said he saw that with you".

(A) "That was the weirdest night in my life. I've never seen that happen before. That totally blew my mind. It was at that point, that I knew that there was something seriously wrong with that house".

(MR) "Now there was a hell of a lot going on at the house, there were even UFO sightings above the property as well. Did you see any strange lights? I know that Sean did with Viv."

(A) "I did yeah. Several times I saw lights up there. They have not been high up they have always been low down and quite small though".

(MR) "Uh huh".

(A) "Not big at all. I think the biggest thing I ever saw was about a foot and a half across".

(MR) "And this I believe was just lights, and not a structured object I take it"?

(A) "Yes, that's all you could see in the dark. It was just like a glow".

(MR) "How far away from the house do you think these lights were Andy"?

(A) "At one point, literally above the greenhouse".

(MR) "Wow, OK".

(A) "Yeah. But they were only small".

(MR) "Did you take any photographs at all, and if so, would they be available to me".

(A) "I wouldn't have any photographs, no".

(MR) "OK. And as far as your take goes on the whole crazy scene that was happening there. What do you think was behind it all. I mean, do you have a bottom line or are you not sure yourself"?

(A) "I'll tell you what I think. The factor there is that the house is on a ley line and a previous Witches house. All Witches built their houses on Ley Lines. And they disturbed the foundations of the Witches house. We believe that the 'frog man', was the Witches familiar".

(MR) "Right".

(A) "So that's that. But Gail, because she was so ill, I believe that 'they' were trying to use her as a 'get out', like a portal to 'get out'".

(MR) "I see, OK".

(A) "That was my feeling. Because it all surrounded Gail. Every noise, every voice was for Gail. She stood in the kitchen one night making some dinner and I was standing in the kitchen talking to her, and she went, *"Andy, look"*, and I said *"What"*, and she said, *"Look out the window"*, and that bloody big man was stood outside looking in through the window. So, I just walked up to the window, put my arm around Gail and said, *"I've got you, don't worry"*, and she said, *"I'm so glad you're here",* and I told her that I was not leaving anytime soon and not to worry, and that I would look after her".

(MR) "Were you aware that Steve Mera was on this case, and if so, was Steve there when you were there"?

(A) "No, not when I was there".

(MR) "So for you, how would you rate this particular case. In all the things that you have done over the years Andy, would you say that this case is up there. How would you give it on a score card so to speak"?

(A) "I'd give it an eight or nine for definite".

(MR) "Do you think that whatever is going on there is still physically there. I think we are in agreement that it had attached itself around Gail, but now that Gail has sadly passed on, do you think that maybe the phenomena has now left".

(A) "Yes, certain amounts, certain things. Those little imps up the loft, they have probably gone now. In fact, Colin actually saw one of them run out his front door. I said to open all the doors to make a way out for them. They went, and I watched them go, and they all headed up towards what used to be that Knights Templar place, so its all connected to that. Me and Viv were up the loft one day because we could hear a woman's voice and we had a K2 meter sat between us which suddenly went missing, and we found it at the other side of the loft!"

(MR) "Viv and I spoke about the Hellfire Club which allegedly had a room at Newstead Abbey which is about half a mile to a mile away from Gail's house. Was that something that you thought about, the strange goings on at that club"?

(A) "No. I didn't really think about the Hellfire Club to be fair".

(MR) "I think that when Gail and Colin had all the other various researchers at their home, who were trying to dot the I's and cross the T's, that the Hellfire Club theory was one of the theories that came up which might explain the strange goings on at their home".

(A) "To be fair, I made good headway at their home. I got rid of quite a lot from there. But there are things there that just won't go, they will be there permanently. You've got to shut doorways down. I actually rerouted the ley line from the garden using my magic staff. And my staff still sits in that garden today. It's made out of Witches hazel with a crystal on top, it cost a bloody fortune to make".

(MR) "When you say that you left it there, did you leave it in the loft, or is it buried in the garden"?

(A) "It's in the garden. I put it right inside where the ley line is which pushed the ley line in a different direction".

(MR) "Some people talk about contagion, and what that means is, that some people who go out and investigate haunted properties, more so in some nasty cases, when they come back to their own home, they find that things have followed them. Was that ever the case with you"?

(A) "Yes, it was for quite some time. Probably for about five months".

(MR) "Really? Wow".

(A) "This is going to sound stupid. But I had unbelievable strength for ages for about five months. One day Wendy and I were shopping at ASDAs in Chelmsford, and I couldn't get the trolley up past the kerb as the trolley was full to the brim, and I just picked it up, and carried it a bit for twenty feet. But I don't remember doing that.

Wendy said that she wished she had recorded that as it was funny as anything. I just didn't think about it. It was just happening. There was this strength there. Now how can I put this? I was getting history repeats, medieval history repeats which was quite weird. When Viv and I went up to the leisure centre place. I was taken back in history there. I could see loads of people running around this little village".

(MR) "Are you saying that you believe you saw into the past, is this what you mean"?

(A) "Yeah. Absolutely. I found, what was potentially a grave there from the Knights Templar which I thought was quite weird. There is a marker there but no gravestone, just a mark with a cross on it. If Gail was alive today, I'd still be there helping her. I was called in as a last chance really. Viv knows what I do, and she said to Sean Cadman that she thinks we need Andy here. And he said, *"Who's he, what does he do"?* So, she told him, and he said yes, let's get him here".

(MR) "Now you did very well there Andy, you did help which is fantastic. Sometimes we know as researchers that there is no easy fix that's the thing. We know that it is not a given. One has to try a whole range of things. Now is there any other thing that you would like to recall and state about this particular case"?

(A) "I was just gutted that so many people got involved. They ruined it. They actually made it a lot worse than it actually was. I'm forever going round repairing what other people do, and that's annoying. They go in half cocked; they don't know what they are doing. They start playing around with things not of this world, they haven't got a bloody clue, they stir it all up. It's just annoying".

(MR) "Yes you are quite right. I know that Gail was quite upset at all these people who came along saying that they would save the day and they charged her money, all to no avail as the phenomena was still there. One chap was paid his hotel and travel expenses and at a meal paid for by Gail and Colin, he said that his spirit guides had told him not to go on this case as it had a Demonic aspect to it, at which point he said he wanted nothing to do with it. This was Jim Bell".

(MR) "Moving on. With this case, you obviously had a big part to play in this, and what you have experienced has been backed up by others, in that they saw and heard the same things as you. In closing Andy, I'd just like to say a big thank you for taking time out to talk to me today, it has been very interesting".

(A) "No problem. I know what I saw".

Clearly then there were indeed some disturbing events that went on at the Lewis household. Little imps running across the loft! Gail, Colin Viv, Sean, and Andy, all said that they heard these footsteps running across the loft all the time that they were there. And what about this big burly menacing fellow in the garden with what looked like an African staff, what was he all about! And then we have the little man who turned into a frog and disappeared in front of both Andy and Sean. And, in his own words, Andy confirmed what Vivien told us earlier, about Andy throwing this Shaman about in the back garden, and of Andy speaking in French, a language that he has never spoken or learned! Clearly there were some upsetting things that happened at that house and in the garden. But what about the Knights Templar angle? Andy, Viv and Sean, all talk about the Knights Templar connections, and we're read about Andy suddenly speaking in a French accent when he was taken over.

The Knights Templar did have many residences in the British Isles, but they only existed for less than two centuries. They had a profound and lasting impact on several English towns. What I learned doing research on the Templars for this book, was that many of the administrative records and court records relating to the Knights Templar, have been lost over the years. I won't go into the history of the Knights Templar here, suffice it to say that the Templars did have a presence in Nottingham and surrounding areas, and that in 1185, a hospital was given over to the Knights Templar at Newark Nottinghamshire in order that sick people could be treated there. Then we have Newark Castle where a number of Templars were imprisoned and keep in dungeons on falsehoods. Many died there in terrible conditions. Newark Castle is around 20 miles away from the Lowe property.

COLLECTING FURTHER INFORMATION

After interviewing Sean Cadman, Vivien Powell, and Andy, I thought I'd ask Sean Cadman for his final thoughts on this case, some of which, I have already covered above.

Sean stated.

"My personal thoughts on the case were that Gail was deliberately attracting things back. Something would always happen when she played her keyboard. No matter how much we said, "Please don't touch it for a while". She would tell us on our following visit that she'd played the keyboard again and stuff had started again. As part of the exorcism, crosses were put all over the place using blessed oil. I remember Viv telling me she'd been and cleaned them all off, because the one on the loft hatch was upside down, when you opened the hatch. Andy who went with her, also removed all the St Benedict medals that had been placed around the property. This property was off the scale.

Whilst we were involved, we witnessed everything from full apparitions, strange lights in the sky, lights shining into windows, audible phenomena from voices to footsteps to loud bangs. The gardens were just as active as the house itself with some crazy things being witnessed that you would not believe and will stay with us forever. The land the property was situated on, had a lot to do with the activity. It was originally a Sherwood Forest settlement, which included the site of a well on a route from Newark to Nottingham".

In February 2023, I received an e-mail from Anthony Beckett, who, along with Steve Mera visited the property. I initially believed that both were involved in this case. Apparently, it was just Steve, and even then, it was just a brief visit. Here is what Anthony Beckett had to say.

Hi Malcolm,

"It's good to hear from you. It's funny you should ask about that case, as I was thinking about it only the other day. Unfortunately, while I was asked to participate in an investigation with Steve, Steve and I didn't go in the end. Another group arrived on the day before Steve, and I had arranged to meet the couple. It was decided that we wouldn't attend (I don't recall by whom). I am not entirely sure if Steve continued at a later date without me. A quick email search just now showed me that Steve told me a couple of details about the case, so it looks like he may have done. I never wrote anything up about the case, but I made a preliminary survey of the geographical area where the house was in advance of my going to visit the couple. Key points from this were, (from memory):"

"The building lay near a minor geological fault to the west. It was possible that the fault stretched to the building, but the geological maps indicated the faulting had been discernible only up to a point nearby.

A professional geologist (my brother) told me that it was plausible that it did continue towards the house. On the east side of the house, a housing development was either in progress or had recently finished (I forget which)".

Author's Comment. The housing development was in progress across the road.

"Steve mentioned to me in a later email only two points in writing on the case:

(1) 'There was a paranormal footprint.'

(2) 'There was no evidence to support any UFO related phenomena taking place'.

"I'm uncertain exactly what point 2 would exclude. I recall having a conversation about light phenomena being present, but perhaps Steve didn't associate that with UFO phenomena".

Kind regards. Anthony Beckett.

I then wrote off to fellow researcher Steve Mera to get his thoughts on the case. I asked about any photographs that he might have taken, and what his impressions of Gail and Colin were. He replied.

"I never took photos of them because it was Sean's case and didn't want to breach any confidentiality. What I can say, is that they were certainly sincere from my interview with them. There were reported time slip incidents, two I believe. They saw people on their grounds and outside their house in period clothing, where they said that the environment looked different. There were the vocals often heard outside their bedroom window, and standard paranormal disturbances taking place in the property. Low severity / average frequency. They did go through hell trying to find people that would take it seriously, but they became the victims of numerous nutters that turned up at their home".

In a further e-mail that I sent to Steve, I asked him when he first attended the property, and I also thanked him for kindly sending me a number of photographs that he personally took at the Lewis home, some of which are featured in this book. One photograph taken by Steve, showed a bright circular light. I asked Steve if this bright light (see photographic section) might be some kind of lens flare or perhaps a streetlight? He replied.

"It was around 2017. The photo shows an orb of some kind, captured in the back garden. However, it could be an illuminated particle via the flash close to the lens. Not too sure. I did not see anything at the time".

THE COLIN LEWIS INTERVIEW

As we have learned, Gail sadly passed away in February 2020. I must admit, I pondered long and hard whether I should telephone Colin to ask if strange things were still happening in his home, as most people felt that Gail was the catalyst or some kind of attractant for paranormal things to happen. But I just had to find out. So, on the 23rd of February 2023, I telephoned Colin, and he told me that he was very, very, poorly at the moment. And what had gone on at his property had nearly destroyed him. I told him that I was sorry to hear of the passing of his wife Gail and asked if things were a bit quieter now in the home. He reiterated that things had tried to destroy him that week, and that he was too ill to talk to me, but he wanted me to call him later on. By the tone of his voice, I could clearly see that yes, he was having a tough time of it, but was glad that he had asked me to call later on. I waited a few weeks, and with a bit of trepidation wondering if he would take my second call, I called him again on Thursday the 9th of March 2023 where I found him to be sounding much better and much more talkative. Indeed, we spoke for over 40 minutes. Admittedly, much of that conversation was about the state of the NHS, police corruption, corrupt politicians, and a whole lot more. What follows, is just a part of that conversation, which I must admit was truly eye opening. He laid his cards out in no uncertain terms. I was left with a much more fuller understanding what this 86-year-old gentleman had to go through. In part, it made for harrowing listening.

Abbreviations

(MR) Malcolm Robinson. **(CL)** Colin Lewis.

(MR) "Hi Colin, it's Malcolm Robinson, we spoke briefly a few weeks ago. I'm calling to see how you are feeling, as you said that you were troubled by what was going on in the house. Are things any better for you just now"?

(CL) "It's one of those things that you learn to live with. I don't want any more bother or people taking an interest anymore. It's one of those things which are best left alone".

(MR) "So you are not looking for any more help"?

(CL) "No. You know what? the amount of help that we should have had, didn't work. Time, and time, and time again. And it cost money. We had a firm in London, a top firm, a college. They said that they would come, and they said they could do this, and they could do that, and they could do the other, and they charged us £800 quid".

(MR) "What! That's terrible, shocking".

(CL) "They came and were here for half an hour and then went away and nothing was any different from when they first came".

(MR) "I'm so sorry to hear that".

(CL) "And this is the problem that you have got. You must know, if you are writing a book about these things, that there are a lot of people who say they are Spiritualists, mediums etc, and they are nothing of the kind. We had them coming here and Gail was making wonderful meals for them. They were coming with their uncles, their aunts, their nieces, their bloody nephews. It was a racket. One man, Geoff, he was very, very, good, but he's dead now. If I was to write a book about Spiritualist mediums etc, people wouldn't believe it. They know that you are in a frightening situation, and they think, *"Right, money"*. I believe in God; I always have believed in God. I've had a guardian angel with me most of my life".

(MR) "Uh huh"

(CL) "The word care has gone. It's all greed now. All people think about now is money, money. That's what it's all about".

(MR) "I'm so sorry to hear that you have had a hard time with fellow researchers. What I can say is, that not everyone will charge, but you are absolutely correct, some of them do. And this really, really annoys me. It really frustrates me. Because as researchers, all we are trying to do is to help people. You've had Sean Cadman, Vivien Powell and I do hope that both Sean and Vivien helped to a degree, I really do. Do you still speak to Sandra Collins?

(CL) "Ah, now there's a story. I should leave that alone. One of the things that I have learned through Spiritualists and mediums etc. Some are jealous about what other people might be able to do".

(MR) "Uh huh".

(CL) "And so that becomes a problem. We've had every sort. One particular man who was supposed to be clever and he could do this and he could do that.

And he said, *"If I come, could you find me a hotel"?* and Gail and I said *"Yes"*. And we paid the money for the hotel for him to stay in. And we gave him a meal at the Hut, which is a restaurant in Ravenshead, and we paid for that. He said that he had other things to do, and we never saw him again".

(MR) "Oh dear".

(CL) "He never even went to the hotel. All he had was a free meal".

(MR) "Was that Jim Bell? Does that name ring a bell?

(CL) "They all ring a bell. I don't believe in Spiritualists. I believe in spirits. I believe that the world is covered in spirits. And we had a plane crash here. And those spirits were trying to get to the light since the plane crash, and we succeeded in getting them there."

Author's Comment. *I asked Colin at this point if he was referring to the Lockerbie plane incident, as I wasn't sure what plane crash he was on about. He replied.*

(CL) "We had a plane crash here in 1944. It was on its way to Ireland, and it crashed into a field across the road from our house. And I was siting on the veranda, and I saw it. And I said to Gail, I've got to go over, there has been a plane crash, and she said where, as there wasn't one that she could see. But I saw one".

(MR) "And this vision occurred at the property that you are staying in just now"?

(CL) "Yes, oh yes".

(MR) "Wow. And did you go over......"?

(CL) "It's a long, long story".

(MR) "Are you still seeing those imps, those little creatures in your house. Are they still there, or are they gone now"?

Author's Comment. Whether Colin didn't understand my question or didn't hear it correctly, but he went back to this vision of a plane crash that he saw across the road from his house. He continued.

(CL) "The pilot and his crew came to this house a few years later, but I'm not going to go down with that story".

(MR) "No that's fine Colin, you don't need to tell me this. But I need to know if you are OK at the moment"?

(CL) "I believe in the spirit world. But the trouble is, and I know how it works, as I've seen it here. People who die naturally go to Heaven and get sorted there. But where people who have been killed in a car crash, or murdered, or killed during the war. People don't realise that their spirit is still there. Those spirits are still walking the planet trying find a way to Heaven. They need all the help they can, and that's where the Spiritualists and mediums are supposed to help, but they don't. 90% don't care. Its all, money, money. Even here it was money, money".

(MR) "I agree with you Colin. They are sadly a lot of people who are out to make money from unfortunate people like yourself. Its very naughty, its very wrong. But I'm glad you said 90%, because that leave's 10% or real bona fide true psychics who do try their very, very best to help people like yourself. But sadly, the vast majority are there to take money and line their pockets. It's not good".

(CL) "The thing that hursts me very, very deeply. Well, when I married Gail, I married an angel. We did everything together.

She was magic, she was wonderful. She cared; she helped people. She did this, she did that. And she got Parkinson's, and I said don't worry we will fight it together. Which we DID. And the Nottingham Hospital gave her some tablets that stopped her from shaking, and she could then paint pictures. She taught herself to play the organ.

She did this, she did that. And then 'they' stopped them, saying that the tablets were so expensive. And then less than a week, she fell and broke her back in two places. And the doctors here said, *"Take paracetamol"* I would have been better asking the ice cream man, and she had broken her back in two places".

(**MR**) "Oh God, that's terrible".

(**CL**) "And I asked God for help in healing if it was possible, and I tried healing on her, twice a day for a week. And she got up and her back was better. And we went to Mansfield hospital for an X-Ray, and they said that there was nothing wrong with her back. So, I said, *"What name have you got there"*. And you know what? It wasn't Gail's name at all!"

(**MR**) "Oh for goodness sake".

(**CL**) "Then they came back with the right name, and they said that her back had been broken in two places but that it had healed up perfectly. So, we got her another doctor who got her back onto those tablets that she was taking, and everything was fine. And then they stopped the tablets again. Now, they can spend millions of pounds looking after murderers, but they can't spend money looking after nice people".

(**MR**) "I totally agree".

(CL) "I saw Gail deteriorate with no help from the doctors or the hospitals. She was 12 stone, and she died in my arms on my birthday weighing less than two stone. There is sadness every day of my life".

(MR) "Colin, I firmly believe in a life after death. That we will all see our own loved ones who have gone before us in a better place. That is a great comfort to me".

(CL) "Oh yes. I do believe this. And I would say that wherever Gail is, she is still keeping an eye on me. I'm sorry, I'm getting upset. You've got one hell of a job if you are writing a book about one thing and another. I could write a book, as thick as a yard about what's been going on. People came here and were supposed to be helping and stayed here got two or three weeks, 'it was a holiday for them'! None of them were bothered".

Author's Comment. At this point in our conversation, the conversation veered away from the strange events that were occurring in Colin's house. Colin went on to discuss other things in his life. Such as the death of his brothers, his wife Gail, and lots of his friends. He said that he had nobody left, other than a family member who lives in Suffolk. Colin then aired his views about politicians of which I wholeheartedly agree with, more so the statement he said that they couldn't find their way out of a chip shop. It would seem that Colin still hadn't lost his sense of humour. He then gave his thoughts about the various strikes here in Great Britain, moreover the doctor and nurses strikes. He stated that if he was a doctor he would never go on strike, even if they stuck a machine gun in his left ear. Colin then explained that when he was younger, he was in the army (Royal Artillery) and later joined the police. He then spoke about building the house that he and Gail lived in. At which point I brought in the aspect of the fields that used to lie across the road from his house which both Gail and Colin fought hard to keep as arable land, as the local council wanted to build houses on. He went on.

(CL) "That land across there was sacred land. And at one time there was a monastery built on that land, it was in the 8th or 9th century. It was like St Paul's Cathedral but only smaller. I know all about it, more than most people. And Gail and I fought the council, and we stopped the builders from building on that land. And then we received a letter from a Labour M.P. who said that they were going to overturn that decision and that they 'would' build houses on it. It was a word called Democracy which no longer exists".

(MR) "Yes I totally agree".

(CL) "You wouldn't believe what I know. I know that there is a tunnel from this land here that goes to Newstead Abbey. I know that there is also another tunnel from this land here which goes to the Hut. *(Author's Comment. The restaurant further up his road which was something else back in the day)* The people who owned Newstead Abbey in those days, paid £35,000 a year to guarantee no building on this land. And then they went and built five bungalows for the staff that worked at Newstead Abbey. And what that did of course, was open the gates for further houses to be built".

Author's Comment. *At this point I wanted to discuss the well that was in Colin's back garden. As you know by reading this chapter, a lot of strange things were seen in the back garden around this covered sunken well. You have read about Andy being taken over in the back garden and throwing a Shaman around. We have learned about Andy and Sean seeing a strange yellow frog that turned into a small man and vanished. And what about the cats that Colin and Vivien saw that barked like dogs? Clearly something was amiss in that back garden. I continued.*

(MR) "Is it true that there is a sunken well in your back garden"?

(CL) "Yes, in our garden. I don't know if you know this, but there was a six wells walk, and that was from Newark to Newstead Abbey and one of the wells was in our garden".

(MR) "It must have been a special well then back in the day".

(CL) "It's in a shocking condition. People that came here told us stories that weren't true".

(MR) "But are you still seeing things in the house though Colin, are things still happening, or have things quieted down now"?

(CL) "Its never going to go away. You see, it's a right of way. It's difficult to tell you really. Things that happened thousands of years ago, created a pathway. It would take to long to tell you".

(MR) "I do accept that whatever was on your land, back in the day, may have some bearing as to what has been happening today".

(CL) "It's still there. You know, people from other planets have been helping this world for thousands of years".

(MR) "Do you regret building your house on this sacred land"?

(CL) "No. When Gail and I built this house, everything was hunky dory, everything was fine. That Labour man, Prescott who overturned our petition and built houses on the land opposite, well, if they were going to haunt anybody, they should have bloody well haunted him".

(MR) "*Laughs.* Yes definitely".

(CL) "It's a wonderful story. The thing about it all, nobody realises until you live amongst it. Its wonderful, its amazing, its fantastic, it's all of these things rolled into one. You mentioned Sandra"?

(MR) "Yes".

(CL) "Well she will say *"Oh, I know a very good lady who is a Spiritualist medium, do you want her to come"?* and I've said, *"Yes if she is good"*. Then Sandra said, *"No, she is not"*. The trouble is, it was jealousy, it's got to be".

(MR) "Are you trying your best just now to ignore what's happening and get on with your life"?

(CL) "I know what's going on. You learn to live with these things. You must know, you've been around long enough to see and to know about these things. Everyday, you are learning something new".

Author's Comment. *At this point Colin spoke about psychic healers, more so about a lady healer called Isa Northage, who had a Sanctuary and Church that was built in the grounds of Newstead Abbey. I continued.*

(MR) "Yes there are some fantastic healers in the world, people who clearly have a tremendous gift that they can use for the betterment of mankind".

(CL) "I have a business which is up for sale at the moment, and that money is going towards helping as many people as I can help".

(MR) "Good for you. That's great".

(CL) "There's a lot of people who I am trying to help at the moment and that's what I am going to do till it's my bugle call".

(MR) "That's so great that you are trying to help other people".

(CL) "That's what I am going to do, and nothing will change that. If it hadn't had a guardian angel with me at all times, my life would have been destroyed on numerous occasions when I was in the army and police force etc. I still believe that I have a guardian angel, even now. Look, do the best you can, that's all you can do".

Author's Comment. At this point in the conversation, it swung around to corrupt politicians and police officers which I won't go into here. But Colin wanted to re-iterate about what he was going to do with the money from the sale of his business. He stated.

(CL) "Nobody cares anymore. Life today, is going to be very difficult for a lot of people, and if I can help as many as I can before I go, that will do me".

(MR) "Bless you, that's a great thing to do, it really is. Like I say, its great that we will see our loved ones who have gone before us again. I believe that you will see Gail again. I lost my brother some years ago, and I know that when it is my time, I will see my brother again, and that's a great comfort".

(CL) "Yes. If you believe, anything is possible".

(MR) "Well it's been a pleasure speaking to you this morning Colin. As long as I know that you are OK, that will do me. You said that it was not as bad as it was, is that correct"?

(CL) "Again it's a long story, it seems impossible really, it did happen, and it does happen, and you can only do what you can do. And that's to look after people, and look after yourself as well, because if you don't look after yourself, you can't look after other people. I've got a lot of work ahead of me, I'm 86 now. Its not going to be easy, but I don't want it to be easy, but its got to be done. And when I get the chance to do it, I shall do it.

A lot of people who came to my house were just a menace. Their heart wasn't in the same place as probably yours and mine. And you know, it's the money. Money is the God now".

(MR) "Well like I said Colin, I wish you well I really do".

(CL) "I know. I hope you can do what you can do. Take care, do the best you can, you can't do any more than that".

(MR) "I wish you well Colin".

(CL) "And I wish you the same".

(MR) "God bless you Colin".

(CL) "God bless you too".

And there you have it. Its fair to say that I wasn't expecting such a long conversation with Colin as I didn't know how much these events had truly affected him. Here was I, another one of those pesky researchers fishing for quotes, hence when he opened up, I rarely broke in and I just let him speak. He went on to speak about other things which had upset him in his life, not related to the haunting, and there were points where I wanted to break in and ask those pertinent questions about the imps in the loft etc, so I failed on that score. Although I did ask that question, but he swerved it and spoke about something else. At the end of the day, it is what it is. Here is a lovely man, still no doubt grieving for his wife, and although yes, I desperately wanted more about the strange goings on in the house, I had to be careful and keep him on the line. I feel that the interview above, confirms the haunting, but its sad that Colin feels that he has to live with what's going on and put up with it. Not a great way to live your life, but then again, what else can you do? One strange thing I did notice as I was interviewing Colin, from round about 23 minutes in, there was a strange 'crackling noise' that appeared during the call. It wasn't overbearing and we could still hear each other. None of us mentioned it. It may well have a natural explanation. Colin might have been using a handset that you can walk about with (although I didn't ask him that)

I knew when I started on this book, that I just had to include the Nottingham Haunting. It was important to document and provide you the reader, with as many facts as possible about this most bizarre case.

Yes, it would have been great to get the testimony from other researchers on this case, namely, Nery Kirby, Don Philips, the Nottingham ghost team that took away the photographs of those cloven hoof prints on the white carpet, which the Lewis couple woke up to one morning, (they never got those photographs back!) And whilst I spoke to Gail a few times on the phone and we sent the odd e-mail to one another, I regret not going to the house myself. But as you have read, there came a point that Gail and Colin had had enough of all the different thrill-seeking researchers coming to their home.

They felt secure with Vivien, Nery, and Andy to look into things. A rapport was built, trust was built, but ultimately the case was never resolved. One person, John Lee, the psychic medium who attended the family home and who placed the medallions around the home and anointed the walls with oils, was sent to prison for reasons which I won't go into here. Nothing to do with the haunting I might add. And whilst I abhor what John was sent to prison for, his testimony and what he did at the Lewis household, should be part of record (rightly or wrongly) I dearly hope, that Colin is allowed to live out the rest of his life peacefully, and when he sells his business, I'm sure it will go to a worthy cause.

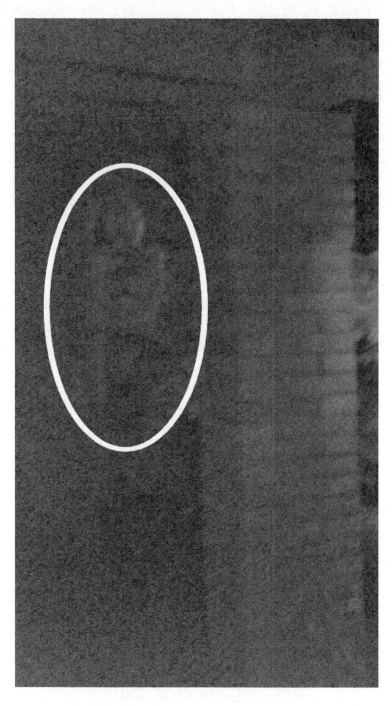

Cropped photo of imp or spirit (c) Sean Cadman

Full photo of garden with imp or spirit. (c) Sean Cadman

Sean Cadman

Orb in garden © Steve Mera

Pillar on Pagoda where Sean saw an 'entity' © Steve Mera

Steve Mera

The Back Garden © Steve Mera

The house and back garden (c) Steve Mera

The Lewis Home (c) Steve Mera

The Pagoda (c) Steve Mera

The side of the Lewis house (c) Steve Mera

St Benedict Medal. Similar to ones placed in house

***

CHAPTER FOUR
THE MEDIA AND THE SUPERNATURAL

"Whoever controls the media, controls the mind".

Singer Jim Morrison.

HOW WEIRD IS WEIRD!

OK, so what do we classify as weird? Many things can be classified as weird, and by that, I mean, strange looking fish which have been sighted deep in the oceans of our world by deep sea submersibles. We can also look at weird tales of re-incarnation and curses, to name but a few. In this chapter we will look at several things, which to this author are downright bizarre. Some of the following tales come from several newspapers from the files of the author. You might want to take them with a pinch of salt. Equally, as to draw comparisons between the British tales that I have to tell, I briefly mention a few similar tales from overseas, purely to allow you the reader to see that this is not just a British phenomenon.

THE FOREIGN ACCENT SYNDROME

We have some weird medical conditions which even today, in the 21st century, medical science is still trying to come to terms with. A 'for instance' would be, the foreign accent syndrome. In her article on this subject featured on the web site, Medical News Today (October 19th, 2018), Maria Cohut writes,

"Imagine this. You were born and grew up in New York, and you have a stereotypically metropolitan American accent. One day, however, as you are

engaged in one of your favourite sports, you receive a heavy blow to the head, and you pass out. A person with foreign accent syndrome has a speech impediment, which causes them to sound as if they are speaking with a foreign accent. When you wake up in the emergency room and call out to the nurse, you realise something shocking has happened to you your New-Yorkese accent is gone, and it has been replaced by what sounds like a strong British English accent. What happened? This thought experiment illustrates an extremely rare condition the foreign accent syndrome. This is a speech impediment, which results from damage to the parts of the brain responsible for coordinating speech. Such damage to the brain can be the result of a stroke or a traumatic brain injury, and the speech impediment that develops makes the person sound like they have suddenly acquired a foreign accent. Researchers note that recorded occurrences of accent 'changes' related to this syndrome, include Japanese to Korean, British English to French, American English to British English, and Spanish to Hungarian. However, some studies suggest that while most cases of foreign accent syndrome may be due to brain injuries, in certain instances, this condition may have a psychogenic origin. "[P]sychogenic [foreign accent syndrome] is related to the presence of a psychiatric or psychological disturbance in the absence of demonstrable neurological damage or an organic condition that might explain the accent."

I don't know about you dear reader, but I have always found this condition truly bizarre. The medical profession still hasn't truly recognised what is going on here, and it would appear, that this strange occurrence features more with women than it does do with men and tends to occur between the ages of 25 to 49 years. Now if I were to put my own spin on this, and coming from a paranormal background, it would be easy for me to say that what is truly happening here, is that somehow, this blow to the head, or the individual

303

coming out of a coma for instance, with this new found language is speaking in a language that they once were well versed in, but not in this lifetime, but in another! In other words, through their genetic makeup, a past life recall of 'voice' is coming through. Sounds fantastic I know, some would say ludicrous, and of course it may well be. But let's stop for a moment and give this theory more credence shall we. Who's to say that what is happening is not true? There is a mountain of evidence out there which purport to showcase past lives, they can't all be deluded? So, for me, it's clearly something worth considering although I dare say a lot of mainstream medical practitioners will not give it the time of day. So, yes, that's weird and joins the many thousands of other weird stuff happening all over the world. Indeed, staying with this theme for a moment and before we go ahead and look at other weird 'stuff'. What about those people who, after having either a heart or lung transplant, suddenly start doing things that they never would have done before their transplant? I'm talking about people who simply hated motorbikes, but after receiving the heart of someone who dies in a motorcycle accident, suddenly have this strange desire to ride a motorcycle, what's going on here? I covered this subject, (Cellular Memory) in a previous book, Paranormal Case Files of Great Britain (Volume 2) available on Amazon and I won't go into that in any great detail here, other than present some 'new cases' that I came across in a British Tabloid, more of which in a moment.

CELLULAR MEMORY

When we speak about things being weird, probably one of the more stranger things would be the 'weirdness' surrounding what's known as 'cellular memory' The main stay of Cellular Memory concerns people who have transplants, be it a heart, liver, or something else.

Then after a short period of time, those people suddenly crave for something be it a blackberry pie, bitter almonds or indeed want to take up a sport like baseball or basketball. All these things that they have never been interested in before! How is it possible, that memory can 'survive' in people's bodily organs, and, when transplanted into someone 'new', somehow give those memories over to the 'new' recipient? It's a fascinating concept and something which to this writer, gives food for thought. In my book, Paranormal Case Files of Great Britain (Volume 2) I gave 6 astonishing examples of Cellular Memory. I'd now like to give a further 4. I came across 8 cases from the Sun Newspaper dated, Saturday January 5th, 2013, featuring 3 females and 5 males of which I am only featuring 4 of those. The feature was a double page spread following on the back of the incredible recent case of Mark Cahill who made medical history as the first man in Britain to have a hand transplant, this was completed in December 2012. I should state that organ transplants have been with us here in the United Kingdom since the second century, and corneal transplants started in 1837, so technically they have been around a long time. The Sun newspaper tells us that around 4,000 transplants occur every year saving more than 1,100 lives. (That figure may well be different now) So, let us take a look at our first case and what this lady had to say about her transplant, but before we do so, it would be fair to point out that when one gets any kind of life saving transplant, that transplant will of course give the recipient a new lease of life, and that 'new lease of life' may well take them into areas that they haven't considered or acted upon before. That said, there are certain changes and attributes that the following people claim to have never had before, which would seem to differ from that equation, as the following would now suggest.

CASE 1. SIMON COOPER. (Liver transplant).
NEW CONDITION. *(Now swears)*

We learn that professional drummer Simon Cooper (29) went into Addenbrooke hospital in Cambridge for a liver transplant and came back out swearing like a trooper! He first noticed it as he came out of surgery and gave out a long line of expletives about how severe the pain was. That in itself may not sound so bad, but up until that time, he had never sworn in his life. His mother had always instilled good manners to Simon as he grew up. However, weeks later into his recovery, he was still swearing. Simon's mother began to think, that perhaps this transplant had somehow changed her son's personality. 13 years later, and Simon has still not shrugged off his swearing bouts. Simon was quoted as saying,

"Mum said that she'd read that transplanted organs could change your personality. I think it's happened to me. And 13 years later I still can't control my tongue. Luckily it hasn't affected my job prospects or my love life. But it does make me wonder about the girl who saved my life".

CASE 2. HENRY KIMBELL. (Kidney transplant).
NEW CONDITION. (Now loves beer)

Our second case concerns 26-year-old Henry Kimbell from Battersea in London, who in point of fact worked with Kidney research UK. It was when Henry was 15 years of age, that he noticed that something wasn't right with his kidneys, he was finding blood in his urine, so his mother rushed him to the doctors. Tests later confirmed that he had Dense Deposit Disease which is a rare genetic kidney infection. Then at 17 years of age, he suffered major renal failure and ended up on dialysis and waited on receiving a new kidney. As luck would have it, his father David was a match on the kidney stakes, and through family love, was more than happy to give his son one of his kidneys.

Sadly however, Henry's body rejected his father's kidney, so the search was on for another donor. One was found, and a further transplant was scheduled. After the transplant and in his recuperation period, Henry had a strong desire for bitter (an alcoholic drink) Prior to the transplant, Henry had always stayed away from bitter, it was not a drink that he liked, and even the smell was enough to put him off drinking it. He now drinks 12 pints of bitter each week. The donor is unknown, so admittedly we don't have any indication if the donor was a heavy bitter drinker.

CASE 3. SHARRON COGHLAN. (Kidney transplant)
NEW CONDITION. (Tastes changed)

With this case, the recipient of the kidney transplant, had her whole tastes in food and lifestyle changed. Sharron Coghlan (45) from Luton in Bedfordshire England, had a kidney transplant in 2011. The kidney came from a 22-year-old man who had lost his life in a car crash. No sooner had Sharron received her new kidney, than her whole lifestyle changed. She started to enjoy things that she had never enjoyed before, such as chick flicks and books, more so war books and historical biographies. Prior to having surgery, she loved sea food, now the thought of eating it would make her feel ill. She now craved brown bread, mustard, and cheese. Sharron describes it as if her taste buds had been swapped over from the donor. Sharron stated,

"I went online and discovered Cellular Memory. Some doctors think it happens, others don't. I am proof that it does. At first it was off putting, but now I consider it an honour. Part of this person's memory is living in me".

CASE 4. BILL WOHL. (Heart transplant)

NEW CONDITION. (Became sport mad)

Our next case features (64) year old Bill Wohl from Arizona in the United States. After receiving a heart transplant at (52) he suddenly found himself wanting to compete at various sporting events, things that he had never wanted to do prior to the transplant. He became so successful, that he won 28 gold medals from triathlon events around the world. Another strange aspect of his newfound love of life, was that he found himself crying to the words of *'Your Love is King'* by the British soul singer Sade. Who, he admits to not knowing who this was prior to his operation. Bill decided to find out who his donor was, and tracked down the brother of the donor, and found out that his donor was one Brady Michaels who died aged 36 in a freak accident whilst setting up a stunt. Brady it would appear, was a man full of the joys of life and loved being involved in outdoor sports. A further surprising thing Bill learned whilst speaking with Brady's brother Chris, was that Brady was a BIG Sade fan! Bill was quoted as saying,

"That's when I said, whoa! Is some sort of connection possible? People think I've become more sensitive. Is there a very real part of who Brady who is, living inside me now"?

What I found most astonishing in this article on Cellular Memory, was one case which described a 27-year-old female who was given a lung to help her recovery. That's all well and good, but the lung she received was from a smoker. Yes, you read that correct! How on earth could the medical profession even contemplate giving someone the lungs of a smoker, it beggars belief.

What makes this case worse, was the fact that the doctors did 'not' tell her that the lung she was about to receive came from a heavy smoker. Sadly, the young lady died, and her father remarked, *"She was dying a death that was meant for someone else".*

A spokesperson at Harefield hospital where the young lady had the transplant stated,

"It is very rare for patients to specify that they do not wish to be considered for clinically healthy lungs from smokers. This is because the risks are much higher if patients decline donor lungs from a former smoker and wait for another set or organs which are both a match and from a non-smoker to become available".

As stated earlier, I covered Cellular Memory in one of my previous books so I won't go into it too much here, what I will say and should point out, that there are many people in the medical profession, who do believe that memories can somehow be stored in the very fabric of our bodily cells, and when transplanted into another human being, that person somehow picks up and acts upon those newly stored memories. Physical therapist assistant Leslie A. Takeuchi, BA, PTA from Orinda California studied the possibility of 'emotions' or 'memories' somehow being stored in the very tissue of human beings and stated, *"Is it possible that our memories reside deep inside our bodily cells in addition to our minds".*

When it comes to cutting edge thought on this issue, Candace Pert a professor at Georgetown University in America who is the author of *'Molecules of Emotion, Why You Feel the Way You Feel'*, discovered what she called 'neuropeptides (or peptides for short). These chemicals can be found in all the tissues, muscles, and major organs of the body.

Candace firmly believes that the mind is not just in the brain, that it exists all throughout our body. The hard drive of our brain, which stores memory, may therefore not be alone as hard drives go.

DON'T WORRY

For those reading this who might themselves be set to undergo an organ transplant and are fearful that they too might somehow receive the thoughts, feelings and likes of the donor, please be aware that this does not happen in all cases, and, as already stated, when anyone received an organ be it a heart, liver, or lung, they will of course enjoy a new sense of freedom, their lives will undoubtably change for the better, and due to this new found sense of life and purpose it goes without saying that they may take up new pursuits. So, there are those that would say that Cellular Memory is nothing more than a person living their newfound life. But then again!

PAST LIFE EXPERIENCES

Staying with the weird and wonderful and again featuring information from my many years of newspaper and magazine files, I would now like to take you on a backwards journey through time. I have always been fascinated by re-incarnation and the claims made by people who have stated that they have lived before, but in a different time and a different place. From the weekend magazine of September 16th, 1981, I give you some weird tales of past lives.

HAVE YOU EVER LIVED BEFORE?

In his double page spread article columnist Jack Pleasant provided his readers with the astonishing work of hypnotherapist Joe Keeton. Born in 1920, Joe has helped thousands of people with their phobias and emotional problems, all of which through the use of hypnosis. During Joe's life, he soon discovered that there were a number of people, who, under hypnosis, started speaking in strange tongues, or stated that they were of a different sex, and that they lived hundreds of years in the past. All of this proved fascinating to Joe, and throughout the course of his life, he managed to cure the ails of those people who through their past life, brought phobias into their present lives. Joe sadly died in 2003. From the following article I take some of the more interesting stories of past lives that were presented.

CASE 1. Sandra Wingfield.
PAST LIFE. A clergyman's daughter who lived 100 years past.

In this case we learn that a Mrs Sandra Wingfield who suffered from backache with no apparent cause, learned after going under hypnosis, that the answer was there all along? After Joe relaxed Sandra and took her through the induction of hypnosis, Sandra suddenly started to pour our long-forgotten memories of being a clergyman's daughter. Her name was Sarah, and she had lived 100 years before, and was the adopted daughter of this clergyman and his wife. Under hypnosis, Sandra went on to state that she became the Governess to the children of a wealthy family in Norwich, and whilst living in this house in Norwich, she fell off the balcony of this house and severely injured her back. Could this be why she is suffering with back pain today, due to this condition in a past life? It may sound crazy but if this was a 'one off' incident then I would tend to agree that it was crazy, but we have to look at the facts and bear in mind that this is a global phenomenon, of people travelling back in time under hypnosis, and having conditions of the past, surface in the future as can be found from the countless books on this subject. But staying with this article. We also learn that another lady came to Joe having problems with claustrophobia (the fear of confined spaces) She had no idea what caused this, but whenever she was in a confined space she would panic and be very fearful. Under hypnosis, she found herself back in Victorian times as the ill-treated daughter of a Liverpool prostitute. Moreover, and more significant, was the fact that her mother used to lock her in the attic whilst she herself went out to prostitute.

CASE 2. Karen M.
PAST LIFE. A 19th Century farrier's wife, living in Surrey England.

Another phobia that was unlocked though hypnosis, was a young lady called Karen M. Growing up, Karen insisted that she did not want any children until she was 26 years of age. She couldn't offer any rational explanation for this, but just knew, that from 26 onwards, that was the only time that she was going to have children. Under hypnosis, she travelled back in time to the 19th century and found herself living as a farrier's wife in Woking Surrey. Her name was Catherine Jeffries, and she died in childbirth at 25. Could this be why Karen living in the 20th century decreed that she would only have children after the age of 25? Or was this just one big coincidence. Joe Keeton himself admitted that cases such as this did not necessarily prove re-incarnation, rather, the information may have been gleamed or picked up in some way from some universal memory bank which we currently don't understand. I personally believe that it could also be genetic. In other words, this might have been the recall of one Catherine Jeffries from this past life, but through the genetic code imprinted in the genes of Karen, or, to put it another way, maybe this 19th century Catherine Jeffries was related to Karen, and through some strange mechanism, under hypnosis, this strange tale unfolded, something akin to cellular memory of which I stated earlier. Just a thought. This article goes on to provide other such stories, only this time coming from celebrities, such as actress Dianne Keen who just somehow knew that in a past life she had lived in Egypt. She claimed that she had very vivid feelings of having lived there before, but more distressingly, she said she saw her current brother, being run over, and killed by a cart in those times. Another actor, Oliver Tobias, is convinced prior to coming to England when he was eight, that he had already lived here before. He stated:

"I remember crying all the way from Dover to London. I seemed to have a fear of something in the past".

Matthew Manning, an English psychic, was quoted in this article as having drawn images from past masters that he claims he has never seen before. Indeed, one such drawing, a sketch of a sad looking monkey, was identified by an expert as an exact replica of a drawing by the 17th century Flemish artists, Savery. This can be found in a museum in Amsterdam, a place, which Manning claimed he had never visited. The subject of re-incarnation is a subject thankfully found in many books, and believe you me, I have only scratched the surface of it here. Rosemary Brown was an English composer and Spiritualist who died in 2001, she claimed that numerous compositions from dead composers came through her mind and onto the keys of her piano. Pieces from composers such as, Bach, Johannes Brahms, Ludwig van Beethoven, Franz Liszt, Frédéric Chopin to name but a few.

There was no denying that many pieces were indeed very similar to those afore mentioned composers, but there were those who said that it was all concocted and was nothing more than a fanciful 'similar rendition' of the style of that composer. But who was right and who was wrong?

BRITT'S LIFE AS A BOY

This was the heading from the News of the World newspaper from November 1980, (I did say some of my press reports go way back!) It gave some interesting information about Swedish actress Britt Ekland and her trip back in time through regressive hypnosis. However, she got so upset about seeing her death in this past life, that the hypnotherapist had to take her out of hypnosis and bring her back to the present. Under hypnosis, she saw herself in a poverty-stricken farmhouse with a man a woman, and children. It wasn't until she went to draw some water from a well, that she saw her reflection of herself. Here is what she had to say about it.

"I see a dark-haired round happy faced boy. I'm very lonely, I'm always playing the flute. I feel very special, very gifted, but I seem to have no hope of getting away. There is a big house, it's like a castle, someone there has heard me playing the flute, they have taken me to live at the castle, and are giving me violin lessons. I play at concerts all over Europe, it's all very exciting, but it's very lonely".

This, however, was not Britt's first experience at living in the past. In a further hypnosis session, she claimed that she lived in the 20th century as a writer and saw herself dying of a chest illness, at which point she had to be brought out of hypnosis.

Author's Comment:

What are we to make of all this? Being a famous actress and star of countless films, could this not be a hidden subconscious memory? A memory perhaps of a movie she once starred in, or even a book that she had read as a child. There is a condition known as cryptomnesia which effectively means that an individual will recall something and mistakenly believe that this thought of theirs is their own, when, in point of fact, they have actually encountered it previously and then forgotten about it. Could this be the case with Britt, or indeed other such cases in which regressive hypnosis has taken people back to allegedly past lives?

THE SECRET GIRL FROM JAMES BOND'S PAST

This was the headline from the same edition of the News of the World dated November 1980, and we learn that James Bond actor, Sean Connery, also shared a past life as someone else. Sean decided to take part in this session with one of Hollywood's top psychics Kebrina Kinkade. The session was conducted at California's famous Beverley Hills Hotel. Here is what Sean had to say about his particular session.

"I'm sliding open a big two-piece door. I'm inside, its rather disappointing and not at all what the building looked like from outside. It's an empty church, there are wine-coloured cushions. Outside there is a pump, I'm lowering a pail to draw water so I can see my reflection" Author's Comment. Similar to what Britt Ekland said in her session) *"I have a very long nose, I don't see any people, but the houses are made of stone and the roofs are red. They appear to be Victorian. I feel I'm in Scotland".*

The newspaper goes on to state that Sean thought he was in the Scottish town of St Andrews, then, after some difficulty, he saw his life as a child. It was a life of squalor. Sean continued.

"My home is quite uncomfortable, and I sleep on the cold floor in a dark corner of the room. Now I can see my mother, she doesn't fit into these surroundings, she is wearing a hoop skirt. Its Dutch clothing and she has large round eyes and a very long nose".

At this point, Sean advanced further in time to 12 years of age and stated.

"I'm still in St Andrews, only I'm taller and I am wearing a black waistcoat. I work for the blacksmith. I soak the horseshoes in cold water after they come out of the fire. I don't see my parents anymore; I think they died of consumption".

Sean then moves forward in time, he is now 17 years of age and a bit of a ladies' man. He states.

"I'm really taken by a woman who owns the local shop. She stands behind the counter wearing a white bonnet and tweed skirt. I just want to stand next to her, she's much older than me but I know we are lovers. I spend a lot of time at her house. The romance lasts until I'm 20, I don't know why it finished".

But Sean isn't finished yet, he goes on to relate to the hypnotherapist about yet another lifetime he saw, this time in Africa. He states.

"I don't know why I'm here. I'm standing on the platform of a railway station watching labourers' work.

I feel like I belong with the kaffirs and black women in this community. I've gone native, sharing two huts with two separate women, they've both given birth to my sons".

At this point, Sean stated that he saw himself lying on the floor of a hut, he continued.

"I think I have just died. I can feel the ground. I see one of my women by me. I think I died from drinking a lot of liquor. They burned me. I can see two men putting me on a pile and setting me on fire. People come by and have a look at me and then wander off and then that's that".

We learn that after he had said these words, Sean opened his eyes, and seemed bemused. He did admit having always been attracted to black women in his present life and then jokingly said, *"But then I love all women, black, yellow and white".*

Author's Comment:

Well again we have to ask ourselves, could this recall not have been scripts from old movies that Sean had read and somehow, his mind constructed these elaborate scenes? It's a possibility. But then of course if this was the case, then this would be a global phenomenon as many people the world over claim similar and different past life experiences. Another famous actor who had his own past life vision revealed to him, was Klute star Donald Sutherland. In its article featured in The News of The World dated September 1981, we learned that actor Donald Sutherland believes that he once 'died'. The story goes that he was working on the movie Kelly's Heroes whilst enduring spinal meningitis when he collapsed. He stated:

"All they say about dying is true. Everything faded away and then there was a wonderful blue tunnel right down my body. There was a light at the bottom of the tunnel, and it seemed to go on forever. It was incredibly seductive. I had to use all the force in my personality to save my own life".

Donald remembers nurses and doctors standing at the end of his bed even though his eyes were closed. He continued.

"I could feel myself trying to run down my arms and move my fingers, but I couldn't do anything. I didn't sleep afterwards. I would wake up after three hours and just sit bolt upright. I guess I was afraid I was going to be dead if I slept too long".

SARAH'S ORDEAL AS A FRIGHTENING OLD WITCH

Staying with the subject of past lives. The News of The World presented another interesting case to its readers in November 1980. It concerned famous actress Sarah Miles, star of movies such as Ryan's Daughter (1970) and Hope and Glory (1987) Surprisingly this article did not say how Sarah went back into a past life, but I'm assuming that it was through hypnosis. Here is what she herself had to say about it.

"I'm a Witch. I have straggly hair, old black clothes, and I'm very old and have a stick. I'm not a bad person. People think I'm a Witch, but I'm really not. I'm a psychic healer before my time. I'm living alone in some kind of derelict castle, it's very old and very dirty. I can see myself beating down high nettles in the garden, they are stinging me as I walk towards the castle. I walk in, there's a big log fire in a huge hall and every kind of animal inside the hall.

There are greyhounds, foxhounds, deer. But what are they all doing inside the castle? Now I can see why I love animals. I care for them. My parents left me this castle and I have made it a home for animals. Everybody thinks that I'm very strange".

Sarah continued.

"I know where I am, I'm in Thaxted, Essex" (Author's Comment, near Sarah's birthplace) *"People are afraid of me, they throw sticks and rocks at me in the street, yet if their animals are ill, they bring them to me to heal. I once tried to help a little boy who was sick in the stomach. He died, and people blamed me, but it wasn't my fault. I see myself going into town, the streets are cobbled and dirty. I think it's about 1725, we get our news from the town crier. I can see an old man, Harry, a merchant. He talks to me at a polite distance, people are afraid of me. It's a lonely life, I have no friends, only the animals".*

After Sarah opened her eyes, she said that she was saddened at what she had seen and felt like her past life was similar to the life that she was leading now. She went onto say that she thinks that she is misunderstood today, just as she was in that past life. She concluded by saying.

"I'm also a healer in this life. When I touch people now, if they're sick, they become well. It's something that I've never quite understood, but I've always been able to do it".

PAST LIFE RECALL

In another one of my extensive news clippings, I came across two people who claimed past lives. The date of the newspaper was January 11th, 1981, but unfortunately, I did not record which newspaper it was.

Here is what it said.

18-year-old Schoolboy James McAvoy from Rainham in Kent England is convinced that the A level exams ahead are nothing compared to his testing time in an earlier life. James stated.

"I know for certain that I have been on Earth before and fought in the Crusades. I can see the whole thing clearly now. I can feel the desert in my blood, the whole atmosphere. I can see the gates of the Holy City of Jerusalem, and I know I've been there. I have seen it in dreams and visions over a period of years, and because of their frequency, I know it's true. This is not a period I have particularly studied at school, but whenever something connected to the Crusades comes up, or I read about it or visit a museum, I instantly feel that it's not new to me. I have seen it all and gone through it before".

The article continues with the testimony of Ronald Cooper from Basingstoke England, a stock controller manager with stationary giant, W.H. Smith. He stated to the newspaper that he had no difficulty in learning the French language as he believed that he had lived before as a Frenchman fighting for Napoleon at the battle of Waterloo. His recollection of his life with Bonaparte's army is uncanny. This feeling that he has lived before has given Ronald an all-consuming interest in the period, but it was not a happy time for him. He claims his subconscious memory told him that he had died in the epic battle, and he knows the exact spot and time. Ronald stated.

"Naturally, I felt that I had to visit the battle scene. When I did, I found it strikingly familiar. And because of my death at the time, also very depressing".

DRACULA WAS A HOLY ROMAN!

This was the title of an undated news cutting from my files which featured the famous actor Christopher Lee, who is of course, best known for his portrayals of vampire Count Dracula. Christopher was regressed to the 15th Century where he saw himself as a titled aristocrat in Rome. Christopher now takes up the story.

"I am standing before a Cardinal, or a Pope, and he is asking me about my journeyings. It has something to do with war for religious reasons. And he is also asking if the marriage for political reasons has been arranged".

At this point in the regression. Christopher suddenly stopped, and said in amazement, that he knew one of his ancestors had arranged the marriage of an Italian noble woman to a King of England. Later on in the regression, Christopher saw himself as a man of 70 lying on his death bed. Christopher again takes up the story.

"I don't see my burial, but now I see a plain stone with a coat of arms on it and the inscription, 'He served God and man'. I see my name, Francesco di Sarsanic, Duke of something. This is extraordinary because my grandfather's name, in this present life, was Francesco and he was the Marquis of Sarsanio."

CAN WE REALLY BE BORN AGAIN?

Growing up in Scotland with this fascination for the supernatural, I was pleased to see a programme on television dedicated to the paranormal which was hosted by Stewart Lamont.

This was in the days before video recorders, and I recall placing my small audio cassette recorder in front of the television to record the sounds of the programme which I would later play back and enjoy. Well in my newspaper files on the supernatural, I came across a large article of which Stewart provides not only his own experience of going under hypnosis where he had a past life but mentions a gentleman by the name of Norman Stewart who featured in his T.V. programme and who related his own past life experience. (Sadly, I didn't take note from which newspaper this came from or on what date.) Let us, however, start with the host of the T.V. programme, Stewart Lamont himself and how he was taken back to a past life. He stated.

"After a few sessions, hypnotist Leonard Wilder suggested that I drift back in time. It was like being sucked into a black whirlpool. A peaceful blackness descended. Gradually I became aware that my body was older and larger. There was a helmet on my head. I felt a belt and the skirt of a tunic beneath my waist. On my legs were woollen tights with leather bindings. Then the realisation hit me. I was a Viking; my name was Haakon. I was able to describe my surroundings and my family back in Norway. But despite this experience, I do not believe in re-incarnation".

However, there is puzzling evidence that some people have experiences in which they get paranormal information about 'past lives'. The existence of child prodigies is often taken as good evidence that we can live again. How else, it is argued, could they have acquired such powers of genius, except by being the reincarnation of a person who already possessed them? And it has been suggested that a person can choose when are where to be born again. Maria do Oliveiro, a Brazilian girl of 28, died after promising her friend Ida Lorenz, that she would be re-born as her daughter.

Ten months later, Ida gave birth to a girl, who, at the age of two and a half, gave detailed knowledge of Maria's life. And there is one example of a child dying and being reborn to its own parents".

"Signora Battista lived in Rome where her daughter Blanche was taught a distinctive cradle song by her French nannie. The little girl died, and the nannie moved abroad. Three years later, during pregnancy, Signora Battista had a dream in which Blanche told her of her intention to 'come back'. The new baby, a girl, never heard the old cradle song, but at the age of six began to sing it clearly. When her astonished parents asked her how she knew the song, she replied, *"It was in my head".* The article then presents the strange tale of Norman Stewart who firmly believes that he has lived before in the town of Strathaven Lanarkshire Scotland, between 1662 and 1722. Norman related that he had always felt drawn to this town and spent many holidays there. He even sketched a bridge, two castles, a prison, a church, and some other features which he claims he recalled from this past life. Then, with some help from his friends, he located each of these features, all in the Strathaven area. But what was the icing on the cake as far as Norman goes and provided him with proof positive, was when he uncovered a series of underground chambers. Until then, no one knew that they even existed. These chambers were so well hidden, they even would be hard to find accidentally. Yet Norman led his friends straight to them. Furthermore, the layout of the chambers corresponded to Norman's earlier sketches before the discovery. The article concluded with T.V. presenter Stewart Lamont's own belief and thoughts on what was behind some of these paranormal happenings. I'll only mention but part of what he said. He stated.

"It would be a foolish person who claimed to have the answer to the weird distortions of natural laws which we called 'psychic phenomena'.

But after examining the experience of many psychics and witnesses who claim no psychic powers whatsoever, I am forced to conclude that they are describing something real. But still, no one understands the laws of the supernatural. That should not surprise anyone. Isaac Newton did not know about electricity, and even his 'truths' had to be changed when Einstein came along. A decade ago, scientist suspected the human memory was like a computer. What we saw and experienced was stored in little signals in the brain. But research shows this picture is not correct. We look at a rose and smell it, but what the 'mind' registers is infinitely more complicated and mysterious than an electrical signal in the brain. The difference between the mind and the brain is a no man's land of knowledge. Whether the mind can exist independently from the brain is the next question. If it can, it would increase the chance that we survive death, taking our memories and dreams with us. The evidence seems to point that way. At the end of it all, psychic phenomena strengthen my belief in the mystery of creation and confirm my faith that there is and end and a purpose in life. To those who dismiss the whole thing as madness or lies, I would say what Lord McLeod said in describing a near miracle, he said" "If you think that's a coincidence, I hope you have a very dull life."

VAMPIRE BEAST ON LOOSE

This was the headline from the Scottish Sunday Mail newspaper of April 7th, 1991, and concerned itself with some kind of weird 'beast' that was killing sheep in the remote Highland Village of Kinlochewe, Wester Ross. Villagers started to find dead sheep in the fields at the end of May that year. Initial thoughts I dare say were of loose dogs, but the villagers soon found out that this could not be the case simply because the nine dead sheep that were found, were completely drained of blood, and had puncture wounds on their necks.

A vet (un-named) was sent for who lived 50 miles away in the town of Dingwall, and he stated,

"I have never seen anything like this before. It's quite a mystery. There was a puncture wound under each ear. These wounds were so definite we thought the sheep had been shot at first, but this is not the case. The attacks appear to be consistent with an animal with a large jaw span, and we are wondering if there is a large cat around".

The article goes on to say that a hotelier by the name of Mark Vincent, claimed to have spotted a large cat like footprint above the snow line in the nearby Ben Eighe Nature Reserve. He stated,

"My son Joss and I could hardly believe our eyes. The print measured at least two and a half inches across".

However, not all villagers believed that a big cat was responsible. Crofter Ewan MacLean was quoted as saying,

"It's possible the killer is an old fox with no back teeth, and therefore unable to eat flesh. It would drink the blood to survive because it can no longer chew".

And that was it, a short and sweet article. I bring it up here because here in the U.K. we are still inundated by sightings of big cats. And whilst admittedly this is not a paranormal thing, it is weird enough to bring it into our weird and wonderful stories. As for me, I believe that these are indeed big cats, exotic pets if you like, bought by exotic owners, who, after a period of time have somehow got fed up with them and released them into the wild, which of course, is a very dangerous thing to do. And maybe the reason why they didn't release them through either a local vet or local zoo, is that they have purchased them illegally and have no official paperwork for them, and of course, bringing them into the U.K. illegally without proper medication would result in a criminal charge.

CURSES

Are there such things as curses, or are they all baloney and make believe? In this section of the book, we'll take a look at some examples of worldwide curses.

THE STORY OF THE BUSBY STOOP CHAIR

The story goes that at the town of Thirsk, North Yorkshire there lived one Thomas Busby. Thomas was a man who enjoyed the odd drink or five, and was regularly seen in his favourite pub, sitting in his favourite chair. Now Busby was not a man to be trifled with, he was a petty thief, and was quick to lose his temper. It seems that he couldn't stay out of trouble and was always getting into fights with the locals. As fate would have it, it was due to his troublesome ways that cost him his life. The fatal events started in the summer of 1702, when Daniel Awety, who was Busby's father-in-law, riled Busby by sitting in his chair without permission or acknowledgment. This duly came to the attention of Busby, and upon entering the pub, saw Daniel sitting where he wasn't supposed to, in his favourite chair. What followed was a blazing row between the two men and fists were thrown. Sometime later that same night, Thomas Busby ended the life of his father-in-law by bludgeoning him to death with a hammer. Needless to say, a trial found Tom Busby guilty as charged, and the sentence was death by hanging on a gibbet which was to be erected outside the pub. But first, Thomas's body was to be covered in tar to help prolong its decomposition. Surprisingly, before he was hanged, there was a show of leniency by the judge, and he offered Thomas one final request. Busby chose to have a final drink. He insisted that his final drink would be taken sitting on his favourite chair. Then, just after he finished his last earthly drink, before he was led him off to his execution, he uttered the following words.

"Death shall come swiftly to anyone that dares to sit in my chair".

Victims of Thomas Busby

The first recorded victim of this apparent curse is an unnamed chimney sweep. Apparently, it was the first time that the chair had been used for quite some time. Now whether the chair had been taken away and stored we are not told. Moreover, as many years had passed, maybe the curse of the chair had been forgotten about. Well, the story goes that not long after finishing his break, and returning to work, this unfortunate chimney sweep fell off the roof to his death. It would appear that Busby's Stoop had claimed the first of its many victims. We then learn that over the course of the next couple of centuries, numerous people felt the need to dare one another to sit in this infamous chair. Most stayed well clear, but there were some who did not. For instance, during the Second World War there were a number of Canadian airmen from the nearby air base at Skipton-on-Swale who, after no doubt much goading, decided to accept the challenge from their fellow airmen. It's said that all who accepted this perilous challenge, never returned from the war, of course that could be put down to pure coincidence, millions of lives were lost in the war after all! Then, twenty years later, 1967 to be precise, two RAF pilots took on the chair's challenge and lost their lives when the car they were traveling in later hit a tree.

Next up to lose at chair roulette, was a bricklayer who was contracted to work on the pub one year. He noticed the chair tucked away in one corner of the basement and decided to rest on it. That very afternoon, he fell to his death. It would appear that nobody could use this chair and survive. History tells us that there were other deaths, one of which was a roofer who was working when the roof suddenly collapsed beneath him. Then there was a cleaning woman who stumbled onto the chair and later suffered an aneurysm. Then there was the unlucky delivery driver who, after sitting on this chair, crashed his delivery van between deliveries just one hour after sitting on the chair. It's claimed that in total, 63 people have lost their lives after sitting in this infamous chair. But again, it could all be down to pure coincidence, right!

Well coincidence or not, enough was enough, and the landlord of the pub which at the time was aptly named, 'The Busby Stoop Inn', decided to remove the chair and stored it away. He then contacted the Thirsk Museum and asked if they would take the chair off his hands. The museum were more than happy to take this chair off his hands, more so because of the tragic circumstances surrounding it. You can still see the chair today which is on public display in the Museum, but the museum are taking no chances, for they placed the chair six feet off the floor and now no one can sit in it unless of course you have a death wish and wait till the staff are not looking and you somehow bring the chair down from its confines and sit on it. Rumour has it, that Busby's ghost can still be seen wandering about the crossroads outside the former inn, which is now an Indian restaurant called, Jaipur Spice. But wait a minute, can this story really be true? Well doing research for this cursed chair, I uncovered the fact that there was a furniture historian who decided to examine this chair, and to his surprise, found that the chair had machine turned spindles, which in effect meant that the chair was not from the time of Thomas Busby.

18th-century chairs were made using a pole lathe. This furniture historian dated the chair to 1840, which was 138 years after Busby's execution.

THE ANGUISHED MAN

This is the name given to a painting by an unknown artist that is owned by Sean Robinson of England. Sean inherited the painting from his grandmother which she kept in her attic for 25 years. She told him that it was haunted and said that she used to see the dark figure of a man around her house. After she died, Sean brought it to his home. When he researched the painting, Sean found out that the painting was completed by an artist hours before he committed suicide. The artist even supposedly mixed his own blood into the painting. Then Sean left the painting in his basement for 10 years. When he took it out of the basement in 2010, and hung it up at home, that's when all the 'spooky' stuff happened. Shortly after hanging it up, various family members saw the dark figure of a man. They would hear strange noises and moaning, and Sean's son was forcibly pushed down the stairs by an invisible force, thankfully coming to no harm. The family also started to hear weird noises. Doors would shut on their own accord. It got so bad that Sean recorded a time-lapse video to catch the painting in the act, and he wasn't disappointed. On his You Tube Channel, you can see the painting, which is resting against a wall, fall over. What appears to be a wispy smoke like substance moves from left to right in front of the camera. These segments were taken in an unoccupied bedroom at night. Sean has invited various paranormal teams into his house to investigate and holds vigils next to the painting. On one occasion as Sean got to the top of his stairs at home, he was surrounded by a strange mist which he described like a thick fog. He initially thought that there was a fire in the house such was this smokey fog like substance. Then, as suddenly as it came, it vanished A psychiatrist surprisingly said that the painting was a portal which could allow people to connect to, or enter into, another dimension, be it spiritual, astral, or out in space. There was even talk of the story surrounding the painting being made into a movie, but that never happened.

There are allegedly hundreds of so called 'cursed' or haunted paintings. Back in the 1950's, an Italian painter by the name of Giovanni Bragolin. (1911–1981). Painted a series of paintings which showed young children with tears in their eyes. It would appear that some of his paintings have caused fear and alarm to some.

THE CRYING BOY PAINTINGS

The Crying Boy Paintings got widespread popularity due to the coverage they received in the British newspaper The Sun. dated 5th September 1985. There was a report in the paper that there had been several devastating house fires that had claimed lives, and while the entire houses were burnt down, only the picture of the crying boy remained unscathed. The story goes that by the end of November, readers of the Sun newspaper believed that this painting was cursed. It even got to the stage where the Sun newspaper organised mass bonfires to get rid of the paintings that had been sent in by readers. According to the Sun newspaper and also the exemplore web site (link in the reference section) it stated the following tragedies from people who had hung this painting up in their home.

• A woman in Surrey lost her house to a fire six months after buying the painting.

• Two sisters in Kilburn had fires in their homes after buying a copy of the painting. One sister even claimed to have seen her painting sway backwards and forwards on the wall.

• A concerned woman on the Isle of Wight attempted to burn her painting without success and then went on to suffer a run of bad luck.

• A gentleman in Nottingham who possessed a print of the painting lost his home, and his family was injured.

• A pizza parlour in Norfolk was destroyed, including every painting on its walls 'except' for The Crying Boy painting.

Indeed, such was the fear of the curse, that the Sun newspaper even stated that a number of sane and rational firefighters, refused to have a copy of The Crying Boy in their homes. After this, it was goodnight, Vienna for the painting. Sales diminished and the end was nigh for the painting.

But wait, this is all a joke, isn't it? There can't be such a thing as a cursed painting. Well one chap felt so, and that was Steve Punt. Wikipedia tells us that Steve who, amongst other things, is a writer and comedian, decided to take a closer look at this painting and its spooky reputation. Steve worked along with a BBC Radio 4 production called Punt PI. And wait for it, wait for it, after testing was conducted at the Building Research Establishment, (BRE) Wikipedia didn't say which one, but the (BRE) has its headquarters in Garston, Hertfordshire, England.

They also have sites in Glasgow and Swansea. Anyway, after testing they said that many prints of the painting had been treated with a varnish which contained fire retardant. Now the string holding the painting was of course just string. It hadn't been treated. The result being that the string holding the painting to the wall would be the first to deteriorate. This of course would result in the painting landing face down on the floor and thus being protected. Ah, don't you just love science and logical explanations. But then again!

THE CHAINED OAK

There is an ancient Oak Tree near the village of Alton, Staffordshire, England, which to some is undoubtedly one of the scariest looking trees you'll ever look at. And why would this be, I hear you ask? Well partly because, would you believe, it's covered in huge, rusted chains. So dear reader, how did this come about? Well, legend has it, that the Earl of Shrewsbury who lived at the grand estate of Alton Towers, was travelling back home one evening when his carriage was stopped by a lone beggar woman. The grubby old lady asked the Earl for a penny and, when he rudely dismissed her, cursed the Earl, stating that for every branch that fell from the old oak tree, a member of his family would perish. Here is where it gets interesting. That night, a great storm ripped one of the limbs from the tree and, by the morning, one of the Earl's family members had passed away horribly. The frightened nobleman then ordered his servants that the Oak should be bound in chains so that no more branches could fall. As the years have rolled by parts of this ancient oak tree have withered away and parts of it have collapsed. An ancient curse then, or an ancient myth? You decide.

THE HAUNTED LEDGER

I've said many times before, that objects of all descriptions, can be haunted. If an object, be it a chair, a medal, a car, indeed anything that a human being has been in touch with for a long time, can leave that individual's own 'vibrations and 'emanations' on that item for ever. This is why some people see ghosts sitting in an old chair. That chair at one time would have belonged to a person who enjoyed sitting in that chair, perhaps reading his newspaper, or reading a book. To all intents and purposes, it was part of him. Along comes an individual with psychic and mediumistic abilities, and they can 'see' that man, that spirit, still sitting in his chair. We call this a 'residual haunting'. In other words, it's like an old video tape that has been played over and over again, till it is more or less lost its colour and playability. Some psychics, have the ability to hold an object given to them by someone else, and proceed to tell that person who once owned the object all about that person. We call this psychometry. It would appear with our next case, that an old shop ledger still retained its owner's persona and wanted something done about it, as we will now see.

The object was a haunted 1915 shop ledger which was the problem. There was a jeweller's shop called 'Shorland Fooks' which stood in the city of Brighton in England for many years, until it was demolished in the 1980's. During the course of the demolition, an old shop ledger was discovered by Tony Benyovits bricked up in one of the walls. Knowing that it was a piece of history, albeit a local one, he decided to keep it, and he took it to his home in Maidstone Kent, which was roughly 65 miles away from Brighton. No sooner had he done so, than strange things started to happen in the family home. Tony's daughter, Josephine stated that bizarre images appeared in her rug. These included a group of men, women, and children, and even a soldier with a horse! There were also strange voices, and spirit manifestations. However, the most peculiar, if not interesting thing that the spirits had to say to Josephine, was that she simply had to return this ledger back to Brighton for the centenary of the diary's first entry, which was December 1915. Clearly, she and her father Tony, felt that they couldn't hold onto this item any longer, more so due to the disturbing paranormal events that were transpiring in the family home. So, she placed a call into Preston Manor in Brighton which itself is reputedly haunted by a lady in white and a lady in grey who silently flit throughout the property. The manor also has its fair share of ghostly voices heard by the staff and visitors alike.

The phone call was taken by venue officer, Paula Wrightson who is reported as saying.

"At first, we weren't sure whether we'd take this apparently ordinary, 100-year-old shop ledger. But the family impressed on us quite how scared they were of having the book in their keeping. When I had a phone conversation with Josephine, she seemed petrified. It sat on my desk for a couple of weeks. During that time, I had a meeting with a spiritual medium who was taking part in an event here, and she said she felt the book had 'bad things' emanating from it. For me personally, the most interesting aspect of the book, is that the entries show what was sold in the shop exactly 100 years ago. But it remains to be seen whether there's more to it than that."

It's not reported if the hauntings associated with the book, have now stopped.

Staying with curses. Famous British actress Joan Collins turned down a movie role for the Curse of Tutankhamun. So stated the News of The World newspaper from November 1980. It stated that Joan was offered the role but decided to consult her astrologer to see if she should do it, but her astrologer stated. *"Don't do it. There are bad associations"* On this advice, Joan turned down the movie and would later learn that actor Ian McShane broke his leg during filming and that there were other injuries to various cast members and crew. Curse, or coincidence?

ESP. TELEPATHY AND CLAIRVOYANCE

In this section, we will take a look at a number of incidents in which people from all walks of life, from the rich and famous to the man and woman in the street, all of whom have had bizarre ESP (Extrasensory Perception) visions of danger and the future. We will also look at telepathy and clairvoyance. See what you make of these. For those not in the know, ESP is the ability to gain information without using any of the five traditional senses which are, taste, touch, sight, smell, and hearing. As for telepathy and clairvoyance, these, to a degree, are similar to ESP. Clairvoyance, also known as 'second sight', implies that some people with this ability, can see events that happen far away without having any previous knowledge of the event. Telepathy is a mental communication between two or more people and has provided in most instances, outstanding results.

ROD SAW ELTON IN DANGER

This was the headline from the News of The World dated November 1980. Apparently, Rod Stewart a firm believer in ESP (Extra Sensory Perception), had a premonition in November 1978 that fellow artist and friend, Elton John was about to have a heart attack. Rod mentioned this to his wife Alana, and both found out a week later that Elton had collapsed, not through a heart attack that Rod had sensed, but due to exhaustion through over work as stated by Elton's doctor.

MICHAEL HAD VISIONS AND HEARD VOICES

So stated the headline from the Scottish Sunday Mail of November 1980 when over a few weeks they featured a few pages devoted to the paranormal titled, 'Supernatural File.' This particular headline concerned the paranormal experiences of the late well-known actor and British comedian Michael Bentine CBE. (26th January 1922 – 26th November 1996) Michael is more well known to fans of the Goon show which featured the comical geniuses of Spike

Milligan, Harry Secombe, and Peter Sellers. In this piece written by Maureen Lawless, she goes on to state numerous bizarre paranormal experiences of our loved comedian. Michael saw the death of his eldest son, Gus (12), weeks before it happened and received strange messages hours before his friend Airey Neave MP was killed by an IRA bomb. Michael relates,

"One day Gus was lying on the floor laughing and he suddenly changed to a corpse in front of my eyes. Then I saw a light aeroplane stall and plunge to the ground. I knew it was precognition (foreknowledge of an event yet to happen). I warned Gus not to fly again".

Sadly Gus (21) did not heed his dad's warning, and, along with a friend Andy, crashed their plane into some woods in Hampshire, the wreckage of which, was hidden for nine weeks. Michael takes up the story,

"Forty-eight hours after he went missing, I was walking in the garden in despair. Then there was a touch on my arm, and I heard Gus say, "Dreadfully sorry Daddy. It wasn't Andy's fault the machine went wrong. They will find us when the leaves fall".

And when those autumn leaves did eventually fall, the wreckage was found. As for the strange experience surrounding Michael's friend Airey Neave. Michael states,

"It was March last year 1979, I was awakened in the middle of the night by a voice saying, 'Blood sacrifice'. Six times the words were repeated, each time I was dozing off. I took it to be a grim warning and thought of my daughter about to fly to South Africa. She had already taken off.

I phoned South Africa and learned that she had arrived safely. Ten minutes later, we heard of Airey Neave's murder. Immediately 'Blood sacrifice' shot through my mind, followed by, 'And all the trumpets sounded for him on the other side'. At the memorial service, the Minister actually said those last words".

Four further strange E.S.P. incidents were featured in the News of the World newspaper dated January 1981. First up was Pamela Vezey, who played Kathleen Brown in the well-known soap serial, Crossroads which was big in the 1980's. She was quoted as saying that she was listening to a lecture in a drama school when she suddenly had a vision. She stated.

"Suddenly I saw a television screen, on it, my mother was being attacked by a dog. She was frightened and calling my name. That evening when I phoned my mother, she sounded strained, and told me that my dog had attacked her. I said, was it at 3 o clock? And she said it was. That was exactly the time I had my vision in the lecture room. I can only believe that though we were miles apart, she had communicated her danger to me through telepathy".

Well know American T.V. star, Robert Stack who played Elliot Ness in the Untouchables series, also believes very strongly in telepathy and ESP. He stated that during the filming of the spoof disaster movie Airplane, he had a vision of trouble involving the film's director. Robert stated.

"That day the director arrived late for the filming, and I told him you were late because your car caught fire. He had to agree, that was just what had happened"!

Another famous actor, American David Janssen who also starred in the hit Television series the Fugitive, also had a bizarre premonition, a premonition that proved to be true as it was fatal. The story goes that David phoned the Hollywood psychic Katrina Kinkade and told her that he saw himself in a dream being carried from his house after a heart attack and then being buried. He asked Katrina what his dream meant as it had really shaken him up, whereupon Katrina told him that he should have a medical check up. Two days later, David Janssen died of a heart attack.

Our next telepathic story comes not from the individual concerned, rather, it came from his mother as a warning to her son. Erik Estrada, star of the hit American television series CHIPS, took a phone call from his mother Carmen one day in which she told him to be careful while riding his motorbike as she had seen him crash his bike in a dream. In the News of the World article dated November 1980, Erik's mother stated.

"Three nights before the accident I'd been dreaming that Erik was in my house. I saw him looking in the papers, looking for a phone number. And I had this feeling that something was going to happen to him".

Carmen, who was 3,000 miles away, was really concerned about her son. Erik promised his mother than he would be OK and would be careful whilst riding his bike. Well, needless to say, that didn't happen. Erik did crash his bike, although the article does not tell us when that accident occurred after his mother's dream. Erik told the newspaper.

"I was lying on my back in hospital and the family were at the foot of the bed. I felt myself going out of my body and walking away from the bed and the family

didn't seem to realise. Then I turned around and saw my body on the bed, and I thought, wow, only 30 years old, too young to die, so I just went back".

Telepathy and seeing the future can be quite disconcerting at times as the following story now illustrates.

THE GRIM NEWS HE SAW COMING

From a newspaper dated January 1981 (paper unknown) we learn of the visions of one Stewart Cummings an antique dealer from Mapperley, Nottingham. Stewart has had lots of premonitions throughout his life, and in this short article he related but a few of them. One day when he was eight years of age and lying in bed due to Tuberculosis, he heard the sound of the postman walking outside on the gravel path. He had this horrible feeling that the postman was bringing him some news which he would find upsetting. He was correct. The letter came from a Christian lady who had been looking in on him from time to time and who had helped to ease his discomfort. The letter went on to say that due to family difficulties, this lady could no longer care for him. Stewart now takes up the story.

"Since then, I have often predicted the future. A vision of the Algerian earthquake came to me hours before it happened while I was eating. I could see the devastation, death, and suffering. But I knew nothing could be done to alter things. I was with a friend when I saw Charlie Chaplin's death. I suddenly blurted out, "The face of a massive international star will appear on the television tomorrow, it will be his death announcement". The next day the death of Charlie Chaplin was broadcast to the world. When this feeling overcomes me, the hairs on my hands and arms stand up rigid".

PSYCHIC WARNING SAVED BIONIC WOMAN'S LIFE

The following concerns former actress Lindsay Wagner who refused to board a waiting jet and escaped America's worst air disaster.

The good thing about Clairvoyance and premonitions, is that one can decide whether or not to heed a warning, and in our following case, this warning saved a young actresses' life. From the Weekend Magazine dated 12th to 18th November 1980 I take the following mind-blowing tale. 31-year-old American actress Lindsay Wagner along with her mother Marilyn, had been waiting to depart on a flight from Los Angeles when Lindsay suddenly had an overpowering feeling of disaster. She just knew that she and her mother 'should not' get on the aircraft, an American Airlines DC-10. She stated.

"I started shaking and my mother who has known about my psychic experiences since I was a child, gave in and agreed to postpone our flight. God how I wish I'd told everybody not to travel on it, but you just feel its hysteria".

All 273 people on board that flight were killed. We learn that twice married Lindsay had her very first psychic experience aged just 14. She stated.

"I saw myself playing a certain role on the screen. I had a clear picture of the house where I would live with my first husband, and I could see a little boy in my life. I got married eight years later and we went house hunting, and one agent took us to a house which was the one which I had seen as a little girl. I didn't need to look inside; I knew exactly what it was like. Unfortunately, the marriage lasted only two months and we didn't live there long.

But soon after moving in, I was offered a role in my first film, 'Two People' with Peter Fonda, I played the mother of a four-year-old boy"

Lindsay went on to tell the writer of this article, Frank Garvan, that she also had another strange experience at an open-air music festival in California, she stated.

"I was there with some friends, and everything seemed lovely until I started to get this awful panicky feeling. My friends told me not to be so silly, but I felt so ill at ease that I had to leave. Next morning, I was told that there had been a police raid soon after I had left, and all my friends had been taken to jail on suspicion of possessing drugs".

On another occasion she had yet another psychic incident where she experienced the suffering of one of her girlfriends who was seriously ill in hospital. She states.

"I sat outside her room, suddenly I appeared to pass out and came out of it just as somebody was calling a doctor. I know that I had been in a trance. I went through strange abstract nightmares. Later, my girlfriend described to me the exact same nightmarish sleep she had experienced that night. I don't have control over these experiences, they just happen. One day, during the time I was working long hard hours making the 'Bionic Woman', I lay down exhausted at home. To my amazement, I floated out of my body and saw myself from above lying on the couch. I had no concept of time or reality. When I finally came to, I was being shaken by a friend who told me that nobody had been able to make contact with me for the previous two days".

THE NIGHTMARE THAT CAME TRUE

Whilst heeding prophetic psychic warnings can save your life, as in the Lindsay Wager case mentioned above, it can be different when you receive a psychic vision, and you don't know whether you should act on it. Will you be believed, or will people laugh at you and think you should be held in a secure unit? That's the dilemma that occurred to one David Booth. This account also comes from the Weekend magazine of 12th to 18th November 1980.

We learn that psychic David Booth (26) from Cincinnati had been having a series of nightmares of a plane crash. In his dreams he saw a jet airliner smash into the ground and burst into flames. Then, just 10 days before this actual crash May 25th, 1979, he had the dream again. David now takes up the story.

"In the dreams I immediately knew there was something wrong with the jet's engines, they weren't making enough noise. It looked as if it was trying to land, but instead it banked, flipped over, and smashed into the ground nose first. There was a tremendous explosion of flames shooting 200ft in the air with clouds of black smoke, it was deafening. I've never had a dream that vivid or terrifying, it was like I was really there, but I couldn't reach out and touch anything. I did everything to stop sleeping from then on. I'd watch T.V. until 2am. One night I got drunk, if I didn't go to sleep, I wouldn't dream I told myself".

But still nothing worked, David was still having these nightmarish visions. Eventually he knew that he just had to call American Airlines and the Federal

Aviation Administration. Ray Pinkerton, assistant sector manager at Cincinnati Airport was on record as saying.

"It didn't sound like a prank, but I could do nothing".

Needless to say, David Booth's vision of an airline crashing into the ground proved all too true as Flight 191 crashed in a fireball at Chicago's O'Hare International Airport. Assistant sector manager Ray Pinkerton continued.

"It shook me. The crash had a number of uncanny similarities to Booth's dreams. He identified the airline. He said the aircraft didn't sound right. It couldn't have sounded right as one engine had fallen off. He told me it turned over and dived into the ground, which is exactly what happened, it's uncanny".

Paul Williams an aviation administrator also stated that Booth kept blaming himself afterwards. Paul further stated.

"He felt as if he had been singled out from every person in the world to be given a picture of what would happen, and he had no means to prevent it".

MARC BOLAN TALKS FROM THE GRAVE

Growing up, I was a big fan of Marc Bolan and T. Rex and always tried to catch his appearances on Top of the Pops back in the 1970's, his glam rock look, was big at the time although admittedly I myself didn't stretch to wearing the make-up and silvery clothes. (I did have the platform shoes however!) In a sensational story in the News of the World paper from November 1980, the reader learned that Marc had spoken from the grave!

Staff writer Michael Parker told us that Marc, who died in 1977, had spoken through a medium. Apparently, Marc's Road manager, Mick O'Halloran who spent nine years with the star, contacted him through a medium.

Mick (38) stated that Marc had contacted him through famous medium, Ronald Hearn during a public demonstration near his home at Ryde, on the Isle of Wight. Mick said that the most astonishing thing was the stance adopted by Mr Hearn while Marc was communicating through him. Mick stated.

"It was exactly the way Marc used to stand on stage. It was so uncanny that you could have replaced Mr Hearn's head with Marc's, and it would have been him to a T. Mr Hearn told me things in which no way could have been public knowledge. He spoke of one incident when I arrived in an American hotel wearing a huge pink wig and Marc fell about laughing. And he recalled two occasions when Marc narrowly missed being electrocuted and crushed to death. I didn't know that, but when I mentioned it to a fan, she said that Marc's father told her the police recovered a half-finished tape after his death. It was all quite uncanny. It sounds fantastic, but it's true and I have no doubt that he will try to get through to me again. He wants his fans to know that he is still very much alive and to thank them for their support and loyalty. I am positive that Marc was speaking through Mr Hearn".

Author's Comment:

Whilst I am a firm believer in Life after death due to the evidence that I personally have looked at over 40 years of research, I am still very sceptical to certain claims, more so the claims regarding famous personalities. I'm not saying that the evidence coming through Mr Hearn was false, it may well have been correct, but there are a number of psychics out there who are more than happy to pull the wool over one's eyes and get paid handsomely for the privilege. All I'm saying is, be careful. And to all paranormal researchers out there. Check the facts, is all as it seems?

Well known and loved television star of the 1970's and 80's, Larry Grayson, was told he would make the big time, years before he found fame. In the magazine Titbits (Date not taken down) columnist Barry Ward presents the story of how Larry who was appearing way down the bill at a variety show in Paignton Devon, England, decided between rehearsals, to take a bus into the neighbouring town of Brixham where he ended up consulting the services of Clairvoyant Mrs Helen Edden, better known as, Madame Credo. The article relates that Helen recalled that first time she saw him, that she could tell straight away he was in show business. She stated:

"I could tell straight away that he was in show business, but at the same time I had this very strong feeling that he was set for better things. I knew he was about to become a star and I told him so. I distinctly remember saying to him, 'Your name will be a household word".

Four months later, in January 1972, Larry was offered his first big break, a spot on a Saturday night T.V. variety show. He made an immediate impact so much so, that he soon got his own show called 'Shut That Door' on I.T.V. In a later visit to the psychic, she told him that he would soon take over from Bruce Forsyth on the hit T.V. show, 'The Generation Game', two years before it actually happened! Larry was quoted as saying:

"My show business career has turned out exactly as Helen said it would. At times I still can't believe this has happened to me"

American Actress and model, Valerie Ritchie Perrine who starred as Honey Bruce in the 1974 film Lenny, woke in the middle of the night with the feeling that her aunt had died. (Date and newspaper not taken down) She then was surprised to see her aunt standing in her room who then spoke to her saying that her legs which had been troubling her, didn't hurt anymore. We are not told how this episode ended other than the very next day, Valerie received a telegram stating that her aunt had died in the night.

THE NIGHT LYNSEY SAW THE LIGHT

English singer songwriter, Lynsey de Paul (11th June 1948 – 1st October 2014) had her own paranormal encounter back in the 1970's as the News of the World reported in November 1980. Here is what she had to say.

"It was in 1977 when I was recording Rock Bottom for the Eurovision Song Contest. With me was my manager, Mike Moran, and a sound engineer. Just after 3:00am, we began to hear what's known as a white noise, the kind of crackling sound you hear when there is interference on a radio. It gradually became so loud that I had to take my earphones off. The engineer was baffled finding nothing wrong with the equipment. When the sound became louder, we all got alarmed. Then suddenly this enormous triangle of white light appeared in the middle of the room. I felt pressure on me from head to foot as though someone had placed an enormous hand on me. I was terrified and burst out crying. The two men with me were also scared. We all saw the light, but I was the only one who experienced that feeling of pressure. The light just disappeared in front of us, and when I recovered, I said, 'have we got a ghost'? The engineer gave me a strange look and told us about strange happenings in the men's loos at this studio.

Apparently, people kept complaining of sharp jabs in the back when they went to the loo, although there never appeared to be anyone there. Sometime later, I met Michael Bentine who is an expert on the paranormal, he explained to me that the white light was a friendly thing, a manifestation of energy that went back as far as the Druids".

DAD BLAMES SPIRITS FOR GIRL'S DEATH

So stated the Scottish newspaper the Daily Record of 27th November 1980. The death of losing your child is always tragic and the grief and heartbreak it can bring can be soul destroying, but this particular death proved more mysterious than any other as the following report will show.

At an inquest into the death of three-year-old Cassandra Wickenden held at Birmingham England, a claim by the father of the child raised quite a controversy. The child's father, Ray Wickenden, claimed that his daughter's death was caused by evil spirits, and that the phantom of a man had been seen in their house having been attracted by his daughter's presence. He further related that a Vicar had conducted an exorcism at the house but his three-year-old daughter had later called the phantom back so that she could play with him. The child's father went on to relate his daughter's strange powers by saying that when she stared at household objects, they would suddenly fall to the ground. She could also move objects in the home just by looking at them. As for her death, he believed that she had started a fire in her bedroom. When the fire took hold, the child's father had fought his way through dense smoke to her room and managed to drop her out of a window down to his wife who was standing outside, sadly she was pronounced dead.

The coroner in the case, Dr Richard Whittington, recorded an open verdict, and would not accept Mr Wickenden's theory about how the fire started. He further stated that although the cause of the fire was unknown, the most likely cause was a cigarette left burning in the room next to the child. However, Cassandra's mother Stephanie stated.

"Nobody had been up there all day. Why don't you believe us"?

After the coroner's verdict, the parents of Cassandra consulted a medium of which Stephanie later was reported as saying.

"The coroner's verdict has put a cloud over our heads. We want to see if we can get the case reopened".

OFFICIAL. YOUR LIFE 'REALLY IS' IN YOUR HANDS

This was the headline of the Scottish Sun newspaper of Tuesday July 24th, 1990, and would go on to state that doctors have now backed up and confirmed that people's lifelines on their hands, really do dictate the life span of that individual. The story goes that a number of doctors examined 100 corpses and based on their lifelines on their hands, corresponded at what age they died! Medics, Paul Newrick, Edwina Affie, and Roger Corrall, decided to look into this seemingly old wife's tale in their study at Bristol's Royal Infirmary. Their findings eventually found their way into the August edition of the prestigious Journal of the Royal Society of Medicine. It was stated that there was a highly significant association between the length of the lifeline and the age at death. The doctors measured the hands from the corpses of 63 men and 37 women and they found a strong statistical correlation particularly on the right hand at death.

They doctors went on to state that if their findings were real, and not merely by chance, then they would appear to support traditional beliefs.

The article finished by some comments that the doctors allegedly made to the newspaper, (comments which I don't believe they said even in jest) but here is what the doctors are alleged to have said.

"The findings could save money for the NHS. A glance at the hands to see whether an illness is a patient's last, could dispense with costly blood tests and X rays. Lifeline measurements are far cheaper than current medical screening, and lucky individuals would be spared the tedium of altering their lifestyle or taking treatment".

SEEING IS BELIEVING

The following article I didn't record the newspaper's name or date it appeared. Nevertheless, it's of interest to be presented here, as it concerns what could be a case of miraculous psychic healing. See what you make of this.

Doctors can't explain it, but 46-year-old Gloria Hughes of Miami Florida knows what cured her blindness, divine intervention. Gloria was blind for two years after a stroke. And then friends took her out to Sunday service at the tiny Solomon Bridge Church of God near Douglas Georgia. Although not particularly religious herself, what followed has made even her doctors talk about miracles. The preacher, Reverend Grady Seawright, unexpectantly called her name saying,

"God's going to do something for this woman tonight".

349

He anointed her forehead with oil. Gloria now takes up the story.

"The minute he touched me it felt like a bolt of electricity shot through me and I collapsed to the floor. My head was pounding, and I thought I was going to have another stroke. My eyes began to ache horribly, and I put my hands over them. When I took them away and opened my eyes, I saw a man standing over me. I shut my eyes again in disbelief, but when I opened them a second time, I could still 'see'".

Dr William Julius who has treated Gloria for 10 years, stated.

"I have never seen a recovery like this one before. As I told Gloria, there must be a God somewhere rooting for her".

Working in the field of the paranormal one hears many unusual stories, for this subject is as wide and diverse with many stories which tax one's mind, none more so I guess that the one that I am about to relate to you.

HAVING A GHOST FOR 25 YEARS!

Scottish actress Adrienne Corri (13th November 1930 – 13th March 2016) has had her own share of supernatural occurrences so stated the Scottish Sunday Mail article on January 11th, 1981. We learn that Clockwork Orange star Adrienne, had been living with a ghost in her house for 25 years! She stated,

"He's very friendly, and the house has such a nice atmosphere that I wouldn't like to try and get rid of him.

Apart from crashing about, he opens doors, and there were times when a picture would fly across the hallway. I shifted it to another wall, and it hasn't moved since.

The only time I get annoyed, was when he persistently threw my bedroom door open. I became so short of sleep, that I used to throw books in the direction I thought he might be in".

DIANE FELT TALONS GRIP HER THROAT

The following experience was featured in a Scottish newspaper, sadly I didn't take note of the newspaper or the date. What I do know, is that it featured amongst my newspaper cuttings from the 1980's, so certainly it's from that time frame. This was quite a serious and disturbing incident and not something that I'm sure you or I would like to experience. Here is what happened.

Mrs Diane Samat of Garthdee, Aberdeen Scotland had a ghostly experience back in 1976 that she would never forget. It's one of those rare ghostly experiences that you certainly don't want to encounter yourself. Indeed, I covered these ghostly attacks in one of my previous books, (Paranormal Case Files of Great Britain Volume 2) available on Amazon. The following case is clearly within that category. Diane was lying in bed when she was astonished to see the figure of a menacing old woman moving towards her. She appeared gaunt and had her arms outstretched displaying 'talon like' hands. No doubt in terror, Diane looked towards her husband who was sleeping peacefully beside her. Suddenly these talon-like hands grabbed Diane by her throat and started to squeeze tightly. All Diane could hear was the gurgling sounds coming from her own throat as the life was being squeezed out of her.

Incredibly her husband lay undisturbed by this scene of terror being played out in front of him. Then suddenly the talon like fingers from this old woman released their grip and this old woman turned away with a sardonic sneer.

Diane somehow knew that this old woman was communicating with her, as she heard (it doesn't say in the newspaper if it was vocally out loud or in her head) the words,

"And now you'll believe in ghosts".

At this point Diane managed to let out a blood curdling scream which thankfully awoke her husband, at which point she saw this old woman's figure suddenly disappear. Diane then related to her husband what she saw, and he instantly recognised the figure of that of his grandmother who, he stated, was a strong-willed woman, now dead, and who had brought him up in Malacca, Malaysia. Apparently, his grandmother was very jealous and possessive in life and had exercised a strong influence on him as a young child. For several days after this horrific experience, Diane had a sore throat where she had been grabbed but thankfully, that was a 'one off' experience and the old woman never returned.

Author's Comment:

With a scenario like this, I would have been inclined to initially believe that this was what's called a hypnopompic hallucination, which effectively means that one can experience a vivid dreamlike situation just as they are falling asleep. This condition is usually very frightening and can seem very real to the person who is experiencing it. They are usually put down to vivid nightmares. What of course makes this scenario different from these other hypnopompic experiences, is of course the fact of what Diane related to her husband and her sore throat afterwards. But of course, the psychologist would say that Diane had seen a photograph of her husband's grandmother, or indeed that he had mentioned her in passing of how she was controlling and manipulative, and somehow Diane had just dreamt up this scenario putting everything in place that she had learned about this woman. This effectively came out in a bizarre powerful dream. But then again!

There are many variations of ghostly sightings, some are felt, some are seen, some are smelled, but there are times when the individual does not see or sense a ghost but still thinks that there might be something amiss. This was the case with English actress Adrienne Posta, star of the movie, 'To Sir with Love' (1967) as stated by the News of the World, January 11th, 1981. Her problems began with her toaster!

No matter how many times she put bread in the toaster or bread under the grill, nothing happened. Repair men could not find any problem, and yet the problem persisted. The toaster worked fine when she took it to her mother's house. What on Earth could be wrong she thought. Deciding that it must be something down to a spirit, she called in the services of Spiritualist Robin Stevens. Adrienne takes up the story.

"He sensed the presence of an old lady who formerly lived in the house and still felt possessive about it. And she disapproved of my wearing make up and burning bread which, she regarded as the stuff of life. Robin called up the old lady's spirit and told her to go with him. Afterwards the toaster and grill worked perfectly. But I felt rotten about turning that old lady out of her house".

AUNT EMILY LOOKED IN ON HER WAY TO HEAVEN

The following account from one of my newspaper accounts dated January 1981 *(I did not record the newspaper)* gives a wonderful account of a woman seeing her dead aunty after she had died. Here is what happened.

It was a few minutes to midnight when Mrs Mavis Martin (49) climbed into bed. Her children had gone down with measles and due to looking after them, didn't have the time to visit her favourite aunt in hospital. Just before she fell to sleep, she heard the distinct sound of footsteps in the living room of which she and her husband decided to get up and have a look. What they saw in the living room would remain with them both for the rest of their lives. Mrs Martin takes up the story.

"Standing the living room in her favourite dress was Aunt Emily. She seemed fussed and worried, but she smiled as she said, "Buggerlugs why didn't you come and see me tonight"?

Mrs Martin continued:

"It wasn't said in an aggressive tone, more appealing. I wasn't frightened, but before I could answer, Aunt Emily just faded away. We decided to let the matter rest for the night and phone her son first thing in the morning. Early next morning before I had the chance to phone, her son was on the doorstep. He told me his mother had died at three minutes to twelve. I automatically replied, "I know". He just burst into tears and came inside. I told him what had happened the previous night and then he told me what had gone on at the hospital. The whole family were there, and auntie had asked for me.

The family told her the children had measles and she accepted it. She didn't remain conscious much longer and deteriorated rapidly, she was only about 64. I've tried to rationalise about what happened, but it's impossible. After all, my husband saw her too.

I'm convinced Aunt Emily loved me so much that she couldn't leave this life without seeing me first. If I couldn't come to her, then she decided to come to me. I truly believe it and I am now content".

The article then goes on to present two further cases where people had encountered a ghost. First up was English actress Debbie Watling who stated.

"I was about eight years old when I first heard strange noises and footsteps. Since then, I've been aware of the ghost. I often hear my name called, and I once saw the face of a pretty girl on the wall. The only time I've been worried was when a hand grabbed mine and tried to pull me out of bed. That was a bit scary".

Debbie's account was followed by actress Elke Sommer who told the newspaper that not only did she share her Beverley Hills house with husband Joe Hyams, but she also shared it with a ghost! She stated.

"Every night we'd hear strange sounds from the dining room. One night we heard a pounding on the bedroom door. Joe unlocked it and smoke poured into the bedroom. The ghost haunted dining room was on fire. Several mediums later said that a spirit started the fire and then warned us".

GHOST HAUNTS CAR'S BACK SEAT

From the Scottish Sun newspaper of July 1986, I give you the following. This story concerns a dead car owner who, it would seem, didn't want to leave his prized possession.

Ben Gale (41) and his wife Julie decided that they needed to buy a new car, and after looking around they decided to buy a Riley Elf. All was well until their friends kept asking them who was the strange man sitting in the back of their car, thinking it all a big joke Ben and his wife laughed it off until one day he

took a photograph of the car as he now wanted to sell it, and the best way to do this was to feature it in the 'For Sale' column in his local newspaper at Eckington near Chesterfield Derbyshire England. And lo and behold, when he looked at the picture he took, there was indeed a man sitting in the back seat. Ben did some digging as to who was the previous owner and he discovered that the car belonged to one Walter Sharp who had since passed on. Ben stated.

"I've never believed in such things, but only this morning I parked the car and when I went back to it, he was sitting there. Walter worshipped that car and maybe wants to remain in it".

Walter's son Grant (26) who was approached to comment on his father being seen in this car, stated.

"Strange things can happen sometimes, and my father believed in life after death".

Author's Comment:

I've said many times before on the lecture circuit and also in my books, that there are a number of differences when it comes to ghosts, they are not all 'see through'. A number of them are solid looking just like you and me. I'm happy to believe that the car's previous owner Walter Sharp, enjoyed his old car just as much in death as he did in life. I'm also sure that as time went on, the appearance of Walter in that car would diminish. Incidentally, I tried to find a photograph of Walter in this car on the internet but didn't come across it.

THE WOMAN WHO MARRIED A GHOST!

OK, as we know, the supernatural can be very strange. There are thousands of crazy stories out there that they surely can't all be true, can they! As I've said many times before, just because something looks and sounds ridiculous doesn't mean to say that it's not true. That said, as a researcher we must get to the truth, sort the wheat out from the chaff, so to speak. I accept that some stories are so farfetched, that even for me, they are hard to believe, but like I say, we should not discount them until we dig into that story and find out if there is any truth in it. Back in 2018 I became aware of a story that sounded so ridiculous that at first, I didn't want to even read it. But curiosity got the better of me, so I jumped in and started to read about a woman who married a ghost!

The story was featured in several newspapers here in the United Kingdom, and many other newspapers across Europe and the rest of the World. This was indeed a BIG story at the time. The following information I have taken from staff writers Charlie Parker and Becky Pemberton from the British Sun newspaper. They told their readers on the 20th of February 2018 the following bizarre tale.

We are told that 45-year-old Amanda Teague who lives in Downpatrick in Northern Ireland and works as a Captain Jack Sparrow impersonator, fell in love, and eventually married a spirit by the name of Jack. Amanda had been married before, and in that six-year marriage, she had five children, now divorced, she was looking for love. So, how did she come to know about this spirit, fall in love, and marry? Well, we are told (and of course we are dealing with newspaper speak here, so much of this could be newspaper spin on what Amanda really said!) Anyway, we are told that Amanda had been searching for a soulmate after getting no-where with 'real men'. I should point out here for the reader, that Amanda was a very spiritual person and into all things psychic, but I guess it was the last thing on her mind when her 'spirit to be lover', would walk into her life. So, how did this spiritual love affair begin? Well, we are told that one night in 2014 as Amanda was lying in bed, she suddenly felt the spirit energy of a man lying beside here. As the weeks rolled on there was this 'spark' or 'energy' between them, much more than she had ever experienced before with her spirit dealings. Jack was a regular 'presence' (if you excuse my pun) in her life, and she was growing more and more fond of his spiritual appearances. Let me now turn to what Amanda said to the English Sun newspaper. She stated,

"He is my soulmate. I am so happy; it is the perfect kind of relationship for me. There are a lot of people out there who don't know about spiritual relationships, but it could be right for them I want to get the message out there."

Now, even although Amanda was a spiritual person herself, she claims never to have seen him in his physical form, that said, she imagines him to be very similar to the character of Captain Jack, who, as we know, is played by Johnny Depp, in the movie series, Pirates of the Caribbean. She stated,

"He is black, so he is not the same colour as Johnny Depp, but he is dark skinned and has very dark jet-black hair, so he tells me."

Amanda said that she initially wasn't that interested in making contact with the spirit, and it wasn't until she realised that she could speak to him through mediumship that gave an added 'edge' to their relationship. This spirit said that his name was Jack, and that he was a thief on the high seas in the 1700s but eventually was caught and executed. Amanda further stated that Jack would sit with her when she watched television or would be in her car when she was out driving. As the weeks drew into months, she started, having strong loving feelings towards him. Then, two years after Jack had made his presence known in January 2016, and as they both were sitting together, he suddenly said, *"We can actually be together you know"*. Amanda went onto say,

"Jack proposed to me. I told him I wasn't really cool with having casual sex with a spirit and I wanted us to make a proper commitment to each other."

I'm sure Amanda never said the words, 'having casual sex with him' to the Sun newspaper, for being a spiritual person, she would know full well, that whilst spirit can indeed 'touch you', it may be taking it too far for a full-blown sexual experience, although that said, I am aware that there are those people who claim to have had 'unwanted' sex with a spirit.

(See my previous book Paranormal Case Files of Great Britain (Volume 1) where I write about a case that our society were involved back in the year 2000 in Greenford London. This case centred around a lady who was plagued by a ghost which was having sex with her on a regular basis.

That case was an 'eye opener' for me, as it was the first case that our society, Strange Phenomena Investigations (SPI) had ever been involved with)

Amanda was quoted as saying in the magazine 'Closer' (12th July 2019) written up by Marianna Manson.

"A lot of people don't understand how you can have sex with a ghost, but we were so connected that I could feel his every movement, even if I couldn't see him. He could touch me intimately and was a great lover."

Amanda was further quoted by Closer Magazine that when she told her children about her intended marriage to her ghost, they were curious but very 'open minded'. Indeed, her eldest daughters agreed to be bridesmaids!

MARRIED

And so it was that Amanda acquired a Shamanic Priest and legal registrar who agreed to marry the 'couple'. Amanda stated that she and Jack had a two-part wedding. The first ceremony was performed by self-described Celtic shaman, Patrick Eamon Carberry, who she said, was a legal wedding officiant in Northern Ireland.

The second ceremony, which was pagan, originated and drew from Wiccan tradition, and was held several months later on a boat in the Atlantic Ocean on July 23rd, 2016. According to an article written by Marisa Iati in the Washington Post online on 14th July 2019, Amanda now identifies mostly as pagan, but said, that she still feels drawn to some elements of Wicca. I also learned through other newspapers, that Amanda wore an 18th century style dress which had a corset top, and that she carried a pirate flag to represent Jack. They had a huge reception where all her family and friends were in attendance, apparently, spirits who knew Jack from his previous life, were also at the happy event. The Washington Post online stated that Winifred McConnell, a registrar in Belfast, stated that a wedding on the Atlantic Ocean could not have been registered in Belfast because marriages must be registered in the district where they took place. We also learn that Amanda said that she and Jack also had a pagan 'handfasting' wedding ceremony in which two witches who were practitioners of Wicca, wrapped cords around the couple's joined hands to symbolise the binding of the pair.

Now, I can hear you ask, *"Is it legal to marry a ghost"?* Well, the Sun newspaper tells us, and I quote,

"There is no provision in U.K. law for posthumous marriages, so the couple took a boat into international waters in the Atlantic Ocean, off the Irish Coast, for their ceremony. Marrying a dead person is legal in certain countries such as France, Singapore, and China, so by going into waters which aren't governed by any particular country, Jack and Amanda's union can be upheld".

We are then told that only 12 people were allowed on this boat, so only a few family members and friends of Amanda joined them at sea. I also hear you ask, *"But how can the marriage be properly agreed upon if the Minister doing the service couldn't hear the groom say I do"?* Well, that was sorted out as well, for Amanda had brought along a Spiritual Medium who 'tuned in' and heard Amanda's chosen one say, *"I Do"*. The full documentation was all signed and we are told that their posthumous relationship has never been questioned by authorities. Amanda stated.

"After the wedding, we were like any other newlyweds. I moved to the coast, as Jack likes to be near by the sea, and we'd go on romantic strolls along the

beach. On Valentine's Day, we went for a curry. The staff did look a bit confused when I asked for a table for two, but I didn't care".

Things were fine for a number of months, but then Amanda and Jack's relationship started to hit the skids. Doing research on this case, I came across an article on the internet from the Irish Central newspaper web site dated July 22nd, 2019, and it made for interesting reading.

DIVORCED

The article tells us that her marriage to 300-year-old Jack the Haitian pirate, had come to an end, after she described him as being an 'energy vampire'. The article goes on to explain to its readers, that Amanda had appeared on the British Talk Show, 'This Morning' to recount her relationship and eventual divorce from 'Jack' *(Which this author has viewed, and I would like to say, that Amanda came over very well. She came over as bright, intelligent and did not fluster at any of the questions that Eamonn Holmes and his fellow presenter Ruth Langsford threw at her).* What I liked about the way Amanda answered her questions on the 'This Morning' show, was when Eamonn Holmes was up front and said, *"Do you think people watching this show right now will think you're mad"!* To which Amanda beautifully replied,

"Seeing spirit, it's no different from people who go to get tarot card readings or people who believe in some sort of God that cannot be seen. Again, if you believe in God or angels, if you believe in anything that's not of this earthly realm, then you believe in spirit. So why would you find what happened to me beyond the realm of possibility?"

I thought that was a beautiful retort. I mean, there are millions of people throughout the world who believe in God (or their own Gods), yet they have never seen him! Another interesting statement that Amanda said on the 'This Morning Breakfast show, was that she claimed to have really struggled with her sexuality from a young age. She further stated that she would probably identify as being on the asexual spectrum, so the physical body isn't really important, it's more about the energy connection or the chemistry. Getting back to the Irish Central story.

Before they informed the readers about Amanda's divorce, they confirmed how the whole scenario unfolded, that Amanda had begun to explore her spirituality in 2010. This was after the death of her son, where she had hopes of finding what she described as, 'a link to the other side'. It took five years before Jack presented himself, and it took a further few months before she fully believed that he was who he said he was, a 300-year-old Haitian pirate. She went on to say that their 'relationship' was more 'intimate' as opposed to 'physical'. It was only a few weeks after their marriage on the High Seas, when Amanda started to notice that things were not quite what they seemed (some would say that was obvious!) She is quoted as saying,

"He was basically like an energy vampire. When spirits stay around too long, they need an energy source and unfortunately Jack was using me as an energy source. He had never accepted his own death, so he wanted to continue living through my body."

Apparently, Amanda consulted with other psychics to see if they could detect what was wrong with their marriage, but they all said that everything was fine. But as the weeks went on, she knew that things were not right.

Her health started to suffer, so much so, that she had a near-fatal bout of sepsis that required emergency surgery in 2018. Amanda went on to say,

"In the end, there were a lot of red flags, and after the operation, I realized that it definitely was him, and it took me a while to figure out whether he knew or not that it was definitely him, that he intended to harm me."

Amanda informed not just the newspapers but mentioned when she was on the 'This Morning' show, that whilst she has had longstanding health problems which apparently won't go away, these were 'not' mental health problems. What was most disconcerting, was when Amanda told 'Jack' to leave. He apparently said that he would kill her if she tried to leave him. It's bad enough in the mortal world if someone is saying that they are going to kill you but coming from a ghost!

When Amanda was interviewed by Closer magazine (mentioned above) she expanded on those health issues, and stated, (and I quote)

"I developed flu-like symptoms, and pain near my bum. I was in so much pain that I called an ambulance. At hospital I was diagnosed with a perianal abscess a collection of pus near the back passage. It was so severe that I was given intravenous antibiotics. At the time, Jack was loving and supportive I had no idea it was anything to do with him. As soon as I thought I was recovering, the abscess came back, and I needed antibiotics again. I noticed that whenever Jack and I had sex, the abscess seemed to get worse, but I put it down to coincidence. By November 2016, I'd also developed psoriasis and my periods had stopped. I spent most of my time in bed, and I was completely miserable". It was at this point, the magazine Closer tells us, that in May 2017, Amanda had had enough

and wanted to move back to Belfast, this caused a heated argument with 'Jack'. Amanda went on,

"We had a huge row and stopped speaking for a couple of weeks. During that time, my health seemed to improve. But when Jack and I reconciled and had sex, the abscess came back, worse than ever. I went to hospital where doctors told me I had contracted life-threatening sepsis and needed to have emergency surgery. Thankfully, the surgery was a success, but I knew I could no longer ignore the connection between Jack and my ill health".

THE SOUL EXTRACTION

According to the Independent Newspaper online dated 15th July 2019, she decided that enough was enough. And so it was, that on January 2018 the couple split up after Amanda had him exorcised. As with the wedding ceremony, she had to use the services of a Shaman in order to get rid of 'Jack' from her life. She called it a 'soul extraction' which is similar to an exorcism. Thankfully this 'soul extraction' worked, and once 'Jack' had left the building, Amanda's health improved dramatically. Marisa Iati in her clever article in the Independent Online (15th July 2019) asked Amanda if after the marriage and subsequent divorce if she regretted marrying 'Jack' to which she replied,

"In a way, I do regret it, and in a way, I don't, because it's given me a lot of lessons,. It's given me a lot of opportunities that I wouldn't have had. I do believe that everything happens to us for a reason. I was stronger than him, ultimately, I'm proud of what I did, and I'm really proud that I've managed to get my life back together. I'm much happier now."

What I found equally interesting, if not a little amusing in the Independent article, was when it was stated that Amanda had appeared on the British television programme, 'Loose Women' (Now there's a title!) where she revealed that when they were out visiting their local pub, not only did she buy herself a drink, but she also ensured to buy 'Jack' her spirit husband a glass of rum as well. Whether Amanda finished off his drink, the article didn't say. Another newspaper stated that 'Jack' had never accepted his own death and wanted to continue living through her body.

SO REAL, OR NOT REAL?

So, I dare say that whilst reading the above, you the reader are wondering if this woman really was sane and of sound mind. As I mentioned earlier, when I watched her appearance on the breakfast television show 'This Morning', (You will find this on You Tube) she came over rational and sound of mind to me. It was therefore interesting to read the article written by Marisa Iati from the Independent online (Monday 15th July 2019) where she incorporated into the article, three well-educated people who each shared their own thoughts about Amanda's claims. Let's take a look shall we at what these three educated individuals had to say. First up, was a T. M. Luhrmann, an anthropology professor at Stanford University who studies the supernatural she was quoted as saying.

"Ms Teague's trauma of losing her young son may have caused her to go into a dissociative, trance-like state that can facilitate dreamlike experiences, instead of becoming memories. The experiences someone has while in trance can remain alive and enable the person to repeatedly return to them. People can also develop ways to perceive that an invisible being is talking back to them, Christians, for example, may consider their spontaneous thoughts to be God speaking, and children often have invisible friends. Whatever the reason for developing a relationship with Jack, marrying a ghost is uncommon in Western

cultures. It has a certain place within paganism. It's not so different from 'invisible others' in general It's not so different than what kids do".

Next to put their tuppence worth in, was David Head, who is a history professor at the University of Central Florida who also studies pirates. He told the Washington Post that after study, he could find no reference to a real pirate named Jack Teague living in the 1700s.

Mr Head went onto say that Haiti was a French colony called Saint-Domingue, and that the name 'Teague' is a generically Irish name. David also drew the comparison to this name 'Teague' as to Jack Sparrow's father in the Pirates of the Caribbean movies, who is called Edward Teague. The Washington Post online further stated that a lot of Amanda's friends at that time, were part of the same spiritual circles, so in that regard they all supported Amanda in regard to her relationship with 'Jack'. Thankfully so did Amanda's children from a previous marriage. However, Amanda's parents were unsure about their daughter's dealings with this 300-year-old ghostly pirate. Mary Rooker, herself a shamanic practitioner from Takoma Park Maryland had this to say about 'soul extractions' and possession.

"In shamanic practice, 'soul extractions', or de-possession, can take various forms. A shaman might grab a ghost and force him to cross over out of the Earthly realm. The shaman might also try to convince the ghost to leave".

According to the Washington Post online, Amanda wanted to warn people about getting involved in New Age Spiritualities. Although Amanda herself was well versed in spiritual matters, it was owing to the loss of her son that drew her more into about finding out what really was on the other side. Sadly, after a period of time with 'Jack' her pirate, she eventually lost control of her life. She stated.

"I would really say to people who are thinking about getting into this, be really, really, really careful. And if somebody is not telling you about the dangerous side of it, run a mile".

She says that she has now cut all ties with the spiritual world. After writing this up, I felt that there had to be more similar stories out there, and there surely were. So, as a few more, 'for instances' let's take a look at a few other cases where people have had intimacy with a ghost. And before you ask, 'no it hasn't happened to the author'!

TALK ABOUT OTHER WORLDLY SEX!

Our first port of call takes us to Bristol England, where a 32-year-old woman called Amethyst Realm claims to have had sexual intercourse with not one, but 20 ghosts! Gordon Bennett, she is taking things a bit far is she not! In an article in the United States Newsweek online dated 12th September 2017, staff writer Maria Perez tells us that Amethyst, is a spiritual guidance counsellor who is happy to tell others that sex with ghosts is much better than sex with men. Amethyst (Like Amanda in our previous story) appeared on the British T.V. show 'This Morning'. She is quoted as saying the following to hosts Philip Schofield and Holly Willoughby.

"It started as an energy, there was pressure on my thighs and breath on my neck. I just always felt safe. I had sex with the ghost. You can feel it. It's difficult to explain. There was a weight and a weightlessness, a physical breath and stroking, and the energy as well".

The Newsweek online, further stated that Realm said that she had been in love with the ghost for three years, when one day her 'real' human lover came home from work early and saw a shadow of what appeared to be a man. Since that first encounter, Realm has gone on to have sex 20 times with various ghosts.

This article also asked the opinions of other people as to what they thought could be behind these intimate sexual encounters. One Rachel Sussman who is a psychotherapist who practices in New York City, had this to say about Realm.

"People have the richest fantasies. If they're getting pleasure from that fantasy, then it is possible. Having sex with a ghost is when it comes to the world of fantasy. It's really whatever gets you through the night".

Sussman stated that with her own personal clients she doesn't judge if they have said that they have had sex with a spirit. As we know, Hollywood stars have their own psychics, but that's one for another day. Patti Negri is one such Hollywood psychic who stated to Newsweek, and I quote,

"Having sex in the spiritual realm, is highly possible, and a lot more common than people would assume. It sometimes happens to women who are afraid of intimacy and want to get into the dating scene".

Alexandra Holzer, the daughter of famous paranormal researcher, Hans Holzer, had this to say.

"Having sex with a ghost can be hard to prove. It's difficult to disprove people's claim to have experienced sexual intercourse with a ghost. Doctors believe that hallucinations caused by dreaming is what is manifesting from this, but you have to keep an open mind in the paranormal, because this is hard to prove".

Needless to say, this story was also big news here in Great Britain. the Daily Mail online dated 14th October 2020, tells us that Realm fell in love with her ghost, a spirit called Ray on a trip to Australia in 2018. Now, like most newspaper stories, we have to take what they say/print with a pinch of salt, but the Mail online goes on to tell us that despite the loved-up couple's holiday getting off to a great start, where Amethyst admitted to the 'This Morning' show's researchers that she and her spirit lover had had sex in the toilet of the plane, things started to go wrong, as we will learn shortly.

Realm states that she was planning to marry and have a baby with her ghostly lover. When asked by Phillip Schofield and Holly Willoughby how she communicated with her ghost, Realm stated that it was through 'energies' and 'feelings'. Staff writer Monica Greep goes on to say that Realm decided to call off the wedding, due to her spirit fiancé behaviour on a holiday to Thailand.

She stated on the programme 'This Morning', that she began to suspect that her ghostly lover was drinking and doing drugs and partying too much. Not only that, but Realm also stated that her spirit would bring back numerous other spirit people into their hotel room. These spirits would stay for days, where they made crashing and banging noises. Realm stated,

"I've never had negative experiences with spirits before, but this was pretty scary, one would just follow me and another one would leave a constant bad smell, things were being moved."

Realm did wonder if it could be the stress of the pandemic which was ongoing at that time, which could be the cause of 'Ray' acting out. What stunned me, as the author of this book, was when Realm stated quite innocently, that (as she put it) Ghosts also have to socially distance from one another, for fear of 'getting ill, she was quoted as saying.

"It affects us all. They'd get ill just as we would". REALLY!

HE HAD TO GO

At first, Realm was unwilling to end their relationship, and tried talking to 'Ray' her sprit, asking him to mend his ways. Indeed, they had planned to get married at Wookey Hole caves in Somerset. She states that she gave him 'chance after chance' but things continued to get worse, and she could see no other way out than to get her spirit lover out of her life. This she did. She did a cleansing with sage. This apparently, didn't go down too well with 'Ray's' other worldly family, who were said to be heartbroken by the news that the marriage was off. But Teague did say that she hasn't ruled out eventually dating another ghost, and was quoted as saying,

"I'm happy free and single at the moment to be honest. It's not put me off spirits, I'm sure eventually I'll be ready for another one".

As with any story of this ilk, the newspaper had to find an expert in psychology or some other discipline to present the 'other side of the coin' so to speak. In other words, if she isn't having sex with her spirit, then what is going on! Step forward Christopher French, who is a professor of psychology at Goldsmiths College, University of London. Chris is the co-author of the book, 'Anomalistic Psychology: Exploring Paranormal Belief And Experience'. Chris stated.

"Ghostly experiences are not anything to do with mental illness. We need to avoid any kind of simplistic notion that anyone who has weird experiences is suffering from a mental illness. What is generally accepted, is that hallucinatory experiences are much more common in the non-clinical, totally well-functioning part of the population than was once appreciated. Anyone can have hallucinations, particularly if you are stressed or sleep deprived".

Chris went on to explain that sex with ghosts' can be explained easily. He states.

"Sleep paralysis is common. 20 to 40 per cent of people say they've experienced it, and it's the state between sleep and wakefulness when you realise you can't move. In a smaller percentage of the population, you get associated symptoms that can be very scary. One that's commonly reported is a sense of a presence something or someone in the room with you. You can also get hallucinations where you see dark shadows or monstrous figures. You can get auditory hallucinations, you hear voices, footsteps, and also tactile hallucinations. You can feel as if you're being held, you might feel as if someone is breathing on the back of your neck, you can feel as if you're being dragged out of the bed.

During a normal night's sleep, you go through different stages and it's REM sleep that's associated with vivid dreams ".

Whilst I would agree with Professor French that this might work in some cases, I certainly wouldn't agree that it would work, or could be attributed to all. Science certainly has a place in the paranormal, so long as it is used and applied carefully and honestly. Science should never throw the baby out with the bathwater, for to do so, may lose science something wonderful.

THE AUSTRALIAN GHOST WHISPERER

From the British Daily Star online, I bring you an Australian 'ghost whisperer' who states that having sex with ghosts, 'is real' and is more common than you think! Features writer Billie Scwab Dunn, brought to the attention of her readers on the 21st of October 2022, the strange life of psychic Caterina Ligato. We are told that Caterina known in Sydney Australian as a 'ghost whisperer' is an 'ageless' spiritual healer who has had psychic ability ever since she was a young child. She first experienced this psychic ability at the age of three, when she saw the spirit of a young man in her house. Not only did Caterina see this strange man, but he also used to play games and run around and chase her. At first, she didn't like this psychic ability and wanted to get rid of it, but after a while, she learned to embrace it and enjoy the comfort and interest that it brought to her. Over time, she developed her psychic skills and over a course of years, she decided to use these 'new found skills' in a professional capacity by becoming a psychic medium. She stated to the Daily Star online.

"A ghost is just a person who no longer has their body, so the same rules would apply. If you don't mind each other's company and make an effort to live together harmoniously, then anything is possible.

However, of course, you live in different realities which isn't exactly natural or normal, so not ideal for a relationship!"

Caterina went on to tell the Daily Star online, about one particular haunted guest house in Australia where a whole host of paranormal things had taken place. There is one man who prefers to book the exact same room each time he visits. There is of course a reason for this, but not one that many would expect! This man claims that a ghost jumps into bed with him! Some people would run away at this, but apparently not this man, as sleeping is the last thing on this ghost's mind. Caterina states.

"I've also heard of people having pleasurable sexual experiences with ghosts, strange but true. People having sex with ghosts is more common than you think. I didn't ask for explicit details, but a friend did tell me they were brought to climax via a sexual encounter with a male spirit. To know more would mean the answer would get a bit more X-rated! Essentially, it's like any sexual experience if it's consensual then there's not really an issue. But if it's not consensual, then it is a huge issue, and the person is best to seek out someone like myself to make sure the spirit moves on. If someone chooses to participate in a consensual experience, that's their choice. It's weird of course, but to each their own!"

She continued:

"When a person has passed over and they remain Earthbound, they may see qualities or traits in people that they're attracted to, and they may follow them home to be around them and experience those things they're attracted to. This happens more often than people realise, especially during ghost tours if a spirit takes a shine to you, you may not be going home alone! They're not always scary experiences, sometimes they can be fun and playful."

Caterina continued that as yet, she has not been approached by any ghostly spirit for an intimate relationship, and of that, she is grateful. She went onto say with tongue in cheek.

"Dealing with human relationships is plenty enough. Although there would be some benefits to a relationship with a ghost, you'd never have to worry about picking up after them, cooking for them, and you'd always get to pick what's on T.V.!"

SUMMING UP

So, there we have it. Some stories of females being intimate with those that have gone to the other side, and one Australian 'ghost whisperer' who states that having sex with ghosts, 'is real' and is more common than you think! Now, that's as maybe, and I'm pretty sure that if I had continued to have trawled the internet, I would have come across plenty more tales of ghostly sex. But as I've mentioned before, we all known that newspapers like to put a spin on any given story, more so on what appears to be crazy stories of the paranormal. Having worked with the media most of my adult life, I have been misrepresented many times myself. It's no fun, and friends get on your back for saying things in the press that you try to say you never said. I know! I've been there. But that aside, sometimes there is no smoke without fire. Somewhere there 'might' be a grain of truth in some of these bizarre tales of sex with ghosts.

Let's be honest, sex with ghosts is not a modern thing. There are tales of people having sex with ghosts right back to antiquity. But does that mean then that there is indeed something in it? That sex with spirits is a done deal! I decided to see what that fountain of knowledge Wikipedia had to say about it all. Much of which I was already aware of.

Sex with spirits even has a name, we call it Spectrophilia. And what that means is, that it's a sexual attraction or fantasy between humans and ghosts, or even, would you believe, sexual arousal from images in mirrors. (Certainly not my mirror!) But mostly the name refers to the alleged phenomenon of sexual encounters between ghosts and humans.

Most, of these sexual encounters are often described as being non-consensual and even unpleasant. Wikipedia also informs us that most traditional ghost stories which includes myths and legends, contain some element of seduction or temptation. A number of myths and legends, tell stories of female ghosts who will lure men to their deaths. One such tale, comes from the Latin American legend of La Llorona. Here in the West, paranormal researchers are aware of the phenomenon known as incubus and succubus. Again, there are many historical tales of this. One thing's for sure, no human wants to be in the grip of a succubus which is described as a demon or evil spirit. This demon will take on the shape of a female human, whose main priority is to seduce men and drain them of their semen or energy, ouch!

On the other side (If you excuse the pun again)! We have the incubus. This is also a demon, however, this demon takes on the shape of a male human form, and much like the succubus, is said to seduce women into sex. The main stay with the incubus, however, is their hope that they can impregnate the female. Most often people may encounter either the incubus or the succubus during sleep paralysis, and to some degree, this phenomenon is likened to the 'old hag' syndrome, where upon awakening, the individual will claim to see a hideous form either lying or sitting on their chest. Many scientists would state that this is nothing real, that it is some form of sleep paralysis. Some go even further, and state that it could be some kind of sexual frustration borne out by the individual which manifests itself in this manner. There is a Folklorist by the name of David Hufford who has estimated that approximately 15% of the population have experienced the incubus or succubus phenomenon at least once in their lives. Wikipedia also inform us that there have been a number of movies which have dealt with this subject, namely, The Entity (1982), Ghostbusters (1984), Star Trek: The Next Generation (Season 7), Ghost (1990), Scary Movie 2 (2001), and Dusk Maiden of Amnesia (2008) And, not to be outdone, The Phantom of the Opera is a story with spectrophilic elements.

So, there is a history of humans being subjected to sexual relations with our dear departed. One might say, *"But surely our own dear departed would never engage is such depravity"*. As a Spiritualist, I firmly believe in a Life After Death, indeed it's much more than a belief, it's an acceptance after studying it for most of my adult life. I've spoken to many people who have been to the 'other side' either through an Out of Body Experience (OOBE) or a Near Death Experience (NDE) I certainly don't accept what some scientists say that its oxygen starvation to the brain, or certain types of drugs that bring this effect on. It's more than that, way more than that. And yes, whilst some drugs may indeed induce a dreamlike quality of an afterlife, it stops far short of what people who have not been on drugs describe.

Anyway, I digress. The point here is, 'who is having sex with the people of the world'! This may sound a bit Hollywood, but I do believe that it is the nastier spirits who engage with this sort of behaviour. Your murderers, paedophiles etc, who have passed on and may tend to hang around the earth plane. The case of Amanda Teague mentioned earlier who actually got married to a 300-year-old Haitian pirate ghost, eventually turned into what she described, as 'an energy vampire' where she felt that her very life and soul was being sucked out of her.

After being initially nice and pleasant with her, her spiritual lover turned vile and nasty, and she realised that she had to get rid of him. Amethyst Realm from Bristol England, claimed to have had sex with 20 ghostly men, and that she enjoyed it, far more than any normal human men. But Amethyst eventually settled for one spiritual lover, who, at the start, was kind, but like Amanda Teague's pirate ghost, turned nasty, and he was out on his ear as well.

I think with both Amanda and Amethyst, that they were looking for something in their lives. Both women, it would appear, were looking for love which may have made them open to other worldly spirits who were ready to attach themselves. But of course, that does not apply to all. There are millions of people out there looking for love who don't (thankfully) have a spirit attachment, so why would these two women be subjected to it? Amanda was very much into spirituality and seeking answers from beyond. But again, I must stress, so are countless others, and they do not have anything happen to them of this nature. If this were the case, then one would imagine that many of these so called 'earthbound spirits' would seek those unfortunate women out there who we call prostitutes. These, women you would think, would be more apt to have unwanted spirit intervention in their lives. I am of course just speculating and trying to come to terms with the reason 'why'. I'm not forgetting a medical possibility here. It would be remiss of me to not have or consider as a contender, a 'medical' episode. Sleep paralysis would not explain both Amanda and Amethyst's long term sexual relationship with their ghostly partners. Could some dissociated identity disorder (DID) state be the root cause here. Many people have suffered from what is known as a 'dissociative state', this comprises of problems with memory, perception, behaviour traits, identity, and can, in some instances, disrupt every area of mental functioning. Some people might feel the presence of other identities. Some of these 'presences' might have their own names, their own voices, mannerisms. In some cases, people who have a dissociative disorder, might also suffer from mental health problems. Could this have been a factor with both cases mentioned above? Again, just speculation on my part. Then there is another candidate that we have yet to bring to bear, as not doubt the sceptics who are reading this book may well have been waiting on, and that is, *'Are these women not just making it all up'?* Yes, that is a possibility, the same however can be said to those people who claim sightings of UFOs and the Loch Ness Monster.

Some people need to feel important in their lives. Some people need to be something other than they truly are, and may concoct the most ridiculous stories, either to fool their friends, or get their five minutes of fame and notoriety in the press or television. Both Amanda and Amethyst appeared on talk shows and appeared in the press. Surely coming out with a story such as this would not be something that you would want in the media? Or would it? Amanda was happy for her friends and family to know about her spiritual lover, was it one of them who leaked the story out to the media? And once the story was 'out there', Amanda had to defend herself and explain to all and sundry what it was all about. One thing's for sure, marrying a dead 300-year-old pirate is news in anyone's books. Newspapers rarely, if ever, pay you. (I should know!) But television is a different kettle of fish, and the suits at T.V. land simply lapped up stories such as Amanda's and Amethyst's. At the end of the day, only Amanda and Amethyst know the truth. Yes, the spirit world is real. Yes, spirits can scratch and harm you (Poltergeists) but having sexual intercourse with humans! Well, who knows!

Alfie. The Crying Boy.

Amanda Teague. Married to a ghost.

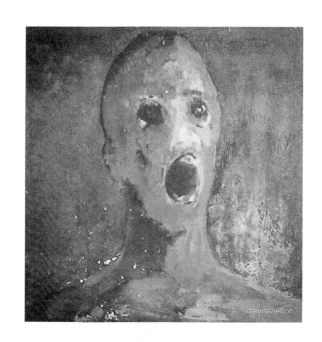

The Anguished Man painting.

The Busby Stoop Chair

The Haunted Ledger.

***

CHAPTER FIVE

THE CONDORRAT HAUNTING

"As we entered the house, I became very aware of a spirit presence, and he was not very happy with us. I followed the vibration around the house, and he was strongest in Susan's bedroom. I hate bullies, and as a result, he found out, as he tried to scare me out of the house with threatening language. In the kitchen, I saw him stand right in front of me wanting a square go".

Steven Bird. SPI's Medium

Location: Condorrat, Cumbernauld, Central Scotland.

Date: 27th February 2022, 5th March 2022, and 14th August 2022.

Principle Witnesses. Susan Strachan (48) Daughter Ciara (17) ex-husband Jim (pseudonym) (58).

SPI Researchers. Malcolm Robinson. Ron Halliday.

SPI Mediums. Ian Shanes. Alyson Dunlop Shanes. Steven Bird.

I learned about this case from the witness herself, 48-year-old Susan Strachan who informed me via e-mail, that there were a lot of paranormal activity occurring in her family home that she shared with her daughter Ciara aged 17. Needless to say, I knew that I would have to act upon this information and find out what was going on behind these paranormal disturbances? I decided to get in touch with a number of people who have assisted my research group, Strange Phenomena Investigations (SPI) throughout the years, in effect, 'getting the old SPI team back together', this was because I had been living in England for 23 years and only came back to Scotland in 2021.

Due to commitments with some of the SPI team, we couldn't get a date that would suit us all to go together, so what we did, was to send Ian and Alyson Shanes, two of SPI mediums, to visit the house first, on the understanding that they wouldn't tell us anything at all that they uncovered, so that we, Team 2, could go in blind. But let's start at the beginning shall we, what are the facts on this case?

THE DISTURBANCES

48-year-old Susan Strachan and her daughter Ciara have lived in the property since 2017. It is a beautifully decorated house, built just over 30 years ago, (the late 1980's) Susan stated to SPI that she has had spiritual activity in her home for around four years. This would comprise of pictures flying off the walls, to a lamp falling over and bending out of shape for no apparent reason. There have been strange unaccounted for bumps and bangs, and the sound of someone running around the house. After a while, she realised that her house must be haunted, as both she and her daughter could not account for all these strange noises and footsteps in a normal manner. It was then that she decided to do something about it. She got various psychics involved, all of whom tried to get rid of the spirit, or spirits from her home. She even stated that she has had random people who she didn't know, come up to her in the street, and say that there was a male spirit from her house which was following her! One psychic told her to throw away a mirror from her bedroom as it contained bad energy and went on to describe a male spirit to her. Susan stated to me that she foolishly had one of those spirit apps on her phone that allegedly can sense spirit, and one night, just after she had fallen asleep, the app sprung into life telling her to leave her ex-husband (Susan's ex-husband occasionally spent the night with her due to the ongoing paranormal disturbances) At this, she asked the spirit to make a noise, at which point a noise came from her room.

She asked again for another noise, and again was granted by a secondary loud noise emanating from somewhere in her room. At this point, her ex-husband Jim (pseudonym) who was lying next to her, shouted at her to switch her phone off. More worrying was the night when Susan was in bed asleep with her ex-husband. Suddenly, her ex-husband was woken up by the most horrendous scream coming from Susan. More worrying, was the fact that neither her ex-husband nor her daughter could wake Susan up. Susan's ex-husband was so scared, that he telephoned their son to come round to the family home. Eventually Susan did wake up but had no recollection of screaming. Knowing that 'something had gone on' she decided to use what's known as a sage stick to cleanse the house. Sage sticks, known as 'smudging', involves burning herbs or resins as a means to cleanse and purify nasty energy from haunted premises. Sadly, Susan's use of the sage stick, only prompted whatever was in the house, to start making itself known again.

As the weeks progressed, more strange things occurred. Susan's electricity key suddenly went missing, and even although both Susan and daughter Ciara searched high and low for it, it wasn't found. That was, until the next day, when it suddenly turned up in the exact same spot where she initially left it. Susan admitted to the author, that she has always had spirit in her life, but nothing that ever really troubled her until now. In February 2022, Susan purchased a motion sensor CCTV camera for her bedroom, in the hopes of capturing her 'strange phenomenon'. Well, she was successful, as the device captured lots of orbs, including, what she described as a 'massive' orb. However, what shocked her the most, was the sound of a male voice saying, *"Hi"*. There was no male presence in her house that night, including her ex-husband! This then was the background of but some of these strange evets that were reported to the author. So, it was clear that SPI just had to act, and hopefully find out who or what was behind these disturbances. It is SPI's remit to not only find out what is the root cause behind any given ghostly account, but also to try and get rid of any ghostly presence that is behind it. This, however, will only be acted upon should we believe that there is a case to go on. In other words, that its real, and not someone out to perpetrate a hoax.

The first to visit the house from SPI, were Ian and Alyson Shanes, who, using their mediumistic abilities, attended the family home to see what they could find. Prior to their visit, I told them absolutely nothing about this house, other than strange things were happening, and I obviously did not go into what those were. Upon completion of their visit, I asked both Alyson and Ian to submit to me, their report of their visit which they duly did. I'd like to point out to the reader, that I 'did not' look over their report prior to attending the family home myself. Here is what Alyson Dunlop Shanes had to say about her visit.

ALYSON DUNLOP SHANES REPORT

SPI's First Visit. (Sunday 27th February 2022)

"Hi Malcolm".

"When I went upstairs with Susan, in the first room (her daughter's) I saw a man standing. He didn't tell me who he was or why he was there. In the middle room, there was a spot halfway in, where I just began shaking, and feeling really sick. I moved towards the window and the feeling disappeared, but when I walked back towards the door at the same spot, I started shaking uncontrollably and again feeling like I was going to be sick. In Susan's bedroom, I saw a child hiding in the corner.

They were afraid of being seen, but I felt they were responsible for the noises of walking/running about upstairs. They told me nothing else as they were too scared".

"I then went into the bathroom, where the main event happened. There was a very aggressive man in there. He was an older man, maybe in his 70s. He told me to get the fuck out. He said I was an 'Interfering bitch' and much more besides. I asked him if that was his 'thing', trying to scare vulnerable women. He kept on hurling abuse at me. I told him that he did not frighten me, and if he didn't leave the house and Susan alone, I'd be back to perform an exorcism. That seemed to shut him up".

Alyson Dunlop

We now take a look at what medium Ian Shanes had to say.

IAN SHANES REPORT

(Sunday 27th February 2022)

"Hi Malcolm".

"The main items that I found in the home, were the two uninvited forms who had been there for a long time. In Susan's bedroom there was a male spirit form who declared himself there to stay, and nobody was able and going to make him go. He saw himself as her 'partner', but that part never happened. I told him who I was and his options, he left soon afterwards, but not before I explained not to return, in my diplomatic way. In her daughter's room there's a mirror, and my attention went there. I asked for whatever was there to show itself or I'd simply end the conversation. Almost immediately a figure began to show itself, but it definitely had a non-human form.

The form changed regularly, in an attempt to intimidate me but I was having none of it. I told it the options, which were different from the others earlier". (Author's Comment. Other's meaning the other psychics who had visited the house before SPI) *"Other information I obtained was of a more positive response for her, especially about her guardian, an Egyptian, and something about her daughter's talents. She was in a good mood and very relieved that we had turned up".*

Ian Shanes.

SPI's SECOND VISIT. March 5th, 2022.

And so it was, that on the 5th of March 2022, Team 2, which included myself the author, fellow researcher Ron Halliday, and medium Steven Bird, headed off in Steven's car to visit the witness at her home in the small town of Condorrat near Cumbernauld. On the way there, Steven kept stating that he was getting the spirit of the perpetrator who was psychically telling him in no uncertain terms, 'not to visit'. Steven said to both Ron and I, that this was a very nasty spirit with an attitude problem, that said, Steven stated that these were the cases that he loved. Coming face to face with a spirit who didn't want to go.

I asked Susan if, prior to coming to live in this property, if she had any previous strange happenings at the house she lived in before this one, she replied that she has always had strange things happening to her. In fact, her last house in Hope Park Drive in Cumbernauld, was also haunted with numerous strange things happening there, it was not a good house at all she said. The following is part of an audio taped interview with Susan Strachan and her daughter Ciara that the author recorded at her home that day. Susan said.

"This is the first house that I can actually say that I felt safe walking down the stairs from the bedroom and walking into the kitchen and not having to look behind me. This house was wonderful. It was only until we got my little dog, who my son has now got, that things started to manifest. Bella, who was a puppy at the time, started to bark upstairs at absolutely nothing. She would then run downstairs into the living room and bark in here, and then it was like she was actually growling at something. Then one night I wasn't actually feeling well, and there was a black bag outside Ciara's room, and I could hear rustling in this black bag. I couldn't fathom out what it was".

At this point, Susan's daughter Ciara takes up the story.

"The only way to describe this noise, would be to imagine that there was a big empty plastic litre bottle of Evian water, and someone was scrunching it up. I had a bottle of water in my room and the water in it was swishing about. At this I got a fright, and I ran into my mum's room".

Susan now described what happened next.

"The only way I can describe what happened next, was like somebody had broken into the house and was running through the kitchen banging. We both screamed the house down, and I had this candelabra in my bedroom, and I was saying, "Get out my house, get out my house", and I was banging this candelabra and then Ciara phoned my ex-husband to come over, and nothing! Nobody else was in the house, nothing was found. No doors or windows were open. I have two chandeliers in the kitchen and the next morning I found that one of the arms was twisted and I took a photograph of it. I had a shop at that time, and I sent the photograph to one of my customers who is a psychic, and she came back to me and said that she felt sick and asked, 'who is the man in your house'?

At this point, Steven Bird, our medium, said that the spirit behind all of these disturbances in her house, was a spirit by the name of Jeffries, at which point Susan said, *"Really, is that what you are getting"?* Susan further stated, *"He doesn't want to go, does he"?* To which Steven replied, *"He is a really nasty bugger, and that's putting it mildly"!* Susan then informed me about a recent event in which a picture flew off her living room wall and landed on her daughter Ciara. There was no wind, and there were no windows open at the time, they couldn't account for this. Then, on another occasion, Ciara was in the living room when she described something like black socks that had been rolled up into a ball. Whatever that was very quickly shot by her and knocked into a lamp with quite a bit of force. Her mother was in the kitchen at this time and no one else was in the living room. Then, on another night, Susan was in a bar in Bothwell which is a small village in South Lanarkshire, when this total stranger came up to her and said not to be frightened, that there was a spirit of a man standing right behind her and he doesn't like the fact that you are talking to my friends. This stranger went onto say that this was not healthy, and that you need to get him out of your house. As Susan was describing all this, Steven interrupted and said that this spirit, was involved in building these houses back in 1978 and that he doesn't want to cross over as he has done bad things, and he was worried in case that he would be judged. But Steven told him, in no uncertain terms, that he 'had to go', that he was causing fear and alarm with his continued presence in the house. Susan than asked, *"Is it him that is doing all these things in our house and making us feel uncomfortable"?* Steven replied, *"Oh yes".*

Susan continued:

"Then there was the occasion when I was at a business meeting and there was a lady who kept looking behind my shoulder and she said to me, "The man has

followed you from your house". I thought, not another person telling me this. I can't believe it! This lady further said that this spirit was swearing and said that he would never leave me".

At this point in our conversation with Susan, you can hear on the audio tape, Steven Bird our psychic shouting out, *"Don't you try and bully me son".* Steven was at this point, walking through the house following this spirit around from room to room where he was being verbally abused by the spirit who no doubt was amazed that Steven had made contact with him.

Susan then recounted:

"I have a friend called Cathy, who is actually a White Witch who said to me that she just had to come to my house, that she needed to get rid of this spirit. Anyway, she came to my house, went into my bedroom, and said that she felt sick, and that he 'the spirit', was bringing other spirit people in, and that 'he' was watching me. I mean, when I came out of the shower, I had to put something straight on, I could feel him watching me. Even when I am in the shower, I feel that I am being watched. Then my friend said that she had managed to get him out and had put a cloak over the mirror. But sadly, it started up again, and during lock down I got somebody else to help me, it was a psychic lady from London who told me on Zoom, that this spirit was always in my bedroom or in the hallway".

Steven interrupted Susan at this point by saying that this spirit, was trying to stop him from talking, and he felt as if this spirit was trying to squash him into the ground. Steven went on,

"I felt him on the stairs going past the corridor and especially in your bedroom. He is in here with us now, and he is telling me that he is ready for me".

Susan continued: *"I've been told several times that he thinks I am his. That I am his partner. And what is worse is, that he doesn't like men".*

I asked Susan, if there was any one thing, or incident, which might have been the catalyst for all the strange phenomenon, she replied:

"I'll tell you when it got worse. I have been separated from Ciara's dad for six years, but he came back last Christmas, and since he has been back, things have got really bad. I have this ghost app on my phone, and two Saturday's ago, it came on by itself and it said, "Leave". Now Ciara's friends know that this house is haunted, and she will have her friends over and things go missing and our electricity always cuts out. Anyway, this Saturday night, I said out loud, "OK, prove that you are here", at which point I heard several loud knocks, and my ex-husband just looked, and said, "Oh no not again". He also said that later that night, he awoke to hear me screaming, like something out of a horror movie. My eyes were wide open, and I was screaming saying "leave me alone, leave me alone". Jim my ex-husband was so scared that he got Ciara and her friends who were at a party to come over, and Ciara said that she was slapping my face and I wouldn't wake up. And then about an hour later when things had quietened down. Jim said that I was quietly sleeping and that I opened up my eyes then a voice, which was 'not' my voice, came out of me saying to Jim, "I can see you, she's mine". My husband and daughter didn't want to tell me everything that happened".

I then asked Susan if she had experienced spirit in other houses, ie, family and friends, to which she replied:

"I don't mind spirits. I can pick up on things. I've got a lot of spirits in here that come and go, I don't mind that. But 'him', I need 'him' gone because I don't like how it makes me feel".

I then stated to Susan that it would appear that she is more psychically aware, to which she agreed. She further stated that she first experienced the psychic world when she was 17. It all happened one night when she was coming home with her friends in the bus, when the bus passed a graveyard, she started to feel ill. She stated to her friends that she needed to get home, and to get home 'now'. She was in so much of a hurry to get home, that she actually got off the bus early and ran to her house. It was at her house when she was given the terrible news that her father had been knocked down and had been killed. I said to Susan that she clearly had a feeling that something wasn't right, that something was wrong, to which she said, *"Oh for sure".*

Susan continued:

"So, three or four months later I went to a Spiritualist Church where there was an empty chair next to me. A lady said we can't have an empty chair, and pointing to me, said "Put it behind you". And then I had a feeling that somebody was wanting me to reach out to them in 'that chair'. It was an overwhelming sensation. Later, as the psychics were going around, one of them said that there was someone in that chair for me. I feel I want to explore this more, but I am too frightened in case I attract people like 'him'.

At this point Steven stated that this spirit was trying to attach himself to him, but he was dam sure that he wouldn't let this happen. I then said to Susan that I would have to ask her some questions, and that I hoped that she wouldn't be offended by them, but I just had to ask them as no doubt the sceptics of the world would surely have asked, 'why I didn't mention such and such'. My first question was, did she or her daughter ever use a Ouija Board, to which she replied, that she did, but that it was just the once, and that was many years ago when she was 16, and she never used it again.

On that occasion, Susan said that she got a spirit come through the board from the town of York in England, and that she had terrified her. I then asked Susan if she was on any medication which might have allowed her to hallucinate or perhaps misperceive something as a ghost? She replied in the negative.

Whilst I had been asking Susan questions, fellow researcher Ron Halliday and been sitting quietly using his dowsing rods in her living room and was astonished when they had crossed over each other immediately. Not only that, but they were also going haywire, they were spinning around, quite a sight to see actually. Ron stated to Susan that the behaviour of the rods, was indicative of some very strong energy in her home. At this point Susan played us some sounds which had come from the CCTV that she had installed in her bedroom. This was a 'sound activated' device which would only come on if there was a sound in the immediate vicinity. We all sat in stoney silence as Susan played the tape for us, within seconds, one could clearly hear the word, *"HEY"*. She then showed us some interesting footage of orbs in her home, which, unlike most orb videos that I've seen, seemed to be intelligent! Steven then asked Susan if she would be kind enough to switch off everything electrical in her house, from televisions to microwaves and anything electric. It was Steven's contention that this spirit, was pulling the energy from the electrical appliances in her home to help make his presence known. During conversation, Susan stated that these blocks of houses, were roughly 50 years old, which would make their erection around 1972 and that there was a lovely old couple who had occupied their house before they moved in. Susan also stated that she has had a well-known psychic, Mary Sanderson (pseudonym) come to the house and do a 'cleansing ceremony', but sadly to no avail, as the paranormal banging's and rapping's still continued.

Steven then said that this spirit, who was called Jeffries, was a sex pest, and certainly didn't want to cross over. I then asked Steven if this spirit would be hard to move on, to which he said, 'most certainly', and that he (Steven) was probably going to have to swear a lot whilst getting rid of him. Steven stated that other than 'Jeffries', he also was getting a few other spirit people in the family home. One was Susan's granny, who was in Susan's home quite a lot. Steven then asked Susan if she could take the name Maggie, but it didn't ring any bells with Susan. In the car coming up to Condorrat, Steven said that he was getting from spirit, the name of Malcolm, but he was unsure as to what capacity this was being thrown at him. Nothing to do with the author of course. Steven was of the opinion that this spirit, this Jeffries chap, was an attachment, and not an errant spirit passing through. He was solely attached to Susan and did not want to leave her. I then asked Susan on a scale of one to ten, how troubling was this spirit entity, to which she replied *"10, no, make that 20, It's also troubling to my daughter"*, she continued.

"Ciara my daughter was in the house herself last week, and this spirit did the same thing. 'He' was running by the room 'he' was banging doors. Ciara was frightened and shouted out, "Mum, Dad", but of course we both were not there".

As I've stated earlier, whilst I was sat interviewing both Susan and her daughter, Steven Bird, our medium was walking around Susan's house where I could hear him swearing and shouting at this spirit to go. He then burst into the living room shouting, *"Malcolm, this needs to be done 'now"* Meaning a 'cleansing'. I certainly didn't want to interrupt what Steven had been doing so I replied that yes, we better get started. As a researcher I always like to entice spirits out, (shall we say!) and I asked if there were any spirits with us right now, to make themselves known to us, 'nothing'.

I then asked Susan to ask the same question, again 'nothing'. Silence prevailed, to which Steven said that 'Jeffries the spirit', doesn't want to play, however, as Steven continued, he has no choice.

MOVING THE SPIRIT ON

It was then time for me to stop asking Susan and Ciara questions, and to let Steven get on with what he does best, and that is getting rid of nasty spirits. At this point, Steven asked Susan to sit on a chair in the middle of the living room with her forearms and hands lying face down on her legs asking her to be as comfortable as she could. Steven then stood in front of her and placed his hands on top of Susan's head and spoke the following words.

"To the Divine Spirit, I call upon the higher side of life to send down angels, to take this spirit away from this lady. I ask that we all be protected from this moment on during this ceremony, and also to ask for this detachment and special protection for myself as I do this job. I ask that this spirit be taken away towards the light, where justice will be dealt in good time and fashion. I ask that this lady live the rest of her life away from negativity, especially of spirits, and I ask that you bless this house once this ceremony is done. I will, on your advice, also use the plant of sage to bless the house afterwards. I ask this with all my love from my heart".

After Steven had finished saying the above words, he then changed tack, and said loudly to the spirit that was attaching itself to Susan,

"You have no permission, GO. Go towards the light, you will not win. GO, to the light. You must leave. You must leave this house and go at once. Leave NOW, the light is there for you. GO......GO NOW. In the name of God's name GO. Take him......Take him now please....thank you. Thank you everyone".

At this point, Steven started to softly weep and left the room for a few moments to compose himself. Ron Halliday then picked up his dowsing rods and we all could clearly see that they were not moving at all. Both rods stayed in line, a massive difference from earlier on when the dowsing rods were constantly crossing over themselves. Ron said, *"Things have changed drastically here"* After which Steven re-joined us in the living room and said that he would have to close things down now. And spoke the following words.

"Great Divine Spirit, thank you for the action from the higher side. Thank you for the deliverance back to spirit where this spirit belongs and where he will meet his judgement according to thy name. Thank you, and if you can bless this house with as much love and light as possible to allow these people here to move on with their lives. I will also do a cleansing ceremony in your name Lord, which is love. Amen".

At this point, I was very keen to ask Steven some quick questions on what he had just done. He replied that it would be fine. Here is what transpired.

Abbreviations

(MR) Malcolm Robinson. **(SB)** Steven Bird) **(SS)** Susan Strachan.

(MR) *"Steven, was the man you just removed from this house, the man that has been attaching himself to Susan?"*

(SB) *"Yes".*

(MR) *"And when you were moving him on, was he reluctant to go?"*

(SB) *"Yes. He was trying to attach himself to me, which is generally what they do. They either go to the weakest source or the strongest source".*

Steven then turned round to Susan and said, *"Don't take this the wrong way, but he has been with you so long that he has weakened you spiritually. And he tried to jump onto me because my aura is massive. But that was never going to happen. It affected me in the way that made me very emotional and tired, and also dizzy as well. But he's gone now."*

(MR) *"You mentioned something about, someone take him away. Was there someone there to collect him?"*

(SB) *"Angels. Two angels came through. I made an outer circle for protection, and although he tried to get to me, he could get to me, but not 'into me'. So, he was trying to put me off the job, but as soon as the angels arrived, white light was created, and then..... 'gone'.*

(SS) *"And he can't come back?"*

(SB) *"No, absolutely gone. But I will cleanse the house, as the house is a mish mash right now of negativity, and that's the last part of my job".*

At this point I tuned to Susan and said that I would give her a call in a few days' time just to see how things are. But I reiterated the points of what had come out of our investigations, and those were.

1) This man died in 1978, and he helped build these houses (as a brick layer)

2) He was a nasty man who attached himself to you and your daughter.

3) But through Steven's work, he was gone now.

We then all spoke about what had just transpired, and Susan stated that this nasty spirit was definitely draining her. That she had on some occasions, no energy whatsoever. Furthermore, she had no interest in her work, no interest in herself, and just didn't want to go out.

Steven broke in and said that this spirit was a self-centred narcissistic sex pest, that's what he was. He was also handy with his fists when he was younger, and he was a hard man. But he came with a lot of s**t. He was a nasty piece of work. He was a hard nasty man, a bully when he was alive. I then asked Steven if he had a rough age of this nasty spirit, to which he replied that he was in his 40's. Steven further described this spirit entity as something like those big sharks which have those little fishes hanging off their underside, he was a bit like that, inasmuch as he was attaching himself to her, feeding off her energy, and using her as a battery source. He can't steal any of your soul, he said to Susan, but he sure can steal some of your energy. Susan then stated that she has definitely felt it more this year, and that her psychic friend Cathy, had said to her that the spirit in her home, was very sleazy, and that she couldn't believe the audacity of this spirit to come back after she had tried to get rid of him. She then went on to say that we had no idea of how much she appreciated SPI being there, and what we had done, that she was ever so thankful. She further stated that this spirit, was all she could think about, that it was taking over her life. At this point I asked Steven what happens now to this spirit. Does he get retribution in the afterlife? Steven replied.

"Oh, he will get way more than that. He will get taken through to a light place, and probably get taken to meet his family. Then he will be taken to a dark place where he will be there until he mends his ways, where he will judge himself and be judged for all the bad things that he has done. The soul knows where to go. It is preprogramed where to go, as it has been here before. What happens is that a white light appears, and it gets bigger and bigger and bigger and there is this urge for the soul to go through it. Unless there is a massive amount of guilt and bad deeds that have been done, then there is an urge for the soul to stay away from it. Because your soul has free will".

Susan then stated that she does feel other spirits in her home, but she doesn't mind them. She then went onto talk about the zoom call that she had had with a famous English psychic who also picked up on a spirit man in her house, but this English psychic had described him as a 1940's gangster. Which, maybe in the sense he was. In that he was evil in his ways and wanting to cause fear and alarm. This psychic also told Susan to get rid of a mirror in her bedroom. She felt that there were things that were attached to that mirror. She said, *"Do not gift the mirror, do not break the mirror and do not sell it"*, and, would you believe it, Susan stated that someone actually stole it from outside our front door! Where she had put it out for collection for the refuse collection. Susan now takes up the story.

"So, I put on my Facebook about this mirror, and that it had negative properties. In fact, STV (Scottish Television) wanted to interview me about it. A lady from STV phoned me, I think it was Beverley Lyons who said that she was really interested to talk to me about this mirror, but there was so much going on at that time with this spirit, that I didn't talk to them. Indeed, the recent pain that I have experienced between my shoulder blades has been horrendous".

Ron Halliday asked Steven if he had been given any psychic impression as to where this 'Jeffries' spirit was from, to which Steven replied that he got the strong impression that he was from Glasgow, and that he was a freelance brickie (Bricklayer) who went from job to job. He never had a home to call his own. Susan went onto say that when this spirit passed over during Steven's 'cleansing ceremony', she had felt very, very, cold, and that her head was really sore, as if it was about to explode. She also said for the record, that her son Mitchell had also experienced the strange goings on in her house. At this point, Steven lit his sage stick and walked through the house doing a further cleansing ceremony and said the following words.

"In the name of God, I ask for a blessing on this house that all energies and all spirits must leave this house at once. And I wish for the energies to stabilise and be positive, in the name of God. I want positivity and love, and I ask for a blessing for this house and protection for this lady and her daughter. All negativity must leave, in the name of God"

I had to laugh when Susan said to me that when she saw Steven Bird our medium coming in her front door, she had said to herself, *"He's not messing about"*. Well, Steven does take his work very seriously indeed. After, Steven, Ron and I had visited Susan's house, I asked both men if they would be kind enough to supply me with their thoughts on their visit. Here is what Ron Halliday had to say.

RON HALLIDAY'S REPORT

"Susan had experienced a variety of supernatural activity in her house over a period of four years: objects went missing, her dog would bark when there was nobody there. She heard the sound of someone running through the kitchen which led her to believe that she'd had a break-in. The chandelier had been twisted, a picture flew off the wall in the sitting room and landed on her daughter Ciara, who was sitting on the couch. And a black ball had shot across the room. However, the main issue was Susan's feeling that a spirit was attached to her. In fact, according to one psychic, a friend, the spirit had followed her to a business meeting. There seemed to be a sexual aspect to the spirit, as both Susan and Ciara felt uncomfortable getting showered as they had the sense that they were being watched. There had been a particularly frightening experience two weeks previously when Susan asleep in bed started screaming but could not be woken up. Jim her ex-husband, heard a voice shouting, 'she's mine! she's mine!"

"Steven Bird, our medium, confirmed that a spirit was attached to Susan and also confirmed Susan's feeling that the spirit was a 'sex pest' who believed that Susan belonged to him, and resented the presence of other men. Steven proceeded to engage forcibly with the spirit who, he said, was a man called Jeffries who had a connection with the house, possibly involved in building it. Steven sat Susan on a chair and putting his hands on Susan's head forced the spirit to leave. He said an angel had come to take 'Jeffries' away. I noticed an immediate lightening of the atmosphere. I had dowsed the sitting room with my rods when we arrived, and they fluctuated wildly. After Steven's 'banishing' they were static. The difference was remarkable. Steven finished by carrying out a cleansing of the house with sage".

Ron Halliday 13th March 2022.

STEVEN BIRD'S REPORT

"On the 5th of March 2022, I accompanied the SPI team to Cumbernauld to help a lady called Susan, I had no previous information about her or the problems that she was experiencing. As we were crossing the Clackmannanshire Bridge, I became aware of a spirit showing himself to me. He was of average height and of stocky build and was laying bricks. I was then made aware of the fact that he was involved in building the houses that she lived in. This spirit then said to me, "Stay Away you cunt"! He said this on several occasions. It was at this point, that I felt Susan had this spirit as an attachment, and not merely as a visitation. So, this changes the game completely. I had spoken to my guide earlier on in the day, and she had reported the fact that the 'Higher Side' were ready, and it was up to me how I wished to proceed. This spirit I felt, was angry and dangerous and a total pest, and as we approached Cumbernauld, I felt him get stronger.

Malcolm was going to Google map the address for me, but I asked him not to, as I felt that spirit would guide me there. Sure enough, that's exactly what happened".

Author's Comment. Incredibly Steven drove to Susan's house as if he had been there a million times before. He only had the address and did not use his satellite navigation to direct him to her door. Spirit, as he states, directed him to her door.

"As we entered the house, I became very aware of a spirit presence, and he was not very happy with us. I followed the vibration around the house, and he was strongest in Susan's bedroom. I hate bullies, and as a result, he found out, as he tried to scare me out of the house with threatening language. In the kitchen, I saw him stand right in front of me wanting a square go". Author's Comment: That is Scottish Language for a fight) *"Unfortunately, angry spirits just get my hackles up, and I stood up to him. 'He' impressed upon me that he was staying, and said, "She's mine, she is gorgeous, I am going nowhere". I said that he had to leave, or be ejected back to spirit and why hadn't he gone when he had died? He told me that he had done many bad things, sexually to other ladies in life, and knew what was going to happen to him if he walked through the white light. I asked him what his name was, and he gave me the name of Jeffries. I also asked how he had died, and he said he died in an accident. He gave me the numbers 78, which I took to be 1978. He then told me 44, which I took to be either 1944, or he was 44 years of age. He was determined to stay, but I felt that Susan's life had been affected dramatically and she was finding it difficult to move on. The situation was also affecting her daughter. My feelings throughout my visit were ones of selfishness and abuse, and these were not conditions that any family should have to endure. I don't feel that this spirit knew Susan in life, but she had just been in the wrong place, and he has*

'attached' himself to her. I was, towards the end of my visit, feeling very frustrated and annoyed with this spirit, when I looked into Susan's aura and knew that this situation needed to be resolved".

"I started the extraction as my own vibration was at its peak. It took a few minutes to complete. During the process I had my guardian and guide present with me, and my grandad Alex and Uncle George. A series of other guides, 'men', stood by me to help, as this spirit was strong. I felt that one was Chinese, and one Indian. Together we created the white light in front of the living room door and two angels appeared simultaneously and took the spirit back to spirit. Afterwards I was exhausted and was told that my work was done, and that this spirit was gone, never to return".

Steven Bird, March 2022

MALCOLM ROBINSON'S COMMENTS

"My sole role of that day was just to record Susan and Ciara's testimony; I would leave the psychic stuff to Steven Bird and the dowsing aspect to Ron Halliday. It was important to get on record, what had been going on in the family home. It was clear to see, that Susan had tried many things to get rid of this nasty spirit in her home, all to no avail. So, it was with fingers crossed that our visit with Steven would do the trick. Team One, which comprised of Ian and Alyson Shanes, had certainly helped the situation, and some interesting information was gained. But again, it looked as if this spirit was in no hurry to depart. When I got home, I listened to the recording that I had made with Susan and daughter in her home. I had hoped to have picked up some spirit voices, more so when Steven Bird was exorcising the spirit from the home, but sadly, no matter how hard I tried to listen out for even the faintest of gasps or words, I couldn't determine any 'extra' voices or sounds that shouldn't have been there.

Now that's not entirely a bad thing, you don't always record what's known as EVP's (electronic voice phenomenon) I was just glad that at least I had recorded the afternoon's events as a record of our visit. So, Susan stated that she had been in the house for six years, but it was only on the fourth year that things started to get spooky. There was two initial years where nothing happened, when all was quiet. We could ask ourselves why!

Needless to say, I telephoned Susan a week or so after our visit to find out if anything paranormal had occurred in her home, hoping that it would be in the negative, as Steven Bird our psychic assured me that he was 99.9% convinced that this spirit had departed, not very happily I should add, but depart he did. Susan stated that her psychic friend Cathy, had said to her that spirit had shown her, that this Jeffries fellow, the spirit that had attached itself to Susan, was shown to her in some kind of underground cave which had a glass door, and that Jeffries was rushing towards the door, banging into it, in an effort to get out. For him, this was a prison. The psychic also saw two Guardian Angels standing outside this prison with him, ensuring that he stayed where he was. Jeffries looked decidedly angry at where he was, but she felt that this was his lot. In other words, this would be his punishment, but if he realised the distress that he had put Susan through, and accepted his punishment, there was a way forward for him to join his family in spirit and be free of his anger and resentment. After sending Susan another e-mail asking how things were, she replied on the 2nd of April 2022 with the following.

Hi Malcolm!

"Things have been quiet, apart from a lot of orb activity, however I don't mind good spirits. A little incident on Wednesday. I've had my son's dog for a couple of days, and she started barking at the stairs again, this went on all day.

She then started barking like crazy and growling and ran upstairs. The next thing it sounded like she was in pain! I ran upstairs and told whoever it was to leave and never upset my dog again! I was pretty shaken. I've got the CCTV working again so I'll keep you updated".

Kind Regards, Susan.

On the 8th of April 2022, Susan e-mailed me again saying.

"He's back. Horrible night. I was on my own with Bella. I've got CCTV of the banging (which he does) and also him speaking again! Here is one of the clips captured last night. There are others with bangs and orbs, but this is the voice saying "Hi" like before, although he says it three times. You can also notice a black shadow. If you could let the guys listen and see what their thoughts are? I'll record over the weekend and let you know if anything else I find".

Kind Regards. Susan.

Upon receiving this e-mail, I must admit I was a bit despondent, as I honestly felt that the work that we had done in Susan's house had put paid to 'Jeffries' efforts to stay. I watched her attached CCTV footage, and one could hear the word *"Hi"*, or was it just me 'thinking' that I heard this word! On the 26th of April 2022, I received another e-mail from Susan which read.

Hi Malcolm,

"Thought I'd update you on what's been happening. Things were fairly quiet, but the past two nights there have been lots of activity and orbs. Last night around 12am, Bella our dog, began barking and growling loudly at the bedroom door, so much so, that Jim let her out again. She ran looking downstairs. As soon as she came back in the room, an orb flew past".

Kind Regards. Susan.

On the 7th of July 2022, I received another e-mail from Susan which read.

"We were both in bed where we heard a male voice calling me a "Fucking Bitch"! Cathy has asked to come next week; she says he's been very active. I posted this to Facebook and other people have heard it as well".

Needless to say, I was quick to get in touch with our medium Steven Bird for his thoughts on this update. He stated, *"It's not him, he is proper gone. Must be another one! The house may need another cleansing".* I also e-mailed Ron Halliday, and he said, *"A persistent spirit! I'm up for another visit. Not sure what else can be done. However, I guess we'll have to try to contact whoever's behind it. Steven seemed convinced that he'd banished the spirit but maybe we're dealing with multiple infestation".* Well clearly that was a possibility. That said, although there were indeed other spirits in the property, it was only 'Jeffries' that was the problem. Alyson Dunlop Shanes our other medium stated,

"Thanks for the update. Sounds bad. I think I'd be inclined to do a house blessing at this point, rather than a full-on exorcism. He's a mean spirited fellow. Very derogatory towards women especially. If I do a blessing or exorcism, I will require assistance from at least one person".

On the 13th of July 2022, I received another e-mail from Susan, which in part read;

Hi Malcolm,

"I feel I may have a demonic presence in my house. He's different from Jeffries. The CCTV has not been working all week going offline throughout the night. Tonight, I put the device in the hall, and I activated the speaker. Oh My God, he said "Susan". Then it sounds like pigs snorting? Something is not good. Ciara is terrified hope you can help".

At this point, Alyson Dunlop Shanes was also e-mailing Susan, and told Susan on the 13th of July 2022, not to put the CCTV camera on, as it was enticing him to continue making appearances, and this was the last thing that she should be wanting. Susan readily agreed. On the 3rd of August 2022, I received another e-mail from Susan, she stated.

Hi Malcolm,

"I was going to contact you; lots more has been going on. I posted some of my videos on Facebook (as everyone is fascinated by them) Due to this, a paranormal team from England contacted me and their medium was concerned as he said that I have several residing spirits and one is demonic! They know you guys are coming on the 14th of August (Author's Comment. We had arranged to go back and visit Susan and Ciara again on that date). *but they want to make the 8 hours round trip as they feel I need help asap! This might be a good thing, as if they can't remove them, then you guys are coming on the 14th.*

SPI's THIRD VISIT. 14th AUGUST 2022

Realistically, we never felt that we had to come back to Susan's property, as we truly felt that 'Jeffries' was 'gone'. Evidently that was not the case, either he was still there, or someone, or 'something' else was there. And so, on the 14th of August, the author, along with fellow researcher Ron Halliday and medium Steven Bird, once more took the journey to Condorrat near Cumbernauld. Susan and Ciara were there to welcome us at the door, and we proceed through to the living room where we sat down to hear all the latest strange goings on. From the audio recording that I made that day, I take (in part) the following. At this point Steven is talking to Susan and he states.

"Once we get rid of 'Jeffries' these other two will just go, because he is holding them together. They are his 'hangers on'.

They worship the ground he walks on, and 'they' are giving him a bit more strength. 'Jeffries 'was taken over', but the problem with the spirit world is the same as this one, it's not a perfect world. He got out. Nobody knows how he got out, but he got out. It's going to be a fight to get rid of him this time. But we will get rid of him, and he won't be back. He was at me this morning when I was putting after shave on and he said to me, "Aye, you're a smelly bastard" He has basically been offensive towards me. He's here, right now, and I 'will' confront him".

At this point I asked Susan to let us know about all the recent paranormal happenings, and how she got on with the paranormal researchers who had travelled up from England to Scotland. She replied.

"When you left the last time, it did get better. Now you left on the Saturday, there was a strange thing that happened on the Sunday. We were talking about 'Jeffries' and a can of cola that was sitting on the floor, just fell over. And I thought, 'Oh No, here we go'" Steven interrupted at this point saying that this might be due to residual energy. And that when you release a spirit, it leaves a lot of energy in the house. That energy will take days and days to dissipate he stated. You can only move energy; you cannot destroy it. When I'm doing this type of work, there is a huge amount of energy that will surge throughout the house, and not all of it goes. Susan continued.

"So, what we have experienced since you left, have been lots of bangs. We also get a lot of sounds, as if somebody is opening the front door, but there is nobody coming in the front door. The middle room has been really 'dodgy' (Ciara pipped up and said, "So is my room") *"I always feel him. I know he is a pervert and that he watches me all of the time. I feel that he is starting to affect me again with my moods and things like that, like he did the last time".*

408

(I asked, Susan. How long after we had left did you start to feel this"? *She replied, "Months. I've been posting the strange videos on Facebook as everybody is fascinated by them. In one of the videos, you see a 'shape' walking upstairs and you hear the words, 'Fucking Bitch'. When you listen to the video, it sounds as if he is wearing heavy boots as he is going up the stairs. I've also been catching here in the living room, strange long orbs. I tried to put the English researchers off, as I didn't want to anger what was here, but they basically begged me to come here because they said that the footage, I had was phenomenal. There were three of them who travelled up to see us from the Midlands area. As soon as the Janet entered our house, (one of their team) she said that she didn't feel comfortable, she looked terrified. She is called an 'empath' and can take in other people's feelings. And Jack, said that its going to be like the conjuring in here tonight".*

"So, what they did was they set up electrical devices in every room in the house. Some of which were motion sensors and torches that would only go off if spirit was around, and they also had lights set up. We went up to my bedroom, and the bed was all nicely made, and one of their team turned round to me and said, "Someone has just sat on your bed", and we looked down, and you could actually see the indentations on the bed. At which point, all their equipment went off". At this point Ciara pipped up and said that wherever you went in the house, all the rooms were absolutely freezing cold. Susan continued. *"We also had a touch teddy, anytime you go near it or touch it, it goes off, well that was going nuts down here in the living room. I took it upstairs and placed it on my bed, and it was the same there as well. Jack, one of the investigators, said that this was the strongest spirit that he has ever encountered in all his investigations.*

I then decided to record in the room, hoping to pick up any spirit, at which point Jack said please stop recording, and then he rose up and was physically sick in the bathroom".

At this point, Steven said that he would like to say a prayer of which the following is but a small part.

"Great divine spirit we ask that you throw a veil of protection around us all. We ask that you return this spirit who is here for no great purpose, to go back to where he came. I ask that this should be done, in your true name, which is love…Amen".

Ciara then spoke again about Jack who had been physically sick in the bathroom and was later joined by Janet, the empath. Ciara said that Janet said to look at Jack's face, as he was being, as she called it, 'overshadowed' and his actual physical face changed. I asked Ciara if she saw Jack's face change, she replied *"Oh yes, as did my mum. I couldn't look at him as I was so scared. His eyes were bulging. He looked raging".* Susan then stated, *"Ciara had to look away and the next thing was that his eyes literally rolled into the back of his head. You could only see the whites of his eyes. Anyway, he managed to come to, and I said to him, "Look, this is too much for you, let's stop this now. And he said "OK". And then I said, "Jack, why are you looking at me like that? And then I realised that he was overshadowed again. It was terrifying".*

I then asked Susan, how did his face look. Was it old, or young? She replied. *"I didn't feel that it looked normal. I didn't feel that it was human. I got the feeling that it was something 'inhumane'. The way his eyes were bulging, it was like a goblin".*

Fellow researcher Ron Halliday asked. *"Susan, could you still recognise that it was him.*

I've seen transfiguration where people's faces totally change, and a completely different face appears…….." Susan quickly injected with, *"I would say it was older wouldn't you Ciara?* Ciara stated. *"I wouldn't, I knew it was him. But it was like his face shape 'changed'.* Susan then said. *"So, then they all came down to the living room and they used their dowsing rods, and 'Jeffries' was talking to me through the dowsing rods. It was incredible. It was left for yes, and right for no. And he was answering a few questions, but the one that really concerned me was, when I said, 'do you want to hurt me'? and he didn't say yes or no! And I asked that several times".*

Ciara then said that Janet, the other psychic, had said that he 'Jeffries', didn't want to hurt her, but if something happens that makes him angry then he might! I then asked both Susan and Ciara that when using the dowsing rods, was the question asked if he, 'Jeffries', would ever leave at all? To which Susan replied that she did ask that question and he said he would not be leaving. Another interesting thing that came through the dowsing rods, was when 'Jeffries' had said that Susan had reminded him of his own wife. It was also asked if he wanted to remain in the house, to which 'Jeffries' replied, 'yes'. I then asked Susan what did this English team do next, did they try and move 'Jeffries' on? She replied yes, but they couldn't do it. They could only move on one spirit person from the house. Susan now takes up the story.

"There was this one person who 'did' want to move on, and his name was John, and he was very thankful to be moved from here. Jack felt that there were another three spirits here, including 'Jeffries' but they were too strong for him to move on" Ciara then stated that Jack, the English medium, had said that 'Jeffries' had also been in her room, watching her and her boyfriend. Susan then said that the last time our research team SPI had left her house, she was really ill

411

and that the headache that she had was unbelievable, so much so, that she had to go to bed. Ciara also said that she too had a horrendous headache.

At this point in the proceedings, Steven Bird, our medium, said that he really had to get on and do his work. He needed to get rid of 'Jeffries' now. We all went quiet, and Steven then said a 'cleansing prayer' after which he remained silent for a time. After a period of around 6 or 7 minutes, Steven began to softy sob. I left it another few minutes, as I could see that Steven was 'coming out' of his process of deliverance. When I asked if I could ask him a question. He replied yes. So, I asked him that when he was doing his deliverance, what was he experiencing? Steven replied.

"I can't tell you the full story, but my Guardian Angel was standing right behind me, and my guide was basically running the process and giving me extra strength. Then the angels came though that wall and a white light opened up, and then there was a bit of a fight to get him through the white light. But the dis-attach happened, and the angels pulled him right through. The other two went through as well, they were the ones that worshiped him. The house is almost cleansed, it's not quite cleansed yet, because there is still an amount of huge energy sitting in this room. The reason I was crying, was because my guardian angel cuddled me, and the sensation is incredible, it's just 'pure love'.

I then asked Steven if 'Jeffries' had put up a fight when he was being taken away. Steven replied. *"Oh, it was a bigger fight this time"*. Susan asked, what was 'Jeffries' saying when he was being taken away, to which Steven replied that he wasn't saying anything, he was just screaming and was trying to hold onto the Earth plane, but he was just not allowed to. Furthermore, he said that Susan wouldn't hear anymore from 'Jeffries', he should have gone the first time but this time, he won't be back.

Ron Halliday then asked Susan if she had felt anything when Steven was doing his cleansing prayer to which Susan replied that she felt as if she was being engulfed by something, and that her hands went freezing cold, to which Steven said that this would be spirit drawing energy from the room. Steven then asked both Susan and Ciara if they have ever fooled around with the occult, or if anyone in their social circle had fooled around with a Ouija board or anything like that, and if there was, to dis-attach from them. He explained that people play with this stuff and don't tell you, so it was important to find out, and stay away from these people. Susan replied that she has been asked this, but they have never played with a Ouija board in this house. At this point in the proceedings, Steven said that he would need to do a closing prayer which he did. He said that 'Jeffries' won't be back, he's gone. Susan then said that she had something else to tell us that had happened last week. This is what she had to say.

"On the phone my gardener said that he would like to come to my house and said that he had been watching my videos online and then he said that his sister is psychic and warned him not to come into my house no matter what. And he has experienced a bit of psychic stuff as well. So, he said to me, put on your CCTV and I will be there in half an hour. So, I put it on in the hall, and I could hear his van outside at which point the CCTV started to squeak and made strange noises and when I played it back, you could actually hear growling voices. And my gardener didn't feel well all weekend. He told me that he had night terrors. And when he was here, he said that he could see a black shadow of a man at my bedroom window willing him to go away. Personally, I feel that I am always going to get spirits here. I'll still keep and use my CCTV". Steven at this point stated, that the CCTV encourages bad spirits, because they like the attention. Also, it's a source of power for them he said.

He further asked her to switch it off, that there wasn't any need for it, to which Ciara said that she was so glad that Steven had said this, as her mother was always switching it on at night trying to capture the spirits. Steven continued saying, *"Spirits like these sorts of things, they have a huge vanity and narcissism. If you've got your CCTV on, they are on the telly"*. I laughed out loud at this and said that I had never thought about it like that. Susan then reiterated what a previous psychic has said which was.

"I was told by a lady that 'Jeffries' was banished to a crystal cave and that he was banging against it going nuts trying to get out. She saw this. It was like a clear glass wall".

Steven explained to Susan that 'Jeffries' wasn't meant to go straight over, that this holding cell was a 'halfway house'. He was meant to stay there as punishment for his deeds and then cross over and then get further punishment. But he got out, but this time he won't be back. Steven further said that one thing about being a medium, is that it's a hard lonely road. People think you are stupid. It affects you in different ways. It tires you out. I asked Susan if she still wants spirit around, or would she miss it if it totally went away? She replied by saying that she knew for a fact, that if she put her CCTV on that night, she would get something coming through. I quickly interrupted her by saying that we didn't want any more spirit attachments linking onto her, and by keeping the desire to capture spirit on her CCTV, this may well induce further spirit happenings. I further stated that she (Susan) was a beacon, she was like a moth to a flame, in the sense that spirit could see her and that 'Jeffries' who was one of the more nastier ones, had attached himself to her. Susan then asked Steven that in his opinion, what was 'Jeffries' doing to her, as in, why was he there? Steven replied, he was a dirty pervert and was wanting to be around her because she was his type of woman.

He more or less had you on his arm saying, 'this is mine, she's mine'. Susan stated, *"That's what he said to the English researchers last week, 'she's mine'. In fact, we asked on the dowsing rods if he helped build these houses, and he said yes!"*

Steven then said that Susan should close herself down, part of which could be helped along if she visited her local Spiritualist Church. Right now, Susan's aura was still bright, and could still attract spirit. Furthermore, Susan's energy is shining like a beacon. 'Energy is energy', 'spirit is energy'. Steven further stated that spirit can see your energy. Susan then asked what was the reason that she was giving out this aura, to which Steven replied that it was just her. That she had psychic ability but doesn't know how to harness it, and this is what has been happening, this is what you have had to deal with. Susan then asked, *"How did 'Jeffries' die"?* to which Steven replied that he felt that something had crushed him, it might have been a fall. Susan then said that when the English researchers were here, and they were standing at the top of the stairs, they had the strong intense feeling that 'something' was wanting to push them down the stairs. She continued. *"That's where I always felt him, standing in the hall at the top of the stairs, or in my bedroom. When I am coming down the stairs, I make sure to hold onto the banister".* Steven said that Susan had to get back to who she was before. Stop searching for spirits, stop the CCTV monitoring, stop thinking about what's gone, and to look forward. She had a right to live, and this has overtaken her life to a degree where it's not healthy. That she needs to get back to being (as he put it) 'you'. Because this isn't you. Susan has let things overtake her. She must get back to being Susan, business, work, holidays, mother, and a nice person. This 'Jeffries' has done nothing but rattle her brain. Susan agreed, and stated that 'yes', she needs to detach herself from 'him' and that she was partly to blame for bringing him back.

AFTER THOUGHTS BY STEVEN BIRD

On the 6th of September 2022, a few weeks after returning from Susan's home, I received an e-mail from Steven Bird our medium regarding that last visit. Here is what he had to say.

"I was aware from a week or two after first visit that 'Jeffries' had escaped from the area he was being held in, and that we had to return to give Susan a permanent fix. Many weeks went by before we eventually went back to her house. That morning (before we left to go to Susan's house) I was shaving, when I felt 'Jeffries' near me and he called me a fat bastard. He was defending his right to keep Susan with him, as in historical words she was his. When we landed at their house, the energy was heavy within. I took a while to tune in and connected with spirit who told me to start the process, as all was in place to take him away for good. When I started, I felt a huge energy engulf me and stay with me for a few minutes. I was surrounded by my grand dad, uncles George and Pat, and my guides Jeremy and Tiberius. Also, ever present was my guardian angel Tryranus who had my back."

"My head felt as if it was going to explode as the process continued, and I was physically shaking throughout. The white light appeared after a few minutes of my healing thoughts towards Susan and her daughter. Then three angels appeared, and 'Jeffries' was livid. He tried to get to me but was held down picked up and taken through the light to accept is punishment. He was left on the Earth plane for initial punishment, but as he was affecting Susan to a great degree, it was declared he should go to spirit. I feel that part of the reason he escaped and went back to Susan was because she was keeping him in the limelight through social media and the CCTV in her house. He felt that this was his permission to return".

CATHY DONALDSON

Susan had mentioned that I should get in touch with one of her psychic friends who had been along to the house, and who had offered help. Her name was Cathy Donaldson (pseudonym) and I duly telephoned her for some comments. Here (in part) was what she had to say.

Abbreviations. (CD) Cathy Donaldson. **(MR)** Malcolm Robinson.

(MR) *"Could you tell me the role you played in helping Susan, and how it started for you".*

(CD) *"Yes. I think that 'he' had been there for a while. My background is that I am not a traditional medium, I've got a few other strings to my bow so to speak. So, it wasn't really from a medium point of view that I went. I was doing a house cleanse for her, and 'he' was coming through very strongly and I got lots of information about him. Her bedroom mirror was terrible, the only way I can describe it, would be like one of those 1950 peep shows with Marilyn Monroe on the bed, 'they' were all coming through from behind the mirror. Low level, low energy men, and 'he' was kind of leading the way. There wasn't as much activity back then as there have been lately".*

Author's Comment. This was just before Covid struck the country so Cathy couldn't really go back over to Susan's house due to the Covid protocols set up by the Government.

(CD) *"When the Covid rules were relaxed, I found out that she had had a few people out to her house to see if they could help, at which point I took a step back, because I thought that she wanted someone else's help. I'm not a pushy person so I just left it".*

(MR) *"When was the first time that you went over to Susan's house, was it 2020"?*

(CD) *"I think it was before that. Because it was before the Covid lockdown maybe early January. But it was definitely before the Covid lock down which came about in March".*

(MR) *"This mirror that you spoke about. Did you say that there were a number of figures coming through it, or appearing in the mirror"?*

(CD) *"They were behind it. So, it was like a portal. So, I covered the mirror up, and put symbols all around it to close it off. With spiritual work like that, you really have to keep it up. It's like housework, you have to keep it up".*

(MR) *"So how many times did you go over to Susan's house"?*

(CD) *"I only went once, and then she got someone from down south. I'm a shamanic practitioner, so I do energy removal from people. But with Susan, I went down the angelic route to remove them and opened up the rainbow bridge and got the angels of the cross to come and get 'him'. He wouldn't go, but they did take him away, but obviously it is a free will thing, and he kept coming back and the more Susan identified with him, as like a member of the family, he has got stronger and stronger with the connection. Anyway, I did go in remotely a few months ago to take 'him' away, and I saw him there as clear as day with angelic beings. The type of energy that 'he' is, is a type of low energy, and he would be taken away by the angelic 'beings' to reflect on his behaviour, and he wouldn't be allowed to come back and re-incarnate in another body until his energy gets really high. But then you get lots of them who refuse to cross over for various reasons. They may think that they don't deserve it, or they don't believe that they are dead, so they want to wreak havoc on people, they want revenge. So 'he' was a very possessive man, a very angry man.*

418

He has become attached to Susan, and it's like an abusive relationship now. But the angels had him. They had him behind something like a clear shop window and he was raging. He was like a bull in a China shop, but he has used as much energy as he could, to get out of that situation. And because he has free will, the angels can't force him to stay there, the angels are hoping that they can educate him to use his energy in a better way. So, he got out, and the other two energies are still in the house, but he was like the ringleader he is almost like a school bully".

(MR) "Did you get an impression of who he was, what he did in life, or anything like that"?

(CD) "The other lady from England got more of that. I got that he was just a little bit older than Susan, maybe 60. He was like one of those Kray Twins those London gangsters. He was very possessive and aggressive, a sort of jack the lad, not a good energy at all".

(MR) "Let's go back to the mirror in Susan's bedroom. Did you see any faces in the mirror and if so, what did they look like? Were they angry, were they trying to speak, how were they dressed"?

(CD) "I don't see it like that. I only see it through 'their' eyes. So, I was on the inside of the mirror looking through into Susan's bedroom. So, I draped the mirror and put symbols all around it. But it's like anything else, you have to keep at it, and as I haven't been there for a while, I don't know if those drapes are still there. I also do a lot of work with the Druids. I've got quite a long ancestral line of Witches. I'm not a Witch or practicing Witch or anything like that. The Druids work with herbs and do rituals and things like that. So, I actually used my ancestral line last night to take 'him' out. So, 'he' is not in the house anymore".

(MR) *"So are you convinced that 'he' 'Jeffries', is definitely away now"?*

(CD) *"Well 'he' has not passed over. The Witch that I worked with last night, she has him. So, it's not a full stop on the case, because we still have to figure out what to do with him. 'He' has been bound, and has been taken out, and she has 'him', in this big kind of metal ball with a big chain on it* (laughs) *which she has taken great delight in doing. She is one of my guides and she really only comes out when people are not being very nice".*

(MR) *"So are you saying that it is your guide that has got 'him'"?*

(CD) *"Well she only comes round when things are very bad. She is not really a guide; she is an ancestral figure. For a long time, she wasn't allowed to come down even near me, my own guides wouldn't let her down because I couldn't cope with her energy. So, she is very hard core, a very powerful energy. She won't see the little man harmed kind of thing. She will step in if things aren't right. She is trying to teach 'him' a lesson now, that there are stronger energies than him, because he has been scaring a lot of people who have been trying to work with him. But I'm not scared of things like that. But my guide has basically got him bound and he is unable to come back, and he is unable to communicate with those other two spirits in the house. In the meantime, I have suggested to Susan, that we do some kind of hecate rituals. (*) put some symbols around the house to keep 'him' out, but she has to disconnect from 'him' herself. Stop the CCTV and giving him energy. If I can think of anything else, I'll get back in touch with you. But yes, at the start it was really creepy. And it was like a peeping glass type scenario where 'he' was watching her in bed and touching her and allowing other low-level spirits to come and watch her too. But she told me that she had now thrown that mirror out, but that's still a porthole somewhere that should be closed off, but we don't know where the mirror is".*

(*) **Author's Comment.** I learned online, that Hecate, Hecat, or Hekate, pronounced, Hê kàh tai, is probably one of the most important Moon goddesses of magic. She apparently rules the astral forms and brings those forms back into Earthly forms, and vice versa. She governs the gates between twilight and the wilderness, and she governs the powers of magic, which includes spells and Witchcraft. Hecate was worshipped by a number of ancient peoples, most notably the Greeks and the Romans. As I was about to finish this chapter, I asked our SPI team once more what they thought about this case. Alyson Dunlop Shanes stated.

AFTER THOUGHTS BY ALYSON DUNLOP SHANES

"Now that I have read Steven and Cathy's reports, it seems clear to me that the entity I spoke with in the bathroom was the same one that Cathy Donaldson saw. She described him exactly how I saw him. A man in his 60s. However, Steven saw a man in his 40s who sounds much younger. That means 'Jeffries' was not the only toxic male entity that was kicking about. For all I know, all the other mediums might have been seeing different male spirits. Like attracts like. I think there may be an awful lot of 'Jeffries'. More like 'The Jeffries Club'. I'm re-thinking this whole case now. Susan needs to stop encouraging this. I feel the current Jeffries is just playing nice for now, perhaps even influencing her thoughts. This entity (or entities) is a liar, a bully, and extremely dangerous to women. I have seen this happen before when people got comfortable with their familiar house ghost. It turned out to be not so friendly by which time it was too late. The ghost had become a negative attachment and was influencing the moods of one of the family members. Simply put, you do not want dead energy in your house. Susan has an incredible amount of energy, but she's giving it all to these negative entities who are flocking around one after the other, feeding off her energy, potentially becoming stronger".

"It's important to bring your energy down at the end of the day, especially if you have a lot of it. Closing the chakras and grounding are amazing spiritual practices that everyone should incorporate into their life. Furthermore, when things are cleared out, it is important to fill that empty space with something else. Some people have a ritual every morning where they open all the doors and windows, sage all the rooms, light candles, and burn incense to welcome the new day. I would encourage Susan to find a way to keep these spirits from returning and keep only positivity and love in her home and heart. In whichever way she connects to the Great Divine Spirit, I would also encourage her to find that connection every day and stop allowing these other negatives into her life. It is asking for trouble. Something bad could very easily happen. I would urge praying to a protective guide, angel, Mary, Jesus, God, or Goddess. Whichever positive beings she is closest with an angel or deity she most trusts".

AFTER THOUGHTS BY RON HALLIDAY

"Hi Malcolm, Alyson expressed some of my own thoughts. The mediums put in a lot of effort to cleanse Susan's house so it's difficult to see how to take it forward. Are we dealing with multiple spirits or an exceptional strong force? Can spirits cooperate to create a maelstrom of activity? I find the situation in Susan's house puzzling, because if house cleansing isn't providing a permanent solution as it should, then other factors may be playing a part"

IS THE CASE STILL ONGOING?

On Friday the 27th of January 2023, Susan dropped me an e-mail with an attached video. The video was quite indistinct, so I asked her what I was supposed to be looking at. In a further e-mail on the 29th of January, she stated that the camera was in her upstairs hall, and it had picked up images and movement.

The camera was apparently static, but on viewing the piece, it appears to be moving around where an indistinct white light source can be seen. Susan claims that she could see a 'man's face'. Sadly, I couldn't. I asked her how were things at home, were any strange events still happening? She replied.

"Yes, still lots of activity Dee Donaldson (pseudonym) did a live piece on Instagram and saw him at the top of the stairs and also a man in the bathroom that you guys picked up before. Usual door sounds as though it's opening and footsteps up the stairs and lots of talking through the CCTV. I don't think 'Jeffries' wants to go, I think I will just need to accept that, but I would love to hear you guys' thoughts on what the CCTV picked up".

Kind Regards. Susan.

FINAL WORDS-SUMMING UP

It was clear that spirits were still in Susan's house, and that 'Jeffries' was not one for disappearing. I asked both mother and daughter to sum up what they felt about the whole situation. Ciara, Susan's daughter was first to put her thoughts forward. She said.

Hi Malcolm,

"At the start it was terrifying what my mum and I witnessed. We thought that no one would believe us. We genuinely thought that on that first night someone had broken in our house, and since then we had him here for years, and the worst part, was when he seemed to possess my mum. My friends and my dad experienced this, and it was the scariest experience ever. He is still here I feel and hear him all the time. I know others are here, but they are just happy being here with us. Thank you for all your help but 'Jeffries' just wants to be here".

Next to sum up what she felt about what had been going on at her house, was Susan. She stated.

Hi Malcolm.

"I've always experienced supernatural things, however that first night with Ciara was honestly indescribable, we both experienced it at the same time. To see my daughter, hide under the covers brought out my mother instinct to confront what we thought was an intruder. Since then, we know it's 'Jeffries' So many have banished him from our house, but he always finds a way back. I'm learning to live with him. He's especially close if I'm unwell. I actually felt him sit beside me a few weeks ago. I think he knows I'm letting him stay. Ciara is not very happy at this, but I know he is terrified to cross over so he can stay. Yes, he does affect things and makes himself known all the time. However, the question is, why does he always find a way back? Love to you Malcolm and the team and thank you for being here for us and believing".

Both Susan and Ciara knew that I was writing about the strange events in their home and would be putting in in this book, I had their blessing to do so. When I finished this chapter, I sent it not only to my SPI team to ensure they were happy with what they said, but also to Susan and Ciara for their final thoughts. In an e-mail that I received from Susan in March 2023 (also sent to the SPI team) she stated the following.

Hi everyone,

"You are all correct it's not safe for us to have these entities here. If I'm completely honest, I do feel that Jeffries is influencing me which makes me feel silly to admit this. However, I've definitely not been the same for a while. I don't want to leave the house for any length of time which is not like me as I'm a social butterfly.

Cathy last week offered to come and move them on, but I had to want them to leave. When we were talking about it, Jeffries actually told Cathy to F**K Off, and apparently, he did the same with Steven when he was in the area. I honestly appreciate everything you have all done and understand how draining it can be on you. I've spoken with Ciara and we both agree it's not safe having them here and I am a little bit scared saying this as I know this will anger Jeffries. Once again thank you to everyone, and I will start practicing how to close down if you can give any advice how to and connect, I'm drawn to the goddess this would be appreciated".

Susan & Ciara

Susan mentioned above that Steven was told to F**K off as he was driving in his car near her area. I decided to telephone Steven and ask him what transpired, and this is what he told me.

"I was just working doing my normal job which takes me all over Central Scotland and I was coming back home to Clackmannan and was driving at the back end of Condorrat, the Glasgow side. I was driving near the bottom end of her street, when all of a sudden, Mr Jeffries popped into my head and said, *"And you can take a f**k to yourself, you can f**k right off"*. And I said, *"Ah, alright, that's fine, I know who you are"*. And he said, *"Yes you do, you won't be doing that again because I am here to stay"*. And I replied *"Ah, is that the case, are you still annoying Susan"*? To which he replied, *"She's mine"!* So, I told him that she was not yours, and that you may think she is yours, but she is not yours and you are meant to stay away from her. I then said to him that I didn't know how he got back, to which he replied, *"Well I did, they sent me back, but I'm not meant to go anywhere near her, but what am I supposed to do, she wants me there?"*.

As this point Steven is in deep conversation with Jeffries and asked him if he was going to 'bother' her and was surprised to learn that he said no that he was sent back to learn lessons. It was only because of Susan's fascination about Jefferies that bound him to her. Steven further stated to the author that his spirit team were continually telling Jeffries to 'stay away' or he would be punished severely.

At the time of writing, March 2023, it would appear that 'Jeffries' does not want to go. It's not for the want of trying from SPI or others. Susan knows that possibly the reason 'Jeffries' is still around (and Ciara her daughter would back this up) is the desire on Susan's part to keep the CCTV on and keep trying to capture sounds and possibly an apparition. Its easy for this author to say, *'Stop it'.* Stop trying to enhance his ability to 'appear' by always thinking about him and sharing your footage of the orbs and sounds to her followers on Facebook. Its human nature to be inquisitive, that's in our DNA. We wonder about the unknown. It's fascinating and entices one's mind to look deeper into it. I get all this, I really do. But then again, Susan could shut down the CCTV and stop thinking about 'Jeffries'. Would that necessarily stop the phenomena from occurring? Who knows. I guess it 'might' be up to Susan. She has her own sage sticks, and could, should she wish, sage her home on a daily basis to see if that helps things. At the end of the day Susan and Ciara have learnt to live with what's going on, and in a way, they are used to things now. I can only hope, that 'Jeffries' does not psychically attack either Susan or Ciara, for that would take it to a different level, and not something I'm sure that both would be happy about.

Ron Halliday (c) Malcolm Robinson

Steven Bird Malcolm Robinson and Ron Halliday

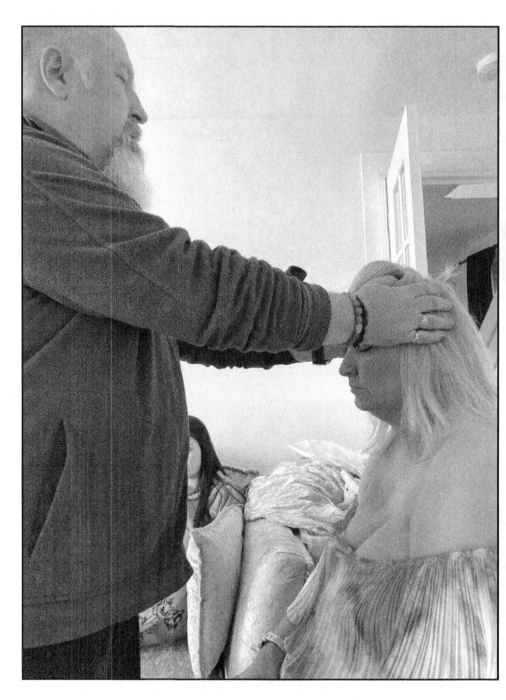

Steven Bird with Susan Strachan (c) Ron Halliday

Susan Strachan and Daughter Ciara (c) Malcolm Robinson

***

CHAPTER SIX
IN CONCLUSION

"Death is not the end, it is simply walking out of the physical form and into the spirit realm, which is our true home. It's going back home. We unzip the body, so to speak, let it fall to the ground and walk through the next door clothed in our spiritual form, which was always there inside the physical body."

Stephen Christopher Dennis.

Since my last book on Paranormal Case files of Great Britain (Volume 3) the big story to hit the world's media, was of course the release of 1,574 pages of once secret Pentagon documents to the public. This related to the Défense Intelligence Agency (DIA) America's secretive UFO programme. This wealth of data included research into the biological effects of UFO sightings on human beings. This stunning report, gained under a Freedom of Information request (FOI) included information regarding UFO abductions and, would you believe, unaccounted for pregnancy! But the big bombshell which really had the public sit up over their cornflakes, was the release by the Department of Defence of three videos which claimed to show true Unidentified Flying Objects. The film clips were taken by pilots of the United States Navy, and were taken over four years, 2004, 2014, 2015, 2019. Not only were these objects filmed, but they were witnessed by many Military and Naval personnel. The first piece of footage was taken by two F/8 18e Super Hornets that were dispatched from the U.S. Aircraft Carrier, USS Nimitz which was roughly 100 miles off the coast of San Diego of the western coast of the United States. Peculiar radar returns were observed near the Island of San Clemente.

This was during a Naval combat training exercise. There had been a period of around a week from the 10th of November 2004 to the 16th of November 2004 where strange aerial objects had been caught by radar operators aboard various vessels in this carrier fleet. Eventually, two Hornet aircraft were despatched to intercept these strange objects. The pilots of these aircraft reported that the speed of the object they chased, was in excess of 2,400mph and they gave it the name of 'Tic Tac' as it resembled the confectionary sweet. Prior to this encounter, it was stated that an American submarine had also observed an object, similar to the 'Tic Tac', speeding just under the surface of the water at around 550mph. However, it was not just the visible testimony coming from the highly trained and observant pilots that drew gasps of astonishment, the radar operators onboard the Naval Fleet were also astonished and mesmerised by the characteristics of these objects. More so because they would descend from around 60,000 feet to 50 feet in a matter of seconds defying the laws of physics. Then they would hover and stay stationary on the radar for a short time then suddenly take off at a terrific velocity.

Needless to say, when all this came out, the media were in a frenzy to learn more. However, the Pentagon were quick to state that there was 'no more' to the USS Nimitz sighting. This was backed up by Sue Gough, a spokesperson for the Defence Department. However, this was not strictly true, further film footage taken by other U.S. Naval ships, namely the USS Princeton, and the USS Theodore Roosevelt, quickly dispelled that. Eventually they admitted that the full report regarding these UAPs, (Yes, they changed the name to Unidentified Aerial Phenomenon) would come out in due course. The USS Theodore Roosevelt named the strange objects that they saw and filmed as 'Gimble' and 'Go Fast'. Let's think about it here. If the objects sighted were our own technology, then we have somehow got around the G Force problem!

Any pilot today currently subjected to the incredible manoeuvrers that these objects displayed, would surely have died due to the G force turns. There is so much more on the internet regarding these incredible events, and I would urge you the reader, to check out this footage online. So, after the release of these mind-blowing files and videos, I waited with bated breath for the promised release of the full report.

AT LAST

Well, the long-awaited report on UAP (Unidentified Aerial Phenomena) by the Office of the Director of National Intelligence, was released on June 25th, 2021, and I guess we shouldn't be surprised that it turned out to be nothing but a damp squid. Some Ufologists had high expectations of something quite considerable coming out of this long-awaited report, in the sense of an acceptance by the United States Government, that yes, planet Earth has seen an intrusion into its air space by vehicles of unknown origin. This report for me was all over the place. It said one thing, then contradicts that one thing further down the report. It is a muddle of words. We are told that most of these objects fall into the category of airborne clutter, the likes of birds, balloons, plastic bags flying in the sky (yes really, plastic bags!) or natural atmospheric anomalies like ice crystals, moisture, and thermal fluctuations.

The bottom line was that limited data left most of the UAP reports unexplained. The investigation into these UAP objects fell between the years of 2004 through to November 2021. I had to laugh where at one point in the report, it states that the sensors mounted on U.S. Military platforms are only designed to fulfill specific missions, and as a result, we are told, are not suited for identifying UAP's.

Really! Overall, the report effectively stated that these UAP reports, probably lacked a single explanation, that said, the report did speculate that some of the UAPs might be Chinese or Russian or from another Governmental entity.

GOOD AND INTERESTING POINTS

The report does state that they found a cluster of UAP reports which were observed around U.S. training and testing grounds. We are also told that in 18 incidents described in 21 reports, observers reported unusual UAP movement patterns or flight characteristics. The report did state that some UAPs may pose a threat to flight safety and National Security, and they accept that some UAPs have been detected near Military facilities or by aircraft which are carrying the United States Government most advanced sensor systems. My, that must be some black plastic bag flying in the wind eh! The report does state that the U.S. Government would continue its research into the UAP phenomenon to learn as much as possible as to what is behind these reports.

THE AUTHOR'S CONCLUDING THOUGHTS ON THIS REPORT

I saw this report as effectively the same old hash. They had to bring out this report simply because of the various U.S. senators asking the Government to come clean on those incredible images that the world saw. Former Senator Harry Reid was instrumental in getting the Freedom of Information files regarding the USS Nimitz and its fleet, released to the American public. The Pentagon and the American Government were backed into a corner, they had to come out with something, and this report is a muddled mess of flowery words each of which, takes you down a different path of thought. I guess we shouldn't have been surprised at this report. Why?

Well because I honestly thought that the subject of UFOs would be proven once and for all at the prestigious National Press Club meeting held back in 2001 in Washington D.C. Attending that meeting with their own UFO sightings, were pilots from around the world and also scientists, ex-Military people, members of Congress and researchers. What they brought to bear at this prestigious meeting, were not just their tales of encountering UFOs, but providing photographic evidence and radar recordings. Here at last, I thought to myself, would finally show to the world the reality of the UFO phenomenon once and for all. Those assembled were high standing people from the United States Air force, Army, and Navy, all seated telling their own stories of the UFOs that they saw. These were not your street drunks, these were men of integrity, who were putting their lives on the line for America, and yet, after their testimony, it was just another day. They were seen, they were heard, and the world moved on. Nothing changed. And whilst other countries throughout the world have started to release their own UFO files, including Great Britain, we are still none the wiser. It is, as we know, a global phenomenon. But here's the rub. What constitutes proof? We have the fantastic footage of UFOs taken by pilots from the USS Nimitz and the USS Princeton but that is not 'physical proof'! It's not hard-core nuts and bolts hold it in your hand 'proof.' UFOs being witnessed by credible observers, be they trained Military or Naval pilots, or strange unexplained objects being seen on radar apparatus by trained radar operators, is not going to convince the world that we are dealing here with a highly intelligent off the world race. We need more. The Governments of our world have always denied that these things exist and have gone to great lengths to convince us. So, one wonders why now? Why are we slowly being drip fed these very tasty morsels? Is there an agenda? Are we slowly being wakened up to the fact that, yes, there is an alien presence and we, the Governments of this world know what's going on?

All this is of course speculative on my part, but it does bear thinking about. People are not so naïve to think that we stand alone in the vastness of the cosmos. Most people would agree that there must be other life 'out there,' but we come back to the 'proof' aspect. We have had the UFO phenomenon for thousands of years now, it goes way back into antiquity where people spread throughout the globe recorded these strange aerial objects. Why don't they land, I hear you ask? Yes, why indeed! For me, I don't think that the United States or Great Britain for that matter, will put their hands up and say, *"Yes, OK guys, you were right all along, we are dealing with an advanced technology from another world"* It isn't going to happen, not for the foreseeable. The only way that we will get our proof is when *'they'* want to come clean and finally show their hand. Only then will the Government back pedal and come clean. So, dear reader, it's now up to *'THEM,'* the craft that stealthily fly in our skies, to make themselves known. My research into the UFO enigma has clearly shown to me that we most certainly are dealing with a superior advanced technology whose agenda we can but speculate. Make no bones about it folks, *'they'* are real alright, and the Governments of this world know this. So, was this Pentagon report a big to do about nothing? Those who have witnessed UFOs, or (UAPs as the Pentagon would prefer to call them) know that what they have seen was not conventional. Like me, I'm sure that they are dismayed that the powers that be, our elected officials, didn't have the guts to trust the people of Earth to accept such a fact, and to prepare mankind for a future 'main intrusion' into our air space by beings that might not have our best interests at heart. But of course, my speculation, is based on the Governments of this world 'knowing' that 'they' are out there. What if they 'don't know'! Maybe one day, further down the line, we will have our interstellar friends join us for either a joyous celebration of life in the cosmos or find out that they don't have our best interests at heart. How would this disrupt world religions?

Well, that's a discussion for another day. Whatever the outcome might be, that day will come, and its best that we all are ready for it, even although the United States Government and others, will continue to muddy the waters of evidence.

THE END OF OUR WORLD!

I watched a series on television entitled, Universe, which was narrated by Brian Cox. He states that our Sun will eventually die 5 billion years from now after it has exhausted all its energy. It makes one think about the world's population at that time, knowing that they are about to die. Families, homes, countries, and civilisations, all gone. Our history, our achievements all gone. Would our world collapse before then? By that I mean anarchy and riots in the streets. People with nothing to lose knowing that soon nothing will matter anyway. I'm glad that we won't be around to see this, or our children. Planet Earth is on borrowed time. Even now mankind is destroying our planet. We are destroying the Amazon rain forest at an alarming rate; we have the nuclear capabilities that could wipe out countries. Mankind won't be here forever, will an alien civilisation step in and save our souls, or are we doomed by the time scale of our dying sun. Either way, mankind if we are not too careful, will be its own worst enemy. Or can mankind be its own saviour by the placement of humanity on other worlds? But that my dear reader, can only happen with cooperation between countries, and an incredible advancement of science for deep space exploration.

Being in the public eye, I do tend to receive a lot of e-mails asking me certain things, from ghosts to UFOs etc. Obviously, I don't have all the answers, I might indeed have none! But I do try and give my own ideas as to what people ask me.

Another point of being in the public eye, is that the media always chase people like me down for a quote, which is fine, if they present the honest and unchanged interview that you give them. I did a piece with the British Daily Star newspaper where I said that in my opinion, these so called 'greys', do not have our best intentions at heart. And I was of course referring to the numerous worldwide UFO abductions where people are taken without their consent and experimented on. I did say that 'some' aliens may be OK, but in the main, mankind has had to put up with their lives being intruded upon where bodily violations have occurred, and for me, that's not on. Anyway, I received an e-mail from someone who I don't know, who took me to task about this. I'll give her name as Barbara, although that's not her real name. Here is what she had to say.

Hi Malcolm,

"I am writing to you because I have read a few articles that you are mentioned in, and it seems like you may be a bit in the dark about some things regarding aliens and UAPs. You don't know me, and I am not any field researcher or anyone noticeable in the field. What I do understand, is the general reasoning behind UFO abductions, and maybe a bit of the entire picture of the history of humanity. Some people I do follow for helpful information are Dolores Cannon (hypnotherapist) and Steven Greer. Dolores's books directly go against your 'aliens aren't peaceful' theory and gives an in-depth account of abductions and the reasonings behind them. PLEASE read these books".

"I have had first hand experiences too, and my partner has direct contact with his 'spirit angel' if you want to call it that, and so I have been able to use that connection to get first hand experiences with the unknown. The majority of aliens are peaceful and have been watching over and caring for the Earth and

humanity for millions of years. We humans are in fact a mess of many 'alien species' DNA. The abductions are just certain races of aliens who are observing/testing certain aspects of 'humanity'. Nothing aggressive or harmful, although it is often perceived that way. (Wouldn't a lab rat be fearful of the giant hands coming down to test on him?). Most people who are being abducted currently, are beings that have agreed to do this kind of work in their human lives, prior to the reincarnation. They don't remember it, because of the way this Earth is set up, but it has been promised all the same. There are innumerous dimensions with varying frequencies, and humanity only lives in the 3D generally. We are not able to see anything above or below that frequency/density. This is the main reason we cannot take clear photos/videos of UAP craft; they are only in our frequency for a split second. Our technology is NOTHING compared to what they have, which is why we aren't seeing any replies on our retro radio transmitters. Aliens don't use radio; it is extremely primitive. There are beings living on Earth, that we are unaware of, and are presented in various ways, ghosts, spirits, shadows, fairies, etc. Governments are well aware of this. I have had experiences having portions of my memory wiped, with physical things happening in the 3D to me that I don't recall. Luckily, I am able to ask my partner directly why these things were done. To put things in perspective, humanity tests lab rats, cats, all sorts of animals and even does human testing. If humanity were given the responsibility to create a new society, you can bet they would be testing DNA and various elements to make sure that society progresses well. This is what aliens are doing on Earth. 'We' are 'them'. Some of us are even 'older' than some species, because they are hybrid human-aliens, created for various purposes. There are negative beings as well, because we live on a planet with the law of duality, meaning there can be no good without the bad (it is all perspective anyways).

They have infiltrated certain powerful areas in order to gain control of the narrative. They are just a few species out of the thousands that are here for goodwill. We ourselves are aliens in this respect, as we have been reborn on this Earth for our personal reasons of growth or help or whatever".

"I hope this sparks an interest in Dolores or the various other experts in the field, for you to dig deeper than just the 3D world, and to stop spreading fear in humanity with your work. Fear is of the ego; thus, it is self-created. Fear is used by religion, government, business, etc in order to control the narrative, please don't do the same".

All is love, light and energy. Best regards, Bob.

I replied.

Hi Barbara,

"Many thanks for your e-mail".

"I'm sure you will agree, that when anyone talks to the newspapers they are not always quoted correctly! I also said that there are some good races out there, but the newspaper hacks were more interested in the juicy bad aliens, sells more newspapers".

"Look, there is an agenda of that there is no question, and yes there are some so called good 'aliens' out there. But let's not forget that some of them are taking people without their consent from the comfort of their own homes and vehicles, for me that's not on. They are not taking us by the hand to walk us to the park and buy us an ice cream. Thankfully (for the moment) things haven't escalated beyond the abductions into people's lives. I have met and interviewed the late Dolores Cannon but she too, did say, that not all aliens have our best

interests at heart. Surely there is a better way to make contact, that to instil fear and alarm into human beings! Make contact, give us your intentions and we can take it from there, that's what I would say to them".

Incidentally, my report from the Daily Star, was reproduced in many other newspapers around the world, it even found it's way into the Jerusalem Post and the International Business Times!

This book contains only a few stories that people have shared with me, I could have added many more. I've mentioned in previous books my beliefs in Life after Death, ghosts, and poltergeists. I won't go into these again here, but suffice it to say, I firmly believe in a Life after Death. In fact, it's not even a belief, it's a culmination of interviews that I have had with people who have had near death experiences. It's also the incredible information coming through 'some' gifted psychic mediums, all of which have shown to me, that there is a continuity of life, 'after' death. This knowledge to me, is a great comfort. More so the knowledge that I will once more meet up with family members who have gone before me. Scientists and free-thinking people have always turned their minds into trying to answer life's mysteries. Why is it that some people see ghosts and UFOs and others don't! What is the mechanism behind their appearance? There are probably more speculations about this than anything else. We humans are a curious lot, we strive for answers, we don't like unsolved mysteries. That's why I love receiving possible answers to these conundrums. A wonderful free thinker was the late Ralph Steadman, a dear friend of mine and someone who I enjoyed many a deep and thought-provoking conversation. He himself, has now passed onto the higher side and I would like to reproduce his own thoughts as to what he calls, 'Co-existence'. Ralph states.

It is possible for different frequencies of vibrations to co-exist within the same object. The example I like to use is that of a sponge, which may or may not contain water. If we look at a sponge, we don't know whether or not it does, unless it is so full that the water is dripping out of it! We look at the sponge containing water, and see only the sponge, not the water! I have used this as an analogy to explain the connection between the physical body and the personality. If we examine the sponge and water closely, we see that the sponge contains holes which hold the water, which give us a way of understanding 'co-existence'. We can imagine objects with vibrations at the bottom of our 'thermometer' as having big holes in them, which can be filled by objects with higher vibrations. So therefore solids, which have the lowest frequencies of all, can play host to any objects higher up the scale. For instance, water can penetrate wood, or even in some cases brick, as liquids have higher frequencies than solids, and carbon dioxide, a gas, can penetrate water, to form fizzy drinks! But everything in existence has its own vibration, and therefore its own frequency, and that includes our own essential self. Scientists might call this our 'consciousness', but I prefer a much simpler everyday word our 'personality'. The personality is made up of several strands, but its predominant frequency is the one in the spiritual section of our 'thermometer', between the level of spiritual sight, and that of 'Pure Thought' (and slightly overlapping both) which leads to some very interesting results! One of the things sometimes demonstrated by spiritualists, is the gift of psychometry, in which the medium is given an object by a client, it might be a ring, a brooch, a watch, or some other personal item and will then give a reading from it, picking up the personality of the one to whom it originally belonged! How on earth can this happen? One would expect the medium to be able to give the reading that's what they are there for, but how do they tie the article up to so quickly to a previous owner?

The answer is very simple! The vibration of the personality of the previous owner has 'soaked itself' into the object, and all that the medium is doing is sensing this vibration and 'milking' it out of the object! This simple fact, the ability of someone's personality to be retained in objects, has enormous repercussions in everyday life. Many people use charity shops, and if the vibrations of previous owners can be absorbed in the items there, usually clothing, then the vibrations of the physical (medical) conditions of those owners can also be absorbed. What if someone has died of some terrible disease? Can some of their symptoms be passed on in their discarded clothing? I myself have had some experience which may be relevant here. For several months I helped to run demonstrations of clairvoyance in a charity shop, which was continually receiving second-hand clothing, and some weeks the energies in the room were so bad, that we had to clear them before we could even start the demonstration!

But now let us turn to the subject of cellular memory. Can conditions around the deceased donor be transmitted through a transplant? There are many documented instances in which the recipient of a transplanted heart or lung has started to get memories associated with the original donor, or even in extreme cases has developed their tastes, habits, interests, or skills. So, the answer must be a resounding 'Yes!', if not more positively 'Of course!' And the reason follows the same logic as the examples outlined above. If the vibrations of the personality can penetrate inanimate objects such as rings or brooches, which someone is merely wearing, how much more so must they penetrate the individual cells of the person's body, with which they are in intimate contact daily! And since the personality contains all the memories and experiences that the individual has ever had, it is not surprising that the recipient of an organ particularly one of the larger organs of the body, could well start to have knowledge of those memories and experiences! But frighteningly, the phenomenon is not confined to incidents where people have had transplants. A far more frequent operation than a transplant is a blood transfusion, and there are recorded clinical incidences of unexpected side-effects from transfusions. It is unlikely that small transfusions would ever have any noticeable side-effect, but major transfusions are quite a different matter. Yesterday I spoke to a friend about this, and she told me of a woman who due to complications during childbirth had to have a massive transfusion. Afterwards her character had changed so much that her own mother, an acquaintance of my friend, said, *'She is no longer my daughter!'* That is only anecdotal evidence, of course, but it is still evidence, nevertheless! Hopefully at some time in the future, scientists and spiritualists might accept to get together and set up joint projects in which to combine the expertise of both sides in order to solve some of the mysteries with which we are still faced with today. All that I can say is, 'Let it be soon!' but I must admit that I'm not holding my breath!

Ralph Steadman.

I felt that I just had to include Ralph Steadman's thoughts in this book. Ralph presents it far more eloquently than I. What Ralph states above, is how I see the strange world of the supernatural. It all has to do with vibrations, frequencies, and dimensions. So, dear reader, we have come to the end of this book. The subject of UFOs and the Paranormal are dear to many people's hearts. We all have our own ideas as to what is behind these mysteries. That they are still elusive is of course frustrating. But at the end of the day, mankind must go forward with his free thinking and try his best to answer these questions, for not to do so would be foolish in the extreme. I hope you have enjoyed reading the strange experiences featured in this book, as I have had in featuring them.

Now I would ask that you go on, and further your paranormal journey. Read as many books on these subjects as you can. There is a lot of nonsense out there, but once you sieve through that, you will be astonished as much as I was, of the valuable and astounding stories that are out there. Enjoy your journey. God bless.

***

REFERENCES

Chapter One. *(Strange Ghostly Occurrences)*

Bizarre Underwater Encounters with Ghosts and Mysterious Monsters (mysteriousuniverse.org)

Strange Tales of Water Ghosts (paranormalauthority.com)

Mysterious Ball Lightning Created in the Lab | Live Science

https://historycollection.com/10-premonitions-of-doom-and-from-history-that-actually-came-true/

Princess Diana death: 'Game-changing' letter predicting death kept secret for six years | Royal | News | Express.co.uk

Top Spooky Spots on Haunted Skye Haunted castles to Ghost cars (spookyscotland.net)

According To Legend, Fairies Inhabit Scotland's Isle Of Skye, Especially In These Locations (thetravel.com)

Face In The Sea Tunnel | Ghost Face In Aquarium | Real Ghost Face | Ghost Bhoot

https://www.the-sun.com/news/5053632/us-government-releases-1500-pages-secret-documents-ufo-programme/

Navy UFO | UFO Sightings | The Truth About the Navy's UFOs (popularmechanics.com)

www.thedeep.co.uk

Wikipedia

Chapter Two. *(The Haunting of Gladstone Villa)*

None.

Chapter Three. *(The Nottingham Haunting)*

House & Abbey - Newstead Abbey

Who was King Ahaziah in the Bible? | GotQuestions.org

Wikipedia

Chapter Four. *(The Media and the Supernatural)*

Amanda Large Teague says she married and divorced a Haitian pirate ghost who inspired Jack Sparrow - The Washington Post Washington Post July 14th, 2019.

Divorcing a ghost: 'Sex with my spirit hubby was great – until he tried to kill me' | Closer (closeronline.co.uk) Closer Magazine online. 12th July 2019.

Who is Amanda Teague? Woman who married the GHOST of a 300-year-old pirate | The Sun The Sun. 20th February 2018.

Irish woman legally marries a 300-year-old pirate ghost | IrishCentral.com Irish Central online January 15th, 2018.

Woman who 'married ghost of 300-year-old pirate' says her beliefs are no different to believing in god | The Independent | The Independent 15th July 2019.

Is It Possible To Have Sex With A Ghost? British Woman Does It—And Is Loving It (newsweek.com) Newsweek U.S. 12th September 2017.

Spectrophilia - Wikipedia

'I'm a psychic and ghost sex is real – it's more common than you think' - Daily Star Daily Star. 21st October 2022.

Woman, 32, calls off her wedding with a GHOST after he 'changed' on holiday | Daily Mail Online Daily Mail online 14th October 2020.

Dissociative disorder - Search (bing.com)

The Curse of Busby's Stoop Chair | Haunted Rooms®

The tale of Busby Stoop and the thug who was hanged there for bludgeoning his goading father-in-law to death | The Northern Echo

https://www.spookyisles.com/busby-stoop/

The Anguished Man - YouTube

The Curse of 'The Crying Boy' Painting - Exemplore

https://en.wikipedia.org/wiki/Chained_Oak

Merlin's Oak - Wikipedia

The haunted book a terrified family gifted to one of our most haunted houses – Museum Crush

Wikipedia.

Chapter Five.   *(The Condorrat Haunting)*

Wikipedia.

Chapter Six.   *(In Conclusion)*

Wikipedia.

Alien expert: They don't come in peace - The Jerusalem Post (jpost.com)

Aliens do not come in peace, claims top UFO expert (ibtimes.co.uk)

***

FURTHER READING

Archives of the Society for Psychical Research. Poltergeist file. P4, 1940/1967.

A Fenland Poltergeist. A.D. Cornell & Alan Gauld. Journal. SPR 40:705 September 1960 343-358.

Are Poltergeists Living or Are They Dead? Ian Stevenson. Journal of the American Society for Psychical Research (SPR) 66, no. 3 (1972): 233–52.

Borley Postscript. Peter Underwood. White House Publications, P.O. Box 65, Haslemere, England. GU27 1XT, ISBN 0-9537721-1-x

Britain's Paranormal Forests. (Encounters in the woods) Peter A. McCue. The History Press 2019. ISBN: 9-780750-991-339

Contagion. Darren W. Ritson & Michael J. Hallowell. The Limbury Press; First edition July 2014. ISBN: 9780956522894

Can We Explain the Poltergeist? A.R.G. Owen (1964). (New York: Garrett)

Encyclopaedia of Ghosts and Spirts. John and Anne Spencer. Headline Book Publishing of 338 Euston Road, London, England NW1 3BH. ISBN 0 7472 7169 0.

Enfield Revisited: The Evaporation of Positive Evidence. Guy Lyon Playfair, and Maurice Grosse. (1988) JSPR 1988-89 Vol 55 No 813 208-219.

Edinburgh After Dark. Ron Halliday. 2013. www.blackandwhitepublishing.com

Famous Scots and the Paranormal. Ron Halliday. 2012 www.blackandwhitepublishing.com

Ghosts Taverns of the North East. Darren W. Ritson and Michael J Hallowell. Amberley Publishing, The Hill, Stroud, Gloucestershire, England, GL5 4EP ISBN978-1-4456-0753-5.

Ghosts at Christmas. Darren W. Ritson. The History Press. November 2010. ISBN: 9780752457673.

Ghosts Over Britain. Peter Moss. Elm Tree Books 1977. ISBN: 10: 024-1897-432.

Ghosts and Hauntings. Dennis Bardens: Fontana Books 1967. ISBN 10: 1859-585-585183.

Haunted Glasgow. Ron Halliday. 2008.www.blackandwhitepublishing.com

Haunted Gardens. Peter Underwood. Amberley Publishing, Cirencester Road Chalford, Stroud, Gloucestershire, GL6 8PE ISBN 978-184868-261-0.

Haunted Wales. Peter Underwood. Amberley Publishing, Cirencester Road Chalford, Stroud, Gloucestershire, GL6 8PE ISBN 978-184868-2634.

Haunted Pubs and Inns of Derbyshire. Jill Armitage. Amberley Publishing, Amberley Publishing, Cirencester Road Chalford, Stroud, Gloucestershire, GL6 8PE ISBN 978-1-4456-0464-0.

Haunted Newcastle. Darren W. Ritson. The History Press. January 2009. ISBN: 9780752448800.

Haunted Durham. Darren W. Ritson. The History Press Ltd. UK. April 2010 ISBN: 9780752454108.

Haunted Northumberland. Darren W. Ritson. The History Press Ltd. UK. August. 2011. ISBN: 9780752458618

Haunted Carlisle. Darren W. Ritson. The History Press. August 2012. ISBN: 9780752460871.

Haunted Berwick. Darren W. Ritson. The History Press. November 2010. ISBN: 9780752455488.

Haunted Wearside. Darren W. Ritson. The History Press. 1 September 2013. ISBN: 9780752460888.

Haunted Tyneside. Darren W. Ritson. The History Press Ltd. November 2011. ISBN: 978075245824.

Human Personality and Its Survival of Bodily Death. Myers, Frederic W. H. Vols. I & II. New York: Longmans, Green & Co., 1954. First published 1903.

In Search of Ghosts. Darren W. Ritson. Amberley Publishing. November. 2008. ISBN: 978184681217.

Investigating the Paranormal. Tony Cornell. New York Press 2002.

Medium. (Memoirs of a Spiritual Medium) Lee Dunn. Printed by Amazon. ISBN: 978-1-6999-73196.

More Anglesey Ghosts. Bunty Austin. Amberley Publishing, The Hill, Stroud, England, UK, ISBN 978-1-4456-0332-2.

More Things You Can Do When You're Dead. Tricia J. Robertson. (2015) White Crow Books. www.whitecrowbooks.com ISBN. 978-1910121-44-3.

Night People. Paul Sinclair. Truth Proof Publishing. (2020) 978-1-8380673-0-4

New Developments in Poltergeist Research in Proceedings of the Parapsychological Association. Hans Bender (1969) 81-102.

On the trail of the Poltergeist. Nanor Fodor. New York, The Citadel Press, 1958.

On the Track of the Poltergeist. D Scott Rogo, Englewood Cliffs, N.J.: Prentice-Hall, 1986.

Please Leave Us Alone. (The true and terrifying story of an Irish family and their desperate fight against the 'Hat Man' and Supernatural forces) Malcolm Robinson. Publish Nation. www.publishnation.co.uk ISBN 9798-4809-72146.

Paranormal County Durham. Darren W. Ritson. Amberley Publishing. June. 2012 ISBN: 9781445606507.

Paranormal Bath. Michael Cady. Amberley Publishing, Cirencester Road Chalford, Stroud, Gloucestershire, GL6 8PE ISBN 1848681763.

Paranormal Dorset. Roger Gutteridge. Amberley Publishing, Cirencester Road Chalford, Stroud, Gloucestershire, GL6 8PE ISBN 978-1-84868-394-5.

Paranormal Hertfordshire. Damien O Dell. Amberley Publishing, Cirencester Road Chalford, Stroud, Gloucestershire, GL6 8PE ISBN 978-1-84868-118-7.

Paranormal Leicester. Stephen Butt. Amberley Publishing, Cirencester Road Chalford, Stroud, Gloucestershire, GL6 8PE   ISBN 978-1-84868-462-1.

Paranormal Lancashire. Daniel Codd. Amberley Publishing, Cirencester Road Chalford, Stroud, Gloucestershire, GL6 8PE   ISBN 978-4456-0658-3.

Paranormal North East. Darren W. Ritson. Amberley Publishing, Cirencester Road Chalford, Stroud, Gloucestershire, GL6 8PE   ISBN 978-1-84868-196-5.

Paranormal South Tyneside. Michael J Hallowell. Amberley Publishing, Cirencester Road Chalford, Stroud, Gloucestershire, GL6 8PE. ISBN 978-1-84868-730-1.

Paranormal Surrey. Marq English. Amberley Publishing, Cirencester Road Chalford, Stroud, Gloucestershire, GL6 8PE. ISBN 978-1-84868-896-4.

Paranormal Sussex. David Scanlan. Amberley Publishing, Cirencester Road Chalford, Stroud, Gloucestershire, GL6 8PE. ISBN 978-1-84868-462-1.

Psychic Quest. Natalie Osbourne Thomason. Claireview Books, Hillside House, The Square, Forest Row, East Sussex, RH18 5ES, ISBN 1-902-636-34-1

Paranormal Encounters on Britain's Roads. Peter A. McCue. The History Press (2018) ISBN: 9-780750-984-386.

Paranormal Case Files of Great Britain (Volume 1) Malcolm Robinson. Publish Nation. www.publishnation.co.uk 2010 & 2017. ISBN: 978-1907126-06-2.

Paranormal Case Files of Great Britain (Volume 2) Malcolm Robinson. Publish Nation. www.publishnation.co.uk 2016. ISBN: 9781-3268-74-22-3.

Paranormal Case Files of Great Britain (Volume 3) Malcolm Robinson. Publish Nation. www.publishnation.co.uk 2018. ISBN: 978-0244-11172-4.

Psychic Quest. Natalie Osbourne Thomason. Claireview Books, Hillside House, The Square, Forest Row, East Sussex, RH18 5ES, ISBN: 1-902-636-341

Poltergeist Over Scotland. Geoff Holder. The History Press 2013. ISBN: 978-0-7524-8283-5.

Poltergeist. A Study In Destructive Haunting, Colin Wilson. New English Library 1981) ISBN: 978-0450048807.

Poltergeists. (A History of Violent Ghostly Phenomenon) P. G. Maxwell-Stuart. Amberley Publishing 2011. ISBN: 978-1-84868-987-9.

Poltergeists, London: Alan Gauld, and A. D. Cornell. Routledge and Kegan Paul, 1979.

Poltergeists: An annotated bibliography of Works in English, circa 1880-1975. Michael Goss. (1979) Scarecrow Press, New York.

Poltergeist in a Scottish Mansion House. J.W. Herries. *Psychic Science.* Vol. 21, No. 3, October 1942, pp.88-92.

Poltergeist Over England. *Three Centuries of Mischievous Ghosts,* Harry Price. London: Country Life, 1945.

'Poltergeist'! A New Investigation into Destructive Haunting. Including the Cage St Osyth' (6th books, Winchester / Washington July 2020). John Fraser.

Pitmilly House. Lorn Macintyre. Priormuir Press, October 2011. ISBN-13: 978-0956768124

Seeing Ghosts. Hilary Evans. John Murray 50 Albemarle Street London England W1S 4BD. ISBN 0 7195-5492-6.

Scottish Haunts and Poltergeists II. JSPR Vol. 42, March 1964, pp.223-7. Lambert, G W.

Supernatural North. Darren W. Ritson. Amberley Publishing November. 2013. ISBN: 9781848682771.

This House Is Haunted. The True Story of a Poltergeist (1980) Guy Lyon Playfair. White Crow Books. ISBN: 978-1907661785.

The Ghost Handbook. John and Anne Spencer. (1998) MacMillan Publishers Ltd. ISBN: 0-7522-1165-X.

The Hat Man. The True Story of Evil Encounters: **Heidi Hollis.** Amazon.co.uk 9780983040194.

Things You Can Do When You're Dead. Tricia J. Robertson. White Crow Books (2013) www.whitecrowbooks.com ISBN. 978-1908733-60-3.

The South Shields Poltergeist. Darren Ritson & Michael J Hallowell. The History Press, October 2009. ISBN. 0752452746.

The Sauchie Poltergeist. (And other Scottish ghostly tales) Malcolm Robinson published by Lulu.com and is available from, www.amazon.co.uk www.amazon.com and www.lulu.com ISBN: 9798 650 294 658.

The Poltergeist Phenomenon. Headline Books, 1996. John and Anne Spencer. ISBN: 0-7472-1801-3.

The Haunting of Willington Mill. Darren W. Ritson & Michael J. Hallowell. The History Press. ISBN: 9780752458786.

The Rochdale Poltergeist. (A True Story) Jenny Ashford and Steve Mera. Bleed Red Books 2015. ISBN-13: 978-15177-56123.

The Andover Case. (A responsive rapping poltergeist). Barrie Colvin Journal of the SPR. 2008. Vol 72, 1-20.

The Poltergeist. William Roll. (1972) Paraview Special Editions; Special edition. March. 2004. ISBN-10: 1931044694.

Truth Proof (The Truth That Leaves No Proof) Paul Sinclair. PBC Publishing (2016) ISBN: 9780-957-500-785.

Truth Proof 2 (Beyond the Thinking Mind) Paul Sinclair. PBC Publishing (2017) ISBN: 978-1-9999165-0-3.

Truth Proof 3 (Bringing Down The Light) Paul Sinclair. PBC Publishing (2019) ISBN: 978-1-9999165-3-4.

Yorkshire Stories of the Supernatural. Andy Owen. Countryside Books, 3 Catherine Road, Newbury Berkshire, England, U.K. ISBN 1-85306-594-3.

SOME BRITISH PARANORMAL SOCIETIES

ASSAP. (The Association for the Study of Anomalous Phenomena) Tel: 020 8798 3981 assap@assap.org http://www.assap.ac.uk/index.html

SPI Scotland. (Strange Phenomena Investigations) Alyson Dunlop https://spiscotland.wordpress.com/ spiscotland@gmail.com

SPI Anglia Region. (Strange Phenomena Investigations) David Young. https://www.facebook.com/groups/358025484712267/

SPI Inverness. (Strange Phenomena Investigations). https://www.facebook.com/Strange-Phenomena-Investigations-SPI-Inverness-383337621775153/

SPI Dundee. (Strange Phenomena Investigations). https://www.facebook.com/spi2015dundee/

SPI Edinburgh. (Strange Phenomena Investigations) Sandra Fraser. https://www.facebook.com/groups/667586660009029/

SSPR. (The Scottish Society for Psychical Research). 020 7937 8984 Innes Smith. https://www.spr.ac.uk/link/scottish-society-psychical-research

SEMR. (Scottish Earth Mysteries Research) Ron Halliday. https://www.facebook.com/ron.halliday.18

Ghost Office. (Hastings, U.K.) (Darren Garcia) www.ghostoffice.co.uk

Fortean Picture Library. The Image Works. http://theimageworks.com/collections-Fortean.php

The Ghost Club. (The World's oldest organisation associated with psychical research). Established, circa 1862. Flat 48, Woodside House, Woodside, London, SW19 7QN https://www.ghostclub.org.uk/index.html

TO CONTACT THE AUTHOR

Research group Strange Phenomena Investigations (SPI) are always interested to hear from anyone who believe that they may have had a UFO or paranormal experience, or indeed may have a photograph or piece of film footage which may appear to show something paranormal. If so, please contact the author at the address below.

(All submissions will be treated in confidence)

Malcolm Robinson

74 Craigview,
Sauchie,
Alloa,
Clackmannanshire,
Scotland,
United Kingdom,
FK10 3HF

www.facebook.com/malcolm.robinson2

You can e-mail the author direct at : malckyspi@yahoo.com

ABOUT THE AUTHOR

MALCOLM ROBINSON

(Founder of Strange Phenomena Investigations) 1979

Malcolm been interested in the strange world of UFOs and the paranormal for as long as he can remember, and in 1979 he formed his own research society entitled, Strange Phenomena Investigations, (SPI). The aims of SPI are to collect, research, and publish, accounts relating to most aspects of strange phenomena, and to purposely endevour to try and come up with some answers to account for what at present eludes us.

MALCOLM'S TELEVISION WORK

Scottish Television News (STV) – Independent Television Network (ITN) – BBC Reporting Scotland – Channel 5 – Sightings (U.S. T.V. Show) – Japanese Television – German Television – Mexican Television – Australian Television – Dutch Television – Italian Television – Strange But True? (With Michael Aspel) – Grampian Television – GMTV (with Eammon Holmes and Lorraine Kelly - The Disney Channel – Loose Lips (with Melinda Messenger and Richard Arnold. - SKY Discovery Channel – SKY History Channel – ITV This Morning (with Philip Schofield and Amanda Holden) – SKY News with Kay Burley, and many more.

DOCUMENTARY MOVIES (That feature Malcolm Robinson)

The Pentagon UFO Files (2022) Space Force, The Dawn of Galactic Warfare (2022) Aliens at Loch Ness (2022)

RADIO

BBC Radio Scotland. - Radio Clyde – Talk FM – BBC Radio Northsound – BBC Radio 4 – Central FM – The Howard Hughes show – And many other local and National radio stations both here in the U.K. and abroad.

ARTICLES

Articles by Malcolm have appeared in many of the world's UFO and Paranormal magazines. Malcolm has assisted many of the U. K's National and Regional newspapers in connection with stories concerning ghosts, poltergeists, and UFOs.

INFO

Malcolm was the very first Scottish UFO researcher to speak in the following countries, United States of America, (Laughlin Nevada). France (Strasbourg) Holland (Utrecht) Ireland (Carrick on Shannon & Galway) Malcolm is also one of the few people on this planet to have gone down into the depths of Loch Ness in a submarine. He is also an international author and lecturer.

AWARDS

2017. UFO & Paranormal researcher of the year. Given at the Paraforce Conference in Witham, Essex, England.

2019: 40 Years Continuous operations of SPI. Given at the Outer Limits Conference in Hull, Yorkshire, England.

2021. The Tartan Skull Award. Presented at the Scottish UFO & Paranormal Conference (over Skype)

**

MORE BOOKS FROM FLYING DISK PRESS

http://flyingdiskpress.blogspot.com/

Printed in Great Britain
by Amazon